CHILDREN O
CHILDREN C. ....

Somewhere beyond the three-mile limit, beyond all nations, in the Ligurian Sea off the coast of Italy, passengers and crew members of the *Star Flyer* gather in the piano bar. The *Flyer*, a four-masted sailing ship, moves smartly before a fair wind. She is a small vessel and those on board have achieved a fine level of camaraderie.

This is their last night at sea. The cruise director from Brazil, the dining room manager from Indonesia, the ship's pianist from Hungary, a waiter from Jamaica, a passenger from America and another from Croatia lead the group in song:

We are the world;
We are the children.
We are the ones that make a brighter day,
*So let's start giving.**

Earlier that evening, at the farewell dinner, Captain Klaus Muller, a German now living in Scotland, had told us that cruising transcends all nationalities.

"Our crew members and passengers are from many nations, but on this ship, we are all one. During the past week, we have found a common language and a common bond. We have sailed together and dined and shared wine together, and we have become friends. We've learned an important truth—that humanism is greater than nationalism. As you leave the ship tomorrow, please take that thought home with you."

Now, in the piano bar, the women from Brazil and America, and the men from Indonesia, Jamaica and Croatia are singing. One by one the others join in. All of them are smiling and some have misty eyes. And the small ship moves freely before a fair wind, beyond the province of all nations, with all of mankind on board.

ß ß ß

BOOKS BY DON AND BETTY MARTIN

NEVADA DISCOVERY GUIDE ● 1996 (Formerly *The Best of Nevada*)
ADVENTURE CRUISING ● 1996
ARIZONA DISCOVERY GUIDE ● 1996 (Formerly *The Best of Arizona*)
UTAH DISCOVERY GUIDE ● 1995
WASHINGTON DISCOVERY GUIDE ● 1994
THE ULTIMATE WINE BOOK ● 1993
NORTHERN CALIFORNIA DISCOVERY GUIDE ● 1993
OREGON DISCOVERY GUIDE ● 1993
THE BEST OF THE WINE COUNTRY ● 1991, 1994, 1995
INSIDE SAN FRANCISCO ● 1991
COMING TO ARIZONA ● 1991, 1993
SAN FRANCISCO'S ULTIMATE DINING GUIDE ● 1988
THE BEST OF THE GOLD COUNTRY ● 1987, 1990, 1992
THE BEST OF SAN FRANCISCO ● 1986, 1990, 1994

ፆ ፆ ፆ

I am fevered with the sunset,
I am fretful with the bay,
For the wander-thirst is on me
And my soul is in Cathay.
— *A Sea Gypsy* by Richard Hovey

ፆ ፆ ፆ

This book is dedicated
to all who, in spirit if not in fact,
go down to the sea in ships.

ADVENTURE CRUISING

By Don W. Martin & Betty Woo Martin

The complete guide to
specialty and small ship cruises

FEATURING "CRUISE CLOSEUPS" OF SEVERAL GREAT VOYAGES

🏴🏴🏴

Pine Cone Press, *Inc.* • Columbia, California

Reaching out and touching a whale can be one of the thrills of adventure cruising. This petting frenzy occurred in Baja California's San Ignacio Lagoon.

Library of Congress Cataloging-in-Publication Data
Martin, Don and Betty—
Adventure Cruising
Includes index.
1. Cruising—description and travel

ISBN: 0-942053-19-2
Library of Congress catalog card number 95-92752

Photography ● **Betty** or **Don Martin,** unless otherwise credited.
Illustrations ● **Bob Shockley,** Mariposa, Calif.
Cover design ● **Dave Bonnot,** Columbine Type and Design, Sonora, Calif.

COVER PHOTOS

FRONT ● *The rainbow-rimmed barkentine Star Flyer sails smartly before a Mediterranean breeze.* — Photo © Harvey Lloyd, courtesy of Star Clippers
BACK ● *The daylight touring yacht Sheltered Seas nudges into LeConte Glacier ice floe in Alaska's beautiful Inside Passage.*
— Photo © Alaska Sightseeing/Cruise West

CRUISE DIRECTORY

PART I: SHIPS AND SAILING

CRUISE CLOSEUPS

INTRODUCTION

Adventure cruises are voyages that focus on appealing destinations and/or the kinds of ships that get you there. These can be high adventure in the high arctic or "soft adventures" on a French canal barge or a Mississippi riverboat. People book these cruises not to lie on sun decks and be pampered, but to experience special kinds of water travel or to visit interesting new places. They travel for the best of all reasons—to discover and to learn.

Adventure Cruising is not a guidebook in the conventional sense. The first section is a detailed directory of hundreds of small ship voyages around the world. This is followed by several "Cruise Closeups," detailed reports of voyages we have taken. If you book a similar trip, your experiences may be entirely different than ours, since specialty cruises tend to be variable. If the voyage we enjoyed is no longer available, odds are that the company has come up with something equally interesting. These are for the most part small ship cruises, permitting flexibility and specialization, things that superliners can't offfer. These little ships and boats often sail off the beaten path, and forgive the fractured metaphor. Thus, their itineraries may change according to whims of wind and tides or even the caprice of the captain. He or she may decide on a different route because the dolphins are jumping or the whales are mating or the river is rising or the shoreline berries are ripe.

Since small ship cruises generally focus on adventure, most have lecture rooms instead of show rooms; on-board field experts instead of hairdressers. You may go ashore in Zodiacs or skiffs, or you may step onto a river pier in a small medieval German town. Your shore excursion may be a musk-ox meadow on Baffin Island or a thousand-year-old wine cellar in Burgundy. Your dinner may be fresh shrimp you helped catch and peel on an Alaskan trawler.

If that is your kind of cruise, this is your kind of book.

Don W. Martin

KNOW OF A GREAT CRUISE? GIVE US THE NEWS!

We're on constant watch for small ship and other specialty cruises to include in future editions of *Adventure Cruising.* If you've taken a small ship cruise not listed in our directory, or if you know of a cruise line or represent a cruise line, please let us know.

Further, we'd like to hear if you catch an error or find stale material in this book. Information contained herein was current at the time of publication, but of course things change. Drop us a note if you find that a cruise itinerary has been altered or discontinued, or if a ship has had an unfortunate encounter with a pier piling and will be in dry dock for a while. Anyone who provides us with a new cruise listing or other useful information will earn a free copy of a *Pine Cone Press* publication. (See listing in the back of this book.) Address your comments to:

Pine Cone Press
P.O. Box 1494
Columbia, CA 95310
e-mail: pinecone@sonnet.com

A BIT ABOUT THE AUTHORS

The Martins have authored more than a dozen guidebooks, mostly under their Pine Cone Press banner. When not tending to their publishing company, they explore America and the world beyond, seeking new places and new experiences for their readers. Both are members of the Society of American Travel Writers.

Don, who provides most of the adjectives, has been a journalist since he was 16, when classmates elected him editor of his high school newspaper. (No one else wanted the job.) After school, he left his small family farm in Idaho and hitch-hiked about the country a bit. He then joined the Marine Corps and served as a military correspondent in the Orient and at bases in California. Back in civvies, he worked as a reporter, sports writer and editor for several West Coast newspapers, then he became associate editor of the California State Automobile Association's travel magazine. He now devotes his time to writing, photography, sipping fine Zinfandel and—for some odd reason—collecting squirrel and chipmunk artifacts.

Betty, a Chinese-American whose varied credentials have included a doctorate in pharmacy and a real estate broker's license, does much of the research, editing and photography for their books. She also has sold articles and photos to assorted newspapers and magazines. When she isn't helping Don run Pine Cone Press, Inc., she wanders the globe—with or without him. Her travels have taken her from Antarctica to Cuba.

They wrote this book's "Cruise closeups" not from brochures or wishful thinking, but from first-hand accounts. They sailed aboard each featured ship and trod each landfall. As a measure of Betty's devotion to the project, she suffers from motion sickness, yet she survived and thrived aboard small ships as they prowled the world's seas and rivers.

Some sailors of yore wore a patch over one eye. Betty wore one, impregnated with scopolamine, behind her left ear.

WALK SOFTLY

It began decades ago with the simple, almost naive phrase: *Take nothing but photographs; leave nothing but footprints.* It has evolved into a new travel consciousness called *eco-tourism*. The message remains the same: As you sail or walk this planet on your journeys of discovery, respect its fragility. Tourism by its very nature promotes crowding and intrusiveness. Crowds tend to litter, trample and tax an area's resources. Here's how you can help make the world a better place to visit and therefore a better place in which to live:

1. Walk softly wherever you travel. A million footprints have preceded yours and millions more will follow. Try to impact an environment as little as possible, whether it be a hiking trail or an old village street. If you can, avoid cruises during peak seasons when resources of popular tourist areas are heavily taxed. (One advantage of small ships is that they don't impact shore stops so heavily.)

2. As a hiker ashore, don't leave established trails and never cut switchbacks; it creates ugliness and erosion. When you see others doing so, tactfully tell them why it's not a good idea.

3. Never toss anything overboard, even if you're far at sea. Your litter may be bad for the sealife below, or it may end up on a pristine shore far away.

4. Obviously, you shouldn't litter on land or sea, but go a step beyond. Pick up what others have left behind. If you see someone littering, offer to carry it out. Perhaps they'll have second thoughts the next time. And remember, cigarette butts are litter—the ugliest kind.

5. Protect all natural and manmade sites and resources. Don't gather "souvenirs" from the wild or from ghost towns or historic sites. A single beach shell or bit of adobe will be missed if thousands of people take one. If you discover a prehistoric artifact, leave it alone. If you move it, you may destroy the story it has to tell.

6. Never put your initials, graffiti or any kind of mark on any structure, cave wall or cliff, tree or stone. And for heavens' sake, please don't deface ancient writings or structures.

7. Respect the traditions and privacy of others. Take time to learn their ways and learn what offends them. There's a difference between honest curiosity and boorish intrusiveness. Ask whose who live in a place if they mind having their picture taken.

8. Recycle and use recycled or recyclable materials whenever possible. When disposing of something, seek out and use recycling bins.

9. Support environmental groups with your actions and your donations. Patronize cruise lines and other travel companies that practice eco-tourism.

10. Most importantly, teach your children these things by word and by example. They are the tourists of today and tomorrow.

Take time to see the sky; find shapes in the clouds
Hear the murmur of the wind, and touch the cool water.
Walk softly; we are the intruders
Tolerated briefly in an infinite universe.
　　　— Jean Henderer, National Park Service (retired)

PART I:
Down to the
Sea In ships

All the rivers run into the sea;
yet the sea is not full;
unto the place from
whence the rivers come,
thither they return again.
— Ecclesiastes 1:7

Passengers help rig the sails of the Star Flyer *during a Mediterranean voyage.*

Chapter one

SHIPS AND SAILING
Seeking adventure on a water planet

In the beginning all cruises were adventures. Boats—or at least the predecessors of boats—were mankind's first vehicles. Initially, they were hollowed out logs and crude rafts. Centuries later, men went to sea in fragile sailing ships, using compasses so inaccurate they could be as much as 40 degrees off. Early mariners had no way to measure the distances they'd traveled, and until the time of Columbus, there was always the risk of falling off the edge. Such voyages certainly *were* adventurous!

No one knows when mankind first left the security of dry land and set forth in a boat. It's likely that some daring citizen of prehistory saw a fallen tree floating downstream and caught a ride. Sitting astraddle wasn't practical, so the dugout evolved, or man may have lashed two logs together to form a raft. As rafts got larger, they began carrying passengers. Thus, not too long after the sunrise of men and women on earth, the cruising industry was born.

Cruising is one of the fastest growing segments of the multi-billion dollar leisure business. It's particularly true for Americans, who comprise more than 80 percent of the world's six million annual cruise passengers. The global cruise count has multiplied nearly five-fold since 1970. The industry is accommodating this growth by building larger and fancier ships. They offer amenities such as multiple restaurant choices (including pizza parlors), shopping arcades and staterooms with verandas. In a multi-billion dollar game of "Can you top this?" Princess Cruises launched the 1,950-passenger *Sun Princess* in late 1995, only to be topped by the 2,600-passenger *Carnival Destiny* a few months later. Princess came right back with an even larger floating resort, carrying a few more passengers and weighing in at 100,000 gross tons.

Down to the sea in droves?

But, wait a minute. Aren't crowds and pizza parlors and shopping arcades the sorts of things that people go on vacation to *escape*?

For a growing segment of the cruise population, this is true. Many people are turning to a different kind of cruising, which features small ships and uncrowded informality. These voyages go by a variety of names—adventure, soft adventure, exploration and expedition cruises. Specialty cruises might be a better term, for these outings often have a theme. They may be centered on the type of vessel—icebreaker, steam paddlewheeler, canal barge—or on its destination. They often focus on a particular part of the world and its environment, be it the Canadian high Arctic, the lesser islands of the Caribbean or Indonesia, or the Mississippi River system.

In calling this book **Adventure Cruising,** we define adventure rather broadly. It can be exploring jungle draped tributaries of the Amazon or going ashore in Germany to see the pulpit where Martin Luther first spoke out against church abuses. Small ship cruises are for the most part learning experiences. Indeed, isn't learning the grandest adventure of all?

Small ships, whether adventure-bound or not, offer many advantages. Obviously, the crowds are thinner for dining, shore excursions and port formalities. Shipboard activities usually are less structured. Passengers may be allowed to drop in on the bridge or peek into the galley. Dining table assignments are rare; open seating is common. On some sailing vessels, passengers can help rig the ship to the wind. Small ships can get into small ports, or pause where there are no ports at all and send passengers ashore by rubber rafts or skiffs. (Can you imagine trying to shuttle 2,600 passengers by Zodiac onto a glacial moraine?) Some expedition ships have bow ramps and can nudge up to any calm shoreline.

One of the nicest aspects of small ship cruising is that passengers get to know one another, and their contact with the crew is more personal. We spent hours aboard a sailing ship in the Caribbean getting navigational lessons from the first mate, and Betty got some great cooking ideas from the chef on a French canal barge. A lecturer on a Baja whale-watching trip was so ac-

We define small ships as those with fewer than a hundred cabins.

commodating that he loaned Betty his spare camera, which was better equipped than ours for filming wildlife. Small ship cruising often appeals to more international travelers, providing an interesting passenger mix. The episode on the opening page of this book wasn't contrived; it happened because our little ship had a great blend of nationalities aboard.

Another advantage—at least for those who love to be on the water—is that small ships offer the sensation of cruising. Large vessels are designed with special stabilizers to muffle the motion of the ocean, to make the cruise as calm as possible, lest a few swells disrupt poolside cocktail service. On smaller craft, you *feel* the sea and it's a glorious feeling! Standing at the bow,

WHAT IF I'M STRANDED?

On large cruise ships, the possibility of being left behind during a shore stop is very real. Usually, passengers are advised that the ship will sail at the appointed hour, with or without them. I once came within thirty seconds of missing a departure from St. Thomas because I stayed ashore until the last minute, figuring I'd catch a cab back. Guess what? When it came time to leave, all of the cabs had been hired by other passengers!

Being stranded on a small ship cruise is much less likely, for obvious reasons. Generally, some kind of check-off board is used when passengers go ashore, and often they're in the company of one of the ship's lecturers or a crew member. Further, someone is much more likely to notice that Charlie's missing when he's one of fifty passengers, and not one of five hundred.

However, suppose you *do* get left behind? Your best piece of survival gear is a phone card; don't leave ship without it. Most cruise lines have shore agents at port stops or at least at their port of debarkation—either company employees or a local tour company that arranges excursions. Give them a call and they'll look after you—although it may mean that you foot the bill for a speedboat or helicopter to catch your disappearing ship. If you're in a foreign language country, head for a hotel or even the police station, where you're likely to find an English speaking person.

If there isn't a port agent available, call home—not your mom, but the main office of the cruise line. Folks there will have radio, phone or FAX contact with the ship.

No, you won't find a shore agent or even a telephone on a remote Baffin Island shore or in a Caboclo village on the Amazon. It's not likely that you'll get left behind on an expedition cruise, however. If the unlikely does happen, seek shelter with the locals and hope that, before too long, somebody asks: "Has anyone seen Charlie lately?"

feet planted on the deck, you sense every movement of ship and sea—that subtle, silky motion of the hull slicing through the water, the firm vibration of the engines or the snap of sails in the breeze. For those who suffer motion sickness, this may be a disadvantage, since small craft dance livelier on troubled waters. If this is a problem, there are hundreds of calm river and canal trips from which to choose.

Staterooms may be more spartan on small ships, although this is not the rule. For the most part, cabins are as comfortable and roomy as those on larger vessels. On some, they're outright elegant. Nor does one suffer food deprivation on these trips. You may not have expansive midnight buffets decorated with ice carvings, but you'll not go hungry. An elaborate buffet is no match for the smell of just-baked muffins or cookies, waiting on deck after you've returned from a long shore hike. Many specialty cruises focus heavily—figuratively and literally—on food service. The chef on our French barge trip shopped at local markets every morning and prepared absolutely elegant meals, matched to regional wines.

Incidentally, this book does not dwell much on shipboard amenities, as do most other cruising guides. (One author fussed that the padding on a cruise ship's deck chairs was too thin.) If we do not spend a lot of time discussing closet space or the wine service, it is on the assumption that these things aren't terribly important to most small ship passengers.

Anything that floats

Early man, a two-legged fish out water, proved remarkably adaptable to life on a planet covered mostly by oceans. Both necessity and curiosity drove primitives to find better ways to float. With water craft, they could navigate rivers and reach offshore islands—or escape from them. They could transport cargo and families with ease. Indeed, most of the early cities of the world were established on waterways or ocean shores, for the keel came long before the wheel. Residents of cities such as Venice and Copenhagen dug canal systems to simplify transit. Rivers and canals also provided transportation between cities.

After that first inquisitive cave kid caught a floating log—and probably gave his little sister a ride—boating evolved rapidly. In fact, some early tribes created boat designs so efficient that they're still used today—the skin kayak of the Arctic and the bark canoes of pre-Columbian America. Archeological evidence proves that Chumash tribes of coastal California paddled canoes to offshore islands long before the first whites invaded their domain. The Pacific islanders' double-hulled canoes—forerunners of the catamaran—evolved hundreds of years before the birth of Christ.

Ancient man probably figured out the oar rather quickly, perhaps by guiding his log with the flat of his hand and then with a widened stick. Such propulsion had its limits; it was difficult to go upstream or too far offshore. When large oar powered galleys were developed, man could travel considerable distances, but not too far from shore. Although slaves provided cheap labor, they were tremendous fuel-burners. It was impossible to carry enough food for long ocean voyages.

The development of the sail finally freed mankind from the land. From that moment forward, adventurers could explore the entire world, since nearly 71 percent of the earth's surface is covered by one vast interconnected ocean. No one knows who developed the sail. Perhaps an ancient man or woman noticed a breeze blowing a fallen leaf across a pond. History does record that Egyptians built the first ocean going vessels. Although none of their boats survive today, models have been found in tombs, along with a parchment containing history's earliest record of a sea disaster. Written by the lone survivor, it chronicles the loss of a 180-foot cargo vessel during a storm on the Red Sea, 4,000 years ago.

The earliest Egyptian ships, perhaps dating back 5,000 years, had a combination of sails and oarsmen. They initially floated the Nile, taking advantage of upstream winds and downstream currents. Soon, they ventured into the Mediterranean, which was to become the cradle of world seafaring. For centuries, Egypt pursued a flourishing trade with settlements of the Red Sea and the southeastern Mediterranean. Among the greatest early seafarers were the Phoenicians, who occupied a narrow coastal shelf at the foot of the Syrian Mountains. Around 3000 B.C., they sailed seaworthy ships with deep hulls and high freeboard. They traded throughout the Aegean and Mediterranean seas and ventured into the Atlantic. One Greek historian says they circumnavigated Africa. There is even speculation that they sailed west and reached the New World.

"However, they could not have made it back," said Klaus Muller, a seafaring historian and the captain of the *Star Flyer,* a modern sailing ship. "The keel had not been developed, and without a keel, it's difficult to tack against the wind. But it was easy to sail west. Just go south until the butter melts, turn right and pick up the trade winds."

About 2000 B.C., Minoans ventured from the island of Crete, reaching landfalls throughout the eastern Mediterranean and as far west as Sicily. Their trading empire eventually fell to Achaean tribes, militant voyagers from peninsulas and islands to the northeast. These were the ancestors of the Greeks. They overran Crete in 1450 B.C. and spread their influence and ships throughout the Mediterranean. From Greek history comes the world's earliest seafaring tale, the ten-year wanderings of Odysseus. It was written 400 years after the fact by that popular Greek travel writer, Homer. This "Odyssey"—during which our hero encountered fierce storms, the nasty one-eyed Cyclops, the enchantress Circe and assorted other maidens—reads like pulp fiction. Much of it was.

"It was easy to sail west. Just go south until the butter melts, turn right and pick up the trade winds."

Rome was never a great seafaring nation, preferring conquest by land. Her boats were used mostly for transit. Even during her peak of power, the Roman Empire was constantly harassed by the nimble ships of the Carthaginians, seafaring descendants of the Phoenicians. Occupying the island of Sicily, Carthage raided Roman coastal settlements with impunity. Finally, during the Punic War, Rome managed to overwhelm her pesky enemy. She sent ponderous, oar-powered troop transports against the smaller Carthaginian ships, trapping them in pincer movements and boarding them to dispatch their crews.

On the other side of the world, around 1000 B.C., Southeast Asians used double hulled canoes driven by woven palm leaf sails to migrate to islands of the South Pacific. About 450 A.D., in one of history's grandest sailing accomplishments, they journeyed 3,000 miles across an empty ocean. Guided by tradewinds and navigating by the stars, they managed to hit the world's most isolated archipelago—Hawaii.

Norse tribes in remarkably advanced vessels began raiding European coastal cities in the eighth century A.D. These fierce Norsemen described their raids as "going a-viking," since *vik* was their word for harbor or bay. Their ships, like those of Mediterranean nations, were powered by oar and sail. They were long and slender with upturned prows—the finest craft of their day. The Vikings achieved a technological breakthrough about 1000 A.D. with the evolvement of the keel. With this stabilizing blade, a ship could run a true course while leaning into the wind, and sail against it by tacking. Thus, they were able to cruise to America and make it back. Archaeological evidence found in Newfoundland proves that Norsemen were the first Europeans to make this round trip; Christopher Columbus came in second.

However, Chris's voyage grabbed the biggest historical headlines. This brash young Italian navigator, sailing under the sponsorship of Ferdinand and Isabella of Spain, had the silly notion that the earth was round. Of course, in seeking a direct sea route to the rich spices of the East Indies, he bumped into the Americas. But never mind. These "west Indies" seemed to offer potential, so he set about to colonize them. He made four round trips, establishing a home and permanent colony on Hispañola, the present Dominican Republic. However, he ran into political trouble, was relieved of his post and sent back to Spain in chains. Eventually freed by a sympathetic Ferdinand and Isabella, he spent the rest of his life exploring his new world. He returned to Spain one last time and died in 1506, at the age of 55.

Columbus certainly proved that ships of the day could cross the great oceans in both directions. In the years that followed, small countries with large fleets ruled much of the world. Spain, Portugal and certainly Great Britain used their sailing skills to become global powers. Of course, wind is a finicky thing; it can blow too hard and sink a ship, or not at all and stall it. The development of the steam engine finally made intercontinental travel safe and reliable. With its development, people began moving freely about the globe. Initially, most of them held one-way tickets—willing settlers headed for new frontiers. Then, about 150 years ago, traveling just for the sake of "seeing the elephant" became popular. Early foundations were laid for the modern cruise industry.

Getting up steam for cruising

It's no coincidence that Great Britain and the United States, two strong participants in cruise travel, were instrumental in refining the steam engine. Invented by England's Thomas Savery in 1698, it was perfected and put to practical use by James Watt of Scotland in 1765. America's Robert Fulton built the first successful steam powered ship, the sidewheeler *Clermont,* which he chugged up the Hudson River in 1807.

Although a few early entrepreneurs—including Fulton—built passenger boats and sold tickets, the root of commercial cruising can be traced to England's Arthur Anderson and Brodie Wilcox. In 1837, they started the Peninsular and Oriental Steam Navigation Company, eventually to become P&O and now Princess Cruises. Two years later in London, Canadian-born Sir Samuel Cunard founded the steamship company that still bears is name. Among other pioneers of pampered sea passage were Nederlandsch-Amerikaansche-Stoomvaart-Maatschappij, started in 1872 and fortunately renamed Holland America Line; and American President Lines, noted early in this century for its elegant *Matsonia* and *Lurline* cruises to Hawaii and the Orient.

Almost from the start, cruise ships were socially structured, often with three classes of service. Millions of immigrants came to America in steerage class, with little more than a place to sleep in the hold. Several decks above, first class passengers dined on fine china and silver, while second class travelers occupied snug staterooms between. Steerage and second class passengers were not permitted to trod on first class decks. Single-class cruising didn't become common until about 30 years ago.

For some, onboard equality wasn't enough. They wanted cruising to come full circle—to become an adventure again. Among the first of these was Swedish-born Lars-Eric Lindblad, who began chartering vessels to the Antarctic in the 1960s. Then in 1969, he designed and outfitted the world's first expedition cruise ship, the *Lindblad Explorer.* Still in service, it features an ice-hardened hull, shallow draft for rivers and a real lecture hall. It has made the rounds of several companies under different names.

Several companies now focus on exploration or expedition cruising. Abercrombie & Kent specializes in polar and tropic cruises as well as land expeditions; the firm now operates the much-traveled *Explorer*. Quark Expeditions offers adventure voyages to the world's most remote corners, including polar cruises on leased Russian icebreakers. Sven-Olof Lindblad, the son of Lars-Eric, operates Special Expeditions, taking passengers to faraway places. Several firms run wildlife cruises to the Baja Peninsula, with a focus on whale watching. Alaska Sightseeing/Cruise West sails the Inside Passage and the Columbia, Snake and Sacramento rivers. Society Expeditions, which suffered financial problems a few years ago, is back in business. Rhode Island shipbuilder Luther H. Blount, who designed early expedition ships and invented the bow lander, operates American Canadian Caribbean Line, specializing in river and offshore trips.

River cruising is one of the fastest growing segments of small ship voyages. From the mid-nineteenth century to the early part of the 20th, steam paddlewheeler were an important means of transit. In North America, they plied Mark Twain's Mississippi and most other southern and mid-America streams. They cruised the Colorado River below the Grand Canyon, the cold Yukon up north and California's Sacramento River. (Historical footnote: The famous Pony Express ended its westward gallop in Sacramento; the young riders rode paddlewheelers from there to San Francisco.)

The advent of rail, truck and air transit brought an end to the steamboat era, and it slowed river and canal traffic throughout the world. Then in 1946, Tom Greene of Cincinnati rescued California's decrepit *Delta Queen* paddlewheeler, restored her and began booking cruises on America's southern rivers. Overseas, abandoned canals were cleaned out, locks were repaired and "hotel barges" were built into the hulls of old cargo carriers. Several companies, such as European Waterways, now book leisurely cruises through the winelands of France and the countryside of England, Holland and Belgium.

The legendary Pony Express ended its gallop in Sacramento; the young riders rode river paddlewheelers from there to San Francisco.

New passenger boats are back on Europe's great rivers. They're squarish and shallow of draft to fit the confines of a river, yet they're sleek and quite stylish within. Some even have retractable pilot houses to duck under low bridges. Firms such as Germany's Peter Deilmann-Reederei operate cruises on the Elbe, Rhine, Danube, Rhône and other rivers.

ᕯ ᕯ ᕯ

The world of adventure cruising—specialty cruising if you prefer—is a world of great versatility. In the next chapter, you'll discover just how widespread small ship cruising has become. We've listed cruises by company, type and region, with enough cross-references to bring an old librarian to tears.

What's your definition of adventure? Walking in the eternal twilight of an Arctic tundra? Petting a whale in a Baja lagoon? Sipping wine in a century-old Burgundy cellar? How about rigging sails to catch the wind in the Ligurian Sea, or witnessing the awesome power of an icebreaker, or watching glaciers calve? Could it be simply drinkin' rum and coconut water on a remote beach in the Belize Barrier Reef? Or seeing, for the first time, the Northern Lights or the Southern Cross?

It's all out there, and more, just waiting for you. Read on, and then go catch your ship.

What would the great world lose, I wonder —
Would it be missed or no —
If we stayed in the opal morning,
Floating forever so?
— Edward Rowland Sill, A Tropical Morning at Sea

Chapter two

SMALL SHIP CRUISES
A comprehensive worldwide directory

For the purposes of this book and for the purpose of avoiding crowds, we define small ships as vessels with fewer than a hundred cabins. We make exceptions for some larger craft whose tilt is primarily educational or exploratory.

We also limit our selections to vacation length cruises, generally five days or more. Dozens of overnighters and quickie cruises are available in various ports, river cities and other tourist centers, and these generally can be booked after you arrive.

We've fashioned this directory so that a quick flip of a page or a hasty consultation with the contents or index will put you in touch with the kind of ship, type of cruise or area of the world that interests you. Having made your choice, refer to the alphabetical list of companies for addresses and telephone numbers. A quick note, FAX or call should result in the delivery of a current brochure with prices and itineraries. Don't be surprised to find itineraries different from those listed here. Cruise companies are constantly fine-tuning or changing their routes to satisfy passenger interests.

Who's running the ship?

Some of the companies listed below operate their own ships or boats, while others are booking agents for cruise lines. Further, some operate their own craft and book for other lines as well. Many firms place blocks of passengers on other ships, sometimes assigning their own escorts or lecturers. Still others are packagers specializing in cruises and tours of specific areas of the world or specific areas of interest. But never mind all that. You'll wind up on the cruise that you've booked, no matter who's running the ship.

Incidentally, what the heck is the difference between a ship and a boat? Any old salt will tell you that a ship sails the seven seas, while a boat or barge plies rivers and other inland waterways. Further, any vessel carried aboard a ship is a boat. Common usage has led to frequent violations of these definitions—guaranteed to get a growl of protest from any old seaman worth his salt.

Cruise pricing

Our pricing guides are very general; coming up with a "typical" daily average cost is an apples and oranges thing. Some cruises involve air flights within the itinerary which may or may not be included in the fare. Some companies include shore excursions in their pricing while others do not; a few firms include gratuities. Virtually all cruise fares cover meals on board while some may or may not include meals during shore transfers or land portions of an itinerary. Most firms will arrange pre-cruise and post-cruise hotels, often at special rates; many can arrange discounted air to your launch point.

Having said all that, we offer these *general* guidelines for a basic cruise package with a standard cabin in high season, not including airfare to and from departure points. These ranges are per person, double occupancy. Single supplements are higher and fares for a third person in a cabin often are considerably lower.

INEXPENSIVE — under $100 per day
MODERATE — $100 to $199 per day
MODERATELY EXPENSIVE— $200 to $299 per day
EXPENSIVE — $300 per day and up

Booking: do it now!

Popular cruises, be they expedition ships or the Love Boat, book up very quickly, so make arrangements early. For some, a *year* in advance is not too soon. Another early-booking advantage is that you have a better choice of cabins; the least and most expensive are the first to go.

MAL DE MER AND OTHER MISERIES

Nothing can spoil a cruise quite so thoroughly as that malady of the seas, motion sickness. As we've already noted, small expedition type ships are more subject to wave action than big cruise vessels.

Motion sickness occurs when the inner ear, which senses movement and issues signals to help keep someone on an even keel, becomes confused by multi-directional activity. You might say your balance mechanism doesn't know which way is up. This is particularly true when you can't control movement and therefore can't anticipate it. For instance, a vehicle driver or small aircraft pilot is much less likely to suffer motion sickness than passengers. They're in control and instinctively sense the directional changes.

This knowledge isn't much help when you're on a rolling ocean, feeling like you're about to die, and then perhaps wishing you would. The captain probably won't let you drive the ship. There is relief out there, of course. Most sufferers are helped by medication, particularly *dimenhydrinate,* better known by its brand name, Dramamine. Other medicines on the market are Marezine and Bonine.

Scopolamine, developed several years ago, was particularly effective because it slows the confusing signals sent to the brain by the inner ear. It was administered through the skin by a transdermal patch, since stomach acid destroys its effectiveness. However, the manufacturer took it off the market, possibly because of problems with the delivery system, and it hadn't reappeared at this writing. It was available by prescription only, so check with your doctor or pharmacist to see if has been re-released. Incidentally, anti-motion drugs should be taken half an hour or more before the motion starts. They work better at preventing motion sickness than curing it.

There are other ways to combat motion sickness. Some say that it helps to go out on deck, stand at the rail and breath the fresh air, and look at the horizon instead of the movement of the ship. If the worst happens, you can lean over the side as you lose your lunch. Remember, *never* do this on the windward side of a ship.

My wife Betty, one of those unfortunate victims of motion sickness, finds the best relief is to lie down in her stateroom and close her eyes. Some say that candied ginger or other ginger products helps because it may contain some natural anti-seasickness ingredients. An elastic band with a plastic disk called a "Sea-Band" supposedly relieves motion sickness by exerting pressure on a particular spot on your wrist. Some say it works; others say it doesn't.

Anti-motion drugs should be taken half an hour or more before the motion starts.

A point to remember: The most stable cabins on rough seas are amidships on lower decks. If motion sickness is a problem, request that location when you sign up for a cruise. The least stable cabins are forward, since the bow of a ship rises and falls more than the stern during rough seas. Further, you'll experience more roll on the upper decks. (The bunker fuel probably gets the smoothest ride.) Crews quarters on old sailing ships usually were "before the mast." Perhaps the ship owners figured it was better to have their crews tossed about than their cargo.

By the way, there is one guaranteed method of avoiding sea sickness: Take only river and canal trips.

The other miseries

Expedition cruises often take you to countries with poor sanitation, exposing you to that other dreaded malady, travelers' diarrhea. In this case, ships offer a definite advantage, since you'll be taking most of your meals aboard. If you do eat ashore, follow these tips to avoid the misery of *tourista.*

1. Remember that it's the water; that's where those nasty little microbes usually lurk. In poor sanitation areas, drink only bottled water, beer or processed soft drinks. Avoid ice cubes and ice cream, since the bugs aren't killed by freezing.

2. If you do dine ashore, eat only freshly cooked food that arrives at your table piping hot. Heat will kill the microbes, but cooked food that gets cold can be recontaminated.

3. Avoid fresh salads or any prepared food that has been washed in water. (I recall a cruise on the Li River in China several years ago, when we watched the ship's cooks wash the salad vegetables in the river; we skipped lunch that day.)

4. Peel fresh fruits or vegetables before you eat them, and take care not to contaminate the part you're eating with the peelings.

5. Follow the other gringos; dine in restaurants—particularly hotel restaurants—that cater to a lot of foreign tourists. To protect their trade, they're generally more careful with sanitation measures. Avoid street stalls and food carts like the plague, lest you catch it.

Hepititis is a much more serious health risk than travelers' diarrhea in countries with poor sanitation, so get a gamma globulin shot before leaving on your cruise.

Hepatitis is a much more serious health risk in countries with poor sanitation, so get a gamma globulin shot before leaving on your cruise. A new type, administered as a shot followed by a later booster, provides much longer protection. Also, contact an overseas medical clinic, or your cruise line about other possible health risks where you'll be traveling.

Remember these pointers, whether you're going to squeaky clean countries or to Timbuktu:

1. Take spare eyeglasses and their lens prescriptions.

2. Take your medications and prescriptions for refills.

3. Advise your cruise staff of any medications you may be taking, or of any medical or physical limitations.

4. Take plenty of mosquito repellent. There's been a recent upsurge of malaria in several tropic countries.

5. Keep a cool head by keeping a hat on it in the tropics.

The vessels listed below may be lovable, but they aren't love boats. Although many have doctors aboard, they can't offer the more extensive medical services of larger cruise ships. Further, they may be taking you to areas where on-shore medical aid is scarce.

Finally, keep in mind that adventure cruises often involve more physical exertion than conventional voyages. Enjoy, discover and learn, but don't overdo it.

Handicapped travelers

Wheelchair travelers or others with mobility problems should inquire about facilities aboard ship or ashore before booking a small ship cruise. Some small ships have facilities for handicapped travelers, while others do not because of their confined spaces. Very few have elevators. And of course, shore excursions tend to be more rigorous on many specialty cruises.

Among agencies that handicapped travelers will find useful are: Travel Information Center, 12th Street and Tabor Rd., Philadelphia, PA 19141, (215) 329-5715; Society for the Advancement of Travel for the Handicapped at 26 Court Street, Brooklyn, NY 11242, (718) 858-5483; and Mobility International USA, P.O. Box 3551, Eugene, OR 97403. The publication, *Access to the World—A Travel Guide for the Handicapped*, by Loise Weiss may be useful. It's published by Holt, Rinehart & Winston of New York and should be available in book stores. A pamphlet, *Access Travel*, is available by writing to the U.S. Government Printing Office, Washington, DC 20402.

EXPEDITION CRUISE COMPANIES

These are cruise lines whose primary focus is exploration and education. Their trips often specialize in the flora, fauna, sociology and/or archaeology of specific areas of the world. They generally have field guide/lecturers aboard.

ABERCROMBIE & KENT INTERNATIONAL, INC. ● *1520 Kensington Road, Oak Brook, IL 60521-2141; (800) 323-7308 or (708) 954-2944.*

A leading adventure travel company, A&K markets cruises and land expeditions around the world. This is the Mercedes of adventure companies, priding itself in thoroughly planned, well executed itineraries.

PRICE RANGE ☼ Moderately expensive to expensive.

PEOPLE RANGE ☼ A&K outings will appeal to active people in all age groups, who want to get off the beaten track and learn as they explore, and then return to comfortable quarters or staterooms at night.

THE DRESS ☼ Strictly casual on some cruises; daytime casual with jackets and cocktail wear for dinner on others.

THE VESSELS ☼ The firm often uses the Explorer, a small craft especially outfitted for expedition travel with a complete lecture hall. Facilities include a dining room and lounge, health club and small pool. The 57 cabins and suites have private baths. Nile cruises are aboard A&K's 23-cabin *Sun Boat II* and 20-cabin *Sun Boat III*, also offering comfortable staterooms with private baths.

SHORE EXCURSIONS ☼ All shore excursions and land extensions are included in the cost of the cruise. Nile trips, which cover the major monuments and tombs of Egypt, are accompanied by an Egyptologist.

THE SEASON ☼ Since A&K's operations are global, season vary.

Sample itineraries

ANTARCTICA AND THE FALKLANDS ☼ Fourteen-day tours from Miami, with a flight to Santiago and then to Tierra del Fuego to pick up the *Explorer* for a cruise through Drakes Passage to the Antarctic Peninsula and its offshore islands. Fifteen-day tours are similar to the above but ending in the Falkland Islands. Nineteen-day Antarctica tour-cruises include stops at King George, Elephant and the South Georgia Islands, and the Falklands.

EGYPT ☼ Combination river cruises and land excursions to the pyramids, tombs and temples along the Nile. Groups—limited to 24 participants—tour Cairo, Aswan, Luxor and other key sites, with air flights to Abu Simbel to visit the temple of Ramses II. Itineraries vary from 11 to 18 days; a 20-day

A California gray whale pops up to check out some adventure cruising visitors to Mexico's San Ignacio Lagoon on the Baja peninsula.

tour includes a flight to Kenya for its game preserves. (**Note:** For details, see Cruise Closeup on page 311)

EUROPE ☼ Three to six-day hotel canal barge cruises in southern and central Burgundy, eastern Loire, the Loire Valley and the Seine/Yonne rivers in France; a Holland tulip cruise and a combined Belgium-Holland trip; an upper Thames voyage in England; and combined Germany-Austria cruises on the Danube.

SOUTH AMERICA ☼ Sixteen and 18-day cruises aboard the *Explorer* on the 2,000-mile navigational length of the Amazon from Belem, Brazil, to Iquitos, Peru. A 10-day cruise on the Upper Amazon from Manaus to Iquitos. Eleven-day Ecuador-Galápagos Island tours with seven days cruising in the islands. Eleven-day cruise-tour of the Galápagos, Quito and Guayaquil. Thirteen-day cruise-tour of the Galápagos, Quito and the Ecuadorian highlands. Ten-day land and water Brazilian rainforest tour with three days on the Amazon, out of Manaus.

ᗺᗺᗺ

ARCTIC ODYSSEYS ● *2000 McGilvra Blvd. East, Seattle, WA 98112; (206) 325-1977; FAX (206) 726-8488.*

Mushing through the Arctic—sometimes literally—is the theme of this company. It offers an assortment of overland arctic trips by air, van, ski and sled dog, plus a cruise up Siberia's Lena River and into the Arctic Ocean.

PRICE RANGE ☼ Expensive.

PEOPLE RANGE ☼ All age groups; outdoor types.

THE DRESS ☼ Casual and warm.

THE VESSEL ☼ A Russian container ship, with accommodations for six in vacated crew's quarters; the cabins have private facilities.

SHORE EXCURSIONS ☼ Included in the price; meeting Russian families, visiting sites of early explorations and observing wildlife.

THE SEASON ☼ Summer.

Itinerary

SIBERIA ☼ An eleven-day tour, starting with a flight from Seattle to Yakutia, then a hydrofoil ride on the Lena River to pick up the ship, which cruises down the Lena and into the Arctic Ocean.

ßßß

BAJA EXPEDITIONS ● 2625 Garnet Ave., San Diego, CA 92109; (800) 843-6967 or (619) 581-3311; FAX (619) 581-6542; e-mail: 72234.1520 @compuserve.com.

Tim Means, who founded Baja Expeditions in 1974 and still runs it, is one of the senior operators of discovery trips down Mexico's fascinating Baja California peninsula.

PRICE RANGE ☼ Moderate.

PEOPLE RANGE ☼ All ages; folks interested in hands-on exploration.

THE DRESS ☼ Strictly casual.

THE VESSEL ☼ The *Don José* is an 80-foot expedition boat with seven cozy cabins, share baths, dining and lounge area, TV/VCR and natural history wildlife library. The firm also has kayaking trips in the Sea of Cortez.

SHORE EXCURSIONS ☼ Hikes along remote beaches, visits to seal, elephant seal, sea lion and bird colonies, pauses at tiny Mexican fishing villages.

THE SEASON ☼ "Whale season" is December through March; other expeditions are scheduled throughout the year.

Sample itineraries

BAJA WHALE WATCHING ☼ Five to seven-day expeditions down the Baja peninsula to observe whales and other wildlife. Most originate in San Diego with a return flight from La Paz. Also camping whale-watching trips with day skiffs in Magdalena Bay.

BAJA WILDLIFE ☼ A variety of other trips focus on blue whales, exotic birds and other wildlife. A ten-day trip traces the route of author John Steinbeck during his exploration of the Sea of Cortez.

BAJA SEA KAYAKING AND DIVING ☼ Kayaking in the Sea of Cortez and offshore islands; and wildlife dives for certificated scuba divers.

ßßß

BRYAN WORLD TOURS ● P.O. Box 4156, Topeka, KS 66604-0156; (800) 255-3507 or (913) 272-7511; FAX (913) 272-6244.

This prairie country firm books Amazon rainforest tours aboard a modern version of the African Queen.

PRICE RANGE ☼ Moderate.

PEOPLE RANGE ☼ Folks more interested in intimate exploration than the comforts of a fancy ship.

THE DRESS ☼ Strictly casual.

THE VESSEL ☼ The *Cichla Ocelaris* is a seven-cabin riverboat with cozy staterooms, a lounge, dining room, bar and small library.

SHORE EXCURSIONS ☼ These are the focus of this trip and they're included in the price. The owner is a native Brazilian and a naturalist who takes his passengers in motorized canoes up small tributaries for caboclo (Indian) village visits and wildlife hikes.

THE SEASON ✿ February through October.

Itinerary

BRAZILIAN RAINFOREST ✿ Twelve-day trips out of Manaus on the Rio Negro and Rio Cuieras, two jungle-draped tributaries of the Amazon.

ఴఴఴ

DOLPHIN CHARTERS ● *1007 Leneve Place, El Cerrito, CA 94530; (800) 472-9942 or (510) 527-9622; FAX (510) 525-0720.*

Ronn Patterson's Dolphin Charters are serious expedition cruises limited to a dozen participants per trip, with a strong focus on the flora, fauna, geology and ecology of the areas they visit.

PRICE RANGE ✿ Moderate.

PEOPLE RANGE ✿ Small groups of people who want to get on intimate terms with the environment.

THE DRESS ✿ Strictly casual.

THE VESSELS ✿ The *Delphinus* is a 50-foot "adventure cruising vessel" with cozy accommodations.

SHORE EXCURSIONS ✿ Included in the price and all accompanied by professional naturalists. These are very comprehensive eye-to-eye with the environment trips.

THE SEASON ✿ Spring through fall.

Sample itineraries

SAN JUAN ISLANDS ✿ Five to nine-day trips, starting at Friday Harbor and ending in Port Moneil, B.C.

CANADA'S INSIDE PASSAGE ✿ Nine and ten-day cruises from Port Moneil through the Gulf Islands to Prince Rupert and Ketchikan.

ALASKA'S INSIDE PASSAGE ✿ Six-day natural history trips out of Ketchikan. Ten-day Inside Passage explorations and photo workshops from Ketchikan to Petersburg. Seven-day Petersburg-to-Petersburg nature trips and photo workshops. Seven- day natural history cruises from Petersburg to Juneau. Thirteen- day trips between Juneau and Petersburg with a focus on Glacier Bay.

ఴఴఴ

EGYPT NATIONAL TOURS, INC. ● *Eastern U.S.: 5974 Cleveland Ave., Columbus, OH 43231; (614) 895-1504. Western U.S.: 1500 E. Tropicana, Suite 100-A9, Las Vegas, NV 89119; (800) 84-EGYPT or (702) 795-3803; FAX (702) 795-3035.*

While this firm packages a variety of conventional tours to Egypt, we've listed it under "Expedition cruise lines" because it arranges cruises aboard tiny *feluccas,* the traditional ancient sailboats of the Nile.

PRICE RANGE ✿ Moderate.

PEOPLE RANGE ✿ Folks willing to rough it on a basic little boat.

THE DRESS ✿ Strictly casual.

THE VESSELS ✿ The *felucca* is a small wooden boat with a triangular sail, little changed through the centuries. It's used mostly for light cargo and day sailing, although passengers on this adventure cruise will eat and sleep aboard.

SHORE EXCURSIONS ✿ Tours to adjacent cities and ruins; most are included in the basic price.

THE SEASON ✿ Most of the year.

Sample itineraries

EGYPT ☼ Twelve-day tour, starting with Cairo, Memphis and a flight to Aswan to begin a five-day *felucca* cruise that ends in Luxor. The firm also has conventional land tours of Egypt, Nile cruises, diving trips to the Red Sea, a ten-day camel caravan tour and 16-day bike tour.

ß ß ß

ESPLANADE TOURS/NOBLE CALEDONIA ● *581 Boylston St., Boston, MA 02116; (800) 426-5492 or (617) 266-7465; FAX (617) 262-9829.*

Noble Caledonia is a London-based expedition travel company whose programs are booked in the U.S. by Esplanade Tours.

PRICE RANGE ☼ Moderately expensive; most cruise prices include air travel.

PEOPLE RANGE ☼ Active people who favor exploration-focused travel.

THE DRESS ☼ Daytime casual; jackets and cocktail wear for dinner.

THE VESSEL ☼ The *Caledonian Star* is a 68-cabin expedition ship with TV/VCRs, private baths and mini-bar/refrigerators. Facilities include a single-seating dining room, lounge, bar, lecture room, library, pool, boutique, beauty salon and laundry. The firm also uses other expedition ships.

SHORE EXCURSIONS ☼ Varied, all accompanied by lecturer/field guides and all included in the cruise price.

THE SEASON ☼ Year around, depending on the area.

Sample itineraries

INDIAN OCEAN ☼ A 17-day cruise from Bombay to the Seychelles, calling on ports along India's Malabar Coast to Sri Lanka, the Maldives and Seychelles. A 21-day voyage from the Maldives and Seychelles to Rangoon, Burma and Bankok. A 19-day cruise along India's west coast to the Maldives and Seychelles. A 14-day cruise across the Indian Ocean to the Red Sea and Suez Canal, from the Seychelles to Cairo.

AFRICA-EUROPE ☼ A 14-day voyage from Alexandria to Tobruk, Tripoli, Tunis and Cadiz. A 17-day cruise from Madrid to Cadiz, Lisbon, Orporto and France's Bordeaux to Dartmouth, England. Several 13-day coastal voyages around the British Isles, from either Dartmouth or London to Edinburgh.

SOUTHEAST ASIA ☼ A 21-day cruise from the Seychelles and Maldives through the Malacca straits to Malaysia and Singapore.

ANTARCTICA ☼ A two-week round trip from Buenos Aires to Antarctica aboard the 38-passenger Russian polar research vessel *Khromov.*

ß ß ß

FAR HORIZONS ● *P.O. Box 91900, Albuquerque, NM 87199-1900; (800) 552-4575 or (505) 343-9400; FAX (505) 343-8076; e-mail: 75473.3100@compuserve.com.*

An archeologist by education and traveler by desire, Mary Dell Lucas created Far Horizons to explore cultures of the ancient and modern world. She personally leads many of her company's archaeological and cultural trips.

PRICE RANGE ☼ Moderate, since it includes air fare from New York.

PEOPLE RANGE ☼ All age groups.

THE DRESS ☼ Casual.

THE VESSELS ☼ Small wooden, locally built motor sailers called *gulets* in Turkey; they have six cabins with private bathrooms. Six-cabin catamaran in the Marquesas.

SHORE EXCURSIONS ☼ Comprehensive, with a strong archeological focus on Turkish, Greek and Roman ruins in Turkey; archeology and wildlife in the Marquesas; all included.

THE SEASON ☼ Spring through fall.

Sample itineraries

TURKEY ☼ Sixteen-day land and sea tour along Turkey's south coast from Istanbul, stopping in Ephesus, then boarding a *gulet* in Marmaris for a five-day cruise to Fethiye, Kalkan, Aperlae, Kekova Island, Arycanda and Antalya. Seven-day tour-cruise from Istanbul to Ankara, Cappadocia, Göreme and other ancient towns, boarding the *gulet* in Antalya, with visits to Perge, Kas, Kalkan, Telmessos, Bodrum and Ephesus.

MARQUESAS ☼ Nine-day prehistory, native village and wildlife exploration of Nuku Hiva, Elaho, Ua Huka, Hiva Oa, Tahuata and other little-visited islands of the lush Marquesa group north of Tahiti.

᠘᠘᠘

GALÁPAGOS, INC. ● *7800 Red Rd., Miami, FL 33143; (800) 327-9854 or (305) 665-0841; FAX (305) 661-1457.*

As the name obviously implies, this firm specializes in Galápagos cruises.

PRICE RANGE ☼ Moderate.

PEOPLE RANGE ☼ All age groups.

THE DRESS ☼ Casual.

THE VESSELS ☼ A variety of small Galápagos Island expedition ships and yachts, ranging from 12 to 100 passengers.

SHORE EXCURSIONS ☼ At least two per day in the various islands, accompanied by a naturalist; included in the cruise price.

THE SEASON ☼ All year.

Sample itineraries

GALÁPAGOS ISLANDS ☼ Three to seven-day cruises; longer voyages are quite comprehensive, visiting some of the outer islands.

᠘᠘᠘

GALÁPAGOS NETWORK ● *7200 Corporate Center Dr., Suite 309, Miami, FL 33126; (800) 633-7972 or (305) 592-2294; FAX (305) 592-6394.*

Another tour specialist in the Galápagos islands, this firm books for Ecuador's EcoVenture.

PRICE RANGE ☼ Moderate to moderately expensive.

PEOPLE RANGE ☼ All age groups.

THE DRESS ☼ Casual

THE VESSELS ☼ The *Corinthian* is a 24-cabin expedition ship. The firm also uses three ten-cabin yachts. All have staterooms with private facilities. The larger *Corinthian* offers amenities such as a dining room and grill, bars, lounge with a big screen TV, library and spa.

SHORE EXCURSIONS ☼ All included.

THE SEASON ☼ All year.

Sample itineraries

GALÁPAGOS ☼ Four and five-day cruises from San Cristobal on the smaller yachts. Three, four and eight-day cruises on the *Corinthian,* visiting most of the major islands of Hood, Floreana, Santa Fe, Santa Cruz, South Plaza, Bartolomé, Santiago, Tower, Fernandia and Isabela.

᭰ ᭰ ᭰

GALÁPAGOS TRAVEL ● *P.O. Box 1220, San Juan Bautista, CA 95045-1220; (800) 969-9014 or (408) 623-2920; FAX (408) 623-2923; e-mail 74072.1127@compuserve.com.*

Never mind that he lives in an old mission town in central California. Galápagos Travel founder Barry Boyce is a leading expert on these islands. He's even written a book: *A Traveler's Guide to the Galápagos Islands.*

PRICE RANGE ☼ Moderate.

PEOPLE RANGE ☼ All age groups.

THE DRESS ☼ Casual.

THE VESSELS ☼ The 16-passenger *San Jacinto* was built specifically for Galápagos expeditions; amenities include private baths, dining room, bar and indoor-outdoor lounges and VCR with a natural history video library.

SHORE EXCURSIONS ☼ Comprehensive; at least two a day and all included in the cruise price.

THE SEASON ☼ All year.

Sample itineraries

GALÁPAGOS ☼ Eleven-day round trips from San Cristobal include Española, Floreana, Santa Cruz, Tower, Isabela, James, Bartolomé, Sombrero Chino and other islands. Fifteen-day cruises add a couple more islands, with more time on Santa Cruz. Shore extensions to Ecuador are available, and special photo trips the Galápagos are scheduled each year.

᭰ ᭰ ᭰

GEO EXPEDITIONS ● *P.O. Box 3656, Sonora, CA 95370; (800) 351-5041 or (209) 532-0152; FAX (209) 532-1979.*

This California firm specializes in Ecuador and the Galápagos Islands, offering several expedition-oriented packages.

PRICE RANGE ☼ Moderately expensive.

PEOPLE RANGE ☼ All age groups.

THE DRESS ☼ Casual.

THE VESSELS ☼ Several motor yachts, sailing yachts and a catamaran are used; three to ten staterooms, all with private baths.

SHORE EXCURSIONS ☼ All island stops are included in the price.

THE SEASON ☼ February through December.

Sample itineraries

THE GALÁPAGOS ☼ Geo's main package provides two days in Quito and six days in the Galápagos, from Baltra or San Cristobal to Española, Santa Cruz, North Seymour, Tower, Santiago, South Plaza and Santa Fe. Other packages are 14 days with two days in the Amazon rainforest headwaters and six in the Galápagos; 13 days with four in Quito and the Ecuadorian highlands, then six in the Galápagos; and 18 days with six in Lima, Cuzco, the Urubamba Valley and Machu Picchu, and then six days in the Galápagos.

᭰ ᭰ ᭰

GEOGRAPHIC EXPEDITIONS ● *2627 Lombard St., San Francisco, CA 94123; (800) 777-8183 or (415) 922-0448; FAX (415) 346-5535; e-mail: info@geoex.com.*

This firm, started as InnerAsia, offers creative adventure travel throughout the world, including several cruises. Trips range from rigorous to easy.

PRICE RANGE ☼ Moderate to expensive.

PEOPLE RANGE ☼ Active travelers in all age groups who want to experience and learn; and to discover out of the way places.

THE DRESS ☼ Varied; mostly outdoor gear.

THE VESSELS ☼ Small sailboats, sailing yachts and expedition ships.

SHORE EXCURSIONS ☼ Moderate to strenuous hikes, explorations of temples, ancient ruins and little-visited cities and villages.

THE SEASON ☼ Varies, depending on the area.

Sample itineraries

TURKEY ☼ Seventeen days touring, hiking and sailing the Turquoise Coast in a *gulet* (small wooden sailing vessel), round trip from Istanbul.

SOUTHEAST ASIA ☼ Eight days touring Thailand and sailing lush islands of the Andaman Sea west of Burma. Seventeen days touring, sailing and river cruising in Thailand. A 17-day exploration of Bali and the Savu Sea, including ten day on a schooner exploring islands between Bali and Timur.

SOUTH PACIFIC ☼ Ten-day and two-week explorations of Polynesia and the Cook Islands aboard the specially-built expedition ship, *World Discoverer*.

ALASKA ☼ Five and eight days cruising Prince William Sound aboard the expedition ship, *Discovery*.

ANTARCTICA ☼ Two-week to 26-day explorations of the Weddell Sea, Antarctic Peninsula and Falklands aboard expedition ships.

ᔭᔭᔭ

INTERNATIONAL EXPEDITIONS ● *One Environs Park, Helena, AL 35080; (800) 633-4734 or (205) 428-1700; FAX (205) 428-1714.*

This expedition company conducts a variety of natural history land tours and several small ship cruises.

PRICE RANGE ☼ Moderately expensive, including air from the U.S. mainland.

PEOPLE RANGE ☼ All age groups

THE DRESS ☼ Casual.

THE VESSELS ☼ *La Esmerelda* is a Brazilian river boat with eight cabins, all with bathrooms; plus a dining room and observation deck. The *Adelaar* is a motor-sailer with seven cabins and shared bathrooms; dining room-lounge and bar.

SHORE EXCURSIONS ☼ All included; wildlife viewing visits to rarely-seen villages on Amazonian tributaries and tours of outer islands of Indonesia.

THE SEASON ☼ July-December in Indonesia; all year on the Amazon.

Itineraries

THE AMAZON ☼ Eight-day cruise aboard the *Esmerelda* on the lesser-traveled Amazonian rivers of Ucayali, Tapiche, Yanayacu and Sabina. Five- day extension to Cuzco and Machu Picchu available.

INDONESIA ☼ Twelve-day land and sea tours, with cruising aboard the *Adelaar* to Gili, Lombok, Moyo, Sumbawa and Komodo islands.

ᔭᔭᔭ

INTERNATIONAL JOURNEYS ● *12995 S. Cleveland Ave., # 117, Fort Meyers, FL 33907; (800) 622-6525 or (941) 278-1955; FAX (941) 278-1004.*

This firm conducts a variety of environmentally-sensitive educational expeditions around the world, including cruises on the upper Amazon.

PRICE RANGE ☼ Moderate.

PEOPLE RANGE ☼ Active outdoor types.

THE DRESS ☼ Casual.

THE VESSELS ☼ The 90- foot *El Arca* and 146-foot *Rio Amazonas* are riverboats with 16 and 20 air conditioned cabins with private baths.

SHORE EXCURSIONS ☼ Three to five trips a day are included in the price. They're accompanied by an American biologist and Peruvian naturalist, up tributaries, into the rainforest and to towns and tribal villages along the way.

THE SEASON ☼ Spring.

Itinerary

THE AMAZON ☼ Eight-day round trip on the upper Amazon from Iquitos, Peru, to Tabatinga, Brazil; seven-day extensions to Machu Picchu available.

℘℘℘

JOURNEYS INTERNATIONAL ● *4011 Jackson Rd., Ann Arbor, MI 48103; (800) 255-8735 or (313) 665-4407; FAX (313) 665-2945.*

This firm offers Galápagos and upper Amazon cruises, plus land trips to Africa, Asia, Indonesia, New Guinea, Australia and the Americas.

PRICE RANGE ☼ Moderate.

PEOPLE RANGE ☼ All age groups.

THE DRESS ☼ Very casual.

THE VESSELS ☼ The *Amazon Explorer* and other small riverboats with three to five cabins on the Amazon; expedition ships and motor yachts in the Galápagos.

SHORE EXCURSIONS ☼ Some are included; others are optional.

THE SEASON ☼ Most of the year, depending on the area.

Sample itineraries

THE AMAZON ☼ Eight-day cruises on the Amazon and Rio Negro from Manaus. Eight-day round trip cruises on the upper Amazon from Iquitos.

THE GALÁPAGOS ☼ Comprehensive 11-day cruises, visiting most of the islands, from San Cristobal or Baltra.

℘℘℘

MALUKU ADVENTURES ● *P.O. Box 7625, Menlo Park, CA 94026-7625; (800) 566-2585 or (415) 731-2560; FAX (415) 731-2579; Web site is http://www.maluku.com; e-mail: maluku@maluku.com.*

"Discovery adventure cruises" are the specialty of this firm, including some combination cruising/diving trips.

PRICE RANGE ☼ Moderate to moderately expensive.

PEOPLE RANGE ☼ Of particular appeal to divers and other aquatic types.

THE DRESS ☼ Very casual.

THE VESSELS ☼ Two motor sailers with four and eight cabins; private baths, dining room-lounge, sun deck and dive base. Also a ten-cabin motor vessel and various charter craft, including a Chinese junk.

SHORE EXCURSIONS ☼ Some are included; others are additional. On diving trips, three dives a day generally are scheduled.

THE SEASON ☼ Year around, depending on the region.

Sample itineraries

INDONESIA ☼ Six to 19-day cruises and combined cruising-diving trips from Bali, particularly around the Moluccans (Spice Islands); stops at Komodo, Gili, Moyo and Indonesian New Guinea (Irian Jaya).

SOUTHEAST ASIA ☼ Seven-day cruises aboard a junk between Saigon and Cambodia, calling on the villages of the Mekong River. Two to 10-day cruises from Phuket, Thailand, around the Andaman Sea in a dorm-style motor cruiser.

℞℞℞

MARINE EXPEDITIONS ● *13 Hazelton Ave., Toronto, Ontario, Canada M5R 2E1; (800) 263-9147 or (416) 964-9069; FAX (416) 964-2366.*

This Canadian adventure travel firm concentrates on the ends of the earth and the middle—the polar regions, the Russian far east and South and Central America.

PRICE RANGE ☼ Moderately expensive to expensive.

PEOPLE RANGE ☼ Serious expedition cruising types.

THE DRESS ☼ Casual.

THE VESSELS ☼ Five ice-rated research vessels with 15 to 54 cabins with private baths; ship facilities include a dining room, small library, lounge, small pool and sauna.

SHORE EXCURSIONS ☼ All included, lead by naturalists and other experts in their fields.

THE SEASON ☼ Year around, depending on the region.

Sample itineraries

ALASKA AND RUSSIA ☼ An eight-day cruise up the Inside Passage; stops include Misty Fjords, Glacier Bay and Sitka National Park. A 12-day cruise from Nome through the Bering Sea to Siberian Russia and Wrangell Island.

ANTARCTICA ☼ Thirteen-day cruises from Santiago through Drake's Passage to the Arctic Peninsula, and to the offshore islands. Eighteen-day cruises, with itinerary similar to the above, plus a stop at the Falkland Islands. Twenty-three day trips to Antarctica, the Falklands and South Georgia.

THE ARCTIC ☼ Twelve-day cruises from Greenland into the Canadian high arctic, exploring Cornwallis Island, Prince Leopold Island, Pond Inlet, Baffin Island and other sites. A 13-day cruise from Reykjavik, Iceland, for a coastal exploration of southern Greenland. A ten-day circumnavigation of Iceland.

BRITISH ISLES ☼ A 14-day "Celtic Expedition" from London around the British Isles to the Faroes and Iceland.

SOUTH AND CENTRAL AMERICA ☼ An eight-day coastal cruise of Venezuela, Panama and Costa Rica. An eight-day voyage with stops at Costa Rica, Nicaragua, Honduras, Belize and its Barrier Reef. An eight-day Belize, Mexico, Cayman Islands and Jamaica cruise. An eleven-day cruise from Nassau to Cozumel and Belize, then through the Panama Canal. Ten-day Chilean fjords cruise and a 20-day voyage down the Peruvian and Chilean coasts to the fjords.

TRANS-ATLANTIC ☼ A 50-day positioning cruise from the Falkland Islands to London, calling on South Georgia, St. Helena, Ascension, the Cape Verdes and other Atlantic islands.

℞℞℞

MELANESIAN TOURIST SERVICES ● *302 W.Grand Ave., Suite 10-B, El Segundo, CA 90245; (310) 785-0370; FAX (310) 785-0314.*

This firm specializes in Papua New Guinea, cruising its rivers and surrounding islands. It also offers many land excursions into New Guinea and helicopter safaris.

PRICE RANGE ☼ Moderately expensive.

PEOPLE RANGE ☼ All age groups; obviously people curious about Papua New Guinea.

THE DRESS ☼ Casual.

THE VESSELS ☼ The *Melanesian Discoverer* is a 25-cabin catamaran with private baths and TVs in each room; restaurant, lounges, library and dive shop.

SHORE EXCURSIONS ☼ All included, featuring trips up shallow tributaries via Zodiac or jetboat to visit remote villages.

THE SEASON ☼ All year.

Sample itineraries

PAPUA NEW GUINEA ☼ A variety of tour-cruise combos up the Sepik River and to the offshore islands; most start and end in Port Moresby. Among the trips are 14-day Sepik River and Trobriand Islands; nine-day Mount Hagen, Sepik River and Bulolo; seven-day Madang and Sepik; 14-day Mendi, Sepik River, Trobriand Islands and Atolau; ten-day Mount Hagen, Trobriand Islands and Atolau; and ten-day Gorka, Mendi, Sepik River and Madang. Also special diving and fishing expeditions.

ß ß ß

NATURAL HABITAT ADVENTURES ● *2945 Center Green Court, Boulder, CO 80301; (800) 543-8917 or (303) 449-3711; FAX (303) 449-3712.*

A global expedition company with a strong environmental thrust, this firm features cruises in the Canadian high arctic and antarctic, Spitsbergen and Franz Josef Land above Norway, Madagascar/Seychelles and other areas. Research programs also are available.

PRICE RANGE ☼ Moderately expensive to expensive.

PEOPLE RANGE ☼ All age groups.

THE DRESS ☼ Casual.

THE VESSELS ☼ A variety of expedition ships, including the 57-cabin *Caledonian Star* with cabin TV and mini-bars; the 50-stateroom Russian icebreaker *Kapitan Khlebnikov* with private baths; and the nine-cabin catamaran *Bottom Time II* with shared baths.

SHORE EXCURSIONS ☼ All included in the tour price.

THE SEASON ☼ All year, depending on the area.

Sample itineraries

ANTARCTICA ☼ A comprehensive 27-day "Ultimate Antarctica" cruise aboard a Russian icebreaker from Santiago through Drake's Passage to the Clarence and South Orkney islands, into the Weddell sea with several mainland Antarctica stops, then to the South Sandwich, South Georgia and Falkland Islands. Twenty-one days from Tierra del Fuego through Drake's Passage to the Antarctic Peninsula and Deception Island to the South Orkneys, South Georgia and Falkland Islands. Twelve to 14-day cruises from Santiago through Drake's Passage to the Antarctic Peninsula.

THE AZORES AND PORTUGAL ☼ Eight to ten-day whale watching cruises between the Azores and Lisbon.

BAJA PENINSULA ☼ Eleven days observing whales and other wildlife on the Baja Peninsula; round trip from La Paz.

CARIBBEAN SEA ☼ Ten day whale-watching trips off the Turks and Caicos archipelago and the Dominican Republic. Eight-day wildlife cruise; round trip from Fort Lauderdale to the Bahamas aboard a sailing schooner.

The Russian icebreaker Kapitan Khlebnikov *crushes through thick pack ice during a Quark expedition to the Canadian high arctic.*

GALÁPAGOS ISLANDS ✿ Seventeen-day "Untouched Galápagos" cruises to some of the archipelago's rarely visited islands. Eleven-day Galápagos cruise to Baltra, Española, Hood, Santa Cruz and other islands.

HIGH ARCTIC ✿ Sixteen-day cruises aboard a Russian icebreaker, circumnavigating Baffin Island in the Canadian high arctic. Fifteen-day cruise aboard a Russian icebreaker from Spitsbergen to Franz Joseph Land.

SEYCHELLES AND MADAGASCAR ✿ Nineteen-day cruise from the Seychelles to Madagascar and several other African offshore islands.

≈ ≈ ≈

NATURE EXPEDITIONS INTERNATIONAL ● *P.O. Box 11495, Eugene, OR 97440; (800) 869-0639 or (503) 484-6529; FAX (503) 484-6531; e-mail: naturexp@aol.com.*

This firm, which specializes in land expeditions over much of the globe, also blocks passage on Society Expeditions' cruises in the South Pacific, arctic and antarctic. See Society's listing below, on page 36.

≈ ≈ ≈

OVERSEAS ADVENTURE TRAVEL ● *625 Mt. Auburn St., Cambridge, MA 02138; (800) 221-0814 or (617) 876-0533; FAX (617) 876-0455.*

This firm markets a variety of land and water trips around the globe, specializing in educational outings for small groups.

PRICE RANGE ✿ Moderate.

PEOPLE RANGE ✿ Active people who like off-the-beaten-path travel.

THE DRESS ✿ Casual.

THE VESSELS ✿ A variety of small expedition ships and motor/sail boats.

SHORE EXCURSIONS ✿ All-inclusive trips offer wildlife hikes, visits to remote villages and major museums and explorations of ancient temples and assorted ruins.

THE SEASON ✿ Year-around, depending on the area.

Sample itineraries

ANTARCTICA ☼ Two-week trips from Tierra del Fuego to the Shetland Islands to visit King George, Half Moon, Deception Islands and other areas of the Arctic Peninsula.

THE ARCTIC ☼ Twelve-day cruises about Hudsons Bay, Baffin Island and Greenland.

ECUADOR ☼ Twelve-day Galápagos wildlife trips to Islas Genovesa, Santiago, Bartolomé and assorted other lesser visited islands.

EGYPT ☼ Sixteen-day Egypt tours including three days cruising the Nile between Aswan and Luxor and a side trip to the Red Sea.

TURKEY ☼ Seventeen-day cruises in the Aegean and Mediterranean seas between Finike and Mamaris, calling on Myra, Kekova, Kas and Oludeniz.

ᕼᕼᕼ

PACIFIC SEA FARI TOURS ● 2083 Emerson Street, San Diego, CA 92106; (619) 226-8224.

A San Diego charter fishing boat company called H&M Landing was the first to begin whale watching trips along Mexico's Baja Peninsula, back in the late 1970s. The company still conducts these Baja trips, operating as Pacific Sea Fari Tours. Whales are only part of the itinerary; these are natural history tours that cover the flora, fauna and geology of this arid peninsula.

PRICE RANGE ☼ Moderate.

PEOPLE RANGE ☼ Anyone in good physical health can handle the shore excursions and wildlife hikes on these trips. Whale-watching is conducted from *pangas,* small outboards operated by Mexican guides accompanied by English-speaking personnel from the boat.

THE DRESS ☼ Casual.

THE VESSELS ☼ The 88-foot *Spirit of Adventure* is a converted charter fishing boats with 14 Pullman type cabins, operated either in conjunction with Pacific Sea Faris or independently as Spirit of Adventure Charters. A companion craft operated by Pacific Sea Fari, the *Big Game* is similar in size and facilities.

SHORE EXCURSIONS ☼ Included in the cruise price, they range from visiting sea elephant colonies to darting among friendly whales in Baja's lagoons.

THE SEASON ☼ These cruises are timed to the migration of the gray whales, from January through early April.

Sample itineraries

BAJA CALIFORNIA ☼ Trips vary from seven to 12 days. Some are round trips from San Diego; others involve a flight back from the Baja Peninsula. Some trips sail around the tip of the peninsula and into the Sea of Cortez. (**Note:** Cruise Closeup on page 165.)

ᕼᕼᕼ

QUARK EXPEDITIONS ● 980 Post Rd., Darien, CT 06820; (800) 356-5699 or (203) 656-0499; FAX (203) 655-6623; e-mail: 76255.3266@compuserve.com

The premier company of high adventure cruising, Quark practically goes from pole to pole. It leases Russian icebreakers for cruises in the high arctic and the antarctic; one nuclear powered ship smashes ice all the way to the North Pole. The firm also packages other cruises and adventure-focused land expeditions from polar regions to the tropics.

PRICE RANGE ✪ Expensive; renting Russian icebreakers doesn't come cheap. The polar cruises include all shore excursions, helicopters for sightseeing and ship to shore transit, expert lecturer/field guides and a parka that you can take home. Other cruises also are all-inclusive.

PEOPLE RANGE ✪ These are active outings, with shore excursions ranging from tundra hikes to explorations of remote villages. Anyone physically fit can keep pace.

THE DRESS ✪ Casual; "formal" means that you remove your parka before going to dinner.

THE VESSELS ✪ The arctic and antarctic ships are Russian icebreakers. The *Kapitan Khlebnikov* and *Kapitan Dranitsyn* are 22,000 horsepower craft; the nuclear powered *Yamal* uses its 75,000 horsepower to cruise all the way to the North Pole, the world's only surface ship capable of doing so. The three icebreakers have about 50 cabins with private baths, dining rooms, small bars and lounges. Other craft include the Russian oceanographic research vessels *Professor Khromov* and *Akademik Shokalski*, with 24 cabins, some with and some without private bathrooms; and the *Alla Tarasova* expedition cruise ship with 52 cabins, all with private baths.

SHORE EXCURSIONS ✪ On the polar trips, visits to remote villages and historic explorers' camps, wildlife spotting hikes over the tundra, helicopter flights to glaciers and Zodiac trips for up-close wildlife observation; all included in the cruise price. Diving, snorkeling, island explorations and studies of flora and fauna on other cruises.

THE SEASON ✪ Summertime, which means July to September in the Arctic and October to early January in the antarctic.

Sample itineraries

AFRICA ✪ An 18-day voyage from South Africa to Tanzania, stopping at Madagascar and its surrounding islands and the Comores island group.

ANTARCTICA ✪ Quark is offering the ultimate polar trip—a 66-day circumnavigation of Antarctica with the *Kapitan Khlebnikov*; the only one ever accomplished by a passenger-carrying ship. Other antarctic itineraries include 12-day round trip voyages from Santiago through Drakes Passage to the South Shetland Islands and several antarctic stops; and 23-day and 24-day cruises between Tasmania and New Zealand through the Ross Sea to the rarely visited empower penguin colonies.

CANADIAN ARCTIC ✪ The *Kapitan Khlebnikov* and/or *Kapitan Dranitsyn* offer several itineraries of nine days or more in the Canadian high arctic. One starts at Resolute far north of the Arctic Circle and explores the coastal wilds of Devon and Baffin islands and Greenland. (**Note:** Cruise Closeup on page 99.) Another itinerary takes adventurers through the legendary Northwest Passage.

EASTERN ARCTIC ✪ At least two itineraries are available in the Europe-Asian arctic—a 13-day trip from coastal Norway to Spitsbergen and Franz Josef Land; and a 20-day cruise from Spitsbergen across the Siberian Sea via the Northeast Passage to Provideniya.

MICRONESIA ✪ A 17-day snorkeling, diving and island-hopping cruise of Micronesia from Truk to Palau aboard the *Akademik Shokalsky*.

NORTH POLE ✪ The *Yamal* departs Helsinki on this 16-day expedition, cruising past Franz Joseph Land and breaking ice all the way to the North Pole and then returning via the Siberian coast to Murmansk.

SEYCHELLES ✿ Twelve-day cruise among the Seychelles aboard the ocean research vessel *Professor Khromov*, featuring stops at rarely visited islands.

SOUTH AMERICA ✿ Six and eleven-day cruise through the Chilean fjords aboard the *Alla Tarasova,* sailing north from Cape Horn

SOUTH PACIFIC ✿ Fifteen-day cruise aboard the *Akademik Shokalski* from Cairns, Australia, to Truk, New Guinea and western Micronesia.

ßßß

RADISSON SEVEN SEAS CRUISE LINE ● *600 Corporate Drive, Suite 410, Fort Lauderdale, FL 33334; (800) 477-7500 or (305) 776-6123; FAX (305) 772-3763.*

Sailing somewhere between expedition cruising and soft cruising, Radisson offers adventure with refinement and panache. Its three vessels, merged under the Radisson Seven Seas label in 1995, are nicely appointed small ships offering the amenities and comforts of most larger vessels.

PRICE RANGE ✿ Expensive.

PEOPLE RANGE ✿ Sophisticated, adventure-bent travelers bored with the Love Boat.

THE DRESS ✿ Casual daytime; moderately dressy "resort wear" for evenings.

THE VESSELS ✿ The 90-cabin *Hanseatic* is the line's true expedition ship, with an ice-hardened hull and a fleet of Zodiacs. It's also elegant, with good-sized staterooms, single-sitting dining, an entertainment lounge, fitness center, spa, sauna and pool. The 177-cabin *Radisson Diamond* is more of a mid-sized cruise ship, with luxury amenities. The 100-passenger *Song of Flower,* built in Japan for the upscale American and European market, also is more of a conventional—if luxury—cruise ship.

SHORE EXCURSIONS ✿ Most are included, ranging from typical Zodiac wildlife stops to excursions in shore cities and prowls through native villages.

THE SEASON ✿ Year around, depending on the area.

Sample itineraries

ASIA/AFRICA ✿ Twenty-day tour/cruise from Nairobi to Bangkok with stops at Mombasa, the Seychelles, Maldives, Sri Lanka, Madras (India), Andaman Island and Rangoon. Eight-day cruise from Singapore to Rangoon, stopping at Kuala Lumpur, Penang and Phuket.

CARIBBEAN ✿ Various itineraries, including eight days from St. Maarten with stops at Puerto Rico, British Virgins, Santo Domingo, Jamaica and the Bahamas; and eight days with stops at St. Kitts, Dominica, Grenada, Bequia, Barbados and Guadeloupe.

CENTRAL AND SOUTH AMERICA ✿ Fourteen-day cruise from Tierra del Fuego to Rio de Janeiro, stopping at the Falklands, coastal Argentina, Uruguay and coastal Brazil. Eleven-day cruises from Tierra del Fuego to the Antarctic Peninsula and the Falkland and South Shetland islands. Fifteen-day coastal Peruvian-Chilean cruise from Esmeraldas to Lima. A 13-day cruise from St. Maarten through the Panama Canal to Costa Rica.

EUORPE ✿ Eight-day Athens to Istanbul cruise with stops at Santorini, Rhodes, Kusadasi and Dikili. Eight day cruise from Rome to Barcelona, stopping at various Mediterranean islands, St. Tropoz, Monte Carlo, Portofino and Livorno.

FAR EAST ✿ Fourteen-day cruise plus four days in Beijing, with shore stops in Shanghai and several other Chinese cities; Cheju-do and Pusan in Korea and Fukuyama, Osaka and Tokyo, Japan.

NORTH AMERICA ✿ Ten-day northeastern U.S.-Canada cruise from Boston along the coast of Maine to the Maritime Provinces and Montréal.

ßßß

SEE & SEA TRAVEL SERVICE ● *50 Francisco St., Suite 205, San Francisco, CA 94133; (800) 348-9778; FAX (415) 434-3409; e-mail: divx-prt@ix.netcom.com; Web site is http://www.divxprt.com/see&sea*

Do you like getting wet and staying wet? This firm books diving trips throughout the world.

PRICE RANGE ✿ Moderate to moderately expensive.

PEOPLE RANGE ✿ Certified divers.

THE DRESS ✿ Wetsuits and scuba gear.

THE VESSELS ✿ A variety of dive boats and expedition craft.

SHORE EXCURSIONS ✿ Wildlife explorations, plus lots of diving.

THE SEASON ✿ Varied, depending on locations.

Sample itineraries

WORLDWIDE ✿ The firm's long list of diving expeditions ranges from the barrier reefs of Australia and Belize to the Caribbean, Hawaii, Galápagos, South Pacific and the Coral Sea of New Guinea.

ßßß

SOCIETY EXPEDITIONS ● *2001 Western Ave., Suite 300, Seattle, WA 98121; (800) 548-8669 or (206) 728-9400; FAX (206) 728-2301.*

Started back in 1972 as one of the world's first adventure travel companies, Society Expeditions is back in business, resuming its role as a leading authority in expedition cruising.

PRICE RANGE ✿ Expensive; these are all-inclusive cruises employing expert guides and lecturers.

PEOPLE RANGE ✿ Travelers with an urge to explore and learn.

THE DRESS ✿ Casual daytime; "casually elegant" in the evening.

THE VESSEL ✿ The *World Discoverer* offers both creature comforts and serious expedition amenities such as a fully-equipped lecture hall and extensive natural history library. The 71 cabins have private baths, desks and large windows. Facilities include single-seat dining, lounge, boutique, fitness center with sauna, salon, laundry and a sun deck with a small pool.

SHORE EXCURSIONS ✿ Led by experienced naturalists, all are included in the cruise price.

THE SEASON ✿ All year, depending on the itinerary.

Sample itineraries

ALASKA/ARCTIC ✿ Twelve and 16-day cruises along the Bearing Strait from Nome to Homer, stopping at Russia's Provideniya, the Pribilofs and the Katmai and Kenai peninsulas. Twelve-day Inside Passage and Gulf of Alaska cruises through Prince William Sound, Glacier Bay National Park, Hubbard Glacier, Prince of Wales Island and Misty Fjords National Monument.

ANTARCTICA ✿ Fifteen to 21-day cruises, with a variety of itineraries including the Antarctic Peninsula, Falkland Islands, Chilean fjords, South Georgia and the Orkneys.

SOUTH SEAS ☼ Nineteen-day cruises "In the Wake of the Bounty" from Santiago to Easter and Pitcairn islands, the Marquesas, Societies and other South Pacific Islands. Twenty-day cruises from Papeete through the Tahitian archipelago to Mataiva, Rangiroa, the Line Islands and Hawaiian Islands. Eleven to 14-day cruises between Papeete and the Cook Islands, stopping at Huahine, Raiatea, Bora Bora, Mopelia, Atiu, Aitutaki and Rarotonga.

ß ß ß

SOUTHERN HERITAGE EXPEDITIONS ● *P.O. Box 209-219, Christchurch, New Zealand; (03) 359-7711; FAX (03) 359-3311.*

This New Zealand based firm runs expedition trips to the antarctic, particularly the Ross Sea.

PRICE RANGE ☼ Expensive.

PEOPLE RANGE ☼ Active people who like chilly adventure.

THE DRESS ☼ Casual day and night.

THE VESSEL ☼ The *Akadehik Shokalski* is a 19-cabin research ship specifically outfitted for polar exploration.

SHORE EXCURSIONS ☼ All-inclusive trips include expeditions ashore to view the wildlife and topography of Antarctica and its offshore islands.

THE SEASON ☼ November through March.

Itinerary

ANTARCTICA ☼ Eight-day to month-long voyages from New Zealand into the Ross Sea, with stops at sub-antarctic islands of New Zealand and the Antarctic Peninsula. The antarctic trips are some of the most comprehensive available. Also, coastal New Zealand fjord and birdwatching cruises and a month-long exploration of south Indian Ocean islands such as St. Paul, Amsterdam and Kerguelen.

ß ß ß

SPECIAL EXPEDITIONS ● *720 Fifth Avenue, Sixth Floor, New York, NY 10019; (800) 762-0003; (212) 765-7740; FAX (212) 654-3770.*

Founded by Sven-Olof Lindblad, the son of expedition travel pioneer Lars-Eric Lindblad, Special Expeditions is one of the major forces in adventure travel, with a varied worldwide program.

PRICE RANGE ☼ Moderate to expensive.

PEOPLE RANGE ☼ All age groups; active people who want to learn as they travel.

THE DRESS ☼ Casual day and evening.

THE VESSEL ☼ The 40-cabin *Polaris* is the mother ship of this large touring company. It's a serious expedition vessel with a combination lounge-lecture room for films, slides and talks. It has single-seat unassigned dining; cabins with private baths, plus a sauna, small shop and salon. The firm also uses other craft, including the 70-passenger *Sea Bird* and *Sea Lion* expedition ships, and the *Sea Cloud,* an opulent four-masted schooner.

SHORE EXCURSIONS ☼ All are included in the cruise price, consisting of field trips led by naturalist guides and lecturers.

THE SEASON ☼ Year around, depending on the area.

Sample itineraries

MEXICO AND CENTRAL AMERICA ☼ An eight-day cruise from Colon, Panama, through the Panama Canal to San Jose, Costa Rica, with stops at wildlife preserves and national parks. An eight-day cruise in the Sea of Cortez aboard the *M.V. Sea Lion*, with a train trip through Mexico's stunning Copper Canyon. Ten-day trips down the Baja Peninsula to observe the gray whales and the wildlife abundance of the Sea of Cortez.

THE NORTHWEST ☼ A seven-day cruise up the Columbia and Snake river system, following the trail of Lewis and Clark. Eight-day sea, land and air explorations of the Inside Passage and Glacier Bay. Twelve-day cruises between Seattle and Sitka, exploring the Inside Passage, Glacier Bay and the Gulf Islands and San Juan Islands. Seven days from Seattle to Vancouver, exploring the San Juan and Gulf Islands and coastal British Columbia.

SOUTH AMERICA ☼ A 17-day tour of Ecuador, including three days in the Amazon, five days in the Galápagos and tours of Quito and Guayaquil.

EUROPE ☼ A 15-day cruise from Dover to Lisbon, pausing at Guimaraes, Oporto, Islas Cies and several ports along the coast of France. An eight-day cruise from Dover to Dublin, exploring Wales and southern England. An eight-day exploration of Ireland. Twelve days cruising from Dover to Helsinki, via Amsterdam and the Kiel Canal. Eleven days exploring the coasts of Sweden, Finland and the Finnish archipelago. Fifteen-day cruise from Lisbon to Naples with visits to Gibraltar, Granada, Sardinia and Malta.

THE CARIBBEAN ☼ An eight-day round trip from Antigua to the Grenadines, Tobago, St. Lucia, Dominica and Iles des Saintes aboard the *Sea Cloud*.

EGYPT ☼ A comprehensive 16-day exploration of Egypt, from Cairo to Abu Simbel, with several days aboard the small riverboat *Hapi*.

℞℞℞

SPIRIT OF ADVENTURE CHARTERS ● *1938 Catalina Blvd., San Diego, CA 92107; phone/FAX (619) 226-1729.*

A pioneer of Baja California whale-watching trips, Mike Keating and his wife Annmarie offer a variety of itineraries from San Diego in their *Spirit of Adventure* expedition ship. Their trips generally are booked through Pacific Sea Fari Tours, or they can be contacted directly. For details, see Pacific Sea Fari Tours listing on page 33. (**Note:** Cruise Closeup on page 165.)

℞℞℞

WILDERNESS TRAVEL ● *801 Allston Way, Berkeley, CA 94710; (800) 368-2794 or (510) 548-0420; FAX (510) 548-0347.*

Wilderness Travel packages a wide variety of expeditions around the world, including several cruises. These are small group outings, generally under 15 people, and all are accompanied by trained lecturer-guides.

PRICE RANGE ☼ Mostly moderate.

PEOPLE RANGE ☼ Outdoor types.

THE DRESS ☼ Casual.

THE VESSELS ☼ Assorted expedition type ships and small sailing craft.

SHORE EXCURSIONS ☼ A great variety of hikes, water activities and such, generally environmentally focused; most are included in the trip price.

THE SEASON ☼ Year around, depending on the area.

Sample itineraries

SOUTH AMERICA ☼ Comprehensive 14-day cruises through the Galápagos Islands. A 16-day "Natural History of Ecuador" tour that includes an eight-day Galápagos cruise. A 16-day "Andes, Amazon and Galápagos" trip; two days on the Amazon and five in the islands. Eleven-day "Hidden Galápagos" and "Enchanted Isles" tours; several days on land and a seven-day cruise.

The fact that the Step Pyramid near Cairo may be the world's oldest surviving manmade objects, dating back to 2500 B.C., probably doesn't impress this local resident. Nile River cruises offer easy access to Egypt's antiquities.

TURKEY ☼ Seventeen-day hiking and sailing trip along the Turquoise coast to Antalya, Marmaris, Phaselis, Finike, and Fethiye, in a *gulet,* a small wooden sailing vessel.

INDONESIA ☼ Eleven-day "cultural cruises" to Lombok, Sumbawa and the Nusa Tenggara island chain (Lesser Sundas), with a stop at the "dragon" island of Komodo.

SOUTH PACIFIC ☼ Eight and nine days aboard a 72-foot sailing ketch with three staterooms with private baths, exploring small islands of the Fiji archipelago and the Vanuatu chain.

ANTARCTICA ☼ The much-traveled *World Discoverer* expedition ship is employed by Wilderness Travel on 15 to 21-day explorations of Antarctica, the Falklands, South Georgia and the Chilean fjords.

ß ß ß

WORLD EXPLORER CRUISES ● *555 Montgomery St., San Francisco, CA 94111-2544; (800) 854-3835 or (415) 393-1565; FAX (415) 391-1145.*

What's a company with a 739-passenger vessel doing in a small ship cruising directory? Although the *Enchanted Seas* is a good sized cruise ship, World Explorer cruises have a strong educational and expeditionary focus, with on-board lecturers and field guides.

PRICE RANGE ☼ Moderate to moderately expensive.

PEOPLE RANGE ☼ People who like educational cruises with cruise ship amenities.

THE DRESS ☼ Casual during daytime, informal for dinner; no ties.

THE VESSEL ☼ The 617-foot *Enchanted Seas* is a 739-passenger cruise ship with the usual on-board amenities of shops, entertainment lounge and fitness center. To make it an expedition ship, the firm has added a 15,000 volume library and classroom facilities for staff and guest lecturers.

SHORE EXCURSIONS ☼ More than 40 optional shore excursions are offered, or passengers can explore on their own.

THE SEASON ☼ Summer in Alaska; winter in Central and South America.

Sample itineraries

ALASKA ☼ Comprehensive 14-day cruises from Vancouver up Alaska's Inside Passage, visiting all Southeast ports, plus Glacier Bay, Hubbard Glacier, Valdez and Victoria.

CENTRAL AND SOUTH AMERICA ☼ Fourteen-day voyages from Nassau, with stops on the Yucatan Peninsula, Honduras, Costa Rica, Panama, Columbia and Jamaica.

฿฿฿

ZEGRAHM EXPEDITIONS • 1414 Dexter Ave., Suite 327, Seattle, WA 98109; (800) 628-8747 or (206) 285-4000; FAX (206) 285-5037.

Another major adventure travel company, Zegrahm packages expedition trips about the globe, often working in conjunction with other firms.

PRICE RANGE ☼ Moderately expensive to expensive.

PEOPLE RANGE ☼ All age groups.

THE DRESS ☼ Casual.

THE VESSELS ☼ The firm books expedition trips on a variety of expedition ships, from the *Explorer, World Discoverer* and *Caledonian Star* to Russian icebreakers.

SHORE EXCURSIONS ☼ All included in the fare.

THE SEASON ☼ All year, depending on the area.

Sample itineraries

ANTARCTICA ☼ Twenty-seven day cruise aboard a Russian icebreaker from Santiago through Drake's Passage to the Clarence and South Orkney islands, into the Weddell sea with several mainland Antarctica stops, then to the South Sandwich, South Georgia and Falkland Islands. Twenty-one days from Tierra del Fuego through Drake's Passage to the Antarctic Peninsula and Deception Island to the South Orkneys, South Georgia and Falkland Islands. Twelve to 14-day cruises from Santiago through Drake's Passage to the Antarctic Peninsula. A two-week circumnavigation of the Falklands and South Georgia from Santiago.

AUSTRALIA ☼ Two-week expeditions in the 42-passenger expedition launch *Coral Princess* along the Kimberly coast of northwest Australia, with explorations of inlets and helicopter flights into the Outback. One-week cruise aboard the *Coral Princess* across the Gulf of Carpentaria, from Darwin past Cape Arnhem and Cape York to Cairns, off the Great Barrier Reef.

POLYNESIA ☼ Nineteen-day cruise aboard Windstar's 70-cabin *Wind Song* from Papeete, Tahiti, to Suva, Fiji, calling on islands of French Polynesia, the Cook Islands and the Vava'u group. Sixteen-day round trip from Papeete aboard the *Windsong*, calling on most of the islands of French Polynesia.

GALÁPAGOS ISLANDS ☼ Ten-day excursions aboard the 18-passenger motor yacht *Flamingo*, calling on most of the islands, including some lesser-visited sites.

HIGH ARCTIC ☼ Sixteen-day circumnavigation of Baffin Island in the Canadian high arctic.

INDONESIA ☼ Eighteen-day cruise aboard P&O Spice Islands' 36-passenger *Island Explorer* along the coast of Irian Jaya and Banda Islands to Bali. A

16-day cruise from the Banda Islands to the Lesser Sundas and Komodo Island to Bali.

SEYCHELLES AND MADAGASCAR ☼ Nineteen-day cruise from the Seychelles to Madagascar and several other African offshore islands.

PASSENGER FERRY LINES

To call the two major operations listed below "ferries" is something of an understatement, since they have passenger cabins and some of the other amenities of regular cruise ships.

ALASKA MARINE HIGHWAY ● *P.O. Box 25535, Juneau, AK 99802-5535; (800) 642-0066 or (907) 465-3941; FAX (907) 277-4829; Web site is http://www/dot.state.ak.us/external/amhs/home.html.*

This "highway" is a wet one—hundreds of miles of mountain-rimmed channels and fjords of Alaska's Inside Passage. The Alaska ferry system serves all the communities in the coastal archipelago complex since none of them are linked by highway. The ferries are the darling of Alaskan tourists, who travel in comfortable cabins or as deck passengers. The big boats haul more than 400,000 passengers each year. Vehicles can be taken in the holds; it's very popular for the RV crowd, although you can't sleep in your rig aboard.

Note: Reservations are required for passenger, staterooms and vehicles, and they must be made *far in advance* for summer sailings, particularly for the initial leg out of Bellingham, Washington, the starting point for the continental U.S.

PRICE RANGE ☼ Inexpensive to moderate.

PEOPLE RANGE ☼ All age groups.

THE DRESS ☼ Casual.

THE VESSELS ☼ The big blue boats of the Alaska Ferry system range in size from 193 to 418 feet. Passenger capacity varies, since many travelers roll out sleeping bags or they're day-trippers. The largest, the 3,946-ton *Columbia* can carry 625 passengers; it has ninety-one cabins with 312 berths.

SHORE EXCURSIONS ☼ None are scheduled, although national forest rangers ride the ferries in summer to give talks and point out interesting landfalls along the route. Also, entertainers come aboard in summer.

THE SEASON ☼ All year, although the ferries are busiest in summer.

Note: Travelers can link to the Alaska Ferry terminal at British Columbia's Prince Rupert by catching B.C. Ferries' *Queen of Prince Rupert* on Vancouver Island near Victoria. Contact BC Ferries, 1112 Fort Street, Victoria, B.C. V8V 4V2; (604) 386-3431; FAX (604) 381-5452.

Itineraries

ALASKA FERRIES ☼ With departures out of its mainland terminal at Bellingham, Washington, the ferries offer frequent service to Inside Passage communities of Ketchikan, Wrangell, Petersburg, Sitka, Juneau, Haines and Skagway. Less frequent service is available to Steward/Hyder, Metlakatla, Prince of Wales Island, and Pelican and Hoonah on Chichagofi Island north of Sitka. Service also is available between Cordova and Valdez across Prince William Sound, from Seldovia and Homer to Kodiak Island, and along the Aleutian chain to Dutch Harbor.

B.C. FERRIES ☼ Daily overnight runs from Port Hardy on Vancouver Island to Prince Rupert on the British Columbia mainland; also service from Prince Rupert to Skidegae on Queen Charlotte Island.

ß ß ß

BERGEN LINE ● *405 Park Ave., New York, NY 10022; (800) 323-7436 for booking information; (800) 666-2374 for brochures; local phone (212) 319-1300; FAX (212) 319-1390.*

Bergen is the American booking agent for the legendary *Hurtigruten,* the coastal passenger-cargo-ferry boats that call on the cities of Norway's northern shores. The firm also books other northern European passenger ferries.

PRICE RANGE ✿ Inexpensive to moderate; lounge passengers with sleeping bags can travel for very little. Cabins with dining room service are about the same as typical cruise ship prices.

PEOPLE RANGE ✿ These trips involve no real physical activity so they're suitable for any age. Shore excursions involve van trips and short walks.

THE DRESS ✿ Casual; some passengers dine in jackets and cocktail wear, but it's optional.

THE VESSELS ✿ The *Hertigruten* hardly fit the profile of small ships; the newer ones have cabin space for 482 passengers and carry a couple of hundred more as day-trippers or sleeping-baggers. However the itineraries to the northernmost reaches of Norway certainly qualify these outings as soft adventure cruises.

SHORE EXCURSIONS ✿ They vary from tours through Norway's northern towns and a visit to the North Cape to scenic overland trips among the fjords. Pre-trip and post-trip rail trips between Oslo and Bergen through a beautiful mountain area are popular. Shore excursions are extra.

THE SEASON ✿ Coastal ferries operate the year around although the best weather and therefore busiest period is summer; fall can be nice and the ships are less crowded.

Itineraries

NORWAY'S NORTH COAST ✿ The ferries offer daily departures between Bergen and Kirkenes. The cruise itself is eleven days round trip and five (southbound) or six (northbound) one way. Air, sea and land packages from the U.S. via Oslo range from 11 to 15 days. Some include a spectacular "Norway in a Nutshell" train trip through the mountains between Oslo and Bergen, and down to the fjord valley of Flam. Some European ground tours include a brief ferry ride. (**Note:** Cruise Closeup on page 211.)

NORWAY TO RUSSIA ✿ Special cruises are offered from Kirkenes through the Kola fjord and into the Barents Sea to the Russian port of Murmansk from mid-June through early August. Sailings are daily except Sunday and Wednesday, and a four-week advance reservation is recommended.

PASSENGER-CARGO LINERS

I f you still have visions of rusty old tramp steamers with a foul-mouthed one-eyed captain, you haven't been on a passenger-cargo liner lately. Many have amenities and comforts to match modern cruise ships. Cargo lines have two good reasons for building passenger facilities into their ships—they're given preferential dock space at ports of call, and they generate additional income. If the banana crop fails along a South Pacific cargo route, the companies can still haul tourists.

We haven't repeated "People range" after each listing unless there are specific age limits, since passenger-cargo liners essentially appeal to the same group—folks who love the sea, with lots of time on their hands.

The Norwegian town of Alesund, draped scenically over a narrow peninsula, is one of the more appealing stops on the Hertigruten *"Coastal Express."*

Freighter travel is almost a cult, and it's supported by two newsletters. *Freighter Space Advisory* is published twice monthly by Freighter World Cruises, Inc., 180 S. Lake Ave., Suite 335, Pasadena, CA 91101; (818) 449-3106; FAX (818) 449-9573. The firm also books passenger freighters and other small ships. *Freighter Travel News* is published monthly by the Freighter Travel Club of America, 3524 Harts Lake Rd., Roy, WA 98580. This newsletter, containing articles on freighter travel and ads from freighter-passenger lines, has been in print for nearly forty years.

ßßß

BANK LINE ● *Dexter House, 2 Royal Mint Court, London EC3N 4XX England; (0171) 265-0808; FAX (0171) 481-4784.*

This firm, allied with United Baltic Corporation (below), offers around the world cruises on four recently refurbished cargo ships.

PRICE RANGE ☼ Moderate.

PEOPLE RANGE ☼ Age limit 82.

THE DRESS ☼ Casual daytime; informal evening wear.

THE VESSELS ☼ Four cargo-container ships, each with four cabins and four double suites for a passenger capacity of 12. Facilities include a lounge, dining room, solarium, gym, pool and sauna.

SHORE EXCURSIONS ☼ On-board British purser can help plan shore stops; port time ranges from one to four days.

THE SEASON ☼ Year-around

Itinerary

THE GLOBE ☼ The four ships depart from one of three cities—Liverpool, Hamburg or Antwerp and cruise around the world, returning in 110 to 115 days. The route takes them through the Panama Canal to Tahiti and other South Pacific islands, New Guinea, Indonesia, Singapore and through the Suez Canal back to Europe.

ßßß

COMPAGNIE FRANÇAISE MARITIME DE TAHITI • *P.O. Box 368-Papeete, 98713 Papeete, Tahiti; (689) 42 63 93; FAX (689) 432 06 17.*

This firm operates a "trading coaster" in the Marquesqas Islands, sailing out of Papeete. It also runs a six-hour passenger ferry between Papeete and Bora-Bora with stops at Huahine, Raiatea and Tahaa.

PRICE RANGE ☼ Inexpensive.

THE DRESS ☼ Casual day and evening.

THE VESSEL ☼ The *Tsaporo 4* is a trading coaster with 12 cabins.

SHORE EXCURSIONS ☼ No planned excursions.

THE SEASON ☼ Year-around.

Itinerary

MARQUESAS ☼ Seven-day cruises from Papeete to Taiohae, calling on Vaitahu, Atuona, Omoa and Vaipaee; four-day return, calling on Hakahau.

ßßß

COMPAGNIE POLYNESIENNE DE TRANSPORT MARITIME • *595 Market St., Room 2880, San Francisco, CA 94105; (800) 972-7268 or (415) 541-0677; FAX (415) 541-0766.*

For many small ship fans, this Tahitian company's ship, the *Aranui* is the Love Boat. It's one of the most popular freighter-passenger cruises in the industry. It's also inexpensive, and for a *real* bargain, travelers can join locals as deck passengers. The atmosphere on this pleasantly funky cruise is so laid back that one travel writer described it as an "un-cruise."

PRICE RANGE ☼ Inexpensive to moderate.

PEOPLE RANGE ☼ All age groups.

THE DRESS ☼ Casual.

THE VESSEL ☼ The *Aranui* is a freighter-mail boat with 36 cabins, most with air conditioning and private baths. Other amenities include a dining room, swimming pool, video room and library.

SHORE EXCURSIONS ☼ Sightseeing tours, picnics and visits to archaeological sites are included.

THE SEASON ☼ All year.

Itineraries

FRENCH POLYNESIA ☼ Sixteen-day round trips between Papeete and Marquesas Islands. Two-day trips from Papeete to the Tuamotu Islands, two days from Tuamotu to the Marquesas and ten days from Nuku Hivato Rangiora.

ßßß

CURNOW SHIPPING, LTD. • *American agents are TravLtips, Inc., 163-07 Depot Rd., Flushing, NY 11358, (800) 872-8584 or (718) 939-2400; and Golden Bear Travel, P.O. Box 6115 (16 Digital Dr., Suite 100), Novato, CA 94948-6115, (800) 551-1000 or (415)382-8900.*

Curnow operates the passenger-freighter-mail ship *St. Helena* between the United Kingdom and South Africa.

PRICE RANGE ☼ Moderate.

THE DRESS ☼ Casual daytime; jacket and tie evenings.

THE VESSEL ☼ Offering more passenger facilities than most freighters, the *St. Helena* has 49 cabins, most with private baths; dining salon, pool, sun lounge, video and book library and small boutique.

SHORE EXCURSIONS ☼ Available at additional cost, including explorations of Ascension Island, city tour of St. Helena and tours of historic sites.
THE SEASON ☼ Year around.

Itinerary

UNITED KINGDOM TO SOUTH AFRICA ☼ Twelve-day cruises from Cardiff, Wales, to Cape Town, South Africa, with port stops at Asension Island and St. Helena.

฿฿฿

FRACHTSCHIFF-TOURISTIK KAPITÄN ZYLMANN • *Exhöft 12, D-24404 Maashold, Germany; (49) 0-4642-6068; FAX (49) 0-4642-6767.*

More than a hundred freighters are represented by this large German booking firm, with fifty or more sea routes.
PRICE RANGE ☼ Inexpensive to moderate.
THE DRESS ☼ Casual; "blue jeans possible always."
THE VESSELS ☼ More than a hundred vessels, ranging from container ships to general cargo and supply ships; passenger capacity ranges from one to a dozen cabins. Most ships have German crews; English is spoken aboard.
SHORE EXCURSIONS ☼ Varied.
THE SEASON ☼ All year.

Sample itineraries

TRANS-ATLANTIC ☼ Popular for American travelers is a 12-day crossing from Richmond, Virginia, to Antwerp, Belgium; others cruise between Hamburg and New York, and Italy and New York.
EUROPE ☼ Various combinations include Rotterdam to Portugal; Rotterdam to Belgium and Ireland; Hamburg to the Scandinavian countries.
GLOBAL ☼ Antwerp to South Africa; Bremen or Hamburg to South America; Hamburg to Casablanca to Antwerp; and Hamburg to the Madeira islands and Spain.

฿฿฿

HORN LINE • *Süderstrasse 75, D-20097 Hamburg, Germany; (040) 23 677-113; FAX (040) 23 677-119.*

This German firm operates several passenger freighter ships out of Hamburg with regular trips to the Caribbean and Costa Rica.
PRICE RANGE ☼ Moderate.
THE DRESS ☼ Casual daytime and evening.
THE VESSELS ☼ Identical cargo ships, each with six passenger cabins.
SHORE EXCURSIONS ☼ None planned.
THE SEASON ☼ All year.

Itinerary

GERMANY TO CENTRAL AMERICA ☼ Thirty-five days between Hamburg and Costa Rica, calling on Dover (England), Antwerp (Belgium), Le Havre (France), Guadeloupe and Martinique in the Caribbean, and Costa Rica.

฿฿฿

IVARAN LINES • *111 Pavonia Ave., Jersey City, NJ 07310; (800) 451-1639 or (201) 798-5656.*

This firm sails the sleek new Norwegian freighter *Americana* from New Orleans down the east coast of South America and a smaller ship from New Jersey to South America.

PRICE RANGE ☼ Moderate.

PEOPLE RANGE ☼ No age limit on the *Americana*; under 80 on the *San Antonio*.

THE DRESS ☼ Casual days, casual to casually dressy evenings.

THE VESSELS ☼ The *Americana* is one of the few passenger-freighters with luxury accommodations. It offers single-seat dining, a swimming pool, sauna and health club, lounge and even a small casino. Passenger capacity is 88, although it usually carries fewer. The *San Antonio* is a more modest 12-passenger freighter; cabins have private bathrooms.

THE SEASON ☼ All year.

Sample itineraries

U.S. TO SOUTH AMERICA ☼ The *Americana* makes 48-day cruises from New Orleans to South America, calling on Houston, La Guaira (Venezuela), Rio de Janeiro, Buenos Aires, Barbados, Puerto Rico, the Dominican Republic and Vera Cruz, Mexico. The *San Antonio* sails from New Jersey, calling on Baltimore, Norfolk, Savannah, Miami and many of the same South American cities as the *Americana*, but no Caribbean ports.

ßßß

MARIS USA, LTD. ● *215 Main St., Westport, CT 06880-3210; (800) 99-MARIS; FAX (203) 222-1500.*

Maris books a variety of passenger-freighters, including around the world cruises.

PRICE RANGE ☼ Inexpensive to moderate.

THE DRESS ☼ Mostly casual.

THE VESSELS ☼ A great variety of passenger-cargo ships, from container vessels and general cargo ships to mail and supply ships. They have from two to 12 cabins.

SHORE EXCURSIONS ☼ Some are included.

THE SEASON ☼ Year around, depending on the area.

Sample itineraries

GLOBAL ☼ The ABC Container line circles the globe from New Orleans in 98 days, with stops in Nova Scotia, England, Germany, Israel, through the Suez Canal to Singapore, Australia, New Zealand and through the Panama Canal to New Orleans.

Other round-trippers booked by Maris: the Bank Line, 110 to 115 days from Europe via Tahiti, Western Samoa, New Caledonia, New Guinea, the Philippines and Singapore. The *DSR Senator,* around the world from Oakland and Long Beach in 84 days, via Japan, Korea, Hong Kong, Taiwan, Singapore, Shri Lanka, Belgium, the Netherlands, England, Germany, the American east coast and through the Panama Canal back to Long Beach. The NSB line, 99 days from Savannah via the Panama Canal to Tahiti, New Caledonia, Taiwan, Hong Kong, New Zealand, the Suez Canal to Egypt's Port Said, Italy, England and New York.

SHORTER CRUISES ☼ Other freighters booked by Maris circumnavigate South America; cruise South America's west coast; cruise from Savannah to South America; sail from England to South Africa; cruise from Wales to South Africa; journey from Florida to the South Pacific, New Zealand and Australia; and from Los Angeles to Australia and New Zealand, ending in Seattle, Washington.

⚑⚑⚑
PATHFINDER ● *P.O. Box 461, Southampton S015 2ZE England; (01703) 33-4415.*

This firm books passengers aboard four container vessels operated by Safmarine shipping company between England and South Africa.

PRICE RANGE ✿ Moderate.

THE DRESS ✿ Casual day and evening.

THE VESSELS ✿ Four 52,000-ton container ships, each with six cabins; air conditioned with TV/VCRs and private baths. Onboard facilities include a laundry, small indoor pool, lounge area, library and bar. Passengers dine with the officers.

SHORE EXCURSIONS ✿ No organized excursions.

THE SEASON ✿ All year.

Itinerary

ENGLAND TO SOUTH AFRICA ✿ About two sailings a month, 15 to 16 days, between Tilbury to Cape Town; port stops may include Amsterdam, Le Havre (France), Puerto Rico, Trinidad, Venezuela, Curacao, Aruba, Columbia, Costa Rica and Jamaica.

⚑⚑⚑
SEA THE DIFFERENCE, INC. ● *420 Fifth Ave., New York, NY 10018-2702; (800) 666-9333 or (212) 354-4409; FAX (212) 764-8592.*

Assorted cargo vessels are booked by this firm, offering a variety of worldwide itineraries.

PRICE RANGE ✿ Moderate.

THE DRESS ✿ Casual.

THE VESSELS ✿ Various cargo ships with one to six cabins; most have refrigerators and private bathrooms.

SHORE EXCURSIONS ✿ None.

THE SEASON ✿ The year around

Sample itineraries

GLOBAL ✿ Among the port combinations are East Coast to Europe, South America and South Africa; Mediterranean to eastern and southern Africa; South Africa to Australia and islands of the Indian Ocean; northern Europe to the Mediterranean; northern Europe to the Canary Islands and Portugal; and northern Europe to South Africa.

⚑⚑⚑
UNITED BALTIC CORPORATION ● *Dexter House, 2 Royal Mint Court, London EC3N 4XY; (0171) 265-0808; FAX (0171) 481-4784.*

United Baltic runs two freighters out of the United Kingdom to ports in northwestern Europe.

PRICE RANGE ✿ Moderate.

THE DRESS ✿ "Smart but casual"; daytime informal, with suits and dressy dresses for dinner.

THE VESSELS ✿ The *Baltic Eagle* is a six-cabin cargo vessel and the *Baltic Eider* is a cargo carrier with a single "owner's suite" cabin; all have private baths and some have refrigerators. Onboard facilities include a TV/video lounge and sauna; passengers dine with the ship's officers. The vessels also can haul private vehicles.

SHORE EXCURSIONS ☼ None scheduled.
THE SEASON ☼ The year around.

Sample itineraries

NORTHWESTERN EUROPE ☼ Twenty-one-day trips from England to Amsterdam, Helsinki and Antwerp; eleven-day round trips between Finland and Belgium; and ten-day Finland-Belgium-Holland voyages.

RIVER & CANAL BOATS & BARGES

This versatile category includes a variety of craft that ply the world's inland waterways—paddlewheelers in America's heartland, canal barges and sleek river boats in Europe and those popular "hotel boats" of the Nile, a great way to see Egypt's antiquities. (**Note:** Some small expedition ships also do river cruises in addition to ocean and coastal waterway voyages. Also, some companies market ocean, river and canal boat cruises. You'll find these mixed itineraries under "Soft adventure cruise lines" below.)

ß ß ß

AMERICAN WEST STEAMBOAT COMPANY ● *520 Pike St., Suite 1400, Seattle, WA 98101; (800) 434-1232 or (206) 621-0913; FAX (206) 623-7809.*

A brand-new made-to-look-old classic steamboat comprises the one-ship fleet of this firm, which cruises the Columbia, Willamette and Snake Rivers.

PRICE RANGE ☼ Moderately expensive.
PEOPLE RANGE ☼ All age groups.
THE DRESS ☼ Casual daytime; casually dressy at night; jackets and cocktail wear requested for captain's dinners.
THE VESSEL ☼ The *Queen of the West* is suitably queenly, with plush Victorian and turn-of-the-century American decor. It has 73 outside staterooms with TV/VCRs (many cabins with verandas; most with desks), a dining room, bar and grill, three bars and a showroom with live entertainment.
SHORE EXCURSIONS ☼ Among shore stops, all included in the price, are Fort Clatsop National Memorial in Astoria, Oregon Trail Interpretive Center in Oregon City, Mount Hood Railroad trip, Maryhill Museum and Stonehenge and a jet boat ride into Hells Canyon.
THE SEASON ☼ Year around.

Sample itineraries

OREGON-WASHINGTON-IDAHO ☼ All are round trips from Portland. Seven-night cruises cover the full navigable length of the Columbia and Snake rivers, from Astoria to Lewiston, with a Hells Canyon jet boat trip. Five-night trips sail through the Columbia River gorge to its confluence with the Snake, then back to the mouth at Astoria. Four night round trips go to Hood River with side trips to Mount St. Helens and the Mount Hood Scenic Railway. Three night cruises go to Hood River and back to Astoria, and two nights jaunts run from Portland to Astoria, with land extensions to Cannon Beach.

ß ß ß

BOLSHOI CRUISES, INC. ● *379 N. University Ave., Suite 301, Provo, UT 84601; (800) 769-8687 or (801) 373-8000; FAX (801) 377-8800.*

This firm is a marketing agent for Russian river cruises between Moscow and St. Petersburg.

PRICE RANGE ☼ Moderate.

PEOPLE RANGE ☼ Various age groups.

THE DRESS ☼ Casual; sportswear for evening.

THE VESSEL ☼ The *MS Maxim Gorki* is a 75-cabin river boat with a restaurant, reading salon, hairdresser, bar and "Music Station" where several classic artists perform.

SHORE EXCURSIONS ☼ Visits to the Hermitage, Russian palaces and cathedrals, village homes, art galleries, and evenings at the opera and ballet. All are included in the cruise price.

THE SEASON ☼ May through October.

Itineraries

RUSSIA ☼ Fourteen-day cruises between Moscow and St. Petersburg, with port calls at Uglitch, Kostroma, Plyons, Kizchi and other towns along the Volga and Svir rivers.

ß ß ß

CRUISE MARKETING INTERNATIONAL ● *1601 Industrial Way, Belmont, CA 94002; (800) 5-RUSSIA or (415) 592-1397; FAX (415) 591-4970.*

This firm markets inexpensive river trips in Russia and the Ukraine.

PRICE RANGE ☼ Inexpensive.

PEOPLE RANGE ☼ Various age groups.

THE DRESS ☼ Casual day and evening.

THE VESSELS ☼ The *Russ* and *Marshall* are small cruise ships with dining room, bar, music salon, boutique, theater and solarium. The 130 cabins have private baths and refrigerators.

SHORE EXCURSIONS ☼ Tours of Moscow, the Kremlin and Red Square, day trip to Zagorsk and visits to the Hermitage, Peter and Paul Fortress and Catherine Palace in St. Petersburg. All are included in the cruise price.

THE SEASON ☼ Spring through summer.

Itineraries

RUSSIA ☼ Two-week cruises between Moscow and St. Petersburg on the *Russ* and *Koshevoy*, with stops at Uglich, Yaroslavi, Kizhi Island, Onega and other communities. Also two-week cruises between Kiev and Yalta/Odessa, calling on Zaporozheye, Yepatoria, Sebastopol, New Kahovka and other cities.

UKRAINE/BLACK SEA ☼ The *Kosshevoy* offers 15-day cruises from Kiev down the Ndieper River to the Black Sea, ending at Yalta.

ß ß ß

DELTA QUEEN STEAMSHIP COMPANY ● *30 Robin Street Wharf, New Orleans, LA 70130-1890, (800) 543-1949; FAX (504) 585-0630.*

This company brought steamboatin' back to life when its founder Tom Greene rescued an old California paddlewheeler in 1946. He refurbished it and put it to work on the Mississippi River system. Three paddlewheelers—one antique and two elegant replicas—now ply the rivers of America's heartland.

PRICE RANGE ☼ Moderately expensive to expensive.

PEOPLE RANGE ☼ These laid-back trips appeal particularly to senior travelers, although some young'uns like to go steamboatin' as well.

THE DRESS ☼ Casual daytime; business and cocktail wear in the evening, with ties for the captain's dinner.

A pair of queens tie up at McFarland Park near Florence, Georgia, on the Tennessee River. The historic Delta Queen *is dwarfed by the new* American Queen.

THE VESSELS ☼ The *Delta Queen* is a completely refurbished 1927 steam-driven paddlewheeler with 87 staterooms. The 207-cabin *Mississippi Queen* and 222-cabin *American Queen* are newly built and cast in the mold of the grand old riverboats.

SHORE EXCURSIONS ☼ Tours, which are extra, include trips to shoreline and neighboring cities, museums and assorted other attractions along the rivers. Pre-tour and post-tour packages in cities of embarkation and debarkation are available.

THE SEASON ☼ The riverboats cruise the year around; spring and fall generally offer the best weather.

Itineraries

SOUTH AND CENTRAL U.S. ☼ The three *Queens* interlace the heartland rivers of America, with cruises from two to 12 days. Several can be linked for those who just want to keep on paddlewheelin'. The riverboats ply the Mississippi, Arkansas, Tennessee, Cumberland, Ohio and Atchafalaya rivers and the intercostal waterway between New Orleans and Galveston. (**Note:** Cruise Closeup on page 133.)

ß ß ß

ERIE CANAL CRUISE LINES ● *114 W. Bayard St., Seneca Falls, NY 13148; (800) 962-1771 or (315) 568-1771; FAX (315) 568-4812.*

These are do-it-yourself cruises on which, as the brochure says: "You are your own captain and crew."

PRICE RANGE ☼ Moderate.

PEOPLE RANGE ☼ Particularly appealing to families.

THE DRESS ☼ Casual.

THE VESSEL ☼ The 42-foot *Canal Cruiser* has two private staterooms and total sleeping accommodations for six, plus a kitchen, dining salon and private bathrooms.

SHORE EXCURSIONS ✿ On your own, exploring small villages, historical sites and wineries, biking or walking along the canal banks.

THE SEASON ✿ The year around.

Itinerary

NEW YORK STATE ✿ One week to ten-day hire boat cruises on the Erie Canal between Waterloo and Fairport; "canallers" pick their own itinerary.

ß ß ß

EUROPEAN WATERWAYS ● *140 E. 56th St., Suite 4-C, New York, NY 10022; (800) 217-4447 or (212) 688-9489.*

This firm conducts leisurely canal and river barge cruises in England, Scotland, Ireland, the Netherlands, Belgium and the winelands of France. European Waterways also organizes chateaux tours in Europe.

PRICE RANGE ✿ Expensive.

PEOPLE RANGE ✿ All age groups.

THE DRESS ✿ Daytime casual; casual to dressy at night.

THE VESSELS ✿ Fully equipped canal barges; three to seven staterooms.

SHORE EXCURSIONS ✿ All included; private wine tastings; tours of ancient villages, castles, museums and historic sites. Some cruises include dinners ashore at noted restaurants.

THE SEASON ✿ April through October.

Sample itineraries
(All are one-week cruises)

GREAT BRITAIN ✿ Windsor to Shillingford aboard the seven-cabin *Actief*. Great Bradford to St. Ives aboard the five-cabin *Barkis* or *Peggotty*. Ireland's Carrick to Athlone on the upper Shannon aboard the five-cabin *Bona Spes*. Scotland's Caledonian Canal and Loch Ness on the four-cabin *Vertrouwen*.

FRANCE ✿ Dijon to Vandessse or Clamency to Auxerre in Burgundy; and Sete to Beaucaire in Provence on the six-cabin *La Belle Epoque*. (**Note:** Cruise closeup on page 230.) Montargis to Chatillon-Sur-Loire on the five-cabin *La Joi de Vivre*. Auxerre to Chevroches on the four-cabin *Penelope*. Tolouse to Agen on the four-cabin *Rosa*. Bordeaux wine country cruise on the five-cabin *Anjodi*.

FRANCE, HOLLAND AND BELGIUM ✿ Strasbourg to Mittersheim or Amsterdam to Amsterdam on the four-cabin *Stella*.

ß ß ß

FRENCH COUNTRY WATERWAYS, LTD. ● *P.O. Box 2195, Duxbury, MA 02331; (800) 222-1236 or (617) 934-2454; FAX (617) 934-9048.*

The waterways of the legendary Burgundy region of France are the pleasant pathways of this canal barge company.

PRICE RANGE ✿ Expensive.

PEOPLE RANGE ✿ All age groups.

THE DRESS ✿ Casual daytimes, "smart casual" evenings.

THE VESSELS ✿ Luxury canal barges with four to nine cabins.

SHORE EXCURSIONS ✿ Private wine tastings, and visits to estates, chateaux, medieval towns and castles, plus a dinner ashore in a noted restaurant; all included.

THE SEASON ✿ April through October.

Itineraries
(All are one-week cruises)

FRANCE ☼ Dijon to St. Léger-sur-Dheune aboard the nine-cabin *Esprit.* Tonnerre to Venarey-les-Laumes on the six-cabin *Horizon II.* Joigny to Clamency aboard the four-cabin *Liberte.* Sens to Ancy-le-Franc on the six-cabin *Nenuphar.*

ß ß ß

KD RIVER CRUISES ● *Eastern U.S.: 2500 Westchester Ave., Purchase, NY 10577; (800) 346-6525 or (914) 696-3600; FAX (914) 696-0833. Western U.S.: 323 Geary St., San Francisco, CA 94102; (800) 858-8587 or (415) 392-8817; FAX (415) 392-8868.*

The Rhine, Danube, Elbe, Moselle, Main, Seine, Rhône and Volga are the playgrounds of this large river cruising company.

PRICE RANGE ☼ Mostly moderate; some moderately expensive.

PEOPLE RANGE ☼ All age groups.

THE DRESS ☼ Casual daytime; jackets and cocktail wear evenings.

THE VESSELS ☼ A variety of 104 to 184-passenger river cruisers, all with private baths, some with TV. One or two seatings at dinner; many with pools, saunas, gift shops and reading rooms.

SHORE EXCURSIONS ☼ Guided tours to villages, historic sites, wineries and such can be purchased as a package.

THE SEASON ☼ Most of the year, depending on the area.

Sample itineraries

GERMANY-HOLLAND ☼ The Rhine: five-day Basel to Amsterdam; five-day Amsterdam to Strasbourg; five-day Cologne to Basel; six days from Amsterdam to Basel; four days from Basel to Cologne. The Rhine-Maine: four-day Cologne to Frankfurt; four-day Frankfurt to Amsterdam.

GERMANY-AUSTRIA-HUNGARY ☼ The Danube: Eight-day Nuremberg to Budapest; eight-day Nuremberg to Vienna; five-day Vienna to Passau.

GERMANY-CZECH REPUBLIC ☼ The Elbe: six-day Berlin and Wittenberg to Prague; six day Dresden to Wittenberg and Berlin; eight-day Hamburg to Dresden; seven-day Prague to Hamburg.

FRANCE ☼ Eight-day Paris to Honfleur on the Seine. Eight-day Losne to Avignon (Geneva) on the Rhône and Saône.

RUSSIA ☼ Eleven-day St. Petersburg to Moscow on the Volga and Svir.

ß ß ß

MID-LAKES NAVIGATION, LTD. ● *P.O. Box 61, Skaneateles, NY 13152-7566; (800) 545-4318 or (315) 685-8500.*

The firm offers two and three-day canal boat cruises on the Erie Canal, and it offers hire boats on the Erie and on Florida's Okeechobee Waterway.

PRICE RANGE ☼ Moderate to moderately expensive.

PEOPLE RANGE ☼ Good family outings.

THE DRESS ☼ Casual.

THE VESSELS ☼ Thirty-three to 44-foot "Lockmaster" canal boats with one or two cabins and full houseboat type facilities.

SHORE EXCURSIONS ☼ On your own, exploring small villages, historical sites and wineries, biking or walking along the canal banks.

THE SEASON ☼ All year.

Itineraries

NEW YORK STATE ☼ Two and three-day cruises on New York's Erie Canal and sail-it-yourself hire boats.

ße ße ße

PETER DEILMANN EUROPAMERICA CRUISES ● *1800 Diagonal Rd, Alexandria, VA 22314; (800) 348-8287 or (703) 549-1741.*

The great rivers of Europe are the objective of this company, which books cruises on the Danube, Elbe, Rhine and Rhone.

PRICE RANGE ☼ Moderately expensive to expensive.

PEOPLE RANGE ☼ These are comfortable, rather luxurious river cruises appealing to all age groups and particularly popular with mature travelers.

THE DRESS ☼ Casual during the day; jackets and cocktail wear preferred at night.

THE VESSELS ☼ Boxy on the outside, elegant within, these are technically "river barges" although they're too pretty for that name. The *Dresden, Prussian Princess, Danube Princess, Mozart* and *Princesse de Provence* have 70 to 100 nicely appointed cabins, and public amenities comparable to larger cruise ships. New to the fleet is the 25-cabin barquentine *Lili Marleen*.

SHORE EXCURSIONS ☼ Most shore trips, which are extra, consist of walking or van trips to the cities along the rivers of Europe. On the Elbe cruise, an extension into Prague is available.

THE SEASON ☼ April to early November.

Sample itineraries

THE DANUBE ☼ Seven-day round-trip sailings from Passau Germany, calling on Vienna, Budapest, and various other cities in Austria and Hungary.

THE ELBE ☼ Week-long sailings from Hamburg into the former East Germany, with stops in old Saxony towns such as Wittenberg, Meissen and Dresden, with a brief dip into the Czech Republic. Land extensions into Prague are available. (**Note:** Cruise Closeup on page 242.)

THE RHINE ☼ Three seven-day itineraries and one ten-day cruise along the Rhine and its tributaries. Among the routes are Basel, Switzerland to Amsterdam; an Amsterdam round trip with stops in the Netherlands and Belgium; cruises through the heart of Germany between Frankfurt and Passau; a Frankfurt-to-Frankfurt Rhine Valley wine country cruise.

THE RHONE ☼ Seven-day trips into the heart of Provence, starting and ending in Lyon.

THE MEDITERRANEAN ☼ The sailing ship *Lili Marleen* offers seven to 14-day cruises in the Mediterranean, primarily to Spanish and Italian ports.

ße ße ße

REGAL CHINA CRUISES ● *57 W. 38th St., New York, NY 10018; (800) 808-3388 or (212) 768-3388; FAX (212) 768-4939.*

This American firm books three German-built ships on the Yangtze River.

PRICE RANGE ☼ Moderate.

PEOPLE RANGE ☼ All age groups.

THE DRESS ☼ Casual; some passengers dress a bit for dinner.

THE VESSELS ☼ The *Princess Jeannie, Princess Elaine* and *Princess Sheena* are near-identical ships with 126 staterooms and suites. They have two restaurants, a bar, ballroom, shops and a business center.

SHORE EXCURSIONS ☼ Guided excursions to shoreside towns and temples are extra; most communities can be reached on foot.

THE SEASON ☼ Late April through November.

Sample itineraries

YANGTZE RIVER ☼ Regal offers a variety of cruises on China's legendary river, including three-day and five-day trips through the Three Gorges between Wuhan and Chongqing, an eleven-day cruise from Shanghai through the gorges to Chongqing and five-day and six-day trips between Shanghai and Wuhan, calling on Jiujiang, Guichi and Nanjing.

ß ß ß

ST. LAWRENCE CRUISE LINES, INC. ● *253 Ontario St., Kingston, Ontario K7L 2Z4; (800) 267-7868 or (613) 549-8091; FAX (613) 549-8410.*

Leisurely riverboat cruises on the St. Lawrence Seaway are the focus of this Canadian firm.

PRICE RANGE ☼ Moderate.

PEOPLE RANGE ☼ Minimum age is 12.

THE DRESS ☼ Casual daytime; cocktail wear and jackets at night.

THE VESSEL ☼ The *Canadian Empress* is a 32-cabin steamboat replica with private baths, grand salon and dining room, small bar and shop.

SHORE EXCURSIONS ☼ Stops at villages, museums and old forts along the way are included.

THE SEASON ☼ May through October.

Itineraries

EASTERN CANADA ☼ Four to six-day cruises on the St. Lawrence Seaway from Kingston to Montreal, Ottawa or Quebec City.

ß ß ß

SONESTA INTERNATIONAL ● *200 Clarendon St., Boston, MA 02116; (800) SONESTA; FAX (617) 421-5434.*

A major hotel chain, Sonesta operates two cruise ships on the Nile.

PRICE RANGE ☼ Moderately expensive.

PEOPLE RANGE ☼ All age groups.

THE DRESS ☼ Casual daytime; jackets and cocktail wear in the evenings.

THE VESSELS ☼ The *Sonesta Sun Goddess* and *Sonesta Nile Goddess* are nicely appointed river craft with 62 and 65 cabins with TV and private baths. Other facilities include a dining room, piano bar, discotheque, pool and sports deck.

SHORE EXCURSIONS ☼ All are included; stops include the temples of Karnak and Luxor, Valley of the Kings, Temple of Khnum, Aswan botanical gardens, Agha Khan Mausoleum, the Aswan High Dam and Temple of Philae.

THE SEASON ☼ All year.

Itineraries

EGYPT ☼ One to six-day Nile cruises, mostly between Aswan and Luxor, with stops at most of the major temple sites.

ß ß ß

UNIQUE WORLD CRUISES ● *39 Beechwood Ave., Manhasset, NY 11030; (800) 669-0757 or (516) 627-2636; FAX (516) 365-1667.*

This firm books rather economical river cruises in Europe and Russia; some have air fare from New York built into the price.

An aged tug pushes barges beneath the imposing cliffs of Qutang Gorge, the smallest and most dramatic of the Yangtze River's Three Gorges. Victoria Cruises offers trips on the Yangtze between Wunan and Chonqing.

PRICE RANGE ☼ Inexpensive to moderate.

PEOPLE RANGE ☼ All age groups.

THE DRESS ☼ Casual daytime, casual to moderately dressy evenings.

THE VESSELS ☼ The *Rouse* is a 103-cabin river cruiser with private baths, dining room, bar, pool, and boutique. The 157-cabin *Furmanov* and *Russ* and the 123-cabin *Korov* are large Russian river cruisers with private baths.

SHORE EXCURSIONS ☼ Most are not included.

THE SEASON ☼ April through October.

Sample itineraries

EUROPE ☼ Ten days on the Danube from Munich to Passau. Fifteen-day tour and cruise with land stops in Berlin, Potsdam, Dresden and Prague, then a cruise from Passau to Munich. Fifteen-day tour and cruise with lands stops in Amsterdam, Cologne, Heidelberg and Nurëmberg, with a cruise from Passau to Munich.

RUSSIA ☼ Twelve to 16-day cruises between Moscow and St. Petersburg on the Volga and Svir rivers. Fourteen-day cruises between Kiev and Odessa on the Dnieper River and Black Sea.

ßßß

VICTORIA CRUISES ● *5708 39th Ave., Woodside, NY 11377; (800) 348-8084 or (212) 818-1680; FAX (212) 818-9889.*

Victoria has built four new river boats designed specifically for cruising through the famous Three Gorges of China's Yangtze River between Wuhan and Chongqing. The firm is American and the vessels are operated by a major Chinese shipping company.

PRICE RANGE ☼ Moderate.

PEOPLE RANGE ☼ All age groups.

THE DRESS ✿ Casual; some passengers don jackets and cocktail wear for dinner although it's optional.

THE VESSELS ✿ The identical *Victorias I, II, III* and *IV* have 77 cabins private baths and TV. Amenities are rather ample for a river boat, including single-seating dining, a nightclub with nightly entertainment, library, beauty salon, fitness center and business center.

SHORE EXCURSIONS ✿ They can be added to the cruise price as an inexpensive package. An English-speaking cruise director—usually an American—takes passengers on shore excursions to shoreside towns and temples. Pre-tour and post-tour packages to other areas of China also are popular.

THE SEASON ✿ March through December; spring and fall offer the best weather and fall is the most popular

Itineraries

YANGTZE RIVER ✿ These are one-way trips through China's famous Three Gorges between Wuhan and Chongqing; six days upstream and four days down, with frequent shore stops. (**Note:** Cruise Closeup on page 275.)

ᛒᛒᛒ

WILLOW WREN CRUISE HOLIDAYS ● *Rugby Wharf, Rugby, CV21 1PB England; phone 1-788-562183.*

This British firm specializes in barge and "narrow boat" cruises along the canals of England and Wales.

PRICE RANGE ✿ Inexpensive.

PEOPLE RANGE ✿ All age groups; these are very leisurely trips.

THE DRESS ✿ Informal day and evening.

THE VESSELS ✿ The seven-cabin "narrowboats" *Tsarina* and *Tsarevna* and six-cabin canal barge *Tranquil Rose.*

SHORE EXCURSIONS ✿ Trips to Windsor Castle, Hampton Court, Oxford College, Warwick Castle and such. Some are included in the cruise price; others are extra.

THE SEASON ✿ Spring through fall.

Itineraries

ENGLAND AND WALES ✿ Seven-day cruises from Rugby to Oxford; from Windsor to Oxford; and seven-day round trips from Bath with stops at Bristol and Bradford on Avon.

SAILING SHIPS

Sailing is cruising in its purest form—with a fair wind and an enchanted tropic isle or exotic port on the horizon. Today's sailing ships offer everything from absolute elegance to barefoot cruising. On some ships, you get to help hoist the sails; on others, you hoist another brew and watch the crew do the work. "The sail will not die as long as men demand their bread and their pleasure from the sea," wrote Claud Farrère.

Some of the ships listed below have auxiliary engines, while others are classic sailing ships, responding only to the winds. For the purist, several craft, most of them refurbished older craft, offer three to six day cruises off the coast of Maine as members of the Maine Windjammer Association. Two, the *Mary Day* and *Nathaniel Bowditch,* are listed below. For information on the others, contact: Maine Windjammer Assn., P.O. Box 1144, Blue Hill, ME 04614; (800) 807-WIND or (207) 374-2955.

🏴🏴🏴
COASTWISE PACKET COMPANY, INC. ● *P.O. Box 429, Vineyard Haven, MA 02568; (508) 693-1699; FAX (508) 693-1881.*

This small firm sails a "pure schooner" along the southern New England coast between Nantucket and Long Island, New York.

PRICE RANGE ☼ Moderate.

PEOPLE RANGE ☼ Ages 10 and above; of appeal to barefoot sailors.

THE DRESS ☼ Casual.

THE VESSEL ☼ The *Shenandoah* is a 108-foot topsail schooner that's all sail with no auxiliary power. Cabins are snug; bathrooms are shared.

SHORE EXCURSIONS ☼ Informal shore explorations at ports along the way are included in the cruise.

THE SEASON ☼ Mid-June to mid-September.

Itinerary

NEW ENGLAND ☼ Six and a half-day round trips from Vineyard Haven, calling on assorted ports in Nantucket Sound and Long Island.

🏴🏴🏴
DIRIGO CRUISES LTD. ● *39 Waterside Lane, Clinton, CT 06413; (860) 669-7068; FAX (860) 669-7068.*

This firm specializes in packaging tall ship cruises in various parts of the globe.

PRICE RANGE ☼ Moderate.

PEOPLE RANGE ☼ All age groups; active folks who like the adventure of true sailing on the high seas.

THE DRESS ☼ Casual

THE VESSELS ☼ Several classic tall ships, including the eight-cabin *Regina Catterina,* 15-cabin *Sir Francis Drake* and 11-cabin *Nathaniel Bowditch.*

SHORE EXCURSIONS ☼ There are few organized excursions but plenty of shoreside activities and water sports available. Passengers can help rig the ship or relax and watch the crew hoist sails to wind.

THE SEASON ☼ The year around, depending on the part of the globe.

Sample itineraries

THE CARIBBEAN ☼ One week cruises from St. Vincent, calling on islands such as Bequia, Young, the Grenadines, Punta Gorda and British Virgins.

NEW ENGLAND ☼ Six-day cruises out of Rockland, Maine, exploring its coast and offshore islands. Six-day voyages out of Boston to coastal communities and offshore islands.

SOUTH PACIFIC ☼ Ten-day cruises from Tonga to Tongatupu, Ha'apai, Vava'u and other South Pacific isles.

SOUTH AMERICA ☼ Seven-day cruises from San Cristobal in the Galápagos to Floreana, Isabela, Sante Fe and ending in Santiago.

🏴🏴🏴
GRAYS HARBOR HISTORICAL SEAPORT ● *P.O. Box 2019 (813 E. Huron St.), Aberdeen, WA 98520; (800) 200-LADY or (360) 532-8611; FAX (360) 538-1321.*

The non-profit historical seaport authority in this Washington community operates a replica of a 200-year-old sailboat that takes serious cruises along the West Coast with volunteer crews.

PRICE RANGE ✿ Inexpensive (volunteer crew costs).
PEOPLE RANGE ✿ Folks serious about learning to sail.
THE DRESS ✿ Casual.
THE VESSEL ✿ The 112-foot brig *Lady Washington* is a working replica of the first American ship to enter waters of the Pacific Northwest in October of 1787. She's as close to the original ship as "historical records and the Coast Guard allow," with facilities for 45 passengers.
SHORE EXCURSIONS ✿ None organized.
THE SEASON ✿ Year around; berths may be available for volunteer crew members.

Itineraries

WEST COAST ✿ A variety of cruises are scheduled along the Pacific Coast, north to Alaska and west to Hawaii and Japan. Brief cruises for the public available at Aberdeen and sometimes at various ports of call.

ß ß ß

GREAT LAKES TALL SHIP ADVENTURES ● *13390 S.W. Bay Shore Dr., Traverse City, MI 49684; (800) 968-8800 or (616) 941-2000.*
Operating on the shore of Lake Michigan, this firm offers cruises about the lake and some of its islands.
PRICE RANGE ✿ Moderate.
PEOPLE RANGE ✿ All age groups.
THE DRESS ✿ Casual.
THE VESSELS ✿ The *Manitou* is a two-masted, square rigged schooner with twelve cozy cabins and share baths. The *Malabar* is a two-master with eight cabins and share baths.
SHORE EXCURSIONS ✿ Island hiking, beachcombing, kayaking and visiting coastal villages; most are included.
THE SEASON ✿ June through September.

Itineraries

LAKE MICHIGAN ✿ A variety of one to six-day cruises from northern Michigan to offshore islands and coastal communities.

ß ß ß

NATHANIEL BOWDITCH ● *P.O. Box 459, Warren, ME 04864; (800) 288-4098 or (207) 273-4062.*
This family owned 82-foot schooner is part of the Maine windjammer fleet.
PRICE RANGE ✿ Moderate.
PEOPLE RANGE ✿ All age groups.
THE DRESS ✿ Casual.
THE VESSEL ✿ The *Nathaniel Bowditch* is a two-masted gaff-rigged schooner with 14 cozy cabins with sinks (share baths and showers), a galley and lounge.
SHORE EXCURSIONS ✿ Exploring Maine's seashore and coastal islands; poking about quaint fishing villages; shore hiking.
THE SEASON ✿ "Schooner Season" is June through early September.

Sample itineraries

MAINE ✿ A variety of trips along the Maine Coast and its islands, ranging from three to six days.

🏴🏴🏴
NORTH END SHIPYARD SCHOONERS ● *P.O. Box 482, Rockland, ME 04841; (800) 648-4544 or (207) 594-8007; FAX (207) 594-8015.*

Three wooden-hulled sailing ships are booked through this organization.

PRICE RANGE ☼ Moderate.

PEOPLE RANGE ☼ People who enjoy pure sailing.

THE DRESS ☼ Casual.

THE VESSELS ☼ The *Heritage* is a modern schooner with classic lines, built in 1983, with 16 cabins. The *Isaac M. Evans*, a former oyster boat dating from 1886, has ten cabins. The *American Eagle*, with 14 cabins, was first launched in 1930. The vessels have share baths; some have cabin sinks.

SHORE EXCURSIONS ☼ Included in the price.

THE SEASON ☼ Primarily spring through fall.

Sample itineraries

☼ All three sailing ships operate off the coast of Maine, calling on seaports and offshore islands; cruises vary in length from three to six days.

🏴🏴🏴
SCHOONER MARY DAY ● *P.O. Box 798, Camden, ME 04843; (800) 992-2218 or (207) 236-8741.*

This one-ship family firm runs voyages along the Coast of Maine in a 90-foot schooner; it's part of the Maine windjammer fleet.

PRICE RANGE ☼ Moderate.

PEOPLE RANGE ☼ All age groups.

THE DRESS ☼ Casual.

THE VESSEL ☼ The schooner *Mary Day* is a two master with 14 cozy cabins (share baths and showers), a galley and lounge.

SHORE EXCURSIONS ☼ Exploring Maine's seashore and coastal islands; poking about quaint fishing villages; shore hiking.

THE SEASON ☼ June through early October.

Itineraries

MAINE ☼ Three to six-day trips along the Maine Coast and its islands.

🏴🏴🏴
STAR CLIPPERS ● *4101 Salzedo Ave., Coral Gables, FL 33146; (800) 442-0553 for booking information and (800) 442-0556 for brochures; the local number is (305) 442-0551.*

What's a barquentine? It's a four-masted schooner with a single brace of square-rigged sails forward to give it speed, stability and more deck space. Star Clippers replicated two of these nineteenth century classics and added modern amenities to offer a realistic yet comfortable sailing experience.

PRICE RANGE ☼ Moderately expensive.

PEOPLE RANGE ☼ All age groups; particularly appealing to those who want to combine pure sailing with modern conveniences.

THE DRESS ☼ Casual; jackets and cocktail wear optional for evenings.

THE VESSELS ☼ The *Star Clipper* and *Star Flyer* are authentic reconstructions of elegant barquentines, with modern amenities such as swimming pools, cocktail lounge, library-reading room and cabin TV/VCRs.

SHORE EXCURSIONS ☼ Van and bus trips and walking tours of port towns and inland communities, with English speaking guides, are additional.

THE SEASON ☼ The year around in the Caribbean, summer in the Mediterranean and September through December in the Far East.

Sample itineraries

CARIBBEAN ☼ One-week round trip cruises from Barbados call on Grenada, Carriacou, St. Vincent and St. Lucia. A second itinerary from San Maarten touches such out-of-the-way ports as Anguilla, Sandy Cay, Norman Island, Virgin Gorda, Monserrat, Dominica and Ilses des Saintes.

MEDITERRANEAN ☼ One week Cannes-to-Cannes cruises sail the Ligurian Sea to Corsica, Sardinia, Giglio, Napoleon's Elba and Portovenere on the Italian mainland. (**Note:** Cruise Closeup on page 257.) Another cruise from Cannes visits several Italian, Turkish and Greek islands and mainland ports, en route to Athens. Others visit Greek and Turkish ports from Mamaris, Turkey, and one itinerary travels the Ionian Sea from Mamaris to Tunis.

TRANS-ATLANTIC ☼ Twenty-six day positioning cruises between the Caribbean and Mediterranean.

SOUTHEAST ASIA ☼ Added in 1996 were one-week cruises along the Malaysian Peninsula with stops in Thailand, Singapore and offshore islands.

ps ps ps

TALL SHIP ADVENTURES ● *1389 S. Havana St., Aurora, CO 80012; (800) 662-0900 or (303) 755-7983; FAX (303) 755-9007.*

Although it's a long way from salt water, this firm specializes in Caribbean cruises aboard the schooner, *Sir Francis Drake.*

PRICE RANGE ☼ Moderate.

PEOPLE RANGE ☼ All age groups.

THE DRESS ☼ Totally casual.

THE VESSEL ☼ The *Sir Francis Drake* is a three-masted schooner with 14 air conditioned cabins, dining room and a salon with bar and TV/VCR.

SHORE EXCURSIONS ☼ Local tours are available at extra cost. The focus here is sailing aboard a tall ship with stops at secluded beaches for water sports, exploring and picnics.

THE SEASON ☼ All year.

Itineraries

CARIBBEAN ☼ Seven-day round trip cruises from Tortola in the British Virgin Islands from November to June. Seven-day one way or 14-day round trip voyages the rest of the year between St. Martaan and Antigua with stops at Tintamarre, St. Barths, St. Eustatius, St. Kitts and Nevis.

ps ps ps

VERNICOS YACHTS ● *566 Seventh Ave., New York, NY 10018; (800) 447-5667 or (212) 221-0006; FAX (212) 764-7912.*

Coupled with Zeus Tours (listed below under "Soft adventures,") this firm specializes in cruises in the eastern Mediterranean.

PRICE RANGE ☼ Moderate.

PEOPLE RANGE ☼ All age groups.

THE DRESS ☼ Casual day and evening.

THE VESSELS ☼ Sailing ship *Galileo Sun* has 18 cabins with private facilities, an on-deck hot tub and salon-dining area. Also in the fleet are the five-cabin *Aromade* and *Hermina* and the four-cabin *Oceanis.*

SHORE EXCURSIONS ☼ None scheduled.

THE SEASON ☼ April through October.

Sample itineraries

EASTERN MEDITERRANEAN ☼ Seven days out of Piraeus (Athens) or Corfu, calling on Paros, Santorini, Lefkas and other Greek islands.

SEYCHELLES ☼ The *Galileo Sun* offers three to seven-day cruises around the Seychelles, from Mahe or Praslin.

ᛒᛒᛒ

VICTORY CHIMES ● *P.O. Box 1401, Rockland, ME 04841; (800) 745-5651 or (207) 265-5651.*

This firm invites tall ship *aficionados* to sail coastal Maine on America's largest windjammer.

PRICE RANGE ☼ Inexpensive to moderate.

PEOPLE RANGE ☼ All age groups.

THE DRESS ☼ Strictly casual.

THE VESSEL ☼ The 180-foot *Victory Chimes* was built in 1900 as a lumber schooner, then refurbished in the 1950s and again in 1988 as a 20-cabin passenger ship. She has no engines except an accompanying motorized yawl boat that can "give her a push in an emergency."

SHORE EXCURSIONS ☼ These consist of dropping anchor in secluded coves and informal exploring. Passengers also can help rig the ship and try their talents at navigation.

THE SEASON ☼ Spring through fall.

Itinerary

COASTAL MAINE ☼ Six-day and three-day trips out of Rockland, calling on Acadia National Park, Boothbay Harbor, offshore islands and shore towns.

ᛒᛒᛒ

WINDJAMMER BAREFOOT CRUISES ● *Box 190120, Miami Beach, FL 33119-0120; (800) 327-2601 or (305) 534-7447; FAX (305) 672-1219.*

Barefoot cruising is just what the term suggests; sailing the briny on classic schooners, bare tootsies planted firmly on varnished decks. Windjammer Barefoot Cruises operates several tall ships—some of them once owned by the rich and famous—and a refurbished small cargo-passenger ship.

PRICE RANGE ☼ Moderate.

PEOPLE RANGE ☼ True lovers of sailing.

THE DRESS ☼ Casual at all times.

THE VESSELS ☼ Classic windjammers, including the 128-passenger *Fantome*, once owned by Aristotle Onassis; the 74-passenger *Flying Cloud*, a former World War II French cadet training ship; the 72-passenger barquentine *Mandalay* originally owned by E.F. Hutton; and the 64-passenger *Yankee Clipper,* an armor-plated yacht captured as a World War II German war prize and later owned by the Vanderbilt family. The *Amazing Grace* is a converted Scottish cargo-passenger ship with a capacity of 94.

SHORE EXCURSIONS ☼ None planned.

THE SEASON ☼ Year around.

Sample itineraries

CARIBBEAN ☼ The tall ships follow a variety of routes through the Caribbean, with six to 13-day cruises calling on lesser-visited islands. Some examples are Tortola to Virgin Gorda, Green Cay, Sandy Cay and Cooper Island; St. Maarten to St. Barts, St. Kitts, Nevis, Anguilla and Montserrat; and

Grenada to Petit St. Vincent, Bequia, Palm Island, Union Island and Carriacou. The *Amazing Grace* offers 13-day cruises between Freeport the Bahamas and Grenada.

MEXICO ☼ The *Fantome* offers six-day cruises out of Cozumel to Cancun and several other Mexican east coast ports.

ß ß ß

WINDSTAR CRUISES ● *300 Elliott Avenue West, Seattle, WA 98119; (800) 626-9900 or (206) 298-3057; FAX (206) 286-3229.*

Windstar ships are elegant motor sailing yachts with six grand sails reaching 204 feet above the water. Think of them as opulently coiffed yachts with stylish staterooms. Cruising emphasis is on water sports and enjoying the good life while sailing in style.

PRICE RANGE ☼ Expensive; elegance has its price. These are one-class cruises—first class, of course—since the ships have identical staterooms.

PEOPLE RANGE ☼ Any age that enjoys the yachting life; these are pampered adventures.

THE DRESS ☼ "Yachting casual" day and evening; some guests dress for the captain's dinner parties.

THE VESSELS ☼ Three vessels, the *Wind Star, Wind Song* and *Wind Spirit* are virtually identical motorized sailing yachts, each with 74 outside staterooms and onboard amenities such as pool and hot tub, sports shop and fitness room, casino, library, gift shop, masseuse and hair stylist.

SHORE EXCURSIONS ☼ Shore trips, which are additional, range from van excursions around tropic islands to port tours. Water play equipment also is available on the ships.

THE SEASON ☼ The "wind fleet" sails the year around, with itineraries in the Caribbean, Mediterranean and French Polynesia.

Sample itineraries

THE CARIBBEAN ☼ Three choices are available, focusing on the Caribbean's smaller islands: Barbados-to-Barbados with stops at Nevis, St. Maartin, St. Barthélemy, Montserrat and Martinique. Barbados round trip with Bequia, Carriacou, Grenada, Tobago and St. Lucia. (**Note:** Cruise closeup on page 182.) St. Thomas round trip, calling on St. Croix, Saba, Montserrat, St. Barthémey, Virgin Gorda and St. John. Most are seven days, with some special nine to 12-day holiday cruises. Sailings are the year around.

THE MEDITERRANEAN ☼ Seven-day Greek isles cruises between Istanbul and Athens, calling on Mykonos, Santorini, Rhodes, Bodrum and Kusadasi. Also seven-day Monte Carlo round trips, departing Monaco for Corsica, Portoferraio, Portovenere, Portofino, Cannes and St. Tropez. These are mostly May through September.

FRENCH POLYNESIA ☼ Seven-day Papeete round trips, touching Huahine, Raiatea, Bora Bora and Moorea. These sail the year-around.

ß ß ß

WORLD OF OZ ● *1427 N. Great Neck Rd., Virginia Beach, VA 24454; (800) 248-0234 or (804) 496-8108; FAX (804) 496-8097.*

Oz is a wholesale tour company focusing primarily on Turkey. Most of its offerings are land tours, although it books "Blue Cruises" in Turkish *gulets,* and it can arrange private yacht charters.

PRICE RANGE ☼ Inexpensive to moderate.

PEOPLE RANGE ☼ All age groups; people willing to experience rather spartan amenities on a Nile cruise.

THE DRESS ☼ Casual.

THE VESSELS ☼ *Gulets* are small wooden ketch-rigged motor sailers built in the coastal towns of Turkey. Those booked by Oz have six cabins with private baths, a dining room and bar; snorkeling gear, sailboard and fishing tackle are available. Cruises also are booked aboard the *Panorama,* a large luxury yacht with 25 fully-furnished staterooms.

SHORE EXCURSIONS ☼ Shore tours, which are extra, include stops at ancient cities, archeological sites and fishing villages.

THE SEASON ☼ Spring through fall.

Itineraries

TURKEY ☼ Seven-day *gulet* cruises out of Bodrum or Mamaris, calling on historic Turkish cities such as Caunus, Mersincik, Ingiliz Limani, Cedreae, Tuzla and Çiftlik. Seven-day cruises between Antalya and Kusadasi aboard the yacht *Panorama,* with stops at Phaselis, Kekova, Kas/Fethiye and Rhodes.

SOFT ADVENTURE CRUISE LINES

Expedition cruising isn't for everyone; some folks would like to see new places and gain new knowledge without trudging over an icy tundra or bobbing about in the cozy confines of a fishing boat turned whale-watcher. "Soft adventure" isn't our term; it was invented by the industry to identify cruises that call on out-of-the-way places and provide educational experiences while offering most creature comforts of conventional voyages.

Many of the firms listed below offer ocean, river, lake and canal cruises, and combinations thereof.

ᛒᛒᛒ

ALASKA SIGHTSEEING/CRUISE WEST • *Fourth & Battery Building, Suite 700, Seattle, WA 98121; (800) 426-7702 or (206) 441-8687; FAX (206) 441-4757.*

Western America and Canada are the focus of this company, which sails the Inside Passage, British Columbia' offshore islands, the Columbia-Snake river systems, and California's San Joaquin Delta and wine country. Many are combined land and water trips, particularly on the Alaska itineraries.

PRICE RANGE ☼ Moderate; these are good buys, since all shore excursions and transfers are included.

PEOPLE RANGE ☼ These trips are popular for all age groups; the easy-going pace on the water particularly appeals to seniors.

THE DRESS ☼ Casual, both day and evening.

THE VESSELS ☼ The firm uses a variety of craft, from motor-yacht "day cruisers" in which passengers sleep in hotels ashore, to expedition style craft with bow ramps for access to remote areas. The overnight vessels have fair-sized staterooms with private baths, dining room-lounges and bars. Some staterooms have TV/VCRs.

SHORE EXCURSIONS ☼ Some shore trips are included; others are extra, ranging from fishing aboard trawlers to helicopter flights over ice fields.

THE SEASON ☼ May to mid-September in Alaska and British Columbia; spring through fall on the Columbia-Snake and October-November and March April in the California wine country.

"Hold it steady!" Pitching in to help haul up a crab trap is part of the fun on this outing aboard a Petersburg fishing trawler. It's an optional excursion available on an Alaska Sightseeing/Cruise West trip up the Inside Passage.

Sample itineraries

ALASKA ☼ Small inlets and icefields bypassed by bigger cruise ships are the focus of the firm's Inside Passage voyages. The call on most Inside Passage towns, along with Glacier Bay National Park and Misty Fjords National Monument. Trips vary in length since several can be linked together to include air, motorcoach and train trips to Fairbanks, Denali National Park, Anchorage and other stops in mainland Alaska. (**Note:** Cruise Closeup on page 114.)

CALIFORNIA DELTA/WINE COUNTRY ☼ Ships depart Sausalito on San Francisco Bay for three-day cruises up the Napa River to the Napa Valley wine country, and the Sacramento River to Old Sacramento State Historic Park.

OREGON-WASHINGTON ☼ Eight-day cruises travel the full navigable length of the Columbia-Snake River system, starting in Portland and reaching Lewiston, Idaho at the end of navigation and Astoria at the mouth of the Columbia. (**Note:** Cruise Closeup on page 147.)

PUGET SOUND AND CANADA'S INSIDE PASSAGE ☼ Eight-day trips from Seattle to explore the Puget Sound, San Juan Islands, Canada's Gulf Islands, Victoria and/or Vancouver.

ৡৡৡ

ALASKA'S GLACIER BAY TOURS & CRUISES ● *520 Pike St., Suite 1400, Seattle, WA 98101; (800) 451-5952 or (206) 623-2417; FAX (206) 623-7809.*

Glacier Bay and beyond is the focus of this firm, with sea and land excursions in Alaska and the Pacific Northwest. The company operates two small expedition ships and books programs on several others, large and small.

PRICE RANGE ✿ Moderate to expensive.

PEOPLE RANGE ✿ Appealing to all age groups.

THE DRESS ✿ Casual.

THE VESSELS ✿ The *MV Executive Explorer* is a yacht style cruiser with 25 cabins with TV, private baths and other amenities. The *MV Wilderness Explorer* is a more modest craft with 18 cabins.

SHORE EXCURSIONS ✿ Some are included; others are additional. They range from poking about shoreside towns to expedition-style wildlife spotting.

THE SEASON ✿ Spring through early fall.

Sample itineraries

ALASKA ✿ A variety of Glacier Bay programs from one to six days, including combined cruising and Glacier Bay Lodge trips. Seven-day Inside Passage cruises including all major port stops, Glacier Bay National Park and Misty Fjords National Monument. Nine and 11-day cruises including the above stops, plus Seattle and Vancouver.

PACIFIC NORTHWEST ✿ A companion firm, YachtShip CruiseLine, Inc., utilizes the *Executive Explorer* and *Wilderness Explorer* in several San Juan, Gulf Island, Victoria and Vancouver outings. Among the itineraries are eight days on the *Executive* from Seattle to Vancouver, then up the Fraser River, through the Gulf Islands and the San Juan Islands; and eight days on the *Wilderness* from Seattle to the San Juans (with kayaking), Victoria, Vancouver Island stops and Vancouver.

誃誃誃

AMERICAN CANADIAN CARIBBEAN LINE, INC. ● *P.O. Box 368, Warren, RI 0288; (800) 556-7450 or (401) 247-0955; FAX (401) 247-2350.*

Positioned somewhere between adventure and soft adventure, ACCL does just what its elongated name says. Its small ships sail the rivers and intercostal waterways of eastern America, the Great Lakes and St. Lawrence Seaway between the U.S. and Canada and they explore islands and rivers of the Caribbean and Central America.

PRICE RANGE ✿ Moderate; these are a very good buy for the price.

PEOPLE RANGE ✿ Cruises are nicely balanced, with interesting shore explorations and activities appealing to younger travelers, yet at a pace suitable for older and less active passengers.

THE DRESS ✿ Casual; some dress a bit for captain's dinners; some don't.

THE VESSELS ✿ These are small expedition ships with 30 to 40 cabins, private baths, dining room, lounge, and BYOB bar counter. Snorkel gear and a glass bottom boat are available. The boats, designed by company president and longtime shipbuilder Luther H. Blount, have front bow landers, permitting them to land just about anywhere. "Blount boats" are used by several other cruise companies as well.

SHORE EXCURSIONS ✿ Many activities, involving swimming, snorkeling, water play and visits to Mayan ruins or town tours, are included; more extensive shore trips can be arranged at additional cost.

THE SEASON ✿ December through April in the Caribbean and Central America; and the year around on various American-Canadian cruises.

Sample itineraries

AMERICAN-CANADIAN WATERWAYS ✿ Voyages include 12 days between New Orleans and Chicago on the Mississippi and Illinois River; 16 days through the Great Lakes, Erie Canal and Hudson River between Chicago and Warren, Rhode Island; a 15-day cruise on the Intercostal Waterway; and 12 days along the Florida Keys. Others are six-day cruises among the islands and waterways of New England; and 12-day itineraries along Erie Canal and St. Lawrence Seaway.

THE CARIBBEAN ✿ Four 12-day itineraries are available: Aruba, Bonaire and Curacao; Trinidad, Tobago and Venezuela's Orinoco River; the Virgin Islands; and Nassau, Exumas and Caicos.

CENTRAL AMERICA ✿ Cruises to ports such as Panama and the canal, Dairen and the San Blas and Pearl Islands. Also explorations of the Belize Great Barrier Reef, Guatemala's Rio Dulce and Honduras. The focus is on snorkeling and other water sports and exploring Central America's towns and Mayan ruins. Most are 12-day cruises. (**Note:** Cruise Closeup on page 196.)

℞℞℞

THE BARE NECESSITIES TOUR AND TRAVEL, INC. ● *1802 W. Sixth St., Suite B, Austin, TX 78703; (800) 743-0405 or (512) 499-0405.*

This company gives new meaning to the term soft adventure cruising. It books clothing-optional voyages aboard several ships (see box), plus nude vacations in resorts.

PRICE RANGE ✿ Moderate to moderately expensive.

PEOPLE RANGE ✿ Well, as a matter of fact, the typical nude cruiser is a college educated upper income person in his and her forties, happily married.

THE DRESS ✿ Although dress codes go out the window—or perhaps the porthole—on these cruises, most nudists prefer to dress for dinner. "Since they're not afraid of no clothing," says company founder Nancy Teimann, "they aren't afraid of adorning." Apparently, costume parties are a real blast.

THE VESSELS ✿ The 90-cabin *Star Clipper* and 74-cabin *Windsong* are among the small vessels booked by Bare Necessities.

SHORE EXCURSIONS ✿ Conventional excursions, some included, some optional; plus nude sunning, swimming and snorkeling at sheltered beaches.

THE SEASON ✿ Year around, depending on the area.

Sample itineraries

As Jimmy Buffet says in his song, *Boat Drinks*: "I wanna go where it's warm!" Nude cruises focus on toasty climes such as the Caribbean, Mediterranean and Tahiti. Cool breezes take on a new significance in this business.

CARIBBEAN ✿ Seven-day round trips from Miami with stops at Nassau, Jamaica and Grand Cayman.

FRENCH POLYNESIA ✿ One-week cruises from Papeete to Raitaia, Moorea, Bora Bora and Huahine.

MEDITERRANEAN ✿ Seven days out of Canne, exploring the French and Italian rivieras.

℞℞℞

CLASSIC CRUISES & TOURS ● *132 E. 70th Street, New York, NY 10021; (800) 252-7745 or (212) 794-3200; FAX (212) 774-1545.*

This firm books voyages on the up-market British Swan Hellenic line's new *Minerva* midsize cruise ship. Although it isn't a small ship, the trips have a strong emphasis on exploration and learning, with onboard lecturers and educational shore excursions. And the cruise calls on some fascinating ports.

SUITES, TIES—AND ALL THE REST—OPTIONAL

Haven't a thing to wear? Bare Necessities may be your travel company. The firm specializes in nude vacations and cruises, chartering vessels from such refined firms as Windstar, Star Clipper and even the veddy British Cunard Lines. These are mostly couples outings. When singles book the cruises, the company ensures that the male-female ratio stays in balance. Further, the cruises aren't really for young voyeurs; 90 percent of those booking clothing-optional cruises are over 35 and most are married.

Nude cruising doesn't mean passengers march *au naturel* up the gangway. Clothing becomes optional once ships hit international waters. Some passengers prefer to keep theirs on; others are part-time nudists during the cruise. Clothes generally are worn at dinner. Remote beaches are used for shore stops, so passengers can frolic without worrying about getting sand down their swimsuits. (Incidentally, nudists refer to those of us who run around fully clothed as "textiles.")

When the firm books a ship, Bare Necessities staff members work with the regular crew to ease the initial shock, and they're given the option of taking the week off. Apparently, no one has.

Nude cruising and vacationing is growing very fast, according to Nancy Teimann, who founded Bare Necessities with her husband in 1992. The firm charters about three cruises a year, and each one has sold out.

"Thousands of people practice social nudism in their own back yard, but don't know there are places to go and enjoy nude recreation while on vacation," she said.

Teimann suggests that clients book at least six months in advance (see listing above). Another firm specializing in uncovered cruising is Travel *Au Naturel* in Land O' Lakes, Florida; (800) 728-0185.

There's apparently plenty of room for expansion in the all-over-tan market. In a recent Roper poll, 40 percent of Americans admitted that they'd skinny-dipped.

PRICE RANGE ☼ Expensive.

PEOPLE RANGE ☼ People who like a blend of conventional cruise luxury with an expedition cruise mentality.

THE DRESS ☼ Casual daytime; casual to dressy in the evening.

THE VESSEL ☼ The opulent new *Minerva* has nearly 200 nicely-attired staterooms and suites, some with private balconies. It offers single-seat non-assigned dining, a pool, gym, conservatory, library, lecture auditorium, beauty parlor and boutique.

SHORE EXCURSIONS ☼ Most are included, and accompanied by local English-speaking guides or lecturer-guides from the ship.

THE SEASON ☼ Year around, depending on the area.

Sample itineraries

THE MEDITERRANEAN ☼ Sixteen-day cruise from Genoa to Venice, with stops at Naples, Messina, Rhodes and several Greek and Turkish ports. Sixteen-day cruise from Venice to Nice, stopping at Croatia, Malta, Libya, Tunisia and several Italian ports. Iberian Peninsula cruise, 13 days from Nice to Barcelona, Cadiz, Lisbon and London. A 16-day voyage from Barcelona, around the edges of Italy, ending in Venice. A 13-day Venice to Athens cruise with stops on the Dalmatian Coast and Greek islands.

NORTHERN EUROPE ✿ A 12-day cruise from London to Leith near Edinburgh, with stops at various United Kingdom ports; and a 13-day cruise to the U.K.'s northern reaches of Scotland, Ireland and the Faros Islands. A two-week cruise from Scotland to Norway, Germany, Denmark, Sweden, Latvia, Russia and Finland.

THE BLACK SEA ✿ Sixteen days from Athens through the Strait of Bosphorus to Black Sea ports in Turkey, Russia, Ukraine, Rumania and Bulgaria.

THE MIDEAST ✿ Sixteen days from Venice to Cyprus, with stops in Croatia, Greece, Turkey, Syria, Lebanon and Israel. Thirteen days sailing from Turkey to Egypt's Port Said, then through the Suez Canal to Jordan.

ß ß ß

CLIPPER CRUISE LINE ● *7711 Bonhomme Ave., St. Louis, MO 63105-1956; (800) 325-0010 or (314) 727-2929.*

With a mix of expedition and soft adventure outings, Clipper offers shore excursions in Zodiacs with onboard naturalists, plus more conventional town tours. Its small shallow draft cruise ships take passengers along the Atlantic Coast, on some American rivers and into the Caribbean and Central America.

PRICE RANGE ✿ Moderate.

PEOPLE RANGE ✿ All age groups.

THE DRESS ✿ Casual.

THE VESSELS ✿ The motor yacht *Yorktown Clipper* has 69 cabins with private baths; dining room, observation lounge and bar. The 51-cabin *Nantucket Clipper* is smaller, with similar facilities.

SHORE EXCURSIONS ✿ Some are included; others are optional.

THE SEASON ✿ Most of the year.

Sample itineraries

ATLANTIC COAST ✿ Eight-day cruises from Jacksonville along the Intercostal Waterway of Florida, Georgia and South Carolina on the *Nantucket Clipper*, with motorboat excursions into the Okefenokee Swamp.

THE CARIBBEAN ✿ Eleven-day cruises aboard the *Yorktown Clipper* from Grenada along the Windward and Leeward Islands to St. Martin, stopping at Bequia, St. Lucia, Dominica, Iles des Saintes, St. Kitts, Saba and Anguilla.

CENTRAL AMERICA ✿ Thirteen-day cruises from Panama to Costa Rica, through the Panama Canal to Darien, several offshore islands and coastal Costa Rica, with shore trips to wildlife refuges.

ß ß ß

CRUCEROS MARITIMOS SKORPIOS ● *Augusto Leguia Norte 118, Las Condes, Santiago, Chile; (56-2) 231.10.30; FAX (56-2) 232.22.69.*

Better known in the north as the Skorpios cruises, this firm specializes in trips through the spectacular fjords of the Chilean coast.

PRICE RANGE ✿ Moderate to moderately high.

PEOPLE RANGE ✿ All age groups.

THE DRESS ✿ Casual; cocktail wear and jackets optional for evening.

THE VESSELS ✿ Three small cruise ships, the *Skorpios I, II* and *III* have 35, 54 and 47 cabins respectively; all with private baths. The *Skorpios III,* launched in 1995, is the fancier of the three, offering roomy cabins with TV/stereos; staterooms in I and II are described as "snug."

SHORE EXCURSIONS ☼ Included in the cruise price, excursions range from Chilean fishing villages visits and thermal baths in Quitralco to motor-boat trips into the narrow fjords.

THE SEASON ☼ All year.

Itinerary

CHILE ☼ Six-day cruises from Puerto Montt (200 miles south of Santiago) along the Chilean fjords to the San Rafael Glacier.

ß ß ß

EUROCRUISES ● *303 W. Thirteenth St., New York, NY 10014; (800) 688-3876 or (212) 691-2099; FAX (212) 366-4747.*

The largest marketer of European cruises in America, this firm runs the gamut from big cruise ships to little vintage steamboats and canal barges.

PRICE RANGE ☼ Moderate to moderately expensive.

PEOPLE RANGE ☼ All age groups.

THE DRESS ☼ Casual daytime and jackets and cocktail wear for evening on some cruises; others are all casual.

THE VESSELS ☼ Several types are used. The *Sergei Kirov* and *Anton Chekhov* are good-sized river cruisers (106 and 118 cabins) that sail the rivers, canals and lakes of Russia. The company also books vintage steamships with 28 or 29 cabins on Swedish waterways. The *Nordbris* is a 19-cabin icebreaker that sails the North Sea. The 120-passenger *Blue Danube* and 148-passenger *Rhine Princess* cruise European rivers.

SHORE EXCURSIONS ☼ Many shore excursions included; some optional.

THE SEASON ☼ April through October.

Sample itineraries

BALTIC SEA ☼ The 200-passenger *Kristina Regina* does a nine-day cruise from Helsinki to Copenhagen, calling on ports in Russia, Estonia, Latvia, Lithuania and Poland.

EUROPEAN RIVERS AND CANALS ☼ The *Rhine Princess* and *Blue Danube* offer eight-day cruises from Holland and up the Rhine to Bastle, Switzerland; six-day Amsterdam to Amsterdam trips on Holland's canals; and eight-day voyages on the Rhine and Moselle.

NORTH SEA ☼ The small icebreaker *Nordbris* sails from coastal Norway to the far northern archipelago of Spitsbergen beyond the Arctic Circle.

RUSSIA ☼ Twelve and 13-day trips along Siberia's Yenisey River in the *Anton Chekhov*. Eleven and 12-day cruises on the Volga River's "Golden Ring" between St. Petersburg and Moscow aboard the *Sergei Kirov*.

SWEDEN ☼ Four and six-day cruises along the Gota Canal, passing through 65 locks between Stockholm and Gothenburg.

ß ß ß

MACKAY INTERNATIONAL, INC. ● *3190 Airport Way, Boise, ID 83705; (800) 635-5336 or (208) 344-1881; FAX (208) 344-1882.*

From far away Boise, this firm books lively Caribbean cruises from Tortola aboard a luxury catamaran.

PRICE RANGE ☼ Moderately expensive.

PEOPLE RANGE ☼ All age groups; the cruise has something of a youthful attitude.

THE DRESS ☼ Casual day and evening.

THE VESSEL ☼ The sail-rigged catamaran *Lionheart* has five cabins with private baths and dining salon. Onboard water play equipment includes inflatable sea kayaks, snorkel gear and water skis; diving ia available with advance arrangement.

SHORE EXCURSIONS ☼ Activities include hiking, shopping, snorkeling and sundry other water sports; some are included in the cruise price.

THE SEASON ☼ Late January through early May.

Itineraries

CARIBBEAN ☼ Seven-day cruises from Tortola among assorted islands of the British Virgins; landfalls include Norman, Peter, Virgin Gorda and Guana.

ß ß ß

MAURITIUS SHIPPING CORPORATION, LTD. ● *Nova Building, One Military Road, Port-Louis, Mauritius; (230) 242-2912; FAX (230) 242-5245.*

Mauritius is a small, densely populated nation in the Indian Ocean, 500 from Madagascar; this firm offers cruises around its coral-rimmed islands.

PRICE RANGE ☼ Inexpensive.

PEOPLE RANGE ☼ All age groups.

THE DRESS ☼ Casual; "smartly casual" in the evening.

THE VESSELS ☼ The *Mauritius Pride* is an eight-cabin motor cruiser; the firm also uses a larger day cruiser for shorter trips.

THE SHORE EXCURSIONS ☼ None scheduled but getting about is easy; English is the official language.

THE SEASON ☼ Most of the year.

Itinerary

MAURITIUS ISLANDS ☼ These are short cruises, one to two days, among the main islands of Mauritius, Rodrigues and Reunion. All-day cruises also are available.

ß ß ß

METROPOLITAN TOURS GALÁPAGOS CRUISES ● *U.S. booking agent: Adventure Associates, 13150 Coit Road, Suite 110, Dallas, TX 75240; (800) 527-2500, (214) 907-0414 or FAX (214) 783-1286.*

Quito's Metropolitan Tours is primarily a land vacation operation, although it also offers Galápagos cruises.

PRICE RANGE ☼ Moderate to moderately expensive.

PEOPLE RANGE ☼ All age groups.

THE DRESS ☼ Casual.

THE VESSELS ☼ The 45-cabin *Santa Cruz*, offering a large dining room, cocktail lounge and boutique, and 20-passenger luxury motor yacht *Isabella II*; both have staterooms with all private baths. A hotel-yacht combination also is available, with nights at Hotel Delfin on Santa Cruz Island and cruises aboard the passenger yacht *Delfin II*.

SHORE EXCURSIONS ☼ Island explorations included in the tour price.

THE SEASON ☼ Most of the year.

Sample itineraries

GALÁPAGOS ISLANDS ☼ For those without a lot of time, Metropolitan offers three-day cruises, hitting the popular northern islands of Bartolomé, Isabela, Punta Espinoza and Fernandina. Four-day cruises cover the southern islands of North Seymour, Punta Suárez, Hood, Punta Cormorant, Floreana, Puerto Ayora, Academy Bay and Santa Cruz. The two can be united into a seven-day cruise, hitting all of these islands. Galápagos cruises can be combined with a variety of land trips.

ßßß

NABILA TOURS & CRUISES ● *605 Market St., Suite 1310, San Francisco, CA 94105; (800) 443-6453 or (415) 979-0160; FAX (415) 979-0163.*
This firm features economically priced fully escorted tours of Turkey, including Aegean and Mediterranean cruises. It also markets Nile river trips.
PRICE RANGE ✿ Inexpensive to moderate.
PEOPLE RANGE ✿ All age groups.
THE DRESS ✿ Casual.
THE VESSELS ✿ Wooden *gulet* sailboats in Turkey; river boats operated by Nabila or Sheraton on the Nile.
SHORE EXCURSIONS ✿ Most are included, featuring guided tours of temples, ruins and historic cities in Turkey and along the Nile.
THE SEASON ✿ April through October.

Sample itineraries

TURKEY ✿ Twelve-day tours of ancient cities and temples, with eight-day "Blue Cruises" in *gulets*. Stops include Bodrum, Caunus, Mersincik, Ingiliz Limani, Cedreae, Tuzla and Çiftlik.
EGYPT ✿ Eight-day to 14-day tours including several days on a Nile riverboat, calling on Aswan, Kom Ombo, Edfu and Luxor.

ßßß

NWT MARINE GROUP ● *17 England Crescent, Yellowknife, Northwest Territories, X1A 3N5 Canada,*
This small family firm runs riverboat trips along the MacKenzie River and Great Slave Lake in Canada's Northwest Territories, and area of 1,322,900 square miles with only 55,000 people.
PRICE RANGE ✿ Moderately expensive.
PEOPLE RANGE ✿ All age groups; seekers of remote places.
THE DRESS ✿ Casual daytime and evening.
THE VESSEL ✿ The *M.S. Norweta* is a 103-foot expedition ship with ten cozy cabins, a lounge, dining room and sundeck.
SHORE EXCURSIONS ✿ Wildlife viewing, visits to native villages and old fur trading posts, fishing, soaking in hot springs and exploring ashore in this wilderness, which is mostly above the Arctic Circle.
THE SEASON ✿ June through August.

Sample itineraries

NORTHWEST TERRITORIES ✿ Four departures each summer, ten and 12 days, between Yellowknife and Inuvik on the Beaufort Sea, cruising the MacKenzie River and the Great Slave Lake. Also, six-day cruises on the Great Slave Lake and into the western entrance to the Northwest Passage.

ßßß

OCEANIC CRUISES ● *5757 W. Century Blvd., Suite 390, Los Angeles, CA 90045; (800) 545-5778 or (310) 215-0191. FAX (310) 215-0346.*
This firm books passage on the small Japanese luxury cruise ship *Oceanic Grace,* with a variety of voyages around Japan and the Far East.

This wild "bull race" through a muddy bog on the island of Sumbawa is one of the spectacles travelers can witness on a P&O Spice Islands cruise.

PRICE RANGE ✿ Expensive.

PEOPLE RANGE ✿ All age groups.

THE DRESS ✿ Casual daytime; jackets or suits and cocktail wear evening; formal wear optional for captain's dinners.

THE VESSEL ✿ The *Oceanic Grace* is an opulent mini-cruise ship with 60 large staterooms equipped with private baths, TV/VCRs, refrigerated bars, couches and desks. Onboard amenities include an attractive dining room, two lounges and bars, beauty parlor, library, pool, sauna and spa, gym, dive platform and even a jogging course.

SHORE EXCURSIONS ✿ Not included; available at each port.

THE SEASON ✿ February through September.

Sample itineraries

JAPAN ✿ A variety of voyages from three to seven days, such as an exploration of the Ogasawara Islands and a southern Japan cruise to Ashizuri and Yakushima and Hahajima islands; these are whale-watching cruises in April. Seven-day Inland Sea cruise from Yokohama to Toba, Aburatsu, Hiroshima and Osaka to Tokyo. Four to 12-day cruises through the Sea of Japan and around Hokkaido.

JAPAN TO CHINA AND KOREA ✿ Nine days from Kobe to Osaka via Yantai and Tianjin. Six-day cruise from Hakata to Cheju, Dairen and Kobe.

MICRONESIA ✿ Twenty-eight days (smaller segments available) from Tokyo to Guam, Ponape, Truk, Palau, Saipan and back to Tokyo.

SOUTHEAST ASIA ✿ Nineteen days (smaller segments available) from Tokyo to Xiamen, Hainan, Danang, Hong Kong, Keelung and Kobe.

ϼϼϼ

P&O SPICE ISLAND CRUISES ● *P.O. Box 3581, Denpasar, Bali 80228 Indonesia; (0361) 286-283; FAX (0361) 386-284.*

The lesser-visited islands of Indonesia are the subject of this Bali-based cruise line—and it has 17,000 from which to choose! Its focus is somewhere between expedition and soft cruising.

PRICE RANGE ☼ Moderate to expensive.

PEOPLE RANGE ☼ All age groups; lots of walking involved but nothing strenuous

THE DRESS ☼ Casual daytime; casual or slightly dressy evenings.

THE VESSELS ☼ the 18-cabin *Island Explorer* and 21-cabin *Spice Islander* are expedition-type catamarans with private baths, dining room and lounge. The *Sea Dancer* is a small conventional type cruise ship carrying 150 passengers.

SHORE EXCURSIONS ☼ Most are included in the price.

THE SEASON ☼ Year around.

Sample itineraries

INDONESIA ☼ A variety of itineraries, including three and four-day excursions on the *Sea Dancer* from Bali to Lombok, Komodo and Sumbawa; seven days from Lombok to Sumbawa, Komodo, Flores, the Solor islands, Aloe and Kupang; 14 days with a similar itinerary plus Roti, Sawu and Sumba; seven-day cruises focusing on Krakatau volcano and rainforests of eastern Sumatra and western Java; and seven-day cruises from Lomboc to Moyo, Komodo, Sumba, Sawu, Roti and Kupang. (**Note:** Cruise closeup on page 291.)

ϼϼϼ

SEABOURN CRUISE LINE ● *55 Francisco St., Suite 710, San Francisco, CA 94133; (800) 929-9595 or (415) 391-7444; FAX (415) 391-8518.*

"Seabourn," it says on page five of the 195-page brochure, "is in a class by itself." It is indeed—simply the world's most luxurious cruise line, according to *Conde Naste Traveler, Fielding's Guide to Worldwide Cruising* and other publications. It can afford to be the best; staterooms—all suites—average more than $500 per day. Of course, that includes airfare to wherever the ships may have wandered. As a further savings, tipping is not permitted.

PRICE RANGE ☼ Very expensive.

PEOPLE RANGE ☼ Those who can afford the absolute best.

THE DRESS ☼ Smartly casual daytime; semi-formal to formal evenings.

THE VESSELS ☼ The opulently appointed *Seabourn Pride* and *Seabourn Spirit* have 100 suites each, plus all the amenities that several hundred dollars a day can buy. They feature five-foot picture windows, fully stocked bars with Hadeland Norwegian crystal for sipping, TV/VCRs, marble baths and walk-in closets. And there's personalized stationery for writing all those "wish you were here" notes. Ship facilities include a posh dining salon, large library, water sports deck, swimming pool, sauna, spa, nightclub and casino.

SHORE EXCURSIONS ☼ Most shore excursions and many land extensions are included.

THE SEASON ☼ All year.

Sample itineraries

SHORT CRUISES ☼ The two ships wander the globe with their pampered passengers, offering cruises varying from a few days to a couple of weeks.

Itineraries—too, too many to mention here—cover Southeast Asia, the Orient and India, the Caribbean and Panama Canal, South America with cruises up the lower Amazon, the Mediterranean and much of coastal Europe including Scandinavia, Africa and the Seychelles, North America and the South Pacific.

LONG CRUISES ✿ For those with time on their hands, "Grand Cruises" include 61 days from Singapore to Seattle; 109-day round trip between San Francisco, the South Pacific and New Zealand; 48-day Haifa to Mombassa to Hong Kong; 41-day Hong Kong to Vietnam, India and Israel; 75 days circumnavigating South America from San Diego to Fort Lauderdale; 25-day trans-Atlantic from Fort Lauderdale to Spain and Portugal via Bermuda and the Canary Islands; 31-day trans-Atlantic from London, Russia, Scandinavia, Iceland and the Maritime provinces to New York; and 35-day Mombassa to Singapore and Hong Kong.

ᚹᚹᚹ

TARA TOURS ● *6595 NW 36th St., Suite 306, Miami, FL 33166; (800) 327-0080 or (305) 871-1246; FAX (305) 871-0417.*

A specialist in South American travel, Tara books moderately priced Amazon and Galápagos cruises.

PRICE RANGE ✿ Inexpensive to moderate.

PEOPLE RANGE ✿ All age groups.

THE DRESS ✿ Very casual.

THE VESSELS ✿ On the Amazon, ten and 20-passenger Amazon river boats with shared baths, lounge, dining area and bar. In the Galápagos, private yachts with ten cabins and private facilities, plus the *Galápagos Explorer*, a small cruise ship with private baths and other amenities.

SHORE EXCURSIONS ✿ All included.

THE SEASON ✿ Most of the year.

Sample itineraries

AMAZON ✿ Eight-day round trip on the upper Amazon from Iquitos to Tabatinga, Brazil. Four to seven-day trips from Manaus to Anavilanhas on the Rio Negro.

THE GALÁPAGOS ✿ Three to seven-day voyages among the Galápagos islands; land extensions to Cuzco, Machu Picchu and other areas available.

ᚹᚹᚹ

TAUK TOURS ● *P.O. Box 5027 (276 Post Road West), Westport, CT 06881; (800) 468-2825 or (203) 226-6911; FAX (203) 221-6828.*

This large tour operator is noted mostly for fully escorted land excursions, although it recently began booking a sleek new sailing yacht, *Le Ponant* and an even sleeker motor cruiser, the *Lady Caterina*.

PRICE RANGE ✿ Expensive.

PEOPLE RANGE ✿ All age groups; adventure travelers who like their creature comforts.

THE DRESS ✿ Casual; dressy at night optional.

THE VESSEL ✿ *Le Ponant* is a 289-foot luxury sailing yacht with 32 fully furnished staterooms, single-seat dining and lounges. The *Lady Caterina* is a posh 165-foot motor yacht with 25 nicely appointed staterooms, single-seat dining, lounges, spa, library and boutique. Both ships offer a variety of water sports gear.

SHORE EXCURSIONS ☼ All included, featuring explorations of assorted ports along the way, plus Mayan ruins in Guatemala.

THE SEASON ☼ January-March in Central America and May-October in the Mediterranean for *Le Ponant* and December through March for the *Lady Caterina* in Belize-Guatemala.

Itineraries

CENTRAL AMERICA ☼ Ten-day tours from San Jose, Costa Rica, including a six-day cruise on *Le Ponant* through the Panama Canal to the San Blas Islands. A nine-day exploration of Tikal and a cruise along the Belize barrier reef and Guatemala's Rio Dulce aboard the *Lady Caterina*.

THE MEDITERRANEAN ☼ A 13-day tour of Provence, the French Riviera and Malta, including a seven-day cruise on *Le Ponant* to Corsica, Ponza, the Amalfi Coast and Sicily.

ß ß ß

TEMPTRESS VOYAGES ● *1600 NW Le Jeuen Rd., Miami, FL 33126; (800) 336-8423 or (305) 871-2663; FAX (305) 871-2657.*

These trips, somewhere between expedition cruising and soft adventure, focus on the shorelines, offshore islands and inland jungles of Costa Rica and Belize.

PRICE RANGE ☼ Moderately expensive, including all shore activities.

PEOPLE RANGE ☼ All age groups; particularly appealing to active people, since the trips offer water sports and nature hikes.

THE DRESS ☼ Very casual.

THE VESSELS ☼ The *MV Temptress Explorer* and *MV Temptress Voyager* are small expedition style ships with 49 and 29 cabins respectively.

SHORE EXCURSIONS ☼ All-inclusive activities consist of nature hikes, temple explorations, river and town tours, snorkeling, sea kayaking, scuba diving and water skiing.

THE SEASON ☼ The year around; high season is November through May.

Itineraries

COSTA RICA ☼ Three-day to six-day voyages around the edges of Costa Rica with frequent trips inland to explore towns, rainforests and ruins.

BELIZE ☼ Three-day to six-day round trips from Belize City, with explorations of the Great Barrier Reef, Sittee River and coastal Belize.

ß ß ß

VOYAGERS INTERNATIONAL ● *P.O. Box 915, Ithaca, NY 14851; (800) 633-0299 or (607) 257-3091; FAX (607) 257-3699.*

Primary target of this firm is South America, particularly the Amazon and Galápagos; it also offers some antarctic trips.

PRICE RANGE ☼ Moderate to moderately expensive; South American trips include air from Miami.

PEOPLE RANGE ☼ All age groups.

THE DRESS ☼ Casual.

THE VESSELS ☼ Various Galápagos ships and yachts; some with private facilities; some shared. The former research vessel *Professor Molchanoz*, 18 basic cabins with private baths, is used in Antarctica.

SHORE EXCURSIONS ☼ Included.

THE SEASON ☼ Year around, depending on the area.

Sample itineraries

SOUTH AMERICA ☼ Eight-day cruises from San Cristóbal, visiting most of the Galápagos Islands. Sixteen-day trips, including Galápagos cruises with shore extensions to Cuzco and Machu Picchu. Twelve-day trips with Galápagos cruise and shore extension to Cotopaxi Volcano National Park and Quito and nearby Indian markets. Fourteen-day tours with Galápagos cruise and an Amazon exploration with overnight stays in river lodges.

ANTARCTICA ☼ Three-week trips from Tierra del Fuego to the Antarctic Peninsula and King George Island aboard the *Professor Molchanov.*

℞℞℞

ZEUS TOURS ● *566 Seventh Ave., New York, NY 10018; (800) 447-5667 or (212) 221-0006; FAX (212) 764-7912.*

Coupled with Vernicos Yachts (listed above under "Sailing ships,") this firm specializes in cruises in the eastern Mediterranean.

PRICE RANGE ☼ Moderate.

PEOPLE RANGE ☼ All age groups.

THE DRESS ☼ Casual day and evening.

THE VESSELS ☼ Zeus employs a small fleet of motor yachts and motor-sailing yachts with four to 21 cabins, all with private bathrooms and salon-dining areas.

SHORE EXCURSIONS ☼ None scheduled.

THE SEASON ☼ April through October.

Sample itineraries

EASTERN MEDITERRANEAN ☼ Seven days out of Piraeus (Athens) or Corfu, calling on Paros, Santorini, Lefkas and other Greek islands. Seven days from Athens into the Aegean Sea, calling on Paros, Santorini, Mykonos and other islands. Seven and 14-day cruises between Athens and Kusadasi, Turkey, calling on Santorini, Rhodes, Mykonos and Turkish islands and ports.

WHITEWATER TRIPS

Why are we including rafting and kayaking trips in an adventure cruising book? Because these certainly *are* aquatic adventures; indeed they're among the more popular water vacations in America. Hundreds of companies large and small offer trips down frothy rivers. We've limited our listings to firms that provide "vacation length" trips of five days or more.

THE POPULAR RIVERS ● The Grand Canyon of the Colorado is the monarch of whitewater runs, with scores of rapids along its 200-mile-plus stretch. To obtain a list of outfitters that run the "Grand," contact River Sub-district, Grand Canyon National Park, P.O. Box 129, Grand Canyon, AZ 86023; (520) 638-7843. Also popular with river runners is the Moab-Canyonlands National Park area in Utah, where the Green and Colorado rivers merge. For a list of operators there, contact the Moab Multi-Agency Visitors Center, P.O. Box 550, Moab, UT 84532; (800) 635-MOAB or (801) 259-8825.

Up in the far north, folks like to bundle up and run the Alsek and Tatshenshini rivers in Canada and Alaska. They flow from the icy heights of Canada's north into the gulf of Alaska, passing through the world's largest non-polar ice fields. Both offer a mix of quiet floating and occasional rapids.

The Tatshenshini runs through wooded areas while the Alsek environment is more barren and glaciated. Several outfits listed below specialize in these streams.

Note: For a detailed list of American whitewater and calm water raft firms and other outdoor vacation companies, contact America Outdoors at P.O. Box 1348, Knoxville, TN 37901; (423) 524-4814.

៲៲៲

ACTION WHITEWATER ADVENTURES ● *P.O. Box 1634, Provo, UT 84603; (800) 453-1482 or (801) 375-4111; FAX (801) 375-4175; e-mail: rafting@xmission.com; Web site is http://www.xmission.com.*

Dating back to the 1950s, AWA is one of America's senior whitewater outfits, offering trips on many of the West's runnable rivers.

PRICE RANGE ☼ Inexpensive to moderate.

THE SEASON ☼ May through September.

Sample itineraries

ARIZONA ☼ Six and seven-day trips down the Grand Canyon.

CALIFORNIA ☼ One to two-day trips on the American and Kern. One to three-day trips on the Tuolumne.

IDAHO ☼ Three to six-day runs on the main and middle forks of the Salmon.

OREGON ☼ Three and four-day trips on the Rogue.

UTAH ☼ Three to five-day trips through Cataract Canyon. Four-day trips on the Green through Desolation Canyon.

៲៲៲

ALASKA DISCOVERY ● *5449 Shuane Dr., Suite 4, Juneau, AK 99801; (800) 586-1911 or (907) 780-6226; FAX (907) 780-6505.*

A "low-impact" wilderness expedition company, Alaska Discovery offers a variety of rafting, canoeing, kayaking and overland trips in Alaska and Canada.

PRICE RANGE ☼ Moderate to moderately expensive.

THE SEASON ☼ Summer.

Sample itineraries

ALASKA-YUKON ☼ Ten-day rafting and hiking along the Kongakut River and the Sheenjek River in the Arctic National Wildlife Refuge; both trips start in Fairbanks. Six and ten days sea kayaking in Icy Bay and along Hubbard Glacier. Eight-day sea kayaking trips in Glacier Bay National Park. Eight days of sea kayaking and canoeing out of Juneau. Ten-day rafting on the Tatshenshini River or 12 days on the Alsek.

៲៲៲

AMERICAN WILDERNESS EXPERIENCE ● *P.O. Box 1486, Boulder, CO 80306; (800) 444-0099 or (303) 444-2622; FAX (303) 444-3999.*

Whitewater rafting and sea kayaking are among the varied outdoor trips packaged by this company, whose motto is "The civilized way to rough it."

PRICE RANGE ☼ Moderate.

THE SEASON ☼ Mostly spring to early fall.

Sample itineraries

NORTH AMERICA ☼ A variety of whitewater trips on the Colorado River through the Grand Canyon and Cataract Canyon, Rogue River in southern

Oregon, Hells Canyon of the Snake River, Canyon of the Lodore on the Green River in Colorado-Utah, and the Salmon River in Idaho. Also sea kayaking, canoeing and some combination trips such as rafting-ranching, rafting-biking and kayaking-biking.

ALASKA ☼ Seven-day small yacht cruising on the Inside Passage and eight-day sea kayaking on Glacier Bay.

ฅฅฅ

ARTA ● 24000 Casa Loma Rd., Groveland, CA 95321; (800) 323-2782 or (209) 962-7873; e-mail: arta-info@arta.org.

Based in the California's Sierra Nevada foothills, this firm specializes in whitewater trips on Western rivers.

PRICE RANGE ☼ Moderate.

THE SEASON ☼ Spring through fall.

Sample itineraries

WESTERN AMERICA ☼ One to 13-day trips on the Colorado River through the Grand Canyon; the American, Tuolumne and Merced in California's Sierra foothills; the North Umpqua, Rogue and Illinois in Oregon; upper Klamath in Oregon-California; the Selway and Salmon in the Idaho Rockies; and the Yampa and Green in Utah.

ฅฅฅ

CANADIAN RIVER EXPEDITIONS ● P.O. Box 1023, Whistler, B.C., Canada V0N 1B0; (800) 898-7238 or (604) 938-6651; FAX (604) 938-6621.

The "best of British Columbia" is the focus of this outdoor travel company; it also seeks out-of-the-way places in the Yukon.

PRICE RANGE ☼ Moderately expensive.

THE SEASON ☼ June through September.

Sample itineraries

YUKON TO ALASKA ☼ Twelve-day combined Tatshenshini-Alsek river trip; and a six and eight-day upper Alsek river trip.

BRITISH COLUMBIA ☼ Eleven-day "Best of British Columbia" is a combined boat, seaplane and raft trip from coastal fjords near Vancouver to Chilko Lake and down the Chilko, Chilcotin and Fraser rivers. Eight-day raft trip on the Gataga and Kechika rivers, out of Fort Nelson.

NORTHWEST TERRITORIES ☼ A one-week kayaking trip through Baffin Island's Lancaster Sound.

ฅฅฅ

CANYONEERS ● P.O. Box 2997, Flagstaff, AZ 86003; (800) 525-0924 or (520) 526-0924; FAX (520) 527-9398.

Of the nearly 20 whitewater companies with permits to run the Grand Canyon of the Colorado River, this outfit is something of a specialist. It runs only the Grand, and it has a variety of other outdoor programs in the area.

PRICE RANGE ☼ Moderate.

THE VESSELS ☼ Large motor pontoons and small oar-powered rafts.

THE SEASON ☼ April through September.

Sample itineraries

GRAND CANYON ☼ The "Extended Grand" is 13-days by oar power from Lees Ferry to Pearce Ferry. Shorter trips vary from three to seven days, often with motor pontoons.

ᏉᏉᏉ

CHILKAT GUIDES, LTD. ● *P.O. Box 170, Haines, AK 99827; (907) 766-2491; FAX (907) 766-2409.*

The Tatshenshini and Alsek rivers of Canada and Alaska are the wilderness playgrounds of this outfit.

PRICE RANGE ☼ Moderately expensive, since outfitting costs are high this far north, and a charter flight is involved.

THE SEASON ☼ Summer.

Itineraries

CANADA-ALASKA ☼ The company's Tatshenshini run is a ten-day, 140-mile float with occasional rapids. The Alsek run, also a mix of flatwater and foam, takes 13 days. The firm also runs half-day trips out of Haines into the world's largest bald eagle preserve in the Chilkat Valley.

ᏉᏉᏉ

DVORAK'S KAYAKING AND RAFTING EXPEDITIONS ● *17921-AC Highway 285, Nathrop, CO 81236; (800) 824-3795 or (719) 539-6851; FAX (719) 539-3378; e-mail: dvorakex@rmii.com.*

Raft and kayak trips down lesser-traveled rivers such as the Dolores and Arkansas are specialties of this outfit, plus classical music journeys with daily concerts.

PRICE RANGE ☼ Moderate.

THE SEASON ☼ April through September.

Sample itineraries

COLORADO-UTAH ☼ Five to seven days on the Arkansas River in Colorado. Five, eight and 12-day trips on Colorado's Dolores River, plus eight-day classical music trips. Five to six-day trips on the Green River in Eastern Utah, plus eight-day classical music trips.

TEXAS ☼ Seven-day trips on the Rio Grande through Big Bend National Park on the Texas-Mexico border.

ᏉᏉᏉ

EARTH RIVER EXPEDITIONS ● *180 Towpath Rd., Accord, NY 12404; (800) 643-2784 or (914) 626-2665; FAX (914) 626-4361.*

This conservation-focused firm runs some of the world's most challenging rivers, often with rapids up to Class V (considered the wildest water runnable.) It's considered a leader in both high adventure outings and environmental activities.

PRICE RANGE ☼ Moderately expensive to expensive.

SHORE EXCURSIONS ☼ Some outings include treks and van trips to explore ancient ruins, temples and such.

THE SEASON ☼ Varies according to the trip.

Sample itineraries

SOUTH AMERICA ☼ Two-week trips originating in Santiago with eight days on Chile's Bio Bio River. Two-week trips from Santiago with rafting, horseback riding and trekking in Patagonia. Ten-day trips in Patagonia with a week in the canyons of the Futaleufu River. Nine days in Venezuela, mostly on the Churun River, with a hike to the base of Angel Falls, the word's highest cataract.

RAPID TRANSIT BY DORY:
The ultimate whitewater trip

When men first challenged the wild rapids of the Colorado River through the Grand Canyon, they used wooden boats. Civil War hero Major John Wesley Powell made the first successful run in 1869, although his long boats proved to be lousy whitewater craft. In fact, his crew roped them down the worst of the rapids. Of course, they had no choice. Inflatables, now employed by virtually every whitewater outfit, hadn't been invented yet. They were offshoots of life rafts developed for World War II pilots.

When leading American environmentalist Martin Litton decided to form a river running company several decades ago, he wanted to use "hardboats" like those first river-runners. However, he needed something more maneuverable than Powell's awkward longboats. He found his answer in the nimble little dory, a small flat-bottom double-prowed fishing boat used for centuries by Portuguese fishermen.

Martin designed a whitewater version of the craft, formed Grand Canyon Dories and began running the great and wild rivers of the American west. River dories are four-passenger craft with the boatman in the middle, and they offer the wildest ride of anything on water. Big rafts plow through the rapids; the dories dance through them. Once people have taken a whitewater ride in a dory, they rarely go back to the "baloney boats."

When Litton retired several years ago—with great reluctance—he sold his operation to George Wendt's outdoor adventure company, OARS. Thus, the tradition continues: OARS runs dories through the Grand Canyon, and on the Salmon, Hells Canyon of the Snake, Owyhee, Grand Ronde, San Juan, Green and Yampa rivers. It's one of the few firms offering the grandest whitewater trip of all—the dory ride.

MEXICO ✿ Ten days, mostly floating the Usumacinta River beneath a jungle canopy, exploring Mayan ruins and wildlife of the area.

TIBET ✿ Seventeen days, with visits to Beijing's Forbidden City and the nearby Great Wall, then several days on the rapids of the upper Yangtze River through the Tibetan wilderness.

CANADA ✿ Eight days, mostly on the little-known but lively Magpie River on the Labrador Plateau of eastern Quebec; a seven-day visit to a small Cree tribe on James Bay, with whitewater runs on the Great Whale River.

ßßß

GLACIER RAFT COMPANY ● *P.O. Box 218, West Glacier, MT 59936; (800) 332-9995 or (406) 888-5454; FAX (406) 888-5541.*

This firm runs the Flathead River near Montana's Glacier National Park.

PRICE RANGE ✿ Moderate.

THE SEASON ✿ Summer.

Itinerary

MONTANA ✿ Five-day trips with two days on the middle fork of the Flathead River and three days horseback riding through northern Montana wilderness areas. Camping or cabin trips are available.

℞℞℞
HOLIDAY RIVER & BIKE EXPEDITIONS, INC. ● *544 E. 3900 South, Salt Lake City, UT 84107: (800) 624-6323 outside Utah or (801) 266-2087; FAX (801) 266-1448.*

These holidays are wet ones, mostly on the rivers of Utah; some include dry land biking.

PRICE RANGE ☼ Moderate.

THE SEASON ☼ Spring through early fall.

Sample itineraries

UTAH ☼ Five to six days through Cataract Canyon on the Colorado and two to three days through Westwater Canyon. Four days on the Green River through Canyon of the Lodor and five days through Desolation Canyon on the Green. Four to five days on the Yampa River through Dinosaur National Monument. Three to four days on the San Juan in southeastern Utah. Also rafting-biking combinations on the Green, Colorado and Yampa rivers.

IDAHO ☼ Five to six days on the main and lower Salmon. Three to five days through Hells Canyon on the Snake River.

ARIZONA ☼ Five to 12 days on the Colorado River through the Grand Canyon.

℞℞℞
NOAH'S WORLD OF WATER ● *P.O. Box 11 (53 N. Main St.), Ashland, OR 97520; (800) 858-2811 or (541) 488-2811; FAX (541) 488-0984.*

Noah runs a variety of whitewater trips on the rivers of Oregon and northern California.

PRICE RANGE ☼ Moderate.

THE SEASON ☼ Spring through summer, depending on the rivers and seasonal runoff.

Sample itineraries

OREGON-CALIFORNIA ☼ Anywhere from half a day to five days on rivers such as Oregon's Rogue, Illinois and Owyhee and northern California's Klamath and Salmon. Most are camping trips, although lodge options are available on some rivers.

℞℞℞
OARS (Outdoor Adventure River Specialists) ● *P.O. Box 67, Angels Camp, CA 95222; (209) 736-4677; FAX (209) 736-2902; Web site is http://www.oars.com.*

One of America's premier river running outfits, OARS hits the rapids of nearly every serious whitewater stream in the West, plus some international rivers. It's also the only major company running whitewater dories (see box), and it offers sea kayak and inflatable kayak trips.

PRICE RANGE ☼ Moderate.

THE SEASON ☼ Year around, depending on the area; spring through early fall in the West.

Sample itineraries

ALASKA/CANADA ☼ Twelve-day trips on the Alsek River and ten-days on the Tatshenshini. Twelve-day trips on the Nahanni in the Yukon and six-days on the Chilko in British Columbia. Six and seven-day sea kayaking trips in the Inside Passage and coastal British Columbia.

ARIZONA ☼ Five to 13-day trips down the Grand Canyon of the Colorado River.

CALIFORNIA ☼ One to three-day runs on the Stanislaus, American, Merced, Tuolumne and Kern rivers in the Sierra Nevada foothills. Two to three-day trips on the Klamath in northern California. Also two to eight-day whitewater raft schools and five and seven-day dory schools on the American River.

IDAHO ☼ Three to 12-day trips through Hells Canyon of the Snake River, the Salmon main and middle forks and Payette River. Also two to eight-day whitewater raft schools and five and seven-day dory instruction on the Snake River near Lewiston.

OREGON ☼ Four and five-day raft and inflatable kayak trips on the Rogue River.

THE SOUTHWEST ☼ Four to six-day trips through Cataract Canyon and Desolation Canyon in Utah; the Dolores, Yampa and San Juan in Colorado and Utah; and the Rio Grande's Big Bend in Texas.

WYOMING ☼ One to five-day float trips and kayak trips on Jackson Lake and the Snake River through Grand Teton National Park. Five-day kayak trip on Yellowstone Lake in Yellowstone National Park.

INTERNATIONAL ☼ Six and seven-day sea kayaking and whale watching trips along Mexico's Sea of Cortez and Baja Peninsula. Fourteen-day whitewater trips on Chile's Bio Bio and nine-day trips on the Zambezi River in Zambia and Zimbabwe.

ᐸᐸᐸ

SIERRA MAC RIVER TRIPS ● *P.O. Box 366, Sonora, CA 95370; (800) 457-2580 or (209) 532-1327; FAX (209) 532-1842.*

Do you want to learn how to handle wild rapids? This outfit, which runs a series of trips on the rivers of California's Sierra Nevada foothills, also conducts whitewater schools up to a week long.

PRICE RANGE ☼ Inexpensive.

SHORE EXCURSIONS ☼ Learning to handle a whitewater raft *is* the excursion!

THE SEASON ☼ May through September.

Itinerary

CALIFORNIA'S SIERRA FOOTHILLS ☼ One to seven-day whitewater rafting schools are conducted on the Tuolumne, Merced and American rivers. The firm also runs one to three-day whitewater trips on the Tuolumne, north fork American and other rivers of the Sierra Nevada foothills.

ᐸᐸᐸ

TAG-A-LONG EXPEDITIONS ● *452 N. Main St. Moab, UT 84532; (800) 453-3292 or (801) 259-8946; FAX (801) 259-8990.*

Cataract Canyon on the Colorado River is the target of this Utah outdoor firm.

PRICE RANGE ☼ Moderate.

THE SEASON ☼ Late spring to early fall.

Sample itineraries

UTAH ☼ Five-day float trips on the Green River. Six-day float and whitewater trips on the Colorado River through Cataract Canyon in Canyonlands National Park to Lake Powell.

🏳🏳🏳
TATSHENSHINI EXPEDITING, LTD. ● *1062 Alder St., Whitehorse, Yukon, Canada Y1A 3W8; (403) 633-2742; FAX (403) 633-6184; e-mail: tatex@polarcom.com*

This far north firm offers whitewater paddle trips on the Tatshenshini and Alsek rivers, plus whitewater raft and kayaking trips in Chile (through its Sports International subsidiary).

PRICE RANGE ☼ Moderate.

THE SEASON ☼ June through mid-August in Canada; mid-January through February in Chile.

Sample itineraries

YUKON TERRITORY ☼ Eleven-day raft trips on the Tatshenshini and Alsek rivers; and six-day raft trips on the Alsek.

CHILE ☼ Twelve-day raft and kayak trips and 16-day advanced kayaker trips on the Bio Bio River.

TYPES OF VESSELS

But, didn't we just list the different types of vessels in the cruise directory above? More or less. However, several of the firms in the directory employ more than kind of vessel. If the specific type of ship or boat is important to you, use this roster. It lists the companies not by the kinds of cruises they offer, but by the specific type of vessels they employ. Obviously, some firms that use more than one kind of craft will appear several times.

Each entry shows the subheading under which the company is listed in the cruise directory above, and the page number.

🏳🏳🏳
Canal barges

Erie Canal Cruise Lines—See listing above under River and canal boats and barges, page 50.

European Waterways—See river and canal boats and barges, page 51.

French Country Waterways, Ltd.—See river and canal boats and barges, page 51.

Mid-Lakes Navigation, Ltd.—River and canal boats and barges, page ??.

Willow Wren Cruise Holidays—See river and canal boats and barges, page 56.

🏳🏳🏳
Catamarans

Galápagos, Inc.—Expedition cruise companies, page 26.
Galápagos Network—Expedition cruise companies, page 26.
Geo Expeditions—Expedition cruise companies, page 27.
Mackay International, Inc.—Soft adventure cruise lines, page 69.
Melanesian Tourist Services—Expedition cruise companies, page 30.
Metropolitan Tours—Soft adventure cruise lines, page 70.
Natural Habitat Adventures—Expedition cruise companies, page 31.
P&O Spice Island Cruises—Soft adventure cruise lines, page 73.

Ɓ Ɓ Ɓ
Cruise ships

Ɓ Ɓ Ɓ
Expedition ships and boats

Ɓ Ɓ Ɓ
Icebreakers

Quark Expeditions—Expedition cruise companies, page 33.
Zegrahm Expeditions—Expedition cruise companies, page 40.

ᗺᗺᗺ
Kayaks
Alaska Discovery—Whitewater trips, page 77.
Alaska's Glacier Bay Tours & Cruises—Soft adventure cruise companies, page 64.
American Wilderness Experience—Whitewater trips, page 77.
Baja Expeditions—Expedition cruise companies, page 23.
Canadian River Expeditions—Whitewater trips, page 78.
Dvorak's Kayaking and Rafting Expeditions—Whitewater trips, page 79.
Great Lakes Tall Ship Adventures—Soft adventure cruise lines, page 58.
Mackay International, Inc.—Soft adventure cruise lines, page 69.
OARS—Whitewater trips, page 81.
Tatshenshini Expediting, Ltd.—Whitewater trips, page 83.
Temptress Voyages—Soft adventure cruise lines, page 75.

ᗺᗺᗺ
Motor launches and yachts
Alaska Sightseeing/Cruise West—Soft adventure cruise lines, page 63.
Alaska's Glacier Bay Tours & Cruises—See soft adventure cruise lines, page 64.
Clipper Cruise Line—Soft adventure cruise lines, page 68.
Galápagos, Inc.—Expedition cruise companies, page 26.
Journeys International—Expedition cruise companies, page 29.
Maluku Adventures—Expedition cruise companies, page 29.
Mauritius Shipping Corporation, Ltd.—See soft adventure cruise lines, page 70.
Metropolitan Tours—Soft adventure cruise lines, page 70.
Tara Tours—Soft adventure cruise lines, page 74.
Tauk Tours—Soft adventure cruise lines, page 74.
Voyagers International—Soft adventure cruise lines, page 75.
Zeus Tours—Soft adventure cruise lines, page 76.

ᗺᗺᗺ
Motor sailers
Galápagos, Inc.—Expedition cruise companies, page 26.
Galápagos Network—Expedition cruise companies, page 26.
Geo Expeditions—Expedition cruise companies, page 27.
Geographic Expeditions—Expedition cruise companies, page 27.
International Expeditions—Expedition cruise companies, page 28.
Maluku Adventures—Expedition cruise companies, page 29.
Metropolitan Tours—Soft adventure cruise lines, page 70.
Overseas Adventure Travel—Expedition cruise companies, page 32.
Special Expeditions—Expedition cruise companies, page 37.
Wilderness Travel—Expedition cruise companies, page 38.
Voyagers International—Soft adventure cruise lines, page 75.
Zeus Tours—Soft adventure cruise lines, page 76.

ßßß
Paddlewheelers

American West Steamboat Company—River and canal boats and barges, page 48.

Delta Queen Steamship Company—River and canal boats and barges, page 49.

ßßß
Passenger-cargo liners
(All except Arctic Odysseys are listed in the "Passenger-cargo section")

Arctic Odysseys—Expedition cruise companies, page 22.
Bank Line, page 43.
Compagnie Française Maritime de Tahiti, page 44.
Compagnie Polynesienne de Transport Maritime, page 44.
Curnow Shipping, Ltd., page 44.
Frachtschiff-Touristik Kapitän Zylmann, page 45.
Horn Line, page 45.
Ivaran Lines, page 45.
Maris USA, Ltd., page 46.
Pathfinder, page 47.
Sea the Difference, Inc., page 47.
United Baltic Corporation, page 54.

ßßß
Passenger ferries
(All are listed under that heading)

Alaska Marine Highway (Alaska ferry system), page 41.
B.C. Ferries (British Columbia Ferry System), page 41.
Bergen Line (Norwegian coastal ferries), page 42.

ßßß
Pure sailing ships (no engines)

Coastwise Packet Company, Inc.—Sailing ships, page 57.
Grays Harbor Historical Seaport—Sailing ships, page 57.
Great Lakes Tall Ship Adventures—Sailing ships, page 58.
Nathaniel Bowditch—Sailing ships, page 58.
North End Shipyard Schooners—Sailing ships, page 59.
Schooner Mary Day—Sailing ships, page 59.
Tall Ship Adventures—Sailing ships, page 60.
Victory Chimes—Sailing ships, page 61.
Windjammer Barefoot Cruises—Sailing ships, page 61.

ßßß
River cruisers

Abercrombie & Kent International, Inc.—Expedition cruise, page 21.
Bolshoi Cruises, Inc.—River and canal boats and barges, page 48.
EuroCruises—River and canal boats and barges, page 69.
International Journeys—Expedition cruise companies, page 28.

KD River Cruises—River and canal boats and barges, page 52.
Nabila Tours & Cruises—Soft adventure cruise lines, page 71.
Peter Deilmann EuropAmerica Cruises—River and canal boats and barges, page 53.
Regal China Cruises—River and canal boats and barges, page 53.
St. Lawrence Cruise Lines—River and canal boats and barges, page 54.
Special Expeditions—Expedition cruise companies, page 37.
Sonesta International—River and canal boats and barges, page 54.
Unique World Cruises—River and canal boats and barges, page 54.
Victoria Cruises—River and canal boats and barges, page 55.

ဩဩဩ
Sailboats and sailing ships

The Bare Necessities Tour and Travel, Inc.—Soft adventure cruise lines, page 66.
Coastwise Packet Company, Inc.—Sailing ships, page 57.
Dirigo Cruises Ltd.—Sailing ships, page 57.
Geographic Expeditions—Expedition cruise companies, page 27.
Grays Harbor Historical Seaport—Sailing ships, page 57.
Great Lakes Tall Ship Adventures—Sailing ships, page 58.
Nathaniel Bowditch—Sailing ships, page 58.
North End Shipyard Schooners—Sailing ships, page 59.
Peter Deilmann EuropAmerica Cruises—Sailing ships, page 53.
Schooner Mary Day—Sailing ships, page 59.
Special Expeditions—Expedition cruise companies, page 37.
Star Clippers—Sailing ships, page 59.
Tall Ship Adventures—Sailing ships, page 60.
Tauk Tours—Soft adventure cruise lines, page 74.
Vernicos Yachts—Sailing ships, page 60.
Victory Chimes—Sailing ships, page 61.
Windjammer Barefoot Cruises—Sailing ships, page 61.
Windstar Cruises—Sailing ships, page 62.

ဩဩဩ
Small river boats

Bryan World Tours—Expedition cruise companies, page 23.
International Expeditions—Expedition cruise companies, page 28.
International Journeys—Expedition cruise companies, page 28.
Journeys International—Expedition cruise companies, page 29.
Tara Tours—Soft adventure cruise lines, page 74.

ဩဩဩ
Firms using specialty craft

Egypt National Tours: *feluccas,* small open sailboats, used for centuries on the Nile—Expedition cruise companies, page 24.
EuroCruises: vintage steamships—Soft adventure cruise lines, page 69.
Far Horizons: *gulets,* wooden Turkish sailing yachts—Expedition cruise companies, page 25.
Maluku Adventures: Chinese junks—Expedition cruises, page 29.

Nabila Tours & Cruises: *gulets,*—Soft adventure cruise lines, page 71.
OARS: dories, descendants of Portuguese fishing boats, used for whitewater rafting—Whitewwater trips, page 81.
Quark Expeditions: oceanographic research vessels—Expedition cruise companies, page 33.
St. Lawrence Cruise Lines, Inc.: small river and lake steamboat—River and canal boats and barges, page 54.
See & Sea Travel Service: dive boats—See expedition cruise companies, page 36.
Southern Heritage Expeditions: polar research ship—Expedition cruise companies, page 37.
World of Oz: Turkish *gulets*—Sailing ships, page 62.

AREAS OF THE WORLD

Where on earth do you want to take your specialty cruise? This list groups cruise companies by the areas in which they operate. The subheadings either indicate specific countries or locales (such as the Amazon, Canada or the Galápagos) that are popular cruising areas, or more generalized regions, since ships often cruise from one country to another. Global travelers will want to consult the final listing, "Worldwide Cruises." It lists companies specializing in long itineraries, including around-the-world voyages.

The companies are listed alphabetically, followed by the subject headings under which they appear in the directory above, and the page numbers.

Africa

Curnow Shipping, Ltd.—Passenger-cargo liners, page 44.
Esplanade Tours/Noble Caledonia—Expedition cruises, page 25.
Natural Habitat Adventures—Expedition cruise companies, page 31.
Pathfinder—Passenger-cargo liners, page 47.
Quark Expeditions—Expedition cruise companies, page 33.
Radisson Seven Seas Cruise Line—Expedition cruise companies, page 35.
Seabourn Cruise Line—Soft adventure cruise lines, page 73.

The Amazon
(Also see South America listing below)
Bryan World Tours—Expedition cruise companies, page ?23
International Expeditions—Expedition cruise companies, pag 28.
Journeys International—Expedition cruise companies, page 29.
Tara Tours—Soft adventure cruise lines, page 74.

Alaska
Alaska Discovery—Whitewater trips, page 77.
Alaska Marine Highway—Passenger ferries, page 41.
Alaska Sightseeing/Cruise West—Soft adventure cruise lines, page 63.
Alaska's Glacier Bay Tours & Cruises—Soft adventure cruises, page 64.

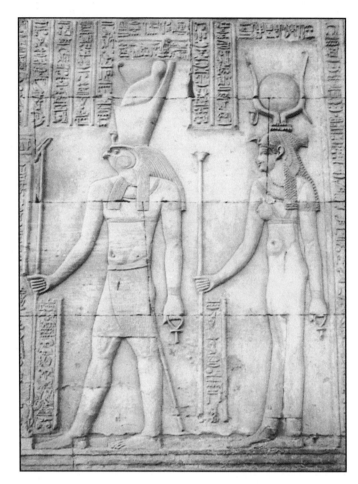

Egyptian gods Horus and Hathor are perpetuated in bas relief at the Temple of Kom Ombo, reached by Abercrombie & Kent outings and other Egypt cruise-tours.

🐚🐚🐚

Antarctica

Overseas Adventure Travel—Expedition cruise companies, page 32.
Quark Expeditions—Expedition cruise companies, page 33.
Society Expeditions—Expedition cruise companies, page 36.
Southern Heritage Expeditions—Expedition cruise companies, page 37.
Voyagers International—Soft adventure cruise lines, page 75.
Wilderness Travel—Expedition cruise companies, page 38.
Zegrahm Expeditions—Expedition cruise companies, page 40.

ßßß

The arctic
(Canadian and Russian arctic; also see Canada and Russia below)

Abercrombie & Kent International, Inc.—Expedition cruises, page 21.
Arctic Odysseys—Expedition cruise companies, page 22.
Bergen Line (Norwegian arctic)—Passenger ferries, page 42.
EuroCruises—Soft adventure cruise lines, page 69.
Geographic Expeditions—Expedition cruise companies, page 27.
Marine Expeditions—Expedition cruise companies, page 30.
Natural Habitat Adventures—Expedition cruise companies, page 31.
Nature Expeditions International—Expedition cruise companies, page 32.
NWT Marine Group—Soft adventure cruises, page 71.
Overseas Adventure Travel—Expedition cruise companies, page 32.
Quark Expeditions—Expedition cruise companies, page 33.
Society Expeditions—Expedition cruise companies, page 36.

ßßß

Australia and New Zealand

Seabourn Cruise Line—Soft adventure cruise lines, page 73.
See & Sea Travel Service—Expedition cruise companies, page 36.
Southern Heritage Expeditions—Expedition cruise companies, page 37.
Zegrahm Expeditions—Expedition cruise companies, page 40.

ßßß

Baja California
(Also see separate listing for Mexico below)

Baja Expeditions—Expedition cruise companies, page 23.
Natural Habitat Adventures—Expedition cruise companies, page 31.
OARS—Whitewater trips, page 81.
Pacific Sea Fari Tours—Expedition cruise companies, page 33.
Special Expeditions—Expedition cruise companies, page 37.
Spirit of Adventure Charters—page 38.

ßßß

British Isles

Bank Line—Passenger-cargo liners, page 43.
Classic Cruises & Tours—Soft adventure cruise lines, page 66.
Curnow Shipping Ltd.—Passenger-cargo liners, page 44.
EuroCruises—Soft adventure cruise lines, page 69.
European Waterways—River and canal boats and barges, page 51.
Marine Expeditions—Expedition cruise companies, page 32.

Pathfinder—Passenger-cargo liners, page 47.
Seabourn Cruise Line—Soft adventure cruise lines, page 73.
United Baltic Corporation—Passenger-cargo liners, page 47.
Willow Wren Cruise Holidays—River, canal boats and barges, page 56.

ꔈꔈꔈ
Canada
Alaska Discovery—Whitewater trips, page 77.
Alaska Marine Highway—Passenger ferries, page 41.
Alaska Sightseeing/Cruise West—Soft adventure cruise lines, page 63.
Alaska's Glacier Bay Tours & Cruises—Soft adventure cruises, page 64.
American Canadian Caribbean Line, Inc.—Soft adventure cruise lines, page 65.
B.C. Ferries—Passenger ferries, page 41.
Canadian River Expeditions—Whitewater trips, page 78.
Chilkat Guides, Ltd.—Whitewater trips, page 79.
Clipper Cruise Line—Soft adventure cruise lines, page 68.
Dolphin Charters—Expedition cruise companies, page 24.
Earth River Expeditions—Whitewater trips, page 79.
Erie Canal Cruise Lines—River and canal boats and barges, page 50.
Geographic Expeditions—Expedition cruise companies, page 27.
Marine Expeditions—Expedition cruise companies, page 30.
NWT Marine Group—Soft adventure cruises, page 71.
OARS—Whitewater trips, page 81.
Radisson Seven Seas Cruise Line—Expedition cruise companies, page 35.
St. Lawrence Cruise Lines, Inc.—See river and canal boats and barges, page 54.
Seabourn Cruise Line—Soft adventure cruise lines, page 73.
Tatshenshini Expediting, Ltd.—Whitewater trips, page 83.

ꔈꔈꔈ
The Caribbean
American Canadian Caribbean Line—Soft adventure cruises, page 65.
The Bare Necessities Tour and Travel, Inc.—Soft adventure cruise lines, page 66.
Clipper Cruise Line—Soft adventure cruise lines, page 68.
Dirigo Cruises Ltd.—Sailing ships, page 57.
Horn Line—Passenger-cargo liners, page 45.
Ivaran Lines—Passenger-cargo liners, page 45.
Mackay International, Inc.—Soft adventure cruise lines, page 69.
Natural Habitat Adventures—Expedition cruise companies, page 31.
Radisson Seven Seas Cruise Line—Expedition cruise companies, page 35.
Seabourn Cruise Line—Soft adventure cruise lines, page 73.
See & Sea Travel Service—Expedition cruise companies, page 36.
Special Expeditions—Expedition cruise companies, page 37.
Star Clippers—Sailing ships, page 59.
Tall Ship Adventures—Sailing ships, page 60.
Windjammer Barefoot Cruises—Sailing ships, page 61.
Windstar Cruises—Sailing ships, page 62.

Three Belizian tykes pose with varying degrees of enthusiasm on a dock in San Pedro, an island village in the Belize Great Barrier Reef.

Central America

American Canadian Caribbean Line.—Soft adventure cruises, page 65.
Clipper Cruise Line—Soft adventure cruise lines, page 68.
Horn Line—Passenger-cargo liners, page 45.
Marine Expeditions—Expedition cruise companies, page 30.
Radisson Seven Seas Cruise Line—Expedition cruise companies, page 35.
Seabourn Cruise Line—Soft adventure cruise lines, page 73.
See & Sea Travel Service—Expedition cruise companies, page 36.
Special Expeditions—Expedition cruise companies, page 37.
Tauk Tours—Soft adventure cruise lines, page 74.
Temptress Voyages—Soft adventure cruise lines, page 75.
World Explorer Cruises—Expedition cruise companies, page 39.

ঠ ঠ ঠ

Egypt

Abercrombie & Kent International, Inc.—Expedition cruises, page 21.
Classic Cruises & Tours—Soft adventure cruise lines, page 66.
Egypt National Tours, Inc.—Expedition cruise companies, page 24.

Nabila Tours & Cruises—Soft adventure cruise companies, page 71.
Overseas Adventure Travel—Expedition cruise companies, page 32.
Sonesta International—River and canal boats and barges, page 54.
Special Expeditions—Expedition cruise companies, page 37.

ເ⊳ເ⊳ເ⊳

Europe
(Also see separate listing for Turkey below)

Abercrombie & Kent International, Inc.—Expedition cruise companies, page 21.
Bergen Line—Passenger ferries, page 42.
Classic Cruises & Tours—Soft adventure cruise lines, page 66.
Curnow Shipping, Ltd.—Passenger-cargo liners, page 44.
Esplanade Tours/Noble Caledonia—Expedition cruise, page 25.
EuroCruises—Soft adventure cruise lines, page 69.
European Waterways—River and canal boats and barges, page 51.
French Country Waterways, Ltd.—River, canal boats and barges, page 51.
Horn Line—Passenger-cargo liners, page 45.
KD River Cruises—River and canal boats and barges, page 52.
Pathfinder—Passenger-cargo liners, page 47.
Peter Deilman EuropAmerica Cruises—River and canal boats and barges, page 53.
Seabourn Cruise Line—Soft adventure cruise lines, page 73.
Special Expeditions—Expedition cruise companies, page 37.
Unique World Cruises—River and canal boats and barges, page 54.
United Baltic Corporation—Passenger-cargo liners, page 47.

ເ⊳ເ⊳ເ⊳

Far East
(China, Taiwan, Japan and Korea)

Earth River Expeditions (Tibet)—Whitewater trips, page 79.
Oceanic Cruises—Soft adventure cruise lines, page 71.
Radisson Seven Seas Cruise Line—Expedition cruise companies, page 35.
Regal China Cruises—River and canal boats and barges, page 53.
Seabourn Cruise Line—Soft adventure cruise lines, page 73.
Victoria Cruises—River and canal boats and barges, page 55.

ເ⊳ເ⊳ເ⊳

Galápagos Islands
(Also see separate listing for South America below)

Galápagos, Inc.—Expedition cruise companies, page 26.
Galápagos Network—Expedition cruise companies, page 26.
Galápagos Travel—Expedition cruise companies, page 27.
Geo Expeditions—Expedition cruise companies, page 27.
Journeys International—Expedition cruise companies, page 29.
Metropolitan Tours—Soft adventure cruise lines, page 70.
Natural Habitat Adventures—Expedition cruise companies, page 31.
Overseas Adventure Travel—Expedition cruise companies, page 32.
See & Sea Travel Service—Expedition cruise companies, page 36.
Special Expeditions—Expedition cruise companies, page 37.

Tara Tours—Soft adventure cruise lines, page 74.
Voyagers International—Soft adventure cruise lines, page 75.
Wilderness Travel—Expedition cruise companies, page 38.
Zegrahm Expeditions—Expedition cruise companies, page 40.

🏴🏴🏴

Indian Ocean
(Seychelles, Maldives and Madagascar)
Esplanade Tours/Noble Caledonia—Expedition cruises, page 25.
Mauritius Shipping Corporation, Ltd.—Soft adventure cruise, page 70.
Natural Habitat Adventures—Expedition cruise companies, page 31.
Quark Expeditions—Expedition cruise companies, page 33.
Seabourn Cruise Line—Soft adventure cruise lines, page 73.
Vernicos Yachts—Sailing ships, page 60.
Zegrahm Expeditions—Expedition cruise companies, page 40.

🏴🏴🏴

Indonesia-New Guinea
(Also see listing for Southeast Asia below)
International Expeditions—Expedition cruise companies, page 28.
Maluku Adventures—Expedition cruise companies, page 29.
Melanesian Tourist Services (New Guinea specialists)—Expedition cruise companies, page 30.
P&O Spice Island Cruises—Soft adventure cruises, page 73.
Seabourn Cruise Line—Soft adventure cruise lines, page 73.
See & Sea Travel Service (Dive specialists)—Expedition cruise, page 36.
Wilderness Travel—Expedition cruise companies, page 38.
Zegrahm Expeditions—Expedition cruise companies, page 40.

🏴🏴🏴

Mediterranean
(Including Italy and Greece)
The Bare Necessities Tour and Travel—Soft adventure cruises, page 66.
Classic Cruises & Tours—Soft adventure cruise lines, page 66.
Natural Habitat Adventures—Expedition cruise companies, page 31.
Peter Deilman EuropAmerica Cruises—River and canal boats and barges, page 53.
Seabourn Cruise Line—Soft adventure cruise lines, page 73.
Star Clippers—Sailing ships, page 59.
Tauk Tours—Soft adventure cruise lines, page 74.
Vernicos Yachts—Sailing ships, page 60.
Windstar Cruises—Sailing ships, page 62.
World of Oz—Sailing ships, page 62.
Zeus Tours—Soft adventure cruise lines, page 76.

🏴🏴🏴

Mexico
Baja Expeditions—Expedition cruise companies, page 23.
Earth River Expeditions—Whitewater trips, page 79.
Natural Habitat Adventures—Expedition cruise companies, page 31.

Pacific Sea Fari Tours—Expedition cruise companies, page 33.
Seabourn Cruise Line—Soft adventure cruise lines, page 73.
Special Expeditions—Expedition cruise companies, page 37.
Spirit of Adventure Charters—Expedition cru ise companies, page 38.
Windjammer Barefoot Cruises—Sailing ships, page 62.

ʁʁʁ

Russia

Arctic Odysseys—Expedition cruise companies, page 22.
Bolshoi Cruises, Inc.—River and canal boats and barges, page 48.
Classic Cruises & Tours—Soft adventure cruise lines, page 66.
Cruise Marketing International—Sailing ships, page 49.
EuroCruises—Soft adventure cruise lines, page 69.
KD River Cruises—River and canal boats and barges, page 52.
Marine Expeditions—Expedition cruise companies, page 30.
Quark Expeditions—Expedition cruise companies, page 33.
Seabourn Cruise Line—Soft adventure cruise lines, page 73.
Society Expeditions—Expedition cruise companies, page 36.
Unique World Cruises—River and canal boats and barges, page 54.

ʁʁʁ

South America

Abercrombie & Kent International, Inc.—Expedition cruises, page 21.
Cruceros Maritimos Skorpios—Soft adventure cruise lines, page 68.
Earth River Expeditions—Whitewater trips, page 79.
Geo Expeditions—Expedition cruise companies, page 27.
International Journeys—Expedition cruise companies, page 28.
Ivaran Lines—Passenger-cargo liners, page 45.
Marine Expeditions—Expedition cruise companies, page 30.
Metropolitan Tours—Soft adventure cruise lines, page 70.
OARS (Chile)—Whitewater trips, page 81.
Overseas Adventure Travel—Expedition cruise companies, page 32.
Radisson Seven Seas Cruise Line—Expedition cruise companies, page 35.
Seabourn Cruise Line—Soft adventure cruise lines, page 73.
Special Expeditions—Expedition cruise companies, page 37.
Tara Tours—Soft adventure cruise lines, page 74.
Tatshenshini Expediting, Ltd. (Chile)—Whitewater trips, page 83.
Voyagers International—Soft adventure cruise lines, page 75.
Wilderness Travel—Expedition cruise companies, page 38.
World Explorer Cruises—Expedition cruise companies, page 39.

ʁʁʁ

South Pacific

The Bare Necessities Tour and Travel—Soft adventure cruises, page 66.
Compagnie Française Maritime de Tahiti—Passenger-cargo liners, page 44.
Compagnie Polynesienne de Transport—Passenger-cargo liners, page 44.
Dirigo Cruises Ltd.—Sailing ships, page 57.
Far Horizons—Expedition cruise companies, page 25.
Geographic Expeditions—Expedition cruise companies, page 27.
Nature Expeditions International—Expedition cruise companies, page 32.
Oceanic Cruises—Soft adventure cruise lines, page 71.

Quark Expeditions—Expedition cruise companies, page 33.
Seabourn Cruise Line—Soft adventure cruise lines, page 73.
See & Sea Travel Service—Expedition cruise companies, page 36.
Society Expeditions—Expedition cruise companies, page 36.
Wilderness Travel—Expedition cruise companies, page 38.
Windstar Cruises—Sailing ships, page 62.
Zegrahm Expeditions—Expedition cruise companies, page 40.

ßßß
Southeast Asia
(Malaysia, Singapore, Thailand, Vietnam, Cambodia)
Esplanade Tours/Noble Caledonia—Expedition cruises, page 25.
Geographic Expeditions—Expedition cruise companies, page 27.
International Expeditions—Expedition cruise companies, page 28.
Maluku Adventures—Expedition cruise companies, page 29.
Oceanic Cruises—Soft adventure cruise lines, page 71.
Seabourn Cruise Line—Soft adventure cruise lines, page 73.
Star Clippers—Sailing ships, page 59.

ßßß
Turkey
Classic Cruises & Tours—Soft adventure cruise lines, page 66.
Far Horizons—Expedition cruise companies, page 25.
Geographic Expeditions—Expedition cruise companies, page 27.
Nabila Tours & Cruises—Soft adventure cruise companies, page 71.
Overseas Adventure Travel—Expedition cruise companies, page 32.
Seabourn Cruise Line—Soft adventure cruise lines, page 73.
Wilderness Travel—Expedition cruise companies, page 38.
World of Oz—Sailing ships, page 62.

ßßß
United States
(Mainland and Hawaii; Alaska listed above)
Action Whitewater Adventures—Whitewater trips, page 77.
Alaska Sightseeing/Cruise West—Soft adventure cruise lines, page 63.
Alaska's Glacier Bay Tours & Cruises—Soft adventure cruises, page 64.
American Canadian Caribbean Line—Soft adventure cruise, page 65.
American West Steamboat Company—River and canal boats and barges, page 48.
American Wilderness Experience—Whitewater trips, page 77.
ARTA—Whitewater trips, page 78.
Canyoneers—Whitewater trips, page 78.
Clipper Cruise Line—Soft adventure cruise lines, page 68.
Coastwise Packet Company, Inc.—Sailing ships, page 57.
Delta Queen Steamship Company—River and canal boats and barges, page 49.
Dirigo Cruises Ltd.—Sailing ships, page 57.
Dvorak's Kayaking and Rafting Expeditions—Whitewater trips, page 79.
Erie Canal Cruise Lines—River and canal boats and barges, page 50.
Glacier Raft Company—Whitewater trips, page 80.

Grays Harbor Historical Seaport—Sailing ships, page 57.
Great Lakes Tall Ship Adventures—Sailing ships, page 58.
Holiday River & Bike Expeditions, Inc.—Whitewater trips, page 81.
Ivaran Lines—Passenger-cargo liners, page 45.
Mid-Lakes Navigation, Ltd.—River and canal boats and barges, page 52.
Nathaniel Bowditch—Sailing ships, page 58.
Noah's World of Water—Whitewater trips, page 81.
North End Shipyard Schooners—Sailing ships, page 59.
Radisson Seven Seas Cruise Line—Expedition cruise companies, page 35.
St. Lawrence Cruise Lines, Inc.—River, canal boats and barges, page 54.
Schooner Mary Day—Sailing ships, page 59.
Seabourn Cruise Line—Soft adventure cruise lines, page 73.
See & Sea Travel Service (Hawaii)—Expedition cruises, page 36.
Sierra Mac River Trips—Whitewater trips, page 82.
Special Expeditions—Expedition cruise companies, page 37.
Tag-A-Long Expeditions—Whitewater trips, page 82.
Victory Chimes—Sailing ships, page 62.

ß ß ß

Worldwide cruises

(Multi-country itineraries; common with passenger-cargo ships)

Bank Line—Passenger-cargo liners, page 43.
Curnow Shipping, Ltd.—Passenger-cargo liners, page 44.
Frachtschiff-Touristik Kapitän Zylmann—Passenger-cargo liners, page 45.
Horn Line—Passenger-cargo liners, page 45.
Ivaran Lines—Passenger-cargo liners, page 45.
Maris USA, Ltd.—Passenger-cargo liners, page 46.
Pathfinder—Passenger-cargo liners, page 47.
Sea the Difference, Inc.—Passenger-cargo liners, page 47.
Seabourn Cruise Line—Soft adventure cruise lines, page 73.
United Baltic Corporation—Passenger-cargo liners, page 47.

ß ß ß

PART II:
NORTH
AMERICA

*Fresh from the sea, this Alaska king crab will be lunch for Alaska Sightseeing/
Cruise West passengers who signed for an optional trip aboard a trawler.*

A ship in the harbor is safe, but that is not what ships are built for.
— **John A. Shedd**

Chapter three

THE HIGH ARCTIC
Breaking ice with Quark Expeditions

P olar bear! On an ice floe, port side!" More effective than a fire alarm, the announcement over the ship's loudspeaker emptied the lecture hall, the library, several cabins and even the bar.

"Just off the bow, ten o'clock!" the loudspeaker voice belonged to one of our lecturers. "It's a female."

We hurried toward the bow, taking the ladders two steps at a time, yet expecting to see only a distant fuzzy white dot, as we had earlier that morning.

This bear, however, was perfectly clear, strolling about on an acre of ice not 200 feet off the port bow. She stopped pacing and stared as the *Kapitan Khlebnikov* carefully crept toward the floe. The great white beast seemed more resentful of our intrusion than afraid. And then, in a daring act of nonchalance, she sat down and yawned. Only when the ship accidentally nudged the ice flow did she exhibit alarm, scrambling quickly to the far edge of her floating domain. Then she calmed down and resumed her pacing, to the cadence of clicking cameras and whirring camcorders. After 15 minutes of this, like a furry Madonna finally tiring of a press photo session, she slipped into the icy sea and paddled away.

CRUISE PLANNER

The cruise • This is a nine-day cruise aboard a Russian ice-breaker leased by Quark Expedition. The trip focuses on the flora, fauna, geology and human history of the far north, and on ice-breaking techniques. Contact Quark Expeditions, 980 Post Road, Darien, CT 06820; (800) 356-5699 or (203) 656-0499, FAX (203) 655-6623, for brochures and schedules. The company, which specializes in educational and adventure outings, also offers Antarctic voyages and it leases the nuclear powered Russian icebreaker *Yamal,* which smashes its way through pack ice all the way to the North Pole.

Getting there • Participants gather in Toronto or Montreal; Air Canada provides the most comprehensive connecting flights from American cities. The cruise package includes overnight lodging in the departure city and a charter flight that takes adventurers north to Resolute, Northwest Territories, where they board the icebreaker.

The ship • The *I/B Kapitan Khlebnikov* is a 429-foot vessel powered by diesel-electric motors capable of generating 22,000 horsepower to propel it through thick pack ice. Built in Finland in 1981, it was refitted in 1992 to modernize the navigational equipment and upgrade passenger cabins and dining areas. Facilities include fifty outside cabins with private baths, plus dining rooms, a bar/lounge and library, indoor pool, gym, sauna and lecture room with a TV/VCR system. The ship's officers are Russian, as are most of the rest of the crew members, with an international hotel staff. Lecturers and guides are mostly American and Canadian.

When to go • Summer is the season for cruises into the Canadian high arctic, since the weather is too severe the rest of the year. These cruises are popular, so book several months in advance. Shoulder season cruises, early July and late August, may have space available for latecomers, and the weather could be fine then.

What to bring • U.S. citizens need only a passport or other proof of birth to enter Canada. Bring warm clothing and wear it in layers, to be shed or added as the capricious arctic sun ducks in and out of clouds. Waterproof rubber boots are essential for slogging around the tundra and a ski mask is handy for Zodiac rides. Attire on board and ashore is strictly casual. Liquor is not sold in most of the Inuit villages in Canada and Greenland, so you'd best bring your own if you want an occasional nip in your stateroom. Dinner wine and full bar service are available aboard.

What's included • All shore excursions and a parka that you can take home are included in the cruise price. Zodiacs and an onboard helicopter are used to take passengers close to wildlife, to beaches for hikes and to the frozen heights of glaciers. Field trips are led by scientists in appropriate disciplines—wildlife and botany, archeology, regional history and glaciology.

What to buy • There's not much to buy in the far north except Inuit souvenirs and many of those made of ivory or fur can't be brought back home. Check U.S. Customs for specific bans on these items.

We were aboard a Russian icebreaker—one of the world's most power-ful—cruising through the long summer days of the Canadian high arctic. Pro-pelled by four diesel-electric engines, she could charge like a mad bull in a china shop through pack ice eight feet thick. On this day, however, the 10,471-ton ship picked her way daintily about floating patches of ice, on the lookout for arctic wildlife. Earlier, in what must have seemed comic irony to the veteran Russian icebreaker crewmen, the *Kapitan Khlebnikov* had gone in deliberate search of thick pack ice, something seamen of old tried mightily to avoid. Our hosts, Quark Expeditions, wanted the captain to demonstrate the ship's ability to crunch jagged paths through the frozen blue seas of the high arctic.

Russia has the world's largest fleet of ice breakers. When the Soviet Un-ion was in power, they were essential in keeping supply lanes open to ice-bound settlements in the northernmost reaches of Siberia. After the breakup of the federation, Russia—now in control of Siberia—saw no economic sense in main-taining these highly subsidized colonies. Many were closed and their residents brought south to warmer climes. Several

After the breakup of the Soviet federation, several Russion icebreakers wound up with no ice to break.

icebreakers wound up with no ice to break. A few years ago, Quark Expedi-tions of Darien, Connecticut, offered to lease some of the idle ships, crews and all.

Quark is thus able to provide polar cruises with a new dimension. Their ships can travel at will, with no concern that ice will block their paths. Actu-ally, watching knife-hulled ships such as the *Khlebnikov* smash through thick pack ice may be the most interesting part of these adventure cruises.

Certainly, polar voyages offer other elements of intrigue: watching polar bears and harp seals hang out on ice floes, studying the stunning blue-white shapes of icebergs and exploring ghostly sites where early arctic explorers perished after running out of luck and provisions. However, few experiences can match the sight and sound of a powerful ship slamming its two-inch-thick steel prow into an eight-foot-thick floe, creating a boiling turquoise cauldron of shattered ice.

On one of Quark's outings, ice-bashing is the primary activity. The 75,000 horsepower nuclear icebreaker *Yamal*, big sister of the *Khlebnikov*, smashes all the way to the North Pole. It's the only surface vessel capable of reaching the top of our planet.

THE ARCTIC: WHAT IT IS

While the crunch to the pole sounded fascinating, we chose a cruise to the Canadian high arctic and Greenland, since it offered a variety of sights and activities. High arctic, indeed! The group gathered in Toronto and then boarded a charter plane for Resolute, a Northwest Territories outpost more than 2,000 north of Toronto, and 200 miles farther north than the most northern part of Alaska.

As we flew north to meet our ship, we browsed through literature pro-vided by Quark, and learned what the arctic is and isn't. Geographers define it as the region of the globe north of the Arctic Circle, located at 66 degrees, 33 minutes north. That, however, is merely a novelty line, marking the point where 24- hour days and nights begin. Folks living on the Arctic Circle get one of each during the year—on June 21 and December 21. As one continues north, the number of 24-hour days and nights increase until you hit the North Pole, which has—as any school kid knows—six months of daylight followed by six months of darkness. Our cruise, about midway between the Arctic Circle and the pole, was in August so we enjoyed long days. The sun, never far above the horizon, would set reluctantly about 2 a.m. then reappear an hour or so later.

Another definition of "arctic" is the region where the median high temperature is 50 Fahrenheit or less, and that certainly was the case during our chilly August visit. The high arctic isn't necessarily the coldest spot in the Northern Hemisphere, since the Arctic Ocean—larger than two Mediterranean seas—tempers the air. Inland Alaska's Fairbanks is often much colder than the Canadian Arctic and it's *below* the Arctic Circle. However, the high arctic is colder in summer. August temperatures can hit 80 degrees in Fairbanks.

Certainly the arctic is not a vast desert wasteland of windswept ice. It *is* technically a desert, receiving less than ten inches of precipitation in most regions. However, it teems with wildlife, including some of the world's greatest concentrations of birds. Walruses and seals hang out along the coast and on ice floes, and musk ox mill about in herds farther inland. Although there are no trees, plants are abundant—grasses, sedges, mosses, lichens and shrubs that manage to eke out an existence in the thin soil layer above the permafrost. Whales are common in these waters, and with luck, visitors may spot narwhals, those strange cetaceans with the single twisted horn that gave rise to unicorn fables.

The arctic is not a vast wasteland of windswept ice. It teems with wildlife, including some of the world's greatest concentrations of birds.

Most of Canada's arctic is within the Northwest Territories, which contains the world's largest archipelago. Islands that we knew only from fifth grade geography—Baffin and Ellesmere—became familiar places during our cruise, as did mysterious Greenland. (No Eskimos in igloos, however. They now go by their ancestral name of *Inuit* and they've surrendered their nomadic ways to live in prefab homes in coastal villages.)

The Northwest Territories cover 1.3 million square miles; that's larger than most countries of the world. Put another way, Canada is the second largest country on the globe after Russia, and the Northwest Territories takes up more than half of its land and water mass.

But enough geography and superlatives. Let's go find a polar bear.

ᐅᐅᐅ

DAY ONE

Our expedition began as we boarded ship in scruffy Resolute, a village on Cornwallis Island, far above the Arctic Circle. Most of our travels would take us still farther north, into the Kennedy Channel between Ellesmere Island and Greenland. Our flight from Toronto landed in near zero visibility, then a bus took us to a gravelly shoreline. There we were met by crewmen in Zodiac—inflatable rafts powered by outboard motors.

"Hi! My name is Grigorey and out there is your big yellow icebreaker!" Our new host poked a finger into an empty fog bank.

The boxy and bold Kapitan Khlebnikov *poses among icebergs in Lancaster Sound off Devon Island.*

The Zodiac zoomed into that blur and shortly, the profile of the *Kapitan Khlebnikov* emerged from the mist. As it came into focus, we decided that our vessel was so homely, it was cute. It resembled a cargo ship onto which, in afterthought, a small six-story apartment building had been plopped. Although it appeared top-heavy, it later proved to be remarkably stable. The nearly landlocked seas in the island-crowded Canadian archipelago are quite calm except during storms. We suffered none of these on our cruise.

On board, we found simple, spacious cabins with old-fashioned portholes that opened to the breezes. A dresser, writing desk, small closet and stall shower would meet all of our terrestrial needs for the next nine days. After unpacking and exploring the ship, dinner was announced. Meal service is casual, with open seating. As on most cruise ships these days, all dining areas are smoke free.

As we began eating, we heard a sonorous crunching sound, like soft thunder, followed by a gentle shudder of the ship.

"That's a sound you'll hear quite often for the next nine days," said a plump lady two seats over. "We're breaking through an ice floe." She grinned and leaned toward us as if sharing a special secret. "This is my fourth icebreaker cruise."

We decided to avoid this woman during the rest of the voyage. She'd give away all the surprises.

Ꮓ Ꮓ Ꮓ
DAY TWO

Human habitation was late in coming to this area," said archeologist Peter Schledermann. We had begun our first full day in the arctic with a morning lecture about those who had come before us. That evening, we would visit Nungavik, a prehistoric site on Baffin Island. "When the Bering land bridge was exposed and the migration to the Americas started, the area here was under a mile-thick sheet of ice, so it couldn't be settled."

The region wasn't occupied until the time of Christ, by a group called the Thule people. Archeological digs revealed that they were hunters who used unusually small projectile points on their spear shafts.

"They were known as the Arctic Small Tool Group." said Schledermann, then he added, without breaking his lecturer's composure: "This was not an indication of a male genetic deformity."

The Baffin Island visit would come after dinner; evening field trips were common on this cruise, taking advantage of the long arctic days. First, we had a date with a few thousand birds. Preparing for an arctic excursion is as complicated as dressing up to be a department store Santa Claus—long-johns, outer wear, parka, life vest and day pack. Finally, we were ready to waddle across the deck, down the ladder and into the Zodiacs.

The nimble craft skimmed easily across the slick surface of Lancaster Sound to an imposing sheer wall, where the edge of Bylot Island dropped abruptly into the sea. Backlighted against the clouds, great swarms of sea birds swirled around the 200-foot cliffs. All the birds here weren't weren't airborne, however. As we drew near, we saw that every niche and cranny of the rough cliff face was occupied by nesting sea birds—mostly kittiwakes, resembling small seagulls, and thick-billed murres, chubby little guys that looked like black-winged footballs. There was no place to land so we putted just beyond the reach of the breakers, watching this wild flying circus. Pirouetting through the sky, clinging to the cliffs or fussing with their pebbled nests, the birds—perhaps 150,000—set up an outerworldly cacophony. Alfred Hitchcock would have loved this place.

After dinner that night, the *Kapitan* dropped anchor in Navy Board Inlet off Baffin Island's Borden Peninsula. The Zodiacs took us ashore for an inspection of rocky rings and chunks of sod that been Thule pithouses five centuries ago. The area was now unoccupied, so we were surprised to see a small group of Thule descendants walking toward us, smiling and waving. Several youngsters gathered

Several children gathered around us, offering that universal child's greeting—bashful grins.

around, studying us with their dark elliptical eyes, offering that universal child's greeting—bashful grins. The Inuit, more recent arrivals to the new world than their Indian cousins to the south, still retain a strong racial resemblance to their Asian ancestors. The kids were fascinated by Betty's Oriental features, perhaps intrigued at seeing an outsider with eyes like their own.

One of the adults, wearing a Toronto Bluejay's baseball cap beneath his parka hood, said they'd come here a week ago to hunt narwhal. They hadn't seen any yet, he said, but they would come.

"Sometimes we can see maybe fifty of them, all swimming in a row," he said, sweeping an index finger toward the inlet.

Several of the children began picking pods of tiny purple plants and eating them. A shy, moon-faced girl offered us a sample. The taste was sort of blandly spicy, or possibly spicily bland.

"Scurvy grass," said our biologist Stephen Johnson. "Early explorers chewed it to prevent scurvy, something they probably learned from the Inuits. It's similar to our mountain sorrel or sour grass."

A female polar bear paces about on an ice floe within two hundred feet of the bow of the expedition ship.

We hiked across the spongy tundra—like walking on a cheap mattress—to one of several Thule sites, a collapsed pithouse filled with scattered bones. Originally, it had a roof of whalebone and sod, and an entrance tunnel that faced the water. The occupants' view, unchanged today except for our ship parked offshore, was quite imposing—low hills across the inlet with glaciers sweeping down to the shore, and a floating sculpture garden of ice shapes in the bay.

ᚦᚦᚦ

DAY THREE

It is difficult to finish a lecture aboard this ship. We were learning that this region was composed of stable, earthquake-free 1.8 billion-year-old metamorphic rock when someone poked his head into the lecture hall.

"Two polar bears have been sighted on an ice floe off the starboard side—a mother and her cub."

Everyone scampered to starboard with such a surge that we were surprised it didn't tilt the ship. By the time we reached the railing the two bears had entered the water and were trying to out-swim the pursuing iron monster. The captain cut back on the engines to ease their panic and we watched them disappear in the ice-filled sea.

That afternoon, we witnessed the gruesome consequence of being too low in the arctic food chain. As we visited another bird-busy seacliff on Coburg Island, we noticed two arctic fox cubs playing on the shoreline. They looked so endearing that Betty wanted to take them home. Then a fledgling murre toppled from its nest above and flopped to the ground; the cubs quickly pounced on the hapless thing. They began a grotesque tug-of-war with the still-screaming creature until each cub wound up with part of the prize.

Back aboard, as we settled in the lecture room for a review of today's events, yet another head thrust through the door. Its voice said, almost apologetically: "Excuse me, but there are several hundred harp seals on ice floes, coming up on the port side."

In less than a minute, lecturer Schledermann stood in an empty hall, a blackboard pointer in his hand, and an understanding grin on his face. The harp seals, still a couple of hundred yards off, looked like dark garden slugs on the frosty ice. As our ship drew near, they began slipping into the water, singly at first, then in pairs, and then *en masse.*

ᐸ ᐸ ᐸ

DAY FOUR

Greenland. The idea of the place had fascinated me since I was a school kid. I would stare at its shape on maps—a bit like a tilted, upside-down Australia—and wonder what was there. I knew that it was first explored in 982 by Norseman Eric the Red, who gave this frozen island a misleading name to encourage settlement. I knew that it now belonged to tiny Denmark and was many times larger than its mother country. But what was *there?*

We learned that it is a bulky extension of this arctic archipelago. It's separated from Canada's Ellesmere Island only by narrow Kennedy Channel, in some places just a mile or so wide. Greenland resembles the rest of these islands, with rocky beaches marked in areas by seacliffs, and spongy tundra lowlands that thaw briefly to bloom in the short summer and then freeze again. Its coastal valleys often are filled with glaciers; the interior hills and mountains are covered by ice. Greenland is wildly beautiful in its own ruggedly icy way, but no different, no more intriguing than the other islands. Up here, of course, *everything* is intriguing to the visitor.

The native people of Greenland, like those of Baffin and Ellesmere, are Inuit. They prefer *not* to be called Eskimo for that was a name imposed upon them by outsiders. Inuit means just what it's supposed to mean: "the people."

We awoke this day in Murchison Sound, offshore of the Greenland Inuit village of Qaanaaq (*ka-NACK*). From the *Kapitan Khlebnikov*, it looked like a mobile home park terraced into a steep slope, since most of the houses were prefabricated. Typical of towns in these reaches, it had no landscaping, no pavement, but friendly and engaging people.

Along the village streets, sled dogs tugged at their tethers, whining and fussing, perhaps wishing that winter would come.

Above town, streaks of snow reached up through shallow ravines toward the Greenland Icecap. Off to the left, a glacier moved in sluggish slow motion toward Kennedy Channel. The people of Qaanaag had a splendid view: the channel decorated with floes and sculptured icebergs from the glacier, and the naked mountains of Ellesmere across the way, streaked with snow and capped with ice.

Along the village streets, sled dogs tugged at their tethers, whining and fussing, perhaps wishing that winter would come. The sleds were still of the traditional wooden variety, although they had Teflon runners. Meat, blackened with dried blood, hung from drying racks near the shoreline. As we walked through the village, a man emerged from one of the houses with a polar bear skull in his hand, snapping the jaw open and shut and grinning at us. When we moved in for photos, he shyly retreated inside.

We hiked uphill to an ivory shop that displayed nicely carved amulets, rings, brooches, earrings and pendants. Made mostly of walrus and narwhal tusks, these were carved by locals to help pass the long winters. Although

A friendly Inuit in the Greenland village of Qamaaq shows visitors a polar bear skull.

walruses aren't considered endangered up here, the United States has imposed a ban on the importation of all ivory, no matter what its source, so none of these could be taken home legally. The shop did a very brisk business that morning.

Our ship pressed northward in the afternoon through Kennedy Channel, allowing us occasional glimpses through a thick overcast of the glistening edge of the Greenland Icecap. We were headed for Siorapaluk (*si-ora-pa-LUK*), which claims to be the world's northernmost town. (A few Russia Siberian settlements might challenge this boast.) As we cruised, an Inuit drum dancer, flown aboard by our resident helicopter pilot, performed ancient and contemporary dances and chants, wearing a polar skin hunting costume. After his show, as we gathered around to admire his attire, he tried to engage

Betty in Inuit conversation. What, he must have wondered, was a good-looking Inuit woman doing, traveling with these Yankees? He handed her his drum and invited her to play. She quickly demonstrated her total lack of musical talent.

Siorapaluk, rather cute from a distance with its red and yellow prefab homes on a steep slope, suffers upon close scrutiny. It's a smaller version of Qaanaaq, although considerably more primitive. It had no streets; only paths connecting a scatter of shabby homes. The per capita sled dog population seemed to be much higher here than in Qaanaaq; we were advised to watch where we stepped.

We chatted with the friendly locals and then some of us—puffing in our heavy parkas—hiked to a ridge far above the village. Our reward was a fine view of the narrow channel and the frozen world that surrounded it.

ᑭ ᑭ ᑭ

DAY FIVE

On this day, we went looking for ice. There was no shortage of this commodity in the high arctic, even in August. We had pushed north beyond where no man lives, into a misty gray cloud-shrouded land of icy waters and naked hills where each shallow valley had its own personal glacier.

The ice thickened as we pressed northward. It was time for the *Kapitan Khlebnikov* to show its stuff. The onboard helicopter was fired up so some passengers could watch the show from the air while others gathered at the bow or on the bridge above. Confronted by a stubborn looking mass of pack ice, the ship made a headlong charge as if deliberately running aground. The knife-edged prow rode up and over the ice and then settled down with a great groaning crunch and backed away. The floe had been dented but not broken; a vee in the ice and a patch

The six-foot-thick floe shattered and parted; chunks of blue ice the size of minivans flipped over slowly, and then danced and spun along the hull.

of red paint marked the point of impact. The ship struck again and a great zig-zagging fracture danced forward through the ice, like slow-motion lightning. The six-foot-thick floe shattered and parted; chunks of blue ice the size of minivans flipped over slowly in a roil of ice water, and then danced and spun along the hull as the ship surged forward through the splintered pack.

Icebreaking involves no sophisticated mechanical devices. Primary weapons are an ice-hardened prow and big engines to drive the ship forward. The bow is covered with a special slippery red Teflon paint so it will ride over the ice and come crunching back down to break it. The paint also keeps the ice from sticking to the prow, making it easier for the ship to work itself free if it becomes wedged.

After cracking an ice floe, the ship follows the fracture's erratic course, easily pushing aside the shattered sides of the pack. In commercial applications, the icebreaker then leads a convoy of other ships to their far north destination.

Our destination, after the *Khlebnikov* proved its mettle, was Pim Island in Lady Franklin Bay, the northernmost thrust in our trek. It was named for the wife of noted arctic explorer Sir John Franklin, although neither had visited this particular site. After her husband had disappeared in 1846 trying to find the Northwest Passage, Lady Franklin in turn spent years and most of her fortune trying to find *him*.

This place also is known as Starvation Bay, for a rather grim reason. The world's first international polar study was conducted in the Canadian arctic from 1881 until 1883, with teams working different areas. Only one group met with disaster, an American team led by Adolphus Greely. After a field trip, they had started back to their base camp by dog sled but were hit by a blizzard and had to hole up on Pim Island. They built hasty rock shelters with canvas roofs, not too different from those used by the early Thule people, and awaited the arrival of a rescue ship. Two vessels attempted to reach them but accidents and bad weather stopped both. During a horrible winter, 20 of the 27 men perished and another died shortly after they were finally rescued the following spring. Those who survived did so by resorting to cannibalism.

Our Zodiac driver followed a slalom course between free-form sculptures of small icebergs to Pim Island's rocky shoreline. We hiked up to Greely's final camp in a shallow ravine littered with broken metamorphic rock. Archeologists who have examined the site, including our Peter Schledermann, a fellow of the Arctic Institute of Calgary, have agreed to leave the area just as it was after the survivors were rescued. We may have been the first cruise ship passengers to visit the site and we saw what those rescuers saw more than a century earlier.

We may have been the first cruise ship passengers to visit the site and we saw what the rescuers saw more than a century earlier.

The low rock structure, originally covered with oars, a longboat and canvas, was still intact, as were ashes from their fires. A few tin cans and bits of rags were scattered about.

"It's ironic," said Peter as we stared solemnly at the littered death camp, "that a primitive people could survive here quite well, without modern weapons or canned food." Stone rings from 3,000-year-old dwellings, still not excavated, were on a nearby rise.

A plaque erected by the National Geographic Society in 1923 marks the site of this tragedy:

To the memory of the dead, who, under Lieutenant A.W. Greely here gave their lives to ensure the final and complete success of the first scientific cooperation of the United States with other nations, 1881-1884.

Twenty-one dead? A complete success?

ᑉ ᑉ ᑉ

DAY SIX

There are no alpine lakes or thick forests in the high arctic; in fact, no trees. You'll see no crystalline creeks lined with willows, or deep red-walled canyons. Yet the scenery can be splendid. Much of it is created by the commodity most plentiful up here—ice.

Particularly spectacular are meltwater floes. These floating ice fields, which have partially melted to form hundreds of thousands of pools, create fantastic mosaics. Meanwhile, on land, glaciers are the arctic's rivers, frozen and wrinkled with deep chasms and cold blue faces that yield merry little creeks and giant icebergs. The bergs are the free-form sculptures of the far

The Quark Expedition onboard helicopter provides passengers with an aerial view of the Kapitan Khlebnikov's ice-breaking techniques.

north: Alice in Wonderland toadstools, translucent fins, icy tapestries and frozen clouds.

Today, we trammeled some of this arctic scenery. During the previous evening and night, we had retreated south through Kennedy Channel and then swung west into Jones Sound between Ellesmere and Devon islands. We put ashore at Craig Harbor, an abandoned Royal Canadian Mountain Police post, from where our 'chopper lifted us high atop Manson Icefield. From this sparkling white ice pasture, the view of the iceberg-littered bay below and its enclosing glacier-clad peaks was rather awesome.

Up here on the glacier, far from anything made of iron, I took my hiking compass from my fanny pack. The needle, confused at first, swung erratically and then pointed south. This was the proper thing to do, since we were between the North Pole and Magnetic North. It's no wonder that explorers got lost in these latitudes!

We did more cruising with crunch that afternoon and evening, cleaving through the beautiful mosaic of a meltwater ice floe. It seemed almost a shame to shatter these striking natural patterns, which stretched ahead to the far horizon.

Evening brings no reason to stop admiring the detail of the summertime arctic. The sun hangs around the horizon until well after midnight. We spent hours on the bow, staring fascinated at the endless shapes and convolutions in the shattering jigsaw puzzle of ice as it parted before us. We were in a blue-on-blue world, from the pale aqua of the arctic sky and the thin blue of the pack ice to deep indigo in some of the icebergs.

🏴 🏴 🏴
DAY SEVEN

On a misty and chilly day, in dark contrast to yesterday's bright sunshine, we crunched more ice and then paused at Grise Fjord on Ellesmere Island to visit with the native folks. Later, we were helicoptered ashore at Truelove Lowlands, a tundra rich in wildlife and little saucer lakes. Our target for the day was a herd of musk ox, known to frequent this rolling expanse of low-lying arctic vegetation. We paused frequently on our hike to get on kneeling terms with multi-colored lichens, arctic poppies and tiny blooms an eighth of an inch across. Our only wildlife sightings were a few tired loons and three distant blurry dots that our leader insisted were musk ox.

After a long hike, we returned to the helicopter landing site, an abandoned science observation station. Several fellow passengers, who'd arrived on a later flight, were talking excitedly about things they'd seen. A bird-watching lady in jodhpurs who seemed always to have a pair of heavy binoculars around her neck, gushed that she had spotted about 500 buntings and dozens of arctic loons.

"Did you see any musk oxen?" Betty asked.

"Those pesky things? They were all over the science station when we got here. We were afraid they'd get too close!"

🏴 🏴 🏴
DAY EIGHT

From an ordinary day to a memorable one. Such is the luck of the weather and animal encounters. We'd sailed north and west around Devon Island during the night and we awoke at anchor, offshore of West Cunningham Glacier. We boarded the Zodiacs, cruised among several small offshore icebergs and then motored slowly along the glacier's fifty-foot face of cracked and marbled blue ice, sparkling in the bright arctic sun. We were then put ashore to tramp along its gravelly moraine and inspect the dozens of tiny meltwater creeks coursing from it.

"Polar bear!"

It was an alert, not an announcement. One of our leaders had spotted a furry white dot, ambling across a far ridge. Although there had never been an incident, our lecturers carried wicked- looking pistol grip shotguns on shore excursions. If this individual came too close, we would return to the Zodiacs. However, it moved away so we continued exploring the glacier while the shore leader kept his binoculars on the departing bear.

Back aboard ship, we came upon the female bear on the small ice patch—the great white lady who opened this chapter. Even though the captain nudged the ship right up to the floe, the bear stayed with us for nearly half an hour. Finally, as camera clutchers were running out of film and polar bear angles, she slipped into the water and idly paddled away.

We put ashore after dinner to explore a narrow peninsula of Devon Island. While others went in search of musk ox, I climbed a high, rocky promontory. My reward was a splendid panorama—dark brown hills brightened by patches of ice, scattered floes in the surrounding seas, distant peaks wearing their blankets of snow, and curving white highways of glaciers. My shipmates were ants far below, prowling around a kettle lake in the tundra—a small scattering of red and navy blue parkas. The Zodiacs, busy during this commute hour, skittered across the calm surface between ship and beach like little black dragonflies.

꽃꽃꽃

DAY NINE

Tomorrow, we would awaken offshore of Repulse, reluctantly abandon our ship and fly south to greener but less intriguing pastures. Before leaving the arctic, we would visit two more places of interest—one geologically fascinating, the other a grim historic site.

Although most of the arctic's cliffs and chasms are of snow and ice, we landed this morning below an imposing 500-foot limestone bluff with eroded fractures similar to those in the American Southwest. Broad alluvial fans at its base spilled into a gravelly beach, invaded here and there by lush green growth. Today's outing, an essential workout after eight days of heavy grazing in the dining room, took us along the beach and through strips of spongy tundra. Tracks and spoor told us this was musk ox country, although they apparently were convening elsewhere. Even in the strongest of our lenses, no black dots appeared.

Our final excursion was to Beechey Island off the southern shore of Devon Island in Lancaster Sound. Here, at the eastern gateway to the Northwest Passage, another tragic chapter was written in the history of arctic exploration. Sir John Franklin, the wealthy, idealistic and stubborn English explorer who discovered the passage, set up camp here in 1846. Although he had found the entrance to the passage, he died before he could attempt a journey through it. Journals found later reported that his behavior had become

At the eastern gateway to the Northwest Passage, another tragic chapter was written in the history of Arctic exploration.

quite erratic and he had headed north by dogsled, ill prepared and poorly equipped, never to be seen again. Everyone in Franklin's party eventually perished. Three of them died here and were buried by surviving companions. Exhumed about a decade ago, they were remarkably intact after a century and a half in permafrost. Their deaths and Franklin's erratic behavior were blamed on lead poisoning from their canned food containers, although some scientists question this.

The party had picked a bleak place for their encampment—a barren gravel beach at the base of equally dismal gray cliffs. We put ashore near the remnants of the Northumberland House, built in the 1850s by a British commander who had come in search of the missing Franklin party. It had been constructed from local stone, plus masts, spars and other pieces of a wrecked whaling vessel that had washed ashore. A few stone walls and scattered wooden fragments remain today.

A one-mile hike along the beach took us to Franklin's last known camp. It is marked now only by graves of the seamen who had died here, and other arctic explorers who had been brought here for burial. In volunteering for arctic exploration, these men had chosen a challenging way to live. Fate had given some of them a grim place to die. One of the grave markers read:

Sacred to the memory of William Brain, died April 30, 1846, age 32 years. Choose ye this day whom ye shall serve. — Joshua 24:15.

..And we entered Prince William Sound... The sky cleared, disclosing to the westward one of the richest, most glorious mountain landscapes I ever beheld—peak over peak dipping deep in the sky, a thousand of them, icy and shining, rising higher...burning bright in the afternoon light...

— John Muir, *Travels in Alaska*

Chapter four

ALASKA BY SEA & LAND
Day-tripping through the North Star State

A laska is too large to be seen just by sea. The forty-ninth state covers 586,412 square miles or 360 million acres, spread over four time zones; it's more than twice as large as Texas. Its coastline is as long as that of the rest of the U.S.

There is of course much more to Alaska than size. It's a state of rich diversity and, perhaps surprisingly, great climatic variety. The far north is predictably cold and chilly, yet summers can be hot in the interior. (When we stepped off a plane in Fairbanks, clutching our down jackets, it was 87 degrees.) Southeast Alaska, warmed by the Japanese Current, is surprisingly temperate the year around, and like much of the rest of the state, it's a grand repository of wildlife. Commented John Haines in his foreword to the Sierra Club edition of *Travels in Alaska* by John Muir:

CRUISE PLANNER

The cruise ● This is one of several combination land and sea expeditions offered by Alaska Sightseeing/Cruise West. Our 13-day itinerary included a four-day Inside Passage voyage with hotel lodging ashore, plus a flight to Fairbanks, a scenic train trip to Denali National Park, a stay at Denali Wilderness Lodge, a motorcoach trip to Anchorage and a one-day cruise through Prince William Sound. For details, contact Alaska Sightseeing/Cruise West, Fourth & Battery Building, Suite 700, Seattle, WA 98121; (800) 426-7702 or (206) 441-8687; FAX (206) 441-4757. In addition to these Alaska excursions, the firm offers Columbia-Snake River cruises out of Portland and voyages from San Francisco Bay to the California wine country and up the Sacramento River.

Getting there ● Passengers for the above itinerary gather in Seattle and are flown to Ketchikan for the first phase—the four-day Inside Passage cruise. At the completion of their sea-and-land outing, they're flown back to Seattle from Anchorage. Most major airlines serve Seattle- Tacoma International Airport, and special air packages can be arranged.

The ships ● The 90-foot *MV Sheltered Seas* and 65-foot *MV Glacier Seas* are "daylight yachts" with ice-hardened hulls designed for nudging through ice floes. Both have dining rooms with single or double seatings (depending on passenger loads), cocktail bars, viewing lounges and ample deck viewing areas. Crewmen with special expertise on Alaska and some guest lecturers provide running commentaries during the cruises. Officers and crew are American.

When to go ● Alaska cruises and air-coach-train sightseeing excursions run from early May through mid-September. Weather is balmy and sometimes chilly from late spring into summer; warmest and sunniest period is late August through September.

What to bring ● This is Alaska, so pack for varied temperatures and bring rain gear. Dress warmly, with good gloves and muffs for the ice floe and glacier cruises. It can be chilly even in mid-summer although many days are quite balmy. Temperatures can reach the 80s and even low 90s in mainland Alaska. Leave suits, ties and cocktail dresses at home; this is a casual outing.

What's included ● The package includes airport transfers, some flights, overnight lodging during land and sea portions, meals aboard the two ships and all transfers between various segments of the trip. Cocktails and wine, and most meals ashore are extra. Some land excursions are included, such as a cruise aboard the riverboat *Discovery* in Fairbanks, the train trip from Fairbanks to Denali National Park, scenic coach trips and a visit to Mendenhall Glacier near Anchorage. Others are extra, ranging from guided walks to trawler fishing to flightseeing. Stays at wilderness lodges can be arranged at additional cost. Available for loan aboard the ships are binoculars and a good selection of books on the area.

What to buy ● Some excellent Native Alaskan ivory and bone carvings, paintings and fur wear are available at shops in various towns. Ample time is provided for shopping.

In these drenched forests and cold, rich waters, we encounter for a last time the original abundance of life, a plenty of bird and fish, of tree life and animal variety.

Southeast Alaska is the state's most visited area, particularly by major cruise lines. More than thirty ships ply these waters, bringing 400,000 visitors a year. This imposing matrix of land and sea is spread over a narrow coastline and a scatter of islands cloaked in spruce and hemlock forests, marked by glacial fjords and slender channels. Here, steep mountains and occasional glaciers plunge into the sea; dolphins and killer whales play in the calm waters; ravens and bald eagles spiral overhead.

However, the Southeast represents only a fraction of the North Star State. We decided to cover more of Alaska by booking a combined sea and land tour with Alaska Sightseeing/Cruise West. This wasn't an unusual approach. Many cruise companies operating in Alaskan waters offer land options as logical extensions of their trips.

> *This imposing matrix of land and sea is spread over a narrow coastline and a scatter of islands cloaked with spruce and hemlock.*

For further variety, we chose a sea-land package with daylight yachting tours, sleeping in hotels ashore at night. This works well for the southeast since all of its communities are relatively small and walkable, and they're isolated from one another by islands and channels. We could explore the area's grand waterways by day and poke about its towns during the long evenings of summer. (The company also offers stay-aboard cruises on its other ships.)

Three small ships, planes, a train and several buses were involved in our complex itinerary. We cruised the Southeast Alaska on the 90-passenger *Sheltered Seas,* explored Fairbanks' Chena and Tanana Rivers during an afternoon outing on the tourist sternwheeler *Discovery III* and sailed across Prince William Sound on the 65-foot motor launch *Glacier Seas.* The first ship is aptly named, for the sheltered waters of the southeast are as calm as a gently flowing river except during occasional wind-blown storms.

Our sea-land voyage began in the Alexander Archipelago, which locals call Southeast Alaska and the cruise industry refers to as the Inside Passage. Other than its coastal towns and occasional mangy patches of clear-cut timber, this area has changed little since John Muir observed it in 1879:

The islands of the Alexander Archipelago, with the straits, channels, canals, sounds, passages and fjords, form an intricate web of land and water embroidery sixty or seventy miles wide, fringing the lofty icy chain of the coast mountains from Puget Sound to Cook Inlet; and, with infinite variety, the general pattern is harmonious throughout its whole extent of nearly a thousand miles.

ps ps ps

DAY ONE

The beauty of Alaska begins from the air—if you are fortunate enough to fly on a clear day. Our outing began with a flight from Seattle to Ketchikan. As we winged over British Columbia and up the Alaskan panhandle, the clouds parted to reveal a glorious landscape of blue-green forested mountains dusted with powdered sugar and interspersed with cobalt blue lakes.

We touched down on Gravena Island, one of the few flat places near Ketchikan. The town itself, across a narrow channel, is a pleasantly rustic

*Like most
Southeast Alaska
towns, Ketchikan
is tiered steeply
against wooded
mountains. This
view is from
Ketchikan
Marina.*

mix of wood frame houses and false front stores, terraced
into steep mountains. The coastal shelf is so narrow that sections of Ketchikan's main street are built on pilings, and many of the homes above town are
served only by stairways.

"We had a little flat land in town," our Alaska Sightseeing/Cruise West
bus driver said as we waited for a ferry to Ketchikan. "But we used it for
baseball diamonds."

The bus, a prim and elderly Ford named Ethel, groaned painfully as it
inched up a steep hill to the Westmark Cape Fox hotel, where we would
spend our first night. Our room offered a fine view of Ketchikan harbor, busy
with float planes that picked landing paths between fishing boats, pleasure
craft and cruise ships.

Ketchikan's business is geared heavily to cruise traffic, since more than
300,000 ship passengers pause in the city each year. Gift salons, souvenir
shops and galleries line the main street, and small squadrons of tour buses
stand ready to take visitors to Totem Bight State Park, the only out-of-town
attraction reachable by road. Misty Fjords National Monument rises in the
cloud-capped hills just above town, and float planes take visitors on flightseeing tours of this huge wilderness area.

A funicular links the hilltop Westmark with downtown, running between the hotel and Creek Street. The "street" is an elevated boardwalk lined with stilt houses that sheltered a flourishing red light district during Ketchikan's early days as a major fishing port. Built over a rushing stream, the houses are now occupied by gift and curio shops. It's not unusual—as you browse from shop to shop—to see salmon migrating upstream, just beneath your feet.

"Creek Street, where fish and fishermen go up the creek to spawn," reads a sign.

You may want to arrive in Ketchikan a day early, since the city has quite a few worthy sights. Your ship schedule may not allow time to explore the Creek Street shops, the excellent new Southeast Alaska Visitor Center, Tongass Historical Museum and the Totem Heritage Center. One also can pick up a walking tour map from the Ketchikan Visitor Information Center at the downtown dock.

ฅ ฅ ฅ

DAY TWO

Tides fluctuate as much as twenty feet in Southeast Alaska, and we couldn't see the top of the *M/V Sheltered Seas* as we approached the dock. It was further dwarfed by the *Regal Princess* parked nearby, a cruise ship so tall that it towered over the highest building in Ketchikan, an eleven-story apartment.

We walked down a steep ramp and stepped aboard our craft, a sleek 90-foot motor launch. The ship offers abundant seating indoors and out for catching the passing scenery and wildlife. With a draft just over six feet, it's capable of cruising into shallow inlets and nudging against icebergs with its specially hardened hull. Our voyage would be accompanied by a running narrative as Captain Jim Cushman or other crew members pointed out landforms and wildlife over the intercom. Most of our time would be spent in narrow channels rimmed by Tongass National Forest, the largest in America with 16.9 million acres.

"If you see anything that looks like wildlife, shout it out," said cruise director Kathleen Pelkan during a morning orientation talk. "Don't be embarrassed if you guess wrong. We've spotted lots of driftwood whales and tree stump bears."

We left Ketchikan under a thick overcast and headed south. Our destination was Misty Fjords National Monument, a 2.2 million acre wilderness of glacial-carved mountains, thick forests and narrow inlets. One of these fjords, Behm Canal, would take us deep into the park's interior. Misty Fjords has no facilities and few trails; it is best seen from the water or air.

We paused frequently to observe bald eagles, or we'd swerve off course to carefully approach a humpback whale...

This would not be a direct commute, of course. This was, after all, an exploration cruise. We paused frequently to observe bald eagles or we'd swerve off course to carefully approach a humpback whale or small pod of killer whales. Bundled against the chill, we lined the boat's rails, watching through binoculars for wildlife. These lenses became almost permanent appendages during the cruise, shed only when we went ashore to our hotel at night. Our first discovery of the morning was a dalls porpoise that sent passengers scur-

A SEASTACK AND A HOT PINK HAT

"That seastack you see off to port is called the New Eddystone Light," said cruise director Kathleen Pelkan as we sailed up Behm Canal. She indicated a slender promontory sitting in mid channel. "It's shaped like the Eddystone lighthouse off Plymouth, England."

She continued over the ship's intercom: "*Eddystone Light* is also the name of an old seafaring song. If anyone knows the words to it, and is willing to sing it into the mike, they'll win a prize."

I grinned and continued staring at the seastack. Betty eyed me curiously.

"What are you smiling about? Do you know the words to that song?"

I nodded. "Burl Ives used to sing it. When I was younger, I collected folk songs—in my head."

"Well, go down there and sing it. You'll win a prize!"

"Not me. I don't perform in public."

Her eyes widened at the prospect of getting something free. "I'll sing it! Write down the words."

"You can't sing."

"Just write down the words. Hurry up!"

I jotted down the first verse; she snatched up the scrap of paper and hurried down to the dining room. Moments later, I heard her halting, flat voice over the intercom:

My father was the keeper of the Eddystone light,
And he slept with a mermaid one fine night.
From this union there came three—
A porpoise and a porgy and the other was me.

She came back shortly, wearing a wide grin and a hot pink *Sheltered Seas* cap. "Look what I won!" Then she flashed a mock frown. "I sounded pretty awful, didn't I?"

I nodded. "You'd best stay with your present line of work."

rying to starboard. Shortly after, we nudged near the shoreline to observe a pair of bald eagles atop a Sitka spruce.

"The way to spot eagles is to look in the trees for a black shape with a white golf ball head," said Kathleen.

Later, a considerable stir swept through the boat when a killer whale was spotted off the port side, easily identified by its tall, erect dorsal fin and white saddle patch. Another appeared to starboard and stayed with us for several minutes, disappearing and then reappearing for quick breaths, cruising a few dozen yards from the ship. Well, of course, we'd seen Shamu at San Diego's Sea World, cavorting about, earning a steady salary of fish. That experience paled at the sight of this free Willy, slicing cleanly through the water, surrounded by his own wilderness world.

We turned into Punchbowl Cove, a glacial-carved granite batholith rimmed by sheer 3,000-foot walls. It was an extraordinary moment, akin to cruising into Yosemite Valley. An Alaskan El Capitan stood before us—a vertical face seamed with ice fractures. Just beyond loomed a thickly forested Half Dome, its face sheared away by a prehistoric glacier. Like glistening strands of hair, half a dozen waterfalls spilled hundreds of feet from tree-cloaked ramparts. In this cove, the monument matches its name. Misty clouds crowned the high peaks, formed by a silent collision of warm waters with icy air sliding down from the heights.

Two Forest Service rangers, camping in Misty Fjords for most of the summer, paddled out in their kayaks and came aboard. They spent the next two hours on the ship's bow—in *shirtsleeves*, yet!—pointing out the wonders of the national monument. This area once was covered by mile-thick ice, which retreated to leave the cliffs, cirques and bowl-shaped valleys. Keeping an eye out for wildlife as they talked, the rangers spotted a female grizzly and three cubs ambling among large boulders on a narrow coastal shelf. Captain Cushman swung the boat to port and eased slowly toward the shoreline. Some of the passengers had trouble spotting the quarry.

> **She grabbed her camera and excitedly took several photographs of rocks—one large and three small.**

"Where are they? I don't see anything that looks like a bear."

"Right there, among the rocks, ma'am. Look carefully." One of the rangers gently swiveled her shoulders in the appropriate direction.

"I don't see them yet. Everything looks like rocks."

As she squinted shoreward through binoculars, the bears—still unseen by her—ambled off to the right and disappeared.

"Oh! I think I see them! Oh, yes!"

She lowered her binoculars, grabbed up her camera and excitedly took several photographs of rocks—one large and three small.

When we returned to Ketchikan, we had time for more sightseeing. I took a tour of Totem Bight State Park and Betty hurried to the new Southeast Alaska Visitor Information Center. More than a visitor center, it's a fine museum that provides a comprehensive introduction to the state. It features a three-dimensional rainforest, native peoples' displays such as a fish camp diorama, and exhibits on the ecosystems and lifestyles of Southeast Alaska.

Totem Bight, with its collection of fourteen poles, was started as a Civilian Conservation Corps project in 1938. Native people were leaving their villages to work in towns and officials were concerned that the art of totem carving would be lost. Carvers were paid to duplicate several decaying poles, which they erected here, along with a "clan house." This is an elaborate board structure that is traditionally occupied by extended families of up to fifty people.

> **You can have your own personal totem carved by a native craftsman for a mere $1,000 per lineal foot.**

As I toured the park, our guide discussed the significance of totems. They have several uses—to symbolically tell tribal legends, to illustrate natural occurrences such as thunder and rain or to display a village's tribal symbol—generally the raven, eagle, beaver, bear, wolf and killer whale. Traditional colors are black, red, orange and turquoise.

The totem carving art is undergoing a renaissance. In fact, you can have your own personal totem carved by a native craftsperson for a mere $1,000 to $1,500 per lineal foot, plus shipping. Fortunately, modern carvers don't have to resort to traditional methods to achieve their colors. For instance, red was produced by chewing dried salmon eggs wrapped in cedar bark.

This pretty Tlingit girl, a member of a tribal dance group in Wrangell, displays her traditional costume.

🏴🏴🏴
DAY THREE

We departed Ketchikan on the *Sheltered Seas* early this morning, northbound for Wrangell and Petersburg. Shortly after breakfast, our first performer of the day appeared. A humpback whale broke the surface, swam a few yards offshore, spouted a couple of times and then—exhibiting a magnificent fluke—went into a deep dive.

"We won't wait around for him to come up," Captain Cushman said over the intercom. "The passageway is about a thousand feet deep here."

We dipped into a narrow side channel and carefully approached a rocky island where a dozen or so shy harbor seals stared nervously at us with their dark, sad eyes. Passengers crowded the starboard rail, clicking their cameras like reporters at a press conference. The seals started slipping into the water as we drew near, so the captain eased the ship away.

Later, we put ashore in Wrangell, a town of 2,500 occupying a slim, wooded coastal shelf. Our stop here would be brief, for we still had to reach Petersburg—several hours northward—by nightfall. We headed for Chief Shakes' house, the town's star attraction. It's another CCC project—a totem park and tribal lodge occupying a small island. Chief Shakes was Wrangell's last traditional Tlingit tribal leader and the structure was dedicated to him when it was completed in 1940. We received an unexpected bonus during our visit. Several young members of a native dancing group, rehearsing behind the tribal house, offered to perform for us. Swirling about in their handsome black and red tribal costumes, they danced with the shy enthusiasm typical of children. Tonight, they'd probably be playing Nintendo or watching *The Simpsons*. But for the moment, they were proud descendants of Alaska's first people, reaching ritualistically into their past.

We received an unexpected bonus during our visit. Several young members of a native dancing group offered to perform for us.

It was late evening by the time we reached Petersburg, yet light was still abundant for this was Alaska of the long summer days. Similar in size to Wrangell, Petersburg would be an ordinary looking town except for its dramatic backdrop—the ragged, snow-streaked Coast Range that separates Southeast Alaska from Canada. Caught in late light as we sailed into the busy fishing port, the peaks were irregular scoops of vanilla marbled ice cream against a pale blue sky.

After checking into the Tides Inn, we walked about town and discovered another pleasing aspect of Petersburg. It began as a fish canning camp, established in 1897 by Norwegian Peter Buschmann, who saw in Southeast Alaska's fjords visions of his homeland. The town still retains its Scandinavian heritage. Hints of Norway appear in the architecture and in *rosemaling* floral decorations on the walls of businesses and homes.

Our walk took us to Eagle's Roost Park, a bit of green above an inlet. Appropriately, a dozen and more bald eagles roosted in fir trees; we counted five on one spindly snag. These grand birds so rare in the lower Forty-eight were as common as crows in Petersburg, and as indifferent to humans. They took flight only when closely approached. They'd spring gracefully into the air, glide to another tree and stare down at us with those piercing eyes.

🐾 🐾 🐾

DAY FOUR

As the *Sheltered Seas* idled in a field of shattered ice, passengers gathered with the captain at the bow to toast LeConte Glacier. The glacier was not in view; nor would we see it this day. For several weeks it had been shedding massive amounts of ice, "calving," as glaciologists like to say. It had filled LeConte fjord with such a vast ice floe that it was impossible for the *Sheltered Seas* to get close enough for a view. It remained hidden, around the next bend.

If our loss was a view of North America's southernmost tidewater glacier, or gain was a fascinating morning cruising and bumping through several miles of the LeConte ice floe. We were surrounded by a frozen wonderland in every hue of blue, from deep cobalt to silken sapphire to phosphorescent turquoise. The day was sunlit and dazzling and the calm sea captured perfect replicas of the hundreds of thousands of ice fragments. Harbor seals on floating ice patches—often mothers with newborn pups—watched us warily and then, as the ship drew near, they slipped silently into the cold sea.

Our narrator during this journey was gregarious Syd Wright, a fisherman and former Petersburg school principal. He talked about Alaska, about the LeConte Glacier ice floe and about his adopted village of Petersburg. He was both an informer and performer—speaking with animation and even singing for us Alaska's state song. As he talked, he passed among us a carved Tlingit mask and rattle, various furs and—good grief!—the penis bone of a killer whale.

"Glaciers, back in their cold solitudes, work apart from men, exerting their tremendous energies in silence and darkness."

When Wright's words faltered—a rare occurrence—he quoted from John Muir's travels in Alaska:

Glaciers, back in their cold solitudes, work apart from men, exerting their tremendous energies in silence and darkness. Outspread, spirit-like, they brood above the predestined landscapes, working unwearied through immeasurable ages, until, in the fullness of time, the mountains and valleys are brought forth, channels furrowed for the rivers, basins made for the lakes and meadows, and long, deep arms of the sea.

After Captain Cushman had cruised into the floating sea of ice as far possible, crew members circulated among us with glasses of champagne and cider. We raised our glasses to toast LeConte Glacier, somewhere out there in its grand and cold solitude. To conclude our icy adventure, several of the crew sang a silly ditty about the Titanic, which ended thusly:

Kerplunk! It sunk;
What a lousy piece of junk.

We hadn't seen the last of Syd Wright. Several of us had signed up for an afternoon fishing excursion aboard his boat. This was not a "party" charter boat but a working trawler. On its cluttered deck was a busy brew of nets, winches, fishing poles, rubber gloves and things I failed to recognize. Syd and his wife Vara had owned the boat for more than a decade, fishing in summers when he was a school administrator, and now fishing more or less full time, since he had more or less retired.

"Trawling is full of surprises. Last year, we caught a Christmas tree."

We cruised out a few miles and unreeled a long trawling net that sank more than a hundred feet to the bottom. Vara held a slow and steady coarse at the ship's wheel while Syd explained the difference between trawling and trolling. The first uses a net that scoops up whatever it encounters along the bottom and the second strings out line with baited hooks.

"Trawling is full of surprises," he said. "You never know what you're going to catch. Last year, we caught a Christmas tree."

No tree this year. He reeled in the net and dumped upon the deck a glistening heap of shrimp, seaweed, small halibut, ugly little mudsuckers and scores of nondescript minnows. Vara began sorting and preparing the shrimp. Betty, with a surge of compassion, knelt among the squiggling mass and started tossing the minnows and mudsuckers back into the sea—not realizing that she was throwing away Syd's bait. Later, he reeled up a crab trap; it was full of tasty, squirming king crabs and *he* began tossing several of them overboard!

"Can't keep any of the females," he explained.

"How can you tell which is which?" I asked.

"Just like women. Their bottoms are bigger."

As the good ship *Chad IV* putt-putted back toward Petersburg, we dined on the seafood prepared by Vara. With eager fingers, we demolished piles of shrimp and plundered the crab, dipping into Vara's special garlic oil or spicy red sauce and tossing the shells overboard. It was a wonderfully decedent, seagoing Roman banquet. It was even the proper thing to do, said Syd. Fish remains—but nothing else—may be thrown into the sea.

And it certainly was one of the tastiest seafood dinners we'd ever devoured.

🐾🐾🐾

DAY FIVE

Petersburg was under a canopy of clouds as we left port and headed for Juneau. We would spend the night there and then hop a plane for Fairbanks to begin the land portion of our tour. A fine diversion was planned en route to Juneau—a cruise up the 25-mile-long Tracy Arm for close encounters with two tidewater glaciers.

As the *Sheltered Seas* cruised toward Juneau, we encountered a pair of humpback whales—mother and child—who kept passengers' cameras and minicams whirring for more than half an hour. Then we swung into Tracy Arm, whose shallow submerged moraine prevents entry by large cruise ships. This is a magnificent passage, one to two miles narrow, walled by 2,000-foot slopes. Waterfalls spilled from the heights; some were thundering cascades, others thin silver strands. Except for the chill in the air and occasional floating ice chunks, these could have been seacliffs in Hawaii.

One young pup poked an urgent flipper into his mother's side as if to say: "C'mon, Mom, let's go! They're getting closer!"

The ice floe thickened and soon we were within view of the ragged mint-blue faces of Sawyer and South Sawyer glaciers. Captain Cushman made a left turn and we bumped through the floe toward Sawyer, a great ice dam wedged between steep granite walls. We crowded the bow for a closer look as the captain urged his boat slowly forward.

Seals basking on icebergs eyed our progress warily. One young pup poked an urgent flipper into its mother's side as if to say: "C'mon, Mom, let's go! They're getting closer!"

As we approached, the glacier—which from a distance appeared as a solid wall of ice—separated into a complex three-dimensional blue badlands of pillars, ridges, creases and canyons.

Captain Cushman's voice came over the intercom: "Through careful calculation, angular estimates and horseback guessing, I've determined that the face of the glacier—above and below water—is a thousand feet high. This is as close as we can approach, because of possible danger from calving."

🏴 🏴 🏴

Juneau was something of an sociological jolt after pleasantly funky Wrangell and Petersburg. It struck me initially as a tough town; I counted half a dozen bars in the short distance from the dock to our quarters at the Baranof Hotel, each smelling of stale cigarette smoke and yesterday's spilled beer. Curio shops outnumbered bars at least three to one, each offering T-shirts, *ulu* knives, postcards, fake gold pans and native crafts real and imagined. Although this is the state capital, we felt no sense of Alaska in downtown Juneau; only a sense of unabashed tourism. (Mixed among the souvenir shops, however, are several fine galleries of Alaskan art.)

One *can* find Alaska in Juneau, however. Plaques along the historic waterfront and in an adjacent park recall the late 1800s, when Joe Juneau and Dick Harris found gold in nearby creek gravel. The Alaska State Museum offers a fine quick study of the state's history, wildlife and ecology. Juneau's setting is certainly a classic slice of Alaska. It perches on a narrow coastal shelf before a 2,000-foot mountain wall, thickly wooded and seamed with waterfall ravines. Just beyond and out of sight is the Juneau Icecap, one of the most imposing ice fields in the world. Flightseeing trips over the cap are popular with visitors.

Like Ketchikan, Juneau's commercial heart beats to the drum of cruise ships. We asked one shopkeeper what time she would open in the morning. "Around eight," she said, then she paused and corrected herself: "No, not tomorrow. The first ship doesn't come in until ten."

🏴 🏴 🏴

DAY SIX

This was mostly a travel day as we competed the transition from sea to land; we would fly from Juneau to Fairbanks via Anchorage. Our tour hosts provided an interesting diversion, however, taking us to the airport by way of Mendenhall Glacier. This is hardly a wilderness experience, since it's reached by paved highway and seen by legions of tourists. We preferred the splendid solitude of the LeConte ice floe and the craggy countenance of Sawyer Glacier. However, this was a fine way to kill time while waiting to crawl into an aluminum tube to be hurled through the air to mainland Alaska.

We'd been here before so—while others in our group took a guided nature walk near the Mendenhall visitor center—we hurried along the East Glacier trail to get closer to the multi-tiered face of the glacier itself. Mendenhall has been receding since the 1700s and is now shrinking at the rate of 35 to 40 feet a year. That big, shy rascal had retreated a good 400 feet since we last saw it seven years ago.

🏴 🏴 🏴

Fairbanks, a community of 30,000 spread over a tree plain between the Alaska and Brooks mountain ranges, is a typical slice of the mainland. It's roots certainly are typical. It was founded in 1901 when E.T. Barnette, a passenger on the paddlewheeler *Lavelle Young* set up a trading post near the merger of the Chena and Tanana rivers. Gold was discovered in the area a few months later and Fairbanks soon boomed into the largest and bawdiest town in Alaska. Its name comes from fair bank, a riverman's term for a shoreline stable enough for a boat landing.

Today's Fairbanks lacks the curio shop overkill of Juneau and Ketchikan. It also lacks their imposing settings between sea and mountain, yet we liked this ordinary-appearing old town. It's a friendly and unpretentious place where strangers say "howdy" as you pass them on the street. Fairbanks just *feels* like Alaska.

The town had the good sense to gather up its architectural heritage and deposit it in a pioneer theme park called Alaskaland. More than a dozen old cabins, mostly log, have been reassembled here, housing assorted boutiques and snack shops. The park also offers a rousing historical pageant called *Riversong*, three museums and a narrow gauge railroad. The star of the pioneer park is the steam-powered sternwheeler *Nenana*. Launched in 1935, she hauled passengers and freight on Alaska's rivers for more than two decades. After years of neglect and an unsuccessful stint as a gimmick restaurant, she was adopted by Fairbanks citizens and is being restored.

We toured Alaskaland until the park closed at 9 p.m., then we went in search of dinner. We retired to our room at the Bridgewater Hotel to work on this chapter, and...

⌂ ⌂ ⌂

DAY SEVEN

...**l**ooked out the window to see that it was 12:02 a.m. and still daylight. This was June 19, one of the longest days of the year, and welcome to mainland Alaska.

A morning tour featured a drive-by of historic Fairbanks, a visit to a gold dredge and a stop at the University of Alaska- Fairbanks Museum, with a fine show on the northern lights. We also paused at a section of the newly-legendary Alyeska Pipeline, through which flows twenty-five percent of America's total oil production.

Our afternoon outing was a voyage aboard the second of three watercraft on our Alaska sea-and-land outing, although this was hardly a cruise. The *Discovery III* is a pretend riverboat with a diesel-powered paddlewheel; it takes boatloads of visitors on short trips along the Chena River. We went aboard, prepared to poke fun at this Disneyesque tourist gimmick and came away impressed with the operation.

The owners have condensed the history of interior Alaska—from Athabascan native to goldseeker to settler—into an afternoon of high-tech entertainment.

The owners, former riverboat captain Jim Binkley and his wife Mary, have condensed the history of interior Alaska—from Athabascan native to goldseeker to settler—into an afternoon of high-tech entertainment. There isn't much to see along the Chena River's wooded shoreline, other than a few modern log cabins, some with sod roofs. However, the Binkleys had set up tableaux along the banks, linked to the boat by wireless microphones. Images are picked up by a video camera and played over TV monitors aboard the ship, for those who choose not to stand at the crowded rails.

Scenarios included a short take-off and landing demonstration by a bush pilot; a ship-to-shore visit with Susan Butcher, four- time winner of the Anchorage-to-Nome Iditarod dog sled race; a view of a fish wheel used by native Alaskans to catch salmon; and a salmon-skinning demonstration at an Athabascan fish camp. Passengers then went ashore at "Camp Chena," a mock Athabaskan village where assorted crafts and hunting techniques were presented by enthusiastic young native Alaskan college students. David Butcher, the Iditarod winner's husband, talked about the curious sport of racing through the wilderness in 50-below temperatures behind a pack of barking dogs.

"A dog in a race consumes about 10,000 calories a day, usually in dried salmon. That's equivalent to a human eating four ten-pound turkeys. No one's sure when natives first started using sled dogs, although the animals came across the Bering land bridge with Alaska's first people, about 10,000 years ago. By the way, we don't use the word huskies up here, because these dogs aren't a particular breed. "

Indeed, the canines in his demonstration corral came in all shapes and sizes. They did share a common disposition: "All of these dogs just love to run. Some of them rack up 25,000 miles or more before they retire from racing. It takes about ten minutes to teach these guys to go and two years to teach them to whoa."

ß ß ß

DAY EIGHT

The next leg on this versatile exploration was a trip south from Fairbanks aboard the Alaska Railroad. The railway was completed in 1915 to haul cargo, prospectors and settlers to the massive interior. Still owned by the state, it now hauls mostly tourists, particularly since it stops at the edge of Denali National Park on its run between Fairbanks and the Seward Peninsula below Anchorage.

This is not a high-speed locomotive, but a slow lane train that sways gently through thick spruce forest and then crawls carefully up beautiful Nenana River Canyon into the park. It's a comfortable train, with parlor cars, dome cars and a dining car. As we chugged through the spruce, a likable on-train tour guide offered a railroad lapel pin as a prize to the first person who spotted a trackside moose or significant other wildlife.

While he talked, a gaggle of garrulous women crowded into the dome car. A few minutes later, a collective high pitched shriek issued from the dome; it sounded like the wail of a stepped-on banshee. At the same instant, we saw an alarmed moose outside, bolting through the brush. The ladies' howls upon spotting the moose apparently had

A few minutes later, a collective high pitched shriek issued from the dome car; it sounded like the wail of a stepped-on banshee.

carried through the glass dome, sending it in terrified flight. They won their pin and I wonder if that moose will ever again be seen at track-side.

At the Denali station, passengers had the choice of touring the national park or continuing by bus to Anchorage. Several of us had signed up for a stay at Denali Wilderness Lodge, a remote hideaway outside the park, reached only by air. Our snug little Cessna winged low through a wooded steep-walled canyon; the ice-sculpted ramparts of the Alaska Range towered high above. The buzzing little dragonfly banked easily and turned into a second canyon, following the course of the glacier-fed Wood River, then the pilot fluttered his craft down onto a gravel landing strip near the lodge. Half an hour after leaving a trainload of chatty tourists, we stood in a splendid, silent cathedral of wilderness.

This is a remarkable place. For three decades it had been a home and commercial hunting lodge for Lynne Castle, a legendary Alaskan guide and bush pilot. It's now owned by former engineer David Thompson and his wife Danielle. No longer a hunting lodge, it's an environmentally sensitive retreat catering to seekers of peace, quiet and camaraderie. This rustic log complex, with a main lodge and several guest cabins, has modern plumbing and generator-produced electricity, bringing almost sinful comfort to the wilderness. The main lodge is an imposing structure, filled with more than a hundred mounted game trophies—from rhinos to moose—collected by Castle. In the evening, guests sink into overstuffed leather chairs and either discuss or ignore the state of the world outside. One can find a quiet corner and curl up with a book, although it's a bit disconcerting to glance up and see a stuffed mountain lion reading over your shoulder.

We dismounted at a fire ring and sat around for a lazy hour or so, telling stories and cremating marshmallows dipped in Bailey's Irish Cream.

Our visit began with a nature walk, during which we learned to identify pretty flowers with ugly names—woolly lousewort, fly-specked orchis and hairy arctic milk vetch. After a hefty dinner of salmon steaks and potatoes, we went for a late evening trail ride. The magnificent peaks of the Alaska range—snow- streaked, glacier-scarred and still bathed in sunlight—jiggled gently as we tenderfeet jostled in our saddles. We dismounted at a fire ring and sat around for a lazy hour or so, telling stories and cremating marshmallows dipped in Bailey's Irish Cream. The sun, understandably reluctant to leave this fine setting, still occupied the sky when we returned to the lodge.

Our senses had been fooled into thinking it was still daytime, so we walked to an observation tower at the airstrip. Here, wide awake and surrounded by peaks the shape of wild ocean waves, we awaited the arrival of summer. At the appointed hour, 12:22 a.m., June 21, the sun painted a few clouds bright orange and then slipped behind one of the snow-dusted peaks. We raised our cups:

"Happy solstice!" we shouted.

"Happy solstice," came the soft cry back.

Of course it wasn't an echo; it was the great land greeting its guests.

ₚₚₚ

DAY NINE

Days pass easily at Denali Wilderness Lodge. We slept through breakfast after our Solstice affair, compensated with a huge lunch and then walked it off with an invigorating hike up one of the surrounding slopes. With guides fore and aft, our band learned more about this special kind of wilderness.

"Winter is the measure of all life here," said one of the guides as we hiked up the rocky shore of a cascading creek. "Only animals that are able to make it through the winter can survive. They have to deal with 50-below temperatures and ten feet of snow. After that, summer is a paid vacation, with lots of plant life for herbivores and plenty of lunch for those higher in the food chain."

Several sea lions snooze aboard a bouy in Prince William Sound.

As we followed a trail through a steep slope of dwarf birch, one of the guides engaged us in a serious scatological discussion, pointing out the difference between moose and caribou droppings. "To help identify them, think of moose scat as Milk Duds and caribou as Raisinettes," she explained.

"I'll try to remember that the next time I go to the snack bar at the movies," I said.

🏴 🏴 🏴

DAY TEN

In Alaska, weather happens. For most of our trip, the days had been alternately sunny or overcast with occasional drizzles, not the kind of weather that would disrupt one's sightseeing. Last night, a serious rain arrived and we were lulled to sleep by the pleasant patter on our cabin roof. When we awoke this morning, the patter was still there. It was still raining during lunch; the surrounding peaks wore floor-length skirts of clouds. We were scheduled to fly out at 12:30 to catch a bus for Anchorage; that was now out of the question. But who wanted to leave? However, we did have one final leg in this complex itinerary—a cruise across Prince William Sound. Other guests had commitments as well. No problem. Our hosts got on the radio-telephone—their only link to the outside world.

Half an hour later, three helicopters flew in; it looked like the opening scene from *M.A.S.H.* We climbed aboard for the most elegant evacuation one

Half an hour later, three helicopters flew in; it looked like the opening scene from M.A.S.H. We climbed aboard for the most elegant evacuation one could experience.

could ever experience. The choppers skimmed the treetops of a lush green valley, flying below the clouds and keeping to the contours of this beautiful land. We were aboard the trailing craft and the two ahead of us seemed suspended on invisible threads, swaying and dancing through the mist. Our little squadron slipped through a cleft in a high ridge and floated low over the Yana River, one of those braided latté colored streams so distinctive to Alaska. Our craft, also hanging from an unseen thread, swung gently from one side of the river valley to the other. Wearing headsets that muffled the noise of our flight, we heard only the occasional comments of our pilot and a tape of velvety music and wildlife sounds.

As we caught our bus at Denali Village and headed south, the low overcast denied us views of Mount McKinley and other monarchs of the Alaska Range. We saw only rolling roadside tundra and thin stands of rather scraggly spruce, which a guide back at the lodge had called pipe cleaners with an attitude. But no matter; that ethereal flight from the wilderness, with its wildlife soundtrack, still played in the CD ROM of my mind.

ß ß ß

DAY ELEVEN

If we had time to sample only one slice of the North Star State, it would be Prince William Sound. This is Alaska incarnate—an awesome mix of craggy mountains, glaciers, slender fjords and spruce thatched islands. It's part of the 4.4-million acre Chugach National Forest, with 2,700 miles of coastline, hundreds of islands and three of North America's largest icefields. The Columbia Glacier is bigger than Greater Los Angeles and much more attractive. In a single day's crossing, we saw dozens of glaciers, a huge flock of kittiwakes, a flotilla of cute little sea otters, a lone puffin, a trio of dancing dolphins and the awesome spectacle of calving icebergs.

Civilization exists only on the fringes of Prince William Sound—the tiny port of Whittier to the west, the Aleyeska pipeline terminal of Valdez northeast and the cute old fishing port of Cordova to the southeast. Getting there is much of the fun. One takes a coach south from Anchorage along scenic Cook Inlet, boards a train that tunnels through the Chugach Mountains to Whittier and then catches a boat.

Our boat was Cruise West's *M/V Glacier Seas*, which makes one-day voyages between Whittier and Valdez. Passengers cruise one way and then fly or bus the other. This is a nimble little day cruiser with ample window seating, a dining area, cocktail bar, the usual loaner binoculars and a small library.

Captain Paul Whitmore of the Glacier Seas *lifts his glass of apple cider to toast Columbia Glacier in Prince William Sound.*

As soon as we sailed from Whittier, we realized that we'd found our favorite piece of the Alaskan pie. We cruised beneath green-clad mountains, mantled with snow and climbing steeply from the blue-green sea. Silken threads of waterfalls coursed down sheer cliff faces. Almost any random glance revealed the icy blue faces of glaciers hanging from high valleys, or creeping patiently toward the waters of the sound.

A short cruise up Barry Arm provided a most remarkable sight—the merger of a trio of tidewater glaciers. Cascade, Barry and Cox, born independently high in the Chugach Mountains, had found a common entry into Prince William Sound. The boat plowed carefully through a virtual clam chowder of crushed ice, drawing within a quarter of a mile of Barry Glacier. Every pair of eyes stared at its snout, for the captain said it had been calving of late. Suddenly, a sharp report like a rifle shot; a shard of ice the size of my first apartment slipped from the gnarled face and dropped soundlessly into the sea. Half a second later the crashing splash of its impact reached our ears. Native Alaskans call this "white thunder." As we stared at a fresh blue wound on the glacier face where the ice had broken free, a gentle wake from the fallen chunk rocked our boat.

And so passed our last day in Alaska. Barry Glacier and then Cascade shed more ice and we left reluctantly after an extended visit. As we continued onward, more sea otters floated past like lazy tourists; bald eagles perched in shoreline trees, indifferent to our passage.

Using a chart of Prince William Sound, Captain Paul Whitmore outlined our irregular exploratory route. Then, he indicated a thin blue line drawn on the chart from Valdez southwest to a point where it became a spreading blur. On March 24, 1989, the oil tanker *Exxon Valdez* was given permission to alter its course to avoid icebergs floating from Columbia Glacier. Later testimony revealed that the helmsman became "confused" when told to change course again to return to the sea lane. The ship slammed into Bligh Reef and 11.2 million gallons of Alaska crude spilled into Prince William Sound. Although estimates vary widely, as many as half a million birds may have died in the oil slick, along with about 5,000 sea otters and 200 harbor seals. About one fifth of the sound's 2,500 miles of shoreline were oiled.

Given time and protected from further abuse, Nature can heal most man-caused wounds. Prince William Sound appeared pristine again...

Given time and protected from further abuse, Nature can heal most man-caused wounds. Prince William Sound appeared pristine again and there was no evidence of the spill along our route. Toward trip's end, we sailed past the tanker terminal outside of Valdez. Prudhoe Bay crude arrives through the Aleyeska pipeline at the rate of 53 million gallons a day and it's stored in 18 monster tanks with a total capacity of nearly a billion gallons. Seeing those tanks on the slope above the water and the waiting tankers below, we felt an odd chill.

The high point of the day came before we sailed past that oil terminal in the port of Valdez. The captain cruised carefully along the submerged moraine of Columbia Glacier, seeking with his depth finder an area low enough to cross. Columbia is currently in "catastrophic retreat" and has pulled back more than five miles since 1983. In its rapid withdrawal, it's shedding a startling number of icebergs, some larger than our ship. We were surrounded by every shape and blue hue of ice; we seemed to have been transported to a set for *Ice Station Zebra*.

When the *Glacier Seas* had penetrated the ice floe as far as safely possible, passengers were handed the traditional glasses of champagne or apple cider.

"Hail Columbia," said Captain Whitmore, lifting his glass of cider. "A toast to our glacier."

"To Alaska," I said.

I still kept in mind a certain wonderful sunset which I witnessed when steamboating was new to me. In the middle distance the red hue brightened into gold...the dissolving lights drifted steadily, enriching it every passing moment with new marvels of coloring. — Mark Twain, *Life on the Mississippi*

Chapter five

SOUTHERN STEAMBOATIN'

Paddlewheeling America on the *Delta Queen*

By some grand coincidence, we experienced the same kind of crimson sunset that had inspired Mark Twain's quill. It happened shortly after the *Delta Queen* left Chattanooga's Ross Landing on a cloudy September evening. The weather had been unseasonably wet during our two days in Chattanooga, provoked by a Caribbean hurricane several hundred miles away. The blow itself never approached Tennessee, although it did push a soggy bank of clouds inland.

After the majestic old riverboat sailed into the Tennessee River—its red orange paddlewheel churning mightily and its steam calliope hooting gaily—we adjourned to the Orleans Room for dinner. Betty glanced out the window and her elliptical eyes widened.

"Wow! Look at that!"

The sun, in its final moments of the day, had broken through the overcast. It painted the surrounding clouds many shades of crimson and sent a

CRUISE PLANNER

The cruise • The Delta Queen Steamboat Company operates three steam-driven paddlewheelers on rivers of the American South and Midwest, with trips ranging from three to fourteen nights. These are leisurely cruises appealing to senior travelers and anyone interested in river lore. Passengers learn about "steamboatin'" and the history and ecology of the Mississippi river system. Our voyage was a six- day, seven-night, 691-mile cruise aboard the *Delta Queen* on the Tennessee, Ohio and Mississippi rivers from Chattanooga to St. Louis. For information on this and other river cruises, contact The Delta Queen Steamboat Co., 30 Robin Street Wharf, New Orleans, LA 70130-1890, (800) 543-1949; FAX (504) 585-0630.

Getting there • Continental Airlines provides comprehensive service to many of the steamboat company's departure and arrival cities. Special "Steamboatin' Plus...Air" combination tickets with various airlines are available through Delta Queen or travel agents. "Steamboatin' Plus...Hotel" packages also are offered at most departure and arrival ports. These are one-night stays *generally in historic hotels that give passengers an opportunity to explore the cities.*

The boats • The *Delta Queen* is the elder stateswoman of the fleet—a 1927 paddlewheeler restored to its brass, teak and frosted glass finery. It's one of the few vintage steamboats still in operation and it shares with San Francisco's cable cars the distinction of being a mobile National Historic Landmark. Decor is Victorian and turn-of-the-century Americana, with crystal chandeliers, iron filigree and Tiffany style stained glass. The 285-foot craft has eighty-seven cabins, two lounges, a New Orleans style dining room, sun decks and a gift shop. Other members of the fleet, built along the classic lines of old paddlewheelers, are the 207-cabin *Mississippi Queen* built in 1976 and the 222-cabin *American Queen,* launched in 1995. Officers and crew are American.

When to go • The three *Queens* operate on assorted rivers throughout the year. Since the American South and Midwest are relatively temperate, there is no best time to go. The firm offers many theme cruises, such as fall foliage, Thanksgiving and Christmas "Old Fashioned Holidays," plus voyages featuring Dixieland, jazz and other regional music.

What to bring • Pack a flexible wardrobe; dress is casual during the daytime, and dressier at night but not formal. Cocktail wear and suits and ties are recommended for the champagne reception and captain's dinner. Expect a little rain much of the year in America's heartland, particularly during the winter and spring, so bring proper apparel. Most spring through fall days are sunny, and it can be rather muggy in summer. Bring binoculars for following river markers and spotting shoreside attractions.

What's included • Reference books on local lore and binoculars for scanning the shore can be checked out during the cruise. Shore excursions are extra, although free shuttle service to town is provided at some shore stops; others are within walking distance.

yellow shard of light across the river. As it dropped below the horizon, the clouds turned a bright orange—the color of our paddlewheel—and then faded to a soft gold. The great writer, checking my copy from above, must have decided to show this obscure author what he'd described more than a hundred years earlier.

ße ße ße

For centuries, men dreamed of plying rivers without the need of oars. Sailing ships could tack into the ocean winds, but river transit was limited. Going downstream was no problem, but how to get back? Streams with powerful currents were virtually "rivers of no return." In the early settlement of the West, many pioneers sailed downstream and then took their boats apart to build their cabins.

Leonardo DaVinci sketched the concept of steam-powered boats in the fifteenth century but it took nearly 400 years for his theory to become reality. America's Robert Fulton built the first practical steam craft, the sidewheeler *Clermont,* which he sailed up the Hudson River in 1807. He launched the first full scale steamboat, the *New Orleans,* on the Mississippi River four years later. He sold five-hour excursion rides for $3 and a local newspaper advised passengers to "carry with them their own provisions" in case of delays. The excursions were a success and the *New Orleans* began regular service on the Mississippi and Ohio rivers.

Moses Rogers built an ocean-going steam craft, the *Savannah,* in 1819. However, no American firm would buy this contraption with a blazing fire on board—fire at sea being a sailor's biggest fear—so Rogers cruised it to Liverpool, England. His departure on May 22 is now observed as National Maritime Day. Failing to find buyers in Europe, he returned to America and—ironically—converted the *Savannah* to sail. In the years following, men overcame their fear of fire on water; steamboats and ocean-going steamships soon dominated world passenger and cargo traffic.

Author Samuel Clemens, briefly a riverboat pilot, made the steamboat legendary with his book *Life on the Mississippi.* He took for himself the name Mark Twain, the riverman's call that the water was at least twelve feet deep—safe for passage. During the nineteenth century, thousands of multi-deck sidewheelers and sternwheelers cruised every navigable river in North America.

Fortunately, Mark Twain's announcement of the death of steamboatin' was premature.

Many early steamboats were elegant vessels with comfortable cabins (initially named for states and thus called staterooms), grand dining rooms and smart salons. Their lower decks were jammed with freight—and chords of wood or tons of coal to keep those boilers percolating. Although steam powered ships dominated the oceans well into this century, river steamer traffic declined late in the 1800s, faced with increasing competition from railroads. Mark Twain declared steamboatin' dead by the 1880s. "I saw half a dozen sleeping steamboats (on the St. Louis waterfront)," he wrote, "where before I had seen a mile of wide-awake ones."

Fortunately, his announcement of the death of steamboating was premature. A few riverboats continued operating into the twentieth century. The *Delta Queen,* built in 1927, cruised for several years on the California Delta—the source of its name. Then, after an inglorious stint as a World War II Navy shuttle on San Francisco Bay, she and her brother craft, the *Delta King,* were

With its big paddlewheel churning lustily, the Delta Queen *cruises down the Tennessee River from Chattanooga.*

retired. Tom Greene, whose parents Gordon and Mary had founded Cincinnati's Greene Line Steamers in 1890, bought the old boat from the government in 1946 for $46,250. He managed to have her towed down the Pacific Coast and through the Panama Canal to New Orleans without sinking her. Upriver in Cincinnati, the Greenes restored her to Victorian opulence. The grand old vessel became the queen of the Greene Line, offering—for the first time in decades—overnight passenger service on the Mississippi river system. The firm later became—under new owners—The Delta Queen Steamboat Company.

The *Delta King,* should you wonder, also was spared the scrap heap, although it doesn't go anywhere. It has been converted into a hotel and theater, permanently anchored at one of its former ports of call—Sacramento. We'll meet the *King* briefly in the next chapter, page 162.

ßßß

CHECKING OUT CHATTANOOGA

More than a score of cities serve as ports for The Delta Queen Steamboat Company's fleet. We had the good fortune of catching the *Queen* in Chattanooga, an appealing city tucked between the banks of the Tennessee River and the ramparts of Lookout Mountain. Once a grimy industrial town, this community of 200,000 has become one of Tennessee's leading tourist destinations.

"We lost our steel mills and gained clean air and a revitalized downtown," said Landon C. Howard, director of marketing for the Chattanooga Area Convention and Visitors Bureau. "A few years ago, the air was so polluted that we had to pack an extra white shirt to work. Now, Chattanooga's air quality is the best of any city of our size in the country."

A key to Chattanooga's revitalization is the $45 million Tennessee Aquarium, completed in 1992. Rated as one of the finest in America, it's housed in an impressive towering glass and steel structure at Ross Landing, a four-acre park on the riverfront. It focuses on the geology, ecology and human history of the Tennessee River from its birth in the Great Smokies to its merger with the Mississippi. It offers a fine introduction to the river system for folks about to board a riverboat, revealing to them not only the complex shoreside environment but the unseen world beneath the hull.

The Chattanooga area offers other lures sufficient to keep visitors occupied for several days. Chickamauga-Chattanooga National Military Park preserves the site of one of the most vicious battles of the Civil War. At nearby Lookout Mountain, visitors can ride an incline railway to Point Park where—

The Tennessee Aquarium offers a fine introduction to the river system for folks about to board a riverboat.

through strong lenses on a clear day—pieces of seven states are visible. Other Lookout Mountain attractions are Ruby Falls, a limestone cavern with a 145-foot underground waterfall; and Rock City Gardens, an area of sculpted rock formations. Back in town, one can stop by the Houston Museum, featuring a huge collection of glassware left by an eccentric lady who went through a dozen or so husbands; and Warehouse Row, a collection of old brick warehouses converted into a shopping complex.

A handy base of operations is the Chattanooga Choo Choo Holiday Inn, occupying the city's turn-of-the-century railroad depot; several of the rooms are in converted rail cars. This was a terminus of the Chattanooga Southern Railway, made famous as the "Chattanooga Choo Choo" by Glen Miller's 1941 song. The world's largest HO gauge model railroad, depicting the city's heyday as a rail center, occupies one of the terminal buildings.

To learn more about the city and its surrounds, contact the Chattanooga Area Convention and Visitors Bureau, 1001 Market St., Chattanooga, TN 37402; (800) 322-3344 or (423) 756-8697. The visitor center is adjacent to the aquarium.

ßßß

DAY ONE

We weren't really finished with Chattanooga, but our waiting riverboat, anchored within sight of the Tennessee Aquarium, gave a throaty warning toot on her steam whistle. The gangway was about to be hauled aboard and she'd be underway by 7 p.m.

I'd deposited our luggage earlier so we procrastinated until 6:45, and then we hurried up the gangway through a light drizzle. Captain Gabe Chengery was announcing the imminent departure of the "legendary *Delta Queen*" as we stepped aboard the cargo deck.

This is a likable old boat. And yes, it's a boat, not a ship. The difference, as we were to learn during a later onboard lecture, is that boats were built for rivers; ships were built for the sea. The *Queen's* public rooms are a blend of Victoriana and turn-of-the-century Americana, with wood paneled walls, ornate settees and walnut tables set with tasseled, tortoise shell lamps. The look is carried into the snug and comfortable cabins. Ours, the New York stateroom, had a brass queen bed with a floral print spread that matched the drapes, a cute little beaded chandelier and brass wall lamps. In his *Life on the Mississippi*, Mark Twain had described a similar boat:

She was as clean and as dainty as a drawing-room; when I looked down her long, gilded saloon, it was like gazing through a splendid tunnel; she glittered with no end of prism-fringed chandeliers. The bar was marvelous, and the barkeeper had been barbered and upholstered at incredible cost.

Our barkeep in the Texas Lounge wasn't upholstered but young and slender and—it appeared—barely old enough to drink. He created a marvelous bloody Mary, which seemed a suitable libation for the boat's departure from Chattanooga. Drink in hand, I headed aft on the Sun Deck to what would become my favorite onboard retreat—beside the steam calliope and above the great paddlewheel. The calliope hissed and whistled and the paddlewheel churned, pushing us slowly from the dock. No, the calliope didn't play *Chattanooga Choo Choo*; our song of departure was *The Tennessee Waltz*. A few onlookers gathered onshore as we pulled away—a black youth tall enough to be an NBA center, with an arm around his waist-high girlfriend; an elderly pair who waved solemnly and looked like they wished they were aboard; a grinning redneck with a turned-around trucker's hat and a point and shoot camera which he pointed and shot frequently, its weak flash falling far short of our departing boat.

> **The calliope hissed and whistled and the paddlewheel churned, pushing us slowly from the dock.**

We weren't really going anywhere, since riverboats often travel by day so passengers don't miss interesting scenery. The captain would cruise past the Chattanooga riverfront a couple of times, and then go downstream to "choke a stump"—tie up to a tree for the night. Answering the call to dinner, we headed down to the Orleans Room. And there, between the gumbo and the fried oysters, we saw the inspiring sunset matching the one Mark Twain had admired a century before:

A broad expanse of the river was turned to blood; in the middle distance the red hue brightened into gold...the dissolving lights drifted steadily, enriching it every passing moment with new marvels of coloring.

Better words than I could find, I thought, watching the clouds change color. Then I recalled what my high school journalism instructor—an awful teacher and a great storyteller—once said:

When words fail you, steal someone else's.

ȸ ȸ ȸ

DAY TWO

Steamboats make special sounds and we awoke to one of these—the swishing sigh of the pitman arm that drives the paddlewheel. We opened our stateroom blinds to low hills thatched with green. Although much of the South is busy with cities, towns and farms, this region of southern Tennessee and northern Alabama was thickly wooded and thinly populated. From Chattanooga, the Tennessee River dipped south into Alabama, swung west and then north, back into its namesake state.

Passengers gather on the bow to watch the Delta Queen *pass through the Tennessee River's Nickajack Lock.*

This was one of two good reasons we'd selected this particular cruise; it offered some hilly scenery instead of the riverside levees of the lower Mississippi. The other reason, of course, was that we wanted to cruise on an original riverboat, although the company's newer *Mississippi Queen* and *American Queen* were larger and offered more amenities.

After breakfast, we attended the first of several lectures about steamboatin' and the Mississippi river system. We learned to spot river markers that would chart our progress along the Tennessee, Ohio and then the Mississippi River for our final leg to St. Louis. We'd go downriver on the Tennessee and Ohio, making a good ten miles an hour, and then upriver on the Mississippi, where our speed would slow to about six or seven.

Riverboat pilots had to know every channel, every bend, every bridge and every sandbar of a river in order to earn a license, we were told. In fact, the final exam was to duplicate from memory—on a blank piece of paper—an exact copy of the navigational chart for a particular stretch of river. One of the *Delta Queen's* pilots, we were told, was licensed for 4,000 miles of the Mississippi river system.

Like most major rivers, the Tennessee has been stairstepped by locks and dams into a series of "navigational pools" to assure enough depth for year-around transit, and for flood control. Many of the dams, of course, also are used for hydroelectric generation and some for irrigation. Most of the Tennessee's facilities are part of the Tennessee Valley Authority, America's first major government-sponsored lock and dam complex. Streams of the South and Midwest are important cargo carriers and we would see in the days to come dozens of "towboats" with their flotillas of barges which, despite the name, were pushed and not towed. (Newer models with flat bows are now called "pushboats.") Trivia fanatics will be happy to learn that one tow with 15 barges can carry the equivalent of 870 freight trucks or 225 rail cars.

We encountered this morning the first of several locks and dams along our route to St. Louis. Passing through Nickajack Lock was no great novelty for us, since we'd cruised the navigable length of the Columbia-Snake rivers a few months earlier. However, our approach to the lock emptied the morning lecture on steamboating. Other passengers bolted from their seats and hurried to the rails to watch the great concrete box swallow up our small paddlewheeler.

Life aboard a steamboat was casual during Mark Twain's day, and so it is today. These cruises are designed for folks seeking relaxation and simple pleasures. Lounging in a rocking chair and watching the shoreline and barge flotillas pass; reading a current best seller or playing bingo in the Texas Lounge; viewing a documentary about the Mississippi River and its influence on America's heartland; touring the galley—these are the simple pleasures of life aboard the *Delta Queen*.

If you need me for anything, you'll find me aft on the Sun Deck, bloody Mary in hand, watching that bright orange paddlewheel churn.

ß ß ß

DAY THREE

We had tied up for the night at Rhodes Ferry Park in Decatur, Georgia, one of hundreds of midsize and somewhat nondescript towns scattered across the Southern landscape. Decatur is not a tourist town. However, it's less than half an hour from Huntsville, Alabama, where the U.S. Space and Rocket Center attracts hundreds of thousands of people annually. More than half the *Queen's* passengers had signed up for a space center bus tour that would depart later this morning.

Our growing waistlines told us that we could afford to miss a meal, so we skipped breakfast and took a hike into town, about half a mile away. Walking to the cadence of Sunday morning church bells, we discovered that Decatur isn't quite as nondescript as it appears from the river. Our route took us through a fine old neighborhood of ancient homes shaded by giant dogwoods and maples. Some had been renovated; some needed it. Many were marked with small signs indicating their vintage and original owners.

We continued into the small

Life aboard a steamboat was casual during Mark Twain's day, and so it is today. These cruises are designed for folks seeking simple pleasures.

business district, a collection of two-story brick and masonry structures shaded by free-standing arcades. Many of the storefronts were empty since much of the town's business had fled to suburban shopping centers. The tired old main street offered a few antique shops although these, like much of the rest of Georgia, were closed on Sunday. The only signs of life in Decatur this early Sabbath morning were three alley cats, two brown squirrels and a roving police car whose occupant waved and grinned at us through his windshield.

A visitor to the Space & Rocket center near Huntsville, Alabama, is dwarfed by the Pathfinder space shuttle sitting atop its giant fuel tank.

Alabama got into the space business because the rolling hills around Huntsville reminded Dr. Wernher von Braun of his Rhine Valley homeland. This we learned as our tour bus rolled past cotton fields toward the Redstone Arsenal and the nearby U.S. Space & Rocket Center. Dr. von Braun, head of America's rocket development program in the 1950s, had toured the country looking for a piece of federal land for a testing facility. He chose this site at the old Redstone Arsenal, once a major munitions depot.

Our bus toured NASA's Marshall Space Center at Redstone, which now serves as command post for the U.S. Spacelab space station, and then we continued to the nearby rocket center. This isn't a working NASA facility but an outstanding museum focused on America's space program. It's also home to Space Camp and Space Academy, where kids and adults are put through simulated astronaut training to stimulate interest in America's various space endeavors. Anyone curious about rocketry and space can consume the better part of a day at this museum, manipulating robotic arms, riding in a multi-axis simulator and viewing static displays and videos. One of the five original Lunar Lander Rovers is here, along with assorted space capsules and mock-up pieces of the Skylab space station. Outside, the space shuttle *Pathfinder* perches atop its two solid fuel booster rockets and giant main fuel tank, dwarfing all who draw near.

After our allotted time, we straggled to our bus like reluctant children, for there was much we hadn't seen. Back aboard the *Delta Queen,* we felt like we'd been pulled through a time warp. Beam us back there, Scotty; we didn't get a chance to ride the Zero G Wall and the Five Degrees of Freedom simulator.

We spent the night near Florence, Georgia, just below Wilson lock. The *American Queen* was moored downstream and Captain Chengery wanted to catch her in the morning before she departed, to give passengers a look at the newest member of the Delta fleet. We tied up at a set of pylons near the lock; a large home sat on a bluff just above. Inside, a lady watching a big screen TV looked up with some surprise to see our riverboat pull abreast of her lawn. She came out on her deck and then down to the edge of the bluff, wearing a robe and a puzzled grin.

"That's a really sharp picture," said one of our crewmen, who was manning a shore line. Her TV was clearly visible from the *Queen*.

"Thanks," the woman said. "And that's quite a ship you've got there."

"Thank you, ma'am, but it's a boat."

ββ β

DAY FOUR

We cleared Wilson Lock, the highest in the Mississippi River system at 94 feet, and headed for our rendezvous with the *American Queen*. She was tied up at McFarland Park near Florence. Folks had come from miles around, it seemed, to see the meeting of the two paddlewheelers. Some had even set up picnics.

The newer boat was a stellar study in gingerbread filigree, topped by two towering "king's crown" smokestacks that dwarfed our craft as we pulled alongside. Our little queen tied up to the big queen's hull and we passengers swarmed aboard the larger craft like curious mice. Public rooms were expansive and opulently dressed in Victorian and vintage American furnishings.

Our little queen tied up to the big queen's hull and we passengers swarmed aboard the larger craft like curious mice.

The dining room was two stories high and a large theater with a thrust proscenium and balconies rivaled the fanciest of early American vaudeville showcases.

"This is really elegant," I commented to one of our crew members, who'd joined us on the tour. "It has more antiques and fancy decoration than our boat."

She shrugged with a smile. "We don't have anything to prove. Our boat *is* an antique!"

The *American Queen* continued upriver that afternoon, calliope shrieking and steam whistle hooting. We boarded tour buses to visit the birthplace of two people who—for quite different reasons—brought fame to this northern corner of Alabama.

William Christopher Handy, the "father of the blues," gained prominence in Memphis and St. Louis, although he was born in Florence in 1873. His childhood log cabin home is now a museum and archive. Although he gained international fame, W.C. was hardly admired at home. His father, a fundamentalist preacher, once said he would rather follow his son's coffin to the graveyard than hear him play "Satan's music."

The area's other noted personage was spoiled by a very indulgent father. She became a "wild child" who finally was tamed and educated by the remarkable efforts of a strong-minded teacher named Annie Sullivan. Helen Keller was born of upper middle class parents in Tuscumbia, a small town near Florence, in 1880. A year and a half later she was stricken with a disease—probably scarlet fever or meningitis—that left her deaf and blind. When Helen was six, her parents hired Miss Sullivan, who managed to penetrate her dark, silent and angry world. Many of you saw this story portrayed by Anne Bancroft and Patty Duke Austin in the Oscar winning film, *The Miracle Worker*. Miss Keller, of course, went on to become the world's leading advocate for the handicapped. Her childhood home, Ivy Green, is now a museum and shrine to one of the most remarkable women of our age.

"He (God) would not let them take away my soul," Miss Keller once wrote. "Possessing that, I still possess the whole."

We would learn, as the days slid lazily past, that the *Delta Queen* was habit-forming. One couple had cruised with the company twenty-six times and twenty-five of these had been on our boat. Another passenger already had made plans for her next four *Delta* cruises.

We understood their affection for this old boat, an affection not dimmed by their brief flirtation with the larger and fancier *American Queen*. Her small size encourages more camaraderie among guests and crew, and we all enjoyed sailing with a sense of history, on a vintage riverboat. Although completely restored and carefully maintained, the *Delta Queen* shows subtle signs of age, like an older woman with a wrinkle here, a tuck there. She's more mature, more experienced and thus more fascinating than a young lady freshly powdered and painted from the beauty parlor.

ßßß

DAY FIVE

Steamboatin' is a term coined by The Delta Queen Steamboat Company to describe the act of cruising lazily down a river. This was one of those steamboatin' days, with no shore stops and a lot of river miles to cover. The *Delta Queen*, in fact, had cruised through the night instead of tying up.

We awoke to a Mark Twain vision of a misty, wooded shoreline, revealing the first touches of fall color. Out on deck, the air was crisp and clear, following several days of overcast which had—in turn—erased the last muggy days of summer. A squadron of ducks formed a loose V-formation overhead, setting their directional finders for the trip south. This particular stretch of the Tennessee River probably had changed little since Twain's riverboating days.

It was a fine day for steamboatin'—a day to relax and go with the flow of the lazy river. Up in the Texas Lounge, our "riverlorian" (a silly name given to the cruise director, who conducts lectures on river lore) was discussing tomorrow's shore stop at Paducah, Kentucky. In the forward cabin lounge, a gentleman nursed a pair of deuces through a

Eight ladies who had volunteered to be "floozies" dressed up in glad rags and paraded to the whistles and giggles of the rest of the passengers.

friendly hand of poker. Two ladies in the Betty Blake Lounge were taking their turns at the second jigsaw puzzle of the trip, the first having been completed yesterday. It was a fine day for silliness, as well. During Riverboat Follies that afternoon, eight ladies who had volunteered to be "floozies" dressed up in glad rags provided by the cruise staff and paraded to the whistles and giggles of the rest of the passengers. Later, several otherwise mature males engaged in an odd-man-out game of swapping silly hats.

However, not all passengers had shifted into the steamboatin' mode. A man in gym sweats leaned against the Texas Deck rail, talking with his broker on a cellular phone. Another had his right ear fused to a transistor radio, obviously guilty of trying to bring in news from the outside world, or even worse, baseball scores.

Yet who are we to talk? Me sitting here, pecking earnestly at my notebook computer; Betty leaning over my shoulder, disagreeing as usual with my selection of adverbs.

ß ß ß

Even without Luwana, the food aboard the *Queen* would have been fine. It was ample, properly seasoned and creatively prepared, with a strong emphasis on regional cuisine. Our waitress Luwana ensured that it *always* arrived at the proper temperature. It is cliché to call a cruise a movable feast. However, it was particularly

> The midnight buffet was served at 10:30, so hungry passengers wouldn't have to wait so long.

true aboard the *Queen*. From early riser breakfast to buffet breakfast or off-the-menu breakfast to buffet lunch or off-the-menu lunch to midafternoon snack to dinner, one had endless opportunities to stuff one more calorie into one's complaining stomach. And the midnight buffet was served at 10:30, so hungry passengers don't have to wait so long.

Luwana was a handsome girl with a coffee latté complexion, honey colored hair and dark brown eyes, and when she smiled, the tiniest hint of dimples formed below her high cheekbones. That smile was so fetching and I was so smitten that food delivered by her always seemed to taste better.

If she brought a braised hiking shoe to my plate, I probably would have just grinned and asked for the salt.

ß ß ß

DAY SIX

If awards were given for Southern hospitality, the good folks of Paducah, Kentucky, would carry off first prize. Employees and volunteers of the Paducah-McCracken County Tourist Commission came aboard to welcome us and pass out brochures. Others were stationed around town, dressed in easy-to-spot red blazers, to answer our questions and point us in proper directions. Sitting at the junction of the Tennessee and Ohio rivers, Paducah is a handsome old city of ornate brick and masonry buildings, tree-lined streets and brick sidewalks. Although it has suffered the usual suburban flight, its downtown area is undergoing a renaissance, with new shops and professional offices going into old store fronts.

The town has two museums and their staffs proved to be as accommodating as the tourist commission folks. The Market House Museum, in an old cargo and marketing building at the waterfront, opened its doors early for us; the Museum of the American Quilting Society offered a special discount to cruise passengers.

Particularly interesting in the Market House Museum was a reconstructed early twentieth drugstore, complete with yesterday's potions lining its shelves. (I discovered why my mother once took daily doses of Lydia E. Pinkham's Vegetable Compound for health purposes; it's 13 percent alcohol.) The quilt museum is fine if one likes quilts—antique and contemporary—and many of the ladies on our cruise did. The museum also caters to husbands, providing comfortable seating while their wives browse among the bedspreads.

Every Southern town seems to be famous for somebody, and Paducah claims three somebodies. It was founded in 1827 by William Clark of the Le-

Downtown St. Louis, with Busch Stadium to the left, presents an impressive picture from view windows in the top of the Peace Arch.

wis and Clark expedition. Later, the town gave birth to Alben W. Barkley (1877-1956), Harry S Truman's vice president; and Irvin S. Cobb (1876-1944), noted humorist, playwright, lecturer, actor and author of 30 books. He coined my favorite quotation, which hangs above my desk:

If writers were good businessmen, they'd have too much sense to be writers.

ᡒ ᡒ ᡒ

"We'll be entering the Mississippi in about five minutes," the captain announced after dinner.

The Tennessee River had been a series of reservoirs for the most part. Now, after a brief downstream passage from Paducah on the Ohio, we'd start cruising upstream on the Mississippi. Free of dams, it offered a good current as it dutifully drained the heartland of America. It was surprisingly narrow here for the Big Muddy; both shorelines seemed within a stone's throw. Their silhouetted trees and grassy banks were visible even in darkness. As we turned into the flow, the *Queen's* paddlewheel churned lustily in the muddy brown water. Our speed slowed to a determined crawl.

Like Forrest Gump, I walk a lot. Although there was no shortage of on-board activities, I spent much of my time trekking around the decks, working off calories and watching the shoreline slip past. Eleven times around the boat was a mile and passengers had a choice of three circuits, since most riverboat decks are all promenade decks. I liked the upper deck where we could walk with the open sky above, the river below and the banks beyond. Striding along, I never missed a thing—-the passing barges, the skittering pleasure boats, the small shoreside towns with their spired steeples and old brick, the bridges that arched overhead.

Past midnight and I still walked the deck, pacing beneath a canopy of stars as the vintage riverboat churned resolutely toward St. Louis. We planned to go ashore early the next morning to explore the Peace Arch and other St. Louis attractions before catching our plane home, so I should have been getting a good night's sleep. Still, I strolled the deck, watching the dark countryside slip past.

I scanned the shoreline for lights and watched the *Queen's* powerful spotlight dart about, seeking out channel markers that would reveal our position to the pilot. Up around a bend, another spotlight knifed across the surface and it seemed for a moment that the two were playing tag. (Do you remember playing spotlight tag on drive-in movie theater screens?) Then a small cluster of lights, which seemed part of the bank, detached itself and floated toward us, materializing as a towboat with several loaded barges.

ط ط ط

DAY SEVEN

Morning and Betty and I we were back on deck, marveling at a splendid vision. The Mississippi was dressed in a predawn fog, like old Southern lace. It was an ethereal scene—an antebellum Brigadoon. Wisps of mist hugged the shoreline and crawled through the trees, becoming whatever the imagination dictated. Look yonder! Could that be the ghosts of Huck Finn and Tom Sawyer on their frail raft? Yet, how could they be ghosts, when they never existed in the first place—except in the mind of Sam Clemens?

On the pre-dawn Mississippi, aboard a riverboat out of yesterday, anything is possible. If we'd wanted reality, we wouldn't be here. We'd be back home, fussing about taxes and opening the mail.

Listen--!

There's an old man called the Mississippi;
That's the old man that I want to be—

ط ط ط

The majestic (Grand) Coulee tells a heroic tale of vanished power far transcending that of Niagara, and beggaring the leisurely story of....even the Grand Canyon of the Colorado.

— A comment in 1923 by Geologist J Harlan Bretz

Chapter six

COLUMBIA-SNAKE RIVERS

Pursuing Lewis & Clark with Cruise West

Great joy in camp. we are in view of the Ocian, this great Pacific Octean which we been so long anxious to see.

If the Mississippi is the mother river of America, the Columbia is the father stream of the American West. Combined with the Snake, it is the second longest river in the U.S. after the Mississippi-Missouri, and the largest stream flowing into the Pacific.

The river network is *big,* carrying 180 million acre feet of water into the ocean each year, while draining 85 percent of the Pacific Northwest. One can forgive intrepid explorer William Clark, not only for his terrible spelling, but for mistaking the lower portion of the river for the Pacific. As Lewis and Clark's Corps of Volunteers for Northwest Discovery pushed downstream on November 7, 1805, the group broke free of a fog and saw a vast expanse of water ahead, more than a mile wide. They made camp that night and Clark wrote in his journal that they had sighted the Pacific. However, this was still the Columbia; the ocean waited several miles downstream.

CRUISE PLANNER

The cruise ● This is a seven-night "soft adventure" cruise up the Columbia and Snake Rivers through Oregon and Washington, with a turn-around at Lewiston, Idaho. Contact Alaska Sightseeing/Cruise West, Fourth & Battery Building, Suite 700, Seattle, WA 98121; (800) 426-7702 or (206) 441-8687; FAX (206) 441-4757. Passengers view the splendor of the Columbia River Gorge, pass through the many locks of the Columbia and Snake, and go ashore frequently to visit nearby communities. They learn about the history of the Lewis and Clark expedition that passed through here and the settlement of the Oregon Territory, plus the geology, flora and fauna of the region. Alaska Sightseeing/Cruise West also has an extensive offering of land and water excursions in the Inside Passage and mainland Alaska. A San Francisco and Sacramento River cruise was added recently; see box on page 162.

Getting there ● Most major airlines serve Portland, and special air-cruise packages can be arranged. Cruises begin and end at River-front Park downtown. Lodging before and/or after the trip can be arranged at the adjacent Marriott Hotel. Passengers gather there for a pre-cruise briefing and then are escorted to the ship.

The ship ● The *MV Spirit of Columbia* is a recently refurbished 143-foot-long craft especially designed for river cruising. A bow ramp permits shore visits without the need for a dock or shuttle boat. It has forty cabins or suites, all with outside views and private baths. Some have refrigerators and TV/VCR combinations. Other facilities include a single-seating dining room that doubles as a lecture room, lounge and bar, and an upper sun deck. Officers and crew are American.

When to go ● Cruises run from late March through mid-November. The best weather is June through early October, although it's often sunny during shoulder seasons, particularly east of the Columbia Gorge, where the ship spends much of the cruise.

What to bring ● Come prepared for varied weather, from often-rainy Astoria to sometimes-hot eastern Washington. However, the area generally is quite temperate. Attire is casual.

What's included ● Airport transfers and all shore excursions are included in the cruise price, plus loaner binoculars for wildlife spotting. Cocktails and dinner wines are available at additional cost. Featured among the shore excursions are a jetboat trip through Hells Canyon of the Snake River, tours of Bonneville Dam and Fort Clatsop National Memorial, a scenic railway ride on Mount Hood and a winery tour. The ship's library offers a good selection of books and videos on the area and its history. Videos and lectures are offered most days, including talks by visiting experts on local subjects.

ß ß ß

Portland's busy and attractive waterfront is the launch point for cruises up the Columbia and Snake rivers.

This is a river of many personalities. It begins as a seepage from Columbia Lake in the western foothills of British Columbia's Rockies, 2,700 feet above sea level. It flows for 1,210 miles, initially with the restless fury of a mountain stream and then with the lazy drift typical of the world's great rivers. Today, dozens of dams and other diversions impede its progress. However, even before they were built, the river had slowed to a crawl as it looped southward through Washington and then west to the Pacific.

The Snake, the Columbia's largest tributary, also is a multi-dimensional river. Born of snowmelt at 10,000 feet near the Continental Divide above Yellowstone National Park, it careens and cascades through southern Idaho, spilling down several braces of rapids, many now muted by dams. After a relatively calm flow through southwestern Idaho, it swings northward to carve Hells Canyon on the Oregon-Idaho border, one of the deepest gorges in America and a popular whitewater run. The stream calms down again, looping north and west into Washington. It joins the Columbia near the eastern Washington-Oregon border.

The *Spirit of Columbia,* operated by Seattle-based Alaska Sightseeing/Cruise West, travels the full navigable length of the Columbia-Snake system, stepping upstream and down through a series of locks. The run covers 470 miles between the Columbia's mouth at Astoria, Oregon, and the lower end of Hells Canyon at Lewiston, Idaho. In doing so, it retraces much of the route of Lewis and Clark and other adventurers, who used this liquid highway to complete their journeys across the continent early in the last century.

One-week voyages begin at the attractive Portland waterfront on the Willamette River, sail north to the Columbia, east through the Columbia River Gorge and then northeast on the Snake River to Lewiston. Returning downstream, the ship bypasses the Willamette and follows the Columbia to its mouth near Astoria for a visit to Fort Clatsop, where Lewis and Clark spent the winter of 1805-06. It then returns to Portland.

Life aboard the *Spirit* is very casual. Service is accomplished with an informal efficiency that's typical of American crews. Food is ample and tasty, focusing on Northwest regional fare. The sixteen American crew members pull multiple duty. The bartender runs the gift shop and serves as the dinner wine host; dining room staff members also are room stewards. Even the captain, Leigh Reinecke, helps steer incoming passengers to their staterooms. A former Coast Guard lifeboat operator, she's one of the few woman skippers in the cruise industry.

These voyages aren't rigorous outings, but are—according to the company—soft adventures that "attract mature travelers...from the mid-40s to the mid-80s." In other words, seniors won't have a problem keeping pace as they explore the geology, history and scenery of the Pacific Northwest. Frequent lectures or videos focus on the area, the library provides a good selection of regional books and the cruise coordinator offers a running commentary as the ship plies the West's mightiest river system.

ß ß ß

DAY ONE

Anyone who books this cruise should plan an extra day or more and treat Portland as the first shore stop. It's one of America's cleanest, safest and most likable cities, brimming with visitor attractions. Particularly appealing is Tom McCall Waterfront Park where the ship docks. It's a complex of parklands, plazas, shops and marinas. Exploring the park, you may find it hard to believe that this once was a scruffy district of old warehouses, bisected by a noisy expressway. The park's namesake, McCall was the governor largely responsible for putting Oregon on the leading edge of the environmental movement, where it remains today. From the waterfront, it's a short walk to downtown shops, museums, galleries and other parks.

Late in the afternoon of our first day, the *Spirit of Columbia* shrugged off its moorings and headed, not for the Columbia River, but south and upstream on the Willamette. The longest northward flowing river in the country, it cuts a liquid swath through 250 miles of western Oregon. The broad, flat Willamette Valley was the goal of many who crossed the Oregon Trail a century and a half ago. Like Lewis and Clark before them, most used rivers to finish their trek. After the long wagon train journey, they piled their belongings on rafts in eastern Oregon and floated west on the Columbia. They then journeyed south on the Willamette to seek their own personal patch of farmland or settle in one of the new towns along the riverbank.

The broad, flat Willamette Valley was the goal of many who crossed the Oregon Trail a century and a half ago.

Our trip south would be brief; Captain Reinecke wanted to show us the good life of the Willamette streamside before heading north into the Columbia. We sailed past the growing Portland skyline, under several bridges and into the suburbs. Here, the bank was cloaked alternately with forest and luxury homes. Some were cantilevered above the river; others were literally on the water, built onto large rafts anchored to the shoreline. Generations ago, explained our cruise director Larry West, their owners paid no property taxes since they didn't occupy land, although that loophole has since been closed.

As we cruised, West pointed out other suburban residents who perched in the trees or circled lazily overhead. This wooded area is busy with ospreys, great blue herons, spiraling vultures and even an occasional bald eagle.

The small ship made a wide U-turn near the community of Selwood and headed back north, picking its way through a maze of Saturday sailors with speedboats, jet skis and water skiers. After ducking under a dozen bridges, it swept into the Columbia, wider than a mile here, and headed upstream. Our river companions were barges heavy with grain, petroleum, wood chips and other cargo, cruises in both directions.

After dinner, we leaned against the rail, inhaled the pleasantly damp, herbal aroma of the river and watched the distant shorelines slip past. This was cruising American style, with its informal attitude, efficiency and good-natured crew. "You didn't finish your broccoli," our waitress had chided me at dinner.

Although we had taken several cruises to research this book and would take many more, it felt great to be on the water again. Tomorrow night, I would finish my broccoli.

ß ß ß

DAY TWO

Five hundred miles upstream, an ice dam suddenly breaks. A massive wall of water spills from an inland sea and surges through the Columbia Basin. It scours new channels through thick layers of basalt and blasts through the Cascade Range to rip out a gorge a thousand feet deep. The mouths of brooks that flowed into the Columbia are left hanging on the new cliff face. Their end-flows become waterfalls—some of the highest in America. The site of Portland is buried under 400 feet of water. Then, within two days, the inland sea is drained, having released a volume of water ten times greater than the flow of all the world's rivers.

Fortunately, this didn't happen while we were cruising upstream on the *Spirit of Columbia.* It occurred during the last Ice Age, between 12,000 and 15,000 years ago. In fact, it may have happened as many as sixty times.

We had anchored for the night on Reed Island east of Portland. Early this morning, over French toast and oatmeal, we entered the Columbia River Gorge, one of the grandest and most unusual landforms in America. It isn't a narrow chasm but a mile-wide river channel, cut through the Cascade Range and marked by thousand-foot basaltic cliffs.

Scientists had wondered for decades how a river could cut its way through a mountain range, leaving sheer walls in its wake.

Scientists had wondered for decades how a river could cut its way through a mountain range, leaving sheer walls in its wake. A remarkable geologist named J Harlen Bretz came up with a wild notion back in 1919—great ice dams once blocked streams in Idaho and Montana, then shattered to send walls of water across Washington and Oregon. Subsequent studies, including aerial photos showing that low hills in the area were actually ancient gravel bars, have proven that he was right.

This fascinating geological story begins with *coulees,* and we aren't referring to Betty's Chinese farm cousins. The name applies to thick sheets of lava—often more than a mile deep—that oozed across the plains of eastern Washington and Oregon millions of years ago, and hardened into basalt. Coulee also refers to canyon corridors cut through this basaltic layer by stream courses.

One of the Columbia River Gorge's best vantage points is the Crown Point Vista House, reached by a short day trip from Portland before or after the cruise.

When the ice dams broke, they scoured deep channels through this basalt, creating the Columbia gorge and other high-walled courses along the river—not in millions of years, but in minutes! They are variously called Spokane Floods, Bretz Floods and Missoula Floods. The first of these drained a thousand mile long inland sea that geologists have named Lake Missoula. When the ice dam burst, 500 cubic *miles* of water roared west across Washington and swept southward into Oregon's Willamette Valley. Within two days, fifty cubic miles of silt and broken lava were strewn over 16,000 square miles. Compared with the Missoula Floods, the recent eruption of Mount St. Helens just across the border in Washington was little more than a geological hiccup.

The basaltic cliffs formed by these floods rose sheer from the shorelines as we cruised eastward. Bathed in the early mists of morning, patched in places with evergreens and marked by silvery veils of waterfalls, they resembled those romanticized paintings popular with nineteenth century artists. From our midstream position in the mile-wide Columbia Gorge, they didn't appear to be a thousand feet high. However, those trains on the water-level railroad weren't H-O gauge Lionels, and the trucks on Interstate 84 just above weren't Tonka toys. Snaking high above the freeway, rarely visible from our river vantage point, was the Columbia Gorge Highway, Oregon's most popular scenic drive. It winds past several waterfalls formed during the catastrophic Ice Age floods. Standing at the rail, we could pick out the distant glistening threads of Bridal Veil, Wahkeena, Multnomah Falls and others.

One of the great advantages of river travel is that there is always something to see. When not admiring the splendor of the Columbia Gorge or following the wary flight of a fishhawk, we watched the comings and goings of water traffic, from tow boats to speedboats. Windsurfers darted about like bright, single-winged butterflies. The breezy gorge is perhaps the world's most popular windsurfing area. It's also popular for sturgeon fishing, and we passed dozens of boats at anchor, with fishing lines dangling in the water. Sturgeon are among the world's largest freshwater fish, ranging up to 12 or more feet and they are, of course, the source of caviar.

"I've got one on! I've got on one!" One of the fishermen, within a few dozen feet of our boat, shouted excitedly as his pole bent suddenly into a deep arc. Moments later, a foaming splash a hundred yards downstream confirmed that he had indeed hooked a big one. His partner in the boat, seeing the audience aboard the *Spirit,* grinned and extended his palms at arms length, an optimistic measure of a big fish yet to be landed.

We couldn't wait to confirm his measurement, since it takes nearly an hour to bring in a big sturgeon. We had to press on to the first of our river locks, at Bonneville Dam. Passing through a lock is simple yet fascinating. The ship sails into an open-ended box, the downstream end is closed and the box is filled with water by gravity until it reaches the river's upper level. The upriver end opens and out you go. Of course, the simple box at Bonneville Dam is 675 feet long and 86 feet wide, and it holds about 17 million gallons of water. The fascination, then, lies in the size. As we entered the lock, it was easy to imagine that we were aboard a *Star Wars* craft, secure on a tractor beam, being drawn into a giant spaceport.

These locks make river navigation possible nearly 500 miles inland to Lewiston; their attendant dams have turned the rivers into a stair-step chain of lakes. Built by the Army Corps of Engineers, the locks are free to all boaters. However, the Bonneville locktender did receive a typical payment from the chef of the *Spirit of Columbia*—three Scandinavian lemon bars left from lunch.

Freed from the lock, our ship put us ashore for a tour of Bonneville Dam. Corps of Engineers ranger Tom Dinsmore, wearing a proper Smoky Bear hat, regaled us with statistics. They are indeed impressive. Bonneville, completed as a Depression era project in 1937, is one of 202 diversions on the Columbia-Snake river system and their tributaries. Among them, they generate 40 percent of all the

Dams on the Columbia-Snake River system generate 40 percent of all the hydroelectric power in the Unites States.

hydroelectric power in the Unites States. No surprise—the Northwest has the cheapest power rates in the country, about four cents a kilowatt. Bonneville was one of the largest dams in the world when it was completed, although it has since been dwarfed by newer ones, including some on the Columbia-Snake system.

The dams have a down side, Dinsmore explained. Although fish ladders have been built to get migrating salmon upstream to spawn, their fingerlings have trouble reaching the ocean. Dams nullify the currents the young fish need to follow, so they tend to get lost. Also, the turbine generators take their toll.

"The generators don't chop the fish into sushi," he explained. "They suffer from cavitation, the huge pressure changes caused by the rotating blades."

Various systems are being employed, including diverters to get them past the many dams, and even fish barges which transport them below Bonneville. We were guided through the powerhouse and then to the fish viewing room, where a fish counter engages in what must be the world's most boring job. Every fish that passes through the ladder system is counted.

WHAT THE SAM HILL?

Samuel Hill was one of the most fascinating characters of the North-west. Some called him a visionary; others said he was a bit daft. Born in 1857 in Deep River, North Carolina, he earned a law degree and headed west to make his mark.

He wound up in Seattle, where in 1886 he was hired as a legal advisor to Great Northern Railway baron James J. Hill (no relation). He later married hill's daughter Mary, although not necessarily for her future inheritance. The young Hill left the senior Hill's employ after a few years and, through clever investments, made his own fortune.

In 1907, he bought 7,000 acres of sun-toasted grassland in Klikitat County, more than a hundred miles east of Seattle, and set about establishing a utopian Quaker farming community. A few Quakers came, decided it was too windy, remote and inhospitable and promptly left. The buildings in the town Sam platted fell to ruin. But never mind that. He began construction of a replica of England's Stonehenge (see story opposite), and an elaborate French style manor, both perched on windy slopes of his property high above the Columbia. Thhe manor was supposed to be his grand residence, but some historians aren't sure. Wrote noted Northwest author Steward Holbrook in The Columbia in 1956:

The reasons for erecting this costly and improbable pile in the vast nothingness of the mid-Columbia were never clear. Probably they were not clear even to Sam Hill himself. At different times over the years he gave various explanations: It was to be some sort of cultural center; again it was to be an international museum; then it was to be a fortress to stop invaders of the United States which—Hill stated—would be Japanese warships...

Whatever its purpose, he named it Maryhill in honor of his wife Mary and their child. However, the senior Mary never went near the place, preferring the urban life of Seattle. But no matter. Since his mansion could be reached only by river, Sam prevailed upon Washington state legislators to build a road to it, through the Columbia River gorge. They showed no interest, so he approached Oregon legislators, who offered limited support, mostly by granting a right-of-way. With his engineer friend Samuel Lancaster, Hill began construction on the Columbia Gorge Highway. It was to become the first scenic highway in America.

The gregarious Hill traveled frequently to Europe, where he accumulated a curious gaggle of friends that ranged from aging American-born Folies-Bergére dancer Loie Fuller to Queen Marie of Romania. In 1926, before his mansion or museum was finished, Sam convinced Loie and Queen Marie to come for a grand dedication. The entourage crossed the Atlantic, crossed the continent and traveled from Portland by Sam's new scenic highway and by boat to Maryhill. There, the Queen delivered a rambling speech about dreamers (while perhaps looking askance at her curious friend), donated a few pieces of furniture and personal items for exhibit, and hastened back to Europe.

Sam died five years later, with his museum still unfinished. It finally was completed through the help of San Francisco sugar heir and philanthropist Alma de Bretteville Spreckles. Maryhill Museum opened to the public on May 13, 1940, the 83rd anniversary of Hill's birth.

"A computer could count the fish," Dinsmore pointed out, "but it couldn't identify the species."

After counting a few fish, we boarded buses for a drive along the Washington side into what has become known as Sam Hill Country. Now east of the steepest part of the gorge, we passed through beige countryside. The Cascade Range forms a rain barrier between the lush western side of the Pacific Northwest and the arid east. Scars of the Missoula floods are even more dramatic here, for no thick forest covers the terraced basaltic cliffs carved by the rushing torrents. Seven thousand acres of this barren countryside was purchased in 1907 by Sam Hill, an idealistic Quaker who had built the Columbia Gorge Highway. He also built two major structures, both curiously misplaced, yet each year they attract hundreds of thousands of visitors.

Time Magazine *called Sam Hill's manor the "loneliest museum in the world."*

We stopped first at Maryhill Museum of Art, housed in an imposing poured concrete chateau which, save for its lawns and wind-bent poplars, would look rather stark on its perch above the Columbia. Despite its remote location—*Time* magazine called it the "loneliest museum in the world"—it out- draws the art museums of both Seattle and Portland. Started by Hill in 1914, it wasn't completed until 1940. It offers an outstanding and eclectic collection of art, from European masters to artifacts of many Native American tribes. Particularly impressive is an August Rodin retrospective with bronzes, clay models and simple figures he sculpted in his early years for food and rent before he became known.

A short drive through more soft brown countryside took us to Sam's other monument, a new world edition of Stonehenge, occupying another slope above the river. According to Sam's hired experts, this was the way the Druid monument looked about 5,000 years ago—a ring of stones connected by capstones, with smaller rings of free-standing stones inside. Hill thought the original Stonehenge had been a sacrificial altar, so he dedicated his to 13 Klikitat County men killed in action during World War I. Experts today think the original was a solar observatory, because of the positions of the stones.

From Stonehenge, we drove to The Dalles, where our ship awaited. (The town's odd name comes from the French word for plateaus, describing several rapid-infested islands in the river. They're now under water, drowned by The Dalles Dam.) Back aboard, we passed through the dam's lock and then continued upstream. We sailed through a barren, treeless area of low basaltic bluffs, buttes and ridges, like a beige Grand Canyon filled to the brim.

After dinner, we were lifted over the John Day Dam. One of the highest single-lift locks in the world, it boosted us 113 feet. Watching a 750-ton lift gate close behind us in the gathering darkness, we again had visions of a set for *Star Wars.*

ß ß ß

DAY THREE

This was a rite of passage day, a long cruise through the flood carved courses of the Columbia and then the Snake rivers, headed for the end of ship navigation at Lewiston. We entered the Snake at mid-morning in the Tri-Cities area of Pasco, Kennewick and Richland. We then shed much of

A huge 750-ton lift gate on the lock at the John Day Dam closes behind the Spirit of Columbia; it's one of the highest lifting locks in the world.

civilization, spending a lazy day cruising past the almost-monotonous stark beauty of columnar basalt bluffs and ridges.

Four dams, built between 1961 and 1975, extend river navigation to the Idaho border. Each---Ice Harbor, Lower Monumental, Little Goose and Lower Granite---steps river traffic up or down more than a hundred feet. By the time we reached Lewiston early in the morning of day four, we would be more than 400 miles east of Portland and 740 feet above sea level.

En route, we paused at Levey Park, an attractive streamside recreation area, for a couple of hours of croquet, leg- stretching, sunning and a barbecue. A bit farther along, we dipped briefly into the Palouse River, where Lewis and Clark paused. This marks the border of "Palouse Country," 4,000 square miles of wind-deposited fine grain loam called *loess*. It comprises the heart of the Washington-Oregon- Idaho wheat country. Wheat, in fact, is one of the primary reasons for the installation of locks on the many Columbia-Snake river dams. One sixth of the world's exported wheat travels down these streams on river barges.

ß ß ß

DAY FOUR

We purchased fish & dogs from those people (Nez Perce), dined and proceeded on. Sixty miles below...we arived at a large southerly fork. This South fork (is the) Lewis River. on this fork a little above its mouth resides a Chief who as the Indians say has more horses than he can count...

On October 10, 1805, Lewis and Clark paddled down the Clearwater River and "haveing passed 5 rapids," entered a larger stream, which Clark named in honor of Lewis. (It has since been re-named the Snake.) They made camp that night, and the next morning, they "set out early and proceeded on." They had entered the river system that would take them to the Pacific. As they left, Clark recorded in his journal that the "Cho-pun- ish or Pierced nose Indians are Stout likely men, handsome women, and verry dressey in their way...." However, in their manner of dress, "the men exposed those parts which are generally kept from view." That, presumably, was a summer uniform.

The Nez Perce were extremely helpful to the Corps of Discovery, which their descendants must have regretted. This was the tribe of Chief Joseph, who was forced into epic flight after white settlers had taken his lands in nearby northeastern Oregon. Later that day, we would pass the point where Joseph and his tribe crossed the Snake River, seeking sanctuary in Idaho and ultimately in Canada.

Two communities have sprouted where the Corps of Discovery made camp among the Nez Perce—Lewiston, Idaho, and Clarkston, Washington. Just beyond this point, the Snake flows from rapid- infested Hells Canyon. It is thus the end of the line for the *Spirit of Columbia.* It was not, however, the end of our Snake River trek. Shortly after breakfast, we would board jetboats and follow the river another seventy miles into Hells Canyon.

Jetboats, should you wonder, are powered by water turbines instead of propellers. They draft only a few inches of water and can skim over rapids efficiently if not gracefully. A jetboater once told me he could operate on a wet sidewalk, although that was a slight exaggeration. Our craft was the *Hells Canyon Rose,* a 1,150-horsepower rig operated by Beamers Hells Canyon Tours. It would take us into the upper reaches of one of America's most rugged and splendid gorges.

Although much of the Snake has been dammed, the stretch through rugged Hells canyon has changed very little. The chasm for the most part is a jagged vee, tilting down from the heights of the Wallowa Mountains in Oregon and Washington and the Seven Devils in Idaho. The craggy, convoluted slopes, mostly treeless, are cloaked in green and tawny grasses, with some

The boat ran a slippery slalom course, slamming through the rapids and dodging logs floating downstream.

ponderosa forests on their upper reaches. The sharp eyes of our boatman spotted occasional bighorn sheep, deer and other creatures as we careened upstream. The boat ran a slippery slalom course, slamming through the outer edges of rapids and dodging logs floating downstream from an unusually heavy spring runoff. (Frankly, we prefer whitewater rafts to this jolting ride.)

At one point in our hasty trip, our boatman slowed his craft to an idle, treaded water against the swift downflow, and pointed out a young bull elk lounging in a grassy meadow near the riverbank. The animal swung its head in our direction, shrugged and returned to its contemplation.

"Some environmentalist want to ban jetboats on this river because they say the noise scares wildlife," our operator said. "As you can see, that animal is absolutely terrified."

The elk looked up again and nodded in agreement.

We had lunch at Copper Creek Lodge, deep into the Hells Canyon wilderness and reached only by boat. After a rural feast of fried chicken, potato salad and biscuits, we hurried back downstream.

ßßß

DAY FIVE

Were they brave, or were they stupid?" The park ranger posed this question during our visit to Whitman Mission National Historic Site near Walla Walla, Washington.

After cruising downstream on the Snake River the night before, we had parked our boat near its confluence with the Columbia. This would be a busy day, as most had been. We would visit the mission site near Walla Walla, pause at a fine community museum at old Fort Walla Walla, return to the ship for lunch and then sip wine at Columbia Crest, the largest winery in Washington.

The museum was interesting, particularly a mockup of an 1886 grain combine drawn by 33 mules that somehow managed not to become entangled in their harness. At Columbia Crest, the wine was fine. After a tour past ranks of stainless steel tanks and rattling high-speed bottling lines, we sipped a bit, decided that the Merlot was particularly good and captured a few bottles for future use.

It was the Whitman mission site, however, that left the greatest impression.

The Whitman tale is legend among Western historians. In 1836, well before traffic was established on the Oregon Trail, missionary-doctor Marcus Whitman and his new bride Narcissa were sent west to establish a religious outpost. They selected a site near the Cayuse village of Waiilatpu. One of the most imperious and independent American Indian tribes, the Cayuse didn't take well to religion, farming or domestic chores that the Whitmans tried to impose. Still, the mission thrived as an important way station as pioneer traffic increased in the area.

In 1847, a measles epidemic brought by emigrants swept through the tribe. They had no resistance to this strange disease and half their small band of 400 perished. The Whitmans were warned repeatedly to leave their mission and seek sanctuary at nearby Fort Walla Walla. The Indians had made threats

The Whitmans insisted on staying, to continue treating stricken Indians they had taken into their mission.

against them, blaming them for the epidemic. They insisted on staying, to continue treating stricken Indians they had taken into their mission. On November 29, a small group of Cayuse stormed the mission, tomahawked Dr. Whitman and shot Narcissa. When the massacre ended, the Whitmans and eleven others were dead and fifty whites were taken hostage. The captives later were ransomed by Peter Skene Ogden of the Hudson's Bay Company.

"So, were the Whitmans stupid for not leaving?" The ranger paused for a moment, then he added: "Let's put it in current perspective. Suppose fire was sweeping through your boat and you were near the gangplank. Would you run for safety, or would you go back and try to save the others?"

With this troubling thought in our minds, we watched a video on the Whitmans, studied exhibits in a fine little museum and then walked about

Little more than a speck below, a jetboat hurries up the Snake River through Hell's Canyon, one of the world's deepest gorges.

the grounds. Lush stands of rye grass lined the pathway from the interpretive center to the original mission site. As we walked, bees buzzed about blooming apple trees, and from somewhere in the rye grass, a red-winged blackbird warbled. It's a pleasant place as massacre sites go.

Only outlines of the original mission remain. On a nearby hill, a monument erected fifty years after the massacre was inscribed simply: "Whitman." Narcissa used to climbed this hill to watch for her husband, returning from some mission of mercy. Ever the optimist, the young woman had written in her diary three years before she died:

Here we are, one family alone, a waymark, as it were, or center post, about which multitudes will or must gather this winter. And these we must feed and warm to the extent of our powers.

We followed a path down off the hill and came upon the Great Grave, where the Whitmans and other victims were buried. We stood there in silence, still wondering: "Were they brave...?"

ß ß ß

DAY SIX

Mount Hood, Oregon's tallest peak at 11,237 feet, had eluded us on the upriver leg, hiding shyly behind cloud cover. This morning, it stood gloriously against the skyline as we cruised into the town of Hood River. An almost symmetrical volcanic cone, it has been compared with Japan's Mount Fuji in shape and splendor.

Hood River, with a population of 4,600, is attractively tiered above the Columbia and rimmed by forests and apple and pear orchards. Its architecture ranges from turn of the century brickfront to art deco and old storefronts house several galleries, antique shops and nearly a dozen windsurfing shops. Because of the prevailing winds puffing up Columbia River Gorge, Hood River is the windsurfing—or sailboarding, if you prefer—capital of the world.

After an early-morning browse through town, we joined the rest of the passengers for the day's outing—a trip into the foothills on the Mount Hood Scenic Railroad. This isn't a steam train but a working diesel locomotive that hauls fruit and lumber when it isn't hauling tourists. The cars are vintage, however—early twentieth century passenger coaches. The train squeaked and groaned as it climbed into Mount Hood's foothills, alternately passing thick stands of evergreens and orderly ranks of pear and apple trees. Occasionally, clumps of trees would part like green curtains for quick glimpses of Mount Hood above us, and massive, broad-shouldered Mount Adams, across the Columbia in Washington.

As we approached the end of our run, in the old fruit packing town of Parkdale, the majestic Hood blossomed into full view. We picnicked in a park and then checked out the tiny town.

Down from the mountain and back on the *Spirit*, we headed again into Columbia Gorge. As the ship sailed into the late afternoon light, we stood on the foredeck and watched a passing panorama of life on the river. Leaning lazily against the rail, we caught glimpses of Mount Hood through gaps in the gorge walls, bright flashes of windsurfers and an occasional osprey, dive bombing for fish to deliver to its nestlings atop a nearby snag.

ßßß

DAY SEVEN

O*! how horriable is the day. waves brakeing with great violence against the Shore throwing Water into our Camp &c. all wet and confined to our Shelters*
Friday November 22nd, 1805

in the evening Seven indians of the Clot sop Nation came over in a Canoe, they brought with them 2 Sea otter Skins for which they asked blue beads &c.
Saturday November 23rd, 1805

After Lewis and Clark reached the mouth of the Columbia, they camped first on the cold, windswept Washington side. The next day, they met several Clatsop Indians, who suggested that their side of the river—in present-day Oregon—was more hospitable. They spent the winter there, naming their camp in honor of the friendly Indians, and headed back home the following spring. It was not entirely a cold and lonely winter, as Clark noted:

An old woman & Wife to a Cheif...came and made a Camp near ours. She brought with her 6 young Squaws I believe for the purpose of Gratifying the passions of the men of our party... Those people appear to View Sensuality as a Necessary evel, and do not appear to abhor it as a Crime in the unmarried state.

We ended our exploration of the Columbia at the Pacific Ocean, near the site where Lewis and Clark had wintered. During the night, we had cruised past the mouth of the Willamette River and followed the Columbia to Astoria. Established in 1811 by John Jacob Astor's American Fur Trading Company, it's regarded by some historians as the oldest American settlement west of the Rockies. Astor himself never set foot in his namesake town.

Mount Hood Scenic Railway passengers pause for a picnic in the hamlet of Parkdale, with snowy Mount Hood offering an imposing backdrop.

An attractive old community terraced into thickly wooded hills, Astoria greeted us at first light. Nothing of its early days remains, since the town burned to the dirt in 1882. However, it offers a fine collection of Victorian homes, plus the outstanding Columbia River Maritime Museum and—just outside of town—Fort Clatsop National Memorial. Our final day would be a busy one.

The *Spirit's* Astoria berth was a rather slender slip near the maritime museum, adjacent to the U.S. Coast Guard cutter *Steadfast*. More easily than I could fit a car into a tight parking space, Captain Reinecke eased her ship into the narrow moorage and snugged it against the dock, without having to use the bow thruster. This was accomplished with cool confidence, under the watchful eyes of several coast guardsmen aboard the *Steadfast*.

"Are those guys friends of yours?" I asked as Leigh cut the engines.

The former coast guardswoman smiled and shook her head. "No, but I knew they were watching me."

We walked to the nearby museum, where enthusiastic docent Bud McKinney took us in hand. This exceptional archive covers every aspect of boating and Northwest maritime history. Because of shifting sandbars and tidal currents, the Columbia was one of the world's most difficult river entrances until dredging and modern navigational equipment eased passage. Pieces of foundered ships and histories of significant shipwrecks are prominent among the museum's displays.

"We've had more than 2,000 craft—big and small—wrecked along our coast and in the mouth of the Columbia," he said. "I could talk about wrecks all day long if you turned me loose."

His favorite story, however, concerns Astoria's bawdy days as a whaling port in the last century. Sailors often jumped ship here, so replacements were shanghaied from houses of ill fame, for which the madam received a fee of $50 each. The town was built on stilts over the river, and prostitutes would slip a mickey into their patrons' drinks and drop them through a hatch into a waiting rowboat. A particularly notorious madam was given a requisi-

CALIFORNIA CRUISIN'—A fine way to sip wine

Alaska Sightseeing/Cruise West offers voyages from San Francisco Bay to the Napa Valley wine country and historic Sacramento aboard the *Spirit of Alaska*. These short cruises leave from the art colony of Sausalito, across the Golden Gate Bridge from San Francisco.

Our cruise, which departed Sausalito on a cool November evening, began with an almost magical vision of the lights of San Francisco, dancing fairy-like off the waters of the bay. The dinner bell sounded and our "wine tour" began well before we reached the wine country. Members of two leading Napa Valley wineries had come aboard to school us in the fine art of wine tasting and appreciation. We learned how to swirl, sniff and sip to pick up all the subtleties of this most civilized beverage. We then settled down to a fine dinner of ling cod *en papillote*, the perfect companion for an outstanding Sauvignon Blanc.

We awoke the next morning in the Napa Valley, for we had cruised up the Napa River during the night. Our hosts had arranged a delightfully busy day in this legendary vale of wine. We first sipped fine sparkling wines in the ancient caves of Schramsberg, whose products once were served at Nixon presidential dinners. We then traveled to Sterling Vineyards, an imposing Moorish style winery perched dramatically atop a bluff above the vineyards, reached by an aerial tram. And then to Rutherford Hill Winery, where we were permitted to practice our newly-achieved skills as winemakers. Tables were set with three different "base wines"—two Merlots and a Cabernet Franc. Our challenge was to blend these into wines of our personal liking. It took me forty-five minutes and perhaps too many sips to arrive at my ideal dinner wine!

Clutching my cherished bottle of *Chateau du Betté*, I hurried to catch the others. We had one more stop—a catered wine tasting dinner served in the aging cellars of a Napa Valley winery. What a grand way to end this day of wine and rosés!

Into the California Delta

From Napa, we cruised through the California Delta, a maze of waterways created by the marriage of several rivers, and then we sailed up the Sacramento River, following the route of early-day paddlewheelers. We put ashore at Old Sacramento State Historic Park to tour vintage brick buildings that house boutiques, restaurants and exhibit centers. This waterfront is soaked with history. It was from here that many fortune- seekers began their search for California gold. Here, the legendary Pony Express and the first Transcontinental Railroad ended their long treks.

In a symbolic linking of yesterday and today, our modern cruise ship tied up next to the old riverboat *Delta King*, which once cruised between San Francisco and Sacramento. It's now permanently moored at Old Sacramento, converted into a hotel, restaurant and theater. The *King's* sister, the *Delta Queen*, now sails the rivers of the American South and Midwest. We were curious to see the *Delta King* since we'd already met the *Queen*; she wrote the previous chapter in this book; see page 133.

To learn more about California's wine country, delta, historic Sacramento and the gold rush, pick up copies of these Pine Cone Press publications—*The Best of the Wine Country, The Best of the Gold Country* and *Northern California Discovery Guide*.   — Betty Woo Martin

tion for three men, but she had only two customers that night. To complete her order, she doped her husband and rolled him down the hatch.

Four years later, his ship returned to Astoria and, being a man of remarkable temperament, he forgave his wife and moved back in. He found a job with the city, repairing pier pilings. After a couple of years on the job, he fell through a hole in a damaged pier and drowned. His wife sued the city for a thousand dollars.

"No way, madam," the judge said at the trial. "Fifty dollars is all you got for him the first time and that's all I'm awarding you now!"

We completed our Astoria visit with a tour to nearby Fort Clatsop and then Cannon Beach, a tourist village on the Pacific with trendy shops and a long, sandy strand. No shred of Lewis and Clark's original log fort survived; it decayed and dissolved back into the forest from which it was hacked. An exact replica has been built, complete with mud-chinked logs and rawhide bunks with deerskin coverlets. Fires stoked by rangers during living history demonstrations give the quarters a properly smoky, musty aroma.

During our visit, costumed docents were making tallow candles, rendering animal fat purchased from local markets for a few cents a pound. It's one of several frontier and Indian skills they demonstrate for tourists, using tools and raw materials that were typical of the period.

"Life was tough then, but people could live off the land, with a little effort," said a young buckskin clad woman wearing granny glasses. "There was game in the forest, and berries on the bushes."

Close inspection revealed that they occasionally supplemented their frontier diet with Quaker granola bars.

ß ß ß

*As idle as a painted ship
Upon a painted ocean.*
**— From The Ancient Mariner
by Samuel Taylor Coleridge**

PART III
Mexico, the Caribbean And Central America

The gleaming white Wind Star *and a weathered fishing boat offer pleasing contrast in the small harbor of Soufriâre on St. Lucia in the Caribbean.*

A curious sea-lion came out to look us over, a tawny, crusty old fellow with rakish mustaches and the scars of battle on his shoulders. Then, satisfied, he snorted and cut for shore and some sea-lion appointment. They always have them, it's just a matter of getting around to keeping them.
— **John Steinbeck,** *The Log from the Sea of Cortez*

Chapter seven

THE BAJA
Communing with whales on the *Spirit*

Its engines purring like a kitten with a cold, the *Spirit of Adventure* slipped through the shallow entrance of Laguna San Ignacio. We were beginning our third day exploring the fauna and flora of Baja California from this small craft. We had walked among elephant seal herds and examined strange desert plants. We'd cruised in skiffs past colonies of squawking sea birds, playful sea lions and shy seals that would take to the water on our approach and then watch us from the surf through their dark, sad eyes.

Although our trip had just begun, we were amazed at the diversity and abundance of wildlife along the Baja coast. We were now entering San Ignacio Lagoon, one of the winter-spring dominions of *Eschrichus robustus*, the Pacific gray whale. Every winter, they migrate several thousand miles from Alaska to the calm lagoons of Mexico's Baja peninsula, where they give birth, mate and then begin their long journey back home.

We'd seen several swimming off the boat as we traveled south from San Diego, their barnacle encrusted backs glistening in the Baja sun. They had for the most part kept their distance. Now, they were all about us, some only yards away, their dark forms slipping silently through the sea. Occasionally,

CRUISE PLANNER

The cruise • This is an eleven-day expedition to observe whales and other wildlife along Mexico's Baja Peninsula. It begins in San Diego, swings around Baja's tip and ends in La Paz. Contact Spirit of Adventure Charters, 1646 Willow St., San Diego, CA 92106, (619) 226-1729; or Pacific Sea Fari Tours, H&M Landing, 2803 Emerson St., San Diego, CA 92106, (619) 226-8224. In addition to this trip, six to fourteen-day Baja wildlife outings are available. Some are San Diego round-trippers; others end in Cabo San Lucas.

Getting there • Trips depart H&M Landing, a five-minute cab ride from San Diego International Airport. Aero California, a privately owned Mexican airline, provides service from Cabo San Lucas (Los Cabos) and La Paz to Los Angeles or Tijuana in northern Baja. For flight reservations and schedule information, call (800) 237-6225. Return flights from Los Cabos or La Paz aren't included in the cruise price, although bus service from Tijuana to San Diego is. Inexpensive parking is available for those who drive to San Diego.

The ship • The *M/V Spirit of Adventure* is an 88-foot diesel powered expedition ship with fourteen small Pullman style cabins. A combination dining room/salon, where all passengers can be seated at once, is set up with a TV/VCR and slide projector for films and lectures. Officers and crew are American.

When to go • Trips are timed to the migration of the gray whales in and out of the lagoons of Baja California, from January through early April. This also is a good time to see herds of elephant seals, sea lions, seals and sea birds that hang out on islands and sheltered coastal coves of the Baja. Peak period for whale watching generally is mid-February through mid-March.

What to bring • Proof of birth such as a drivers' license or passport are needed by American citizens, along with a Mexican Tourist Card, which is arranged by your hosts. Casual attire is the uniform of the day. Layered clothing is appropriate for the arid, warm-to-chilly winter-spring weather of Baja California, when temperatures can range from 90 in the daytime to 50 at night. Bring binoculars and a telephoto lens for all that wildlife.

What's included • All excursions are included in the cost of the cruise. They consist mostly of onshore hikes to assorted wildlife rookeries led by naturalists, and skiff cruises for close-up observation of whales and other creatures in and out of the water. There are also stops for snorkeling and other water sports. If you want to photograph whales, save your film until you enter the lagoons. They'll appear frequently as the ship cruises offshore, but rarely within good camera range. A limited number of swim fins, masks and snorkels is available, although you may prefer to bring your own. Snorkeling is particularly good in the Sea of Cortez.

What to buy • There are no town stops on this particular itinerary, except La Paz at the end of the trip, where you may have a few hours to shop for typical Mexican handicrafts and curios before your flight back to Tijuana. Some trips end at Cabo San Lucas, which also has the usual handicraft and curio shops.

they arched their backs above the water to breath through their blowholes with whispered sighs and then settle below the surface to again become shadowy shapes.

Suddenly, a few feet off the bow, a huge whale lurched into the air, nearly clearing the water, and then fell back with a mighty splash. One of the German passengers nearly dropped his camcorder.

"Mein Gott!" he exclaimed.

ß ß ß

Although whales aren't the only objects of study on these voyages down the Baja peninsula, they certainly are the stars of the show.

The order of *cetacea*—fish-like mammals—has fascinated scholars, poets and curious onlookers ever since Jonah was swallowed by a "great fish" which presumably, although never identified, was a whale. The event never happened, of course; Jonah couldn't have made it past the baleen. The story, which originated not as Biblical writing but as an anonymous tale in the fourth century B.C., was allegorical. Jonah represented the people of Israel, who would be swallowed up by the warlike Assyrians unless these aggressors could be convinced of the power of God. Jonah was dispatched by the Almighty to give them The Word but he chickened out and fled the Assyrian capital by ship. A great storm besieged the craft and the frightened crew, believing it was God's wrath against Jonah, threw him overboard. He was promptly swallowed by a great fish and imprisoned inside for three days until he agreed to return and face the Assyrians. To ensure that he accomplished his assigned task, God ordered the fish disgorge him back on the Assyrian shore.

Whales have been around for more than 50 million years, descended from creatures that—having originally come from the sea—returned to it. Evidence such as finger-like bones in their flippers and useless hipbones still suspended within their mass prove that their ancestors walked on land. After surviving those 50 millennia, whales were nearly exterminated by relentless hunting in fewer than a hundred years.

Whaling has been going on for centuries, but only with the development of fast moving motor driven ships and exploding harpoons has the species been seriously threatened. Considerable public sympathy for whales and their smaller dolphin and killer whale kin has been generated in recent decades by movies, TV shows, folk songs and—of course—whale watching trips. Only a couple of nations now hunt whales commercially.

Pacific gray whales have the longest migration pattern of any mammal, a 9,000-mile swim from Alaska's Bering Sea to the Baja Peninsula.

Pacific gray whales have the longest migration pattern of any mammal, a 9,000-mile round trip from Alaska's Bering Sea along the coast of North America to the Baja peninsula. They feed on plankton and shrimp-like krill in arctic waters and then in October as the days begin to cool, they begin their long trip south. In the still waters of Baja bays and lagoons they give birth, mate (beneficiaries of a handy thirteen-month gestation cycle) and start north with their new calves.

Hundreds of thousands of people take short day trips off the American west coast to watch these great beasts pass, particularly on their northbound trek, when mothers and calves travel closer to the coast to avoid marauding killer whales. However, the ultimate whale watching experiences are in Baja

Spirit of Adventure *passengers enjoy an afternoon of swimming and snorkeling in the Sea of Cortez; the woman to the left is in mid-air, taking a plunge.*

California, the only place where whales allow visitors to approach so closely that they sometimes can actually touch them. Grays aren't the largest of whales, but at forty to forty-five feet and more than thirty tons, they're certainly impressive beasts. Getting cozy with an animal of that size is one of humankind's most fascinating encounters with the wild.

Many Baja trips—such as the one we were taking—are further enhanced by the presence of onboard experts, who conduct shore excursions and evening lectures. Our authority was friendly, gregarious Pieter Folkens, whose extensive knowledge of sea mammals contributed greatly to ours. Folkens is one of the world's leading illustrators of marine mammals and a creator of animated replicas for films such as *Free Willie* and the whale-based *Star Trek IV: The Voyage Home.*

If whales are the stars of the Baja show, they're surrounded by a fascinating supporting cast. Other sea mammals appear frequently as character actors, ranging from playful and gregarious sea lions and shy harbor seals to the ponderous elephant seals. Dolphins and porpoises, distant whale cousins, dance about the water, often riding the ship's wake just inches off the bow. Bird life is abundant; voyagers will see curious orange-billed oyster catchers, ungainly brown pelicans that become suddenly graceful when they explode into flight, and all manner of loons, grebes and the ubiquitous seagull.

The Baja itself is a major attraction. This arid peninsula, 800 miles long and less than a hundred miles wide, is one of the world's most untouched regions, despite its proximity to the United States and mainland Mexico. Although towns are clustered at its northern border with California and resorts thrive at the southern tip, the rest of Baja has been for the most part left to nature. Mountainous desert terrain, sizzling hot summers and scant rainfall—ten inches a year or less—have discouraged settlement.

Big fish, small ship

Only small ships with shallow drafts can cross the sandbars into Baja California's lagoons for closeups of the gray whale. The first whale watching trips, developed by H&M Landing of San Diego, were conducted in sportfishing boats. In recent years, larger craft have been used although the shallow lagoons still limit their size.

Cozy is a proper way to describe accommodations aboard the 88- foot *Spirit of Adventure*, which we boarded in San Diego Bay for our February trip south. Two bunk beds, a small closet, two drawers under the lower bunk and a storage compartment comprised the accouterments in our small cabins. Four bathrooms—three with showers—were down the hall. More accurately, they were up a short gangway and aft.

A small kitchen was amidships, where the cook (on our cruise, a hefty gentleman appropriately nicknamed Bubba) and his assistant prepared and served a startling variety of food. Three large meals were augmented by the mid-morning and mid-afternoon emergence of muffins, cookies, fruit and beverages. Forward was the multi-function salon, the ship's activity center. This was the dining room, lecture hall, bar (self-service beer and soft drinks), natural history library and—for those who write books as they travel—the composing room.

Snug yet comfortable, capable of skimming over the shallows and thrusting its slender bow into small coves, remarkably stable at sea, our *Spirit of Adventure* was aptly named.

ළ ළ ළ

DAY ONE

San Diego on this cool February night was a low-lying garland of lights strung around the city's huge natural harbor. As our ship cleared the bay and pressed southward on a calm, windless sea, that garland of lights appeared to unravel and follow us. It marked the heavily populated coastal corridor between San Diego and the Mexican border, about 20 miles south. Before morning, however, our little 88-foot craft would take us to some of the most remote regions of the Western Hemisphere.

Betty and I were exhausted—her through a marathon of flights, me through worry—so we retired early and were soon drummed to sleep by the thrumming of the *Spirit's* diesel engines. Through the nervous miracle of flight, Betty—who had been on a press trip to Cuba—left Havana that afternoon and, after three plane changes, arrived in San Diego half an hour before the ship was scheduled to depart. My task—having arrived in San Diego earlier—was to meet her at the airport, seize her roll-on baggage and get her to the ship on time.

ළ ළ ළ

DAY TWO

First call to breakfast!" Walter's announcement seemed distant, vague, perhaps part of some culinary dream.

"Last call to breakfast!" We awoke with a start, scrambled quickly into our clothes—no simple task in our cozy cabin—and stumbled up the gangway. Although it seemed only minutes, an hour had passed since the first break-

Like liquid ghosts, these dolphins ride the bow wake of the Spirit of Discovery, skimming just beneath the surface.

fast call. As we slept, the ship had paused in Ensenada to clear Mexican customs and we were headed for our first stop—the island bird rookery of Todo Santos. Walter, the cook's assistant, handed us plates laden with scrambled eggs and ham with buttered English muffins on the side.

We had eaten only a few bites when Skipper Mike Keating called: "Dolphins off the bow!"

It would be the first of many interrupted meals. We hurried forward to discover a small and certainly frisky herd of bottlenosed dolphins playing tag with the ship's prow. In graceful liquid ballet, they sliced through the water, running easily with the ship, surfacing for a quick puff of a breath, occasionally rolling sideways to glance up at us. Although the ship moved along at a good fifteen knots, these "bow riders" kept pace easily, like jet propelled torpedoes. The rapid undulations of their flat tails—their means of propulsion—were barely discernible. About a dozen dolphins rode the bow. We saw others slanting toward the ship from afar, like free safeties taking an angle on a runaway ball carrier.

We soon realized that—much to our satisfaction—our blithe *Spirit* rarely traveled in a straight line or set a predictable pace. Our first whale sighting—three grays headed back to Alaska—sent our southbound ship in a wide turn to follow them briefly north while eager cameras and minicams clicked, whirred and purred. Later that day, a group of small

"You shouldn't bother. When you kill one fly, a thousand come to the funeral."

dolphins came to play in the ship's wake, bouncing off the ripples and leaping high in the air.

The ship followed a *general* course, of course, with planned stops at islands, bays and lagoons where wildlife flourished. Off Todo Santos, we boarded skiffs for a close-up cruise around the island's rough, rocky shoreline. Uninhabited except for seasonal fishermen, it was a few acres of rough lava, currently wearing a green derby from recent rains. Thousands of sea birds occupied its nooks and crevices; others swam in lazy circles above. Offshore ridges and seastacks, through which our boat operator ran a tricky slalom course, were painted with the birds' personal patina. Our skiff driver began pointing out residents of the island.

"See that little black guy with the beak like a carrot? That's a black oystercatcher."

Others presenting themselves for identification included double crested cormorants, California brown pelicans, frigate birds and assorted gulls including the ubiquitous California gull ("Garbage gull," said our driver with disdain.) Returning to the ship, we could smell fresh blueberry muffins as we climbed the ladder from the skiff. They had just emerged from Bubba's oven and they were excellent. Normally, the skiffs land on Todo Santos, but the island was busy with a recent hatching of kelp flies so we had stayed just offshore. Even so, a few followed us back on board. Betty, jealously guarding her blueberry muffin, busied herself trying to swat them.

"You shouldn't bother," said one of the passengers from Switzerland. "When you kill one fly, a thousand come to the funeral."

That evening, as the dining room became—at the flick of a slide projector switch—the lecture hall, we learned about tomorrow's shore excursion, San Benito Island. It's home to that great, ponderous and comical genetical aberration, the northern elephant seal. If Mother Nature ever held an ugly contest, the adult male of this species would carry away the prize.

᠊ᢣᡲᢣᢥ

DAY THREE

Through the night and into the morning, the *Spirit of Adventure* pressed southward to keep its date with Mister Ugly and family. We put ashore at a scruffy, littered seasonal fishing village on San Benito Island and walked past discarded oil drums to the first of several rocky bays where the elephant seal herds spend the winter and spring.

A "beachmaster" elephant seal (right) on San Benito Island battles to protect his harem from an intruder. It's hard to determine who's side the ladies have taken.

These ungainly beasts occupy dozens of sheltered coves along the Baja coast and their range extends north into California. The females resemble oversized seals, while nature endowed males with a floppy proboscis that indeed suggests a seagoing elephant. They're much larger than the females, up to twenty feet long and weighing 8,000 pounds.

Elephant seals are practically indifferent to humans, except that males may charge an intruder during breeding season. This indifference almost resulted in their downfall. Heavily hunted for their oil, they were thought to be exterminated by the turn of the century. Then, in 1912, a herd of about 125 was found on Guadalupe Island off the Baja peninsula. Placed under full protection, they have made an amazing comeback, with numbers now estimated at 60,000, extending over much of their original range.

For those who have never seen these ungainly creatures, they present a startling sight. They are favored objects on these natural history voyages to the Baja, perhaps second only to the great gray whales. Several Germans in our group gasped in amazement when we came upon the first bay occupied by a large group of elephant seals.

They spend much of their time dozing in the sand, looking like giant slugs. Still, there is constant motion within these colonies. They shift and squirm and grunt and snort and gurgle and roll and undulate and scratch themselves rather absent mindedly with their flippers. Small pups squall as adults roll over them, seemingly oblivious to their presence.

Dominant males—called beachmasters—accumulate, copulate with and protect a group of females. Younger bachelor males sulk around the fringes of the herd, either on the beach or just offshore. They occasionally challenge the harem keepers and attempt to mate with wayward females. They raise themselves on their haunches, trying to look as big as possible, throw their heads back and emit a strange hollow, snorting sound—something akin to a two-cylinder tractor engine. The challenge is soon answered. Females and pups ignore the coming conflict; they continue grunting, snorting, squealing and squalling. This could be the sound track for that great, noisy night club scene in one of the *Star Wars* films.

The challenges often erupt into brief, vicious battles, either on the beach or in the shallow surf. The snorting, undulating beasts hurl themselves at one another, biting, slapping with their floppy trunks and pushing like primeval sumo wrestlers. The battles, often bloody, rarely last more than a minute, usually ending with the challenger beating a hasty and undignified retreat into the surf. The beachmasters—shoulders, head and snout marked with old battle wounds and perhaps a couple of brand new ones—rear up in a final gesture of victory, and then settle back into the sand.

Back aboard the ship, we continued south briefly. Then we dropped anchor and boarded the skiffs for a shoreline cruise past an uninhabited island where large colonies of sea lions dwelt. They swam out to meet our boats, cavorted about in the water, played tag with the skiffs and with one another, yapping like happy puppies greeting their masters.

That evening, as our ship continued southward, dinner was interrupted by a call from Pieter: "Bio-luminescent dolphins! Starboard bow!"

Forks were dropped as we hurried forward to see several dolphins riding the bow. Their swift passage activated luminous plankton, coating them with a shimmering, soft blue velvet glow. Ghost dancers off our bow; a fine way to end a fascinating day along the Baja coast.

The next day would be even better. Tomorrow, we would pet whales.

ʁ ʁ ʁ

DAY FOUR

The *Spirit of Adventure* entered broad San Ignacio Lagoon at mid-morning, virtually surrounded by whales, swimming within a few dozen yards of the ship. Their spouts resembled dust devils on the calm water. The skipper found a suitable parking place and the anchor went down.

Three Mexican *pangas*—Fiberglas motorboats—came alongside to take us on our personal encounters with whales. This was our third Baja cruise, so we knew what was to come. The ritual was simple. The *pangas* would cruise slowly about the bay, seeking out whales and then moving in their direction. Initially, officials were concerned that these close approaches might disturb the whales. However, as the years passed, the great creatures became more and more comfortable with their visitors, eventually even allowing themselves to be petted. Particularly approachable whales—recognized from year to year by scars and barnacle patterns on their back—became known as "friendlies." Often, these would be a mother with her new calf.

As the years passed, the giant creatures became more comfortable with their visitors, eventually even allowing themselves to be petted.

Although we'd visited whales before, we were greenhorns compared with *Spirit of Adventure* owner Keating. He started working as a deck hand on fishing boats out of San Diego's Mission Bay in 1971 at the age of 16 and got

ELEPHANT SEALS FOR THE KILLING

Charles Melville Scammon, an American whaling captain who started the slaughter of gray whales in Baja lagoons in the middle 1800s, also was a remorseless killer of elephant seals. In his book, *Marine Mammals of the North-Western Coast*, he described his technique:

The sailors get between the herd and the water: then, raising all possible noise by shouting, and at the same time flourishing clubs, guns, and lances, the party advances slowly toward the rookery. Occasionally an overgrown male will give battle or attempt to escape; but a musket ball through the brain dispatches it; or someone checks its progress by thrusting a lance into the roof of its mouth, which causes it to settle on its haunches, when two men with heavy, oaken clubs give the creature repeated blows about the head until it is stunned or killed. After securing those that are disposed to show resistance, the party rushes on to the main body.

The onslaught creates such a panic among these peculiar creatures that, losing all control of their actions, they climb, roll and tumble over each other. We recollect in one instance, where sixty-five were captured, that several were found showing no signs of having been either clubbed or lanced, but were smothered by numbers of their kind heaped upon them.

The whole flock, when attacked, manifested alarm by their peculiar roar, the sound of which, among the largest males, is nearly as loud as the lowing of an ox, but more prolonged in one strain, accompanied by a rattling noise in the throat.

Owing to the continual pursuit of the animals, they have become nearly if not quite extinct on the California coast, or the remaining few have fled to some unknown point for security.

his skipper's license four years later. The following year, he was among the first boatmen to begin running whale-watching trips in the lagoons of Baja California, working for H&M Landing. Initially, Mike recalls, the whales were wary of these intruders, then they became more approachable when they realized the curious boat people meant no harm.

"I'll never forget my first close encounter," he said. "A gray whale came right up behind my skiff. It really spooked me and it took a while to realize that he just wanted to be friends." It was one of the first friendly whale encounters on record.

Mike bought the *Spirit of Adventure* in 1987, which he and his wife Annmarie operate in conjunction with H&M.

Shortly after we began our outing, a mother and her calf practically adopted our three *pangas,* making frequent passes, coming alongside to be petted, passing beneath our boats to disappear briefly into the deep and then reappear. Most of the passengers, who until now had seen whales only from a distance, squealed with delight, tripping over one another to touch and photograph the friendlies.

When the whales weren't near our boats, they were in performance a short distance away. We witnessed "spy-hopping," when the grand beasts would appear suddenly from the deep and push their snouts skyward. Some experts theorize that they were simply having a look around; others say it was to rinse water through their baleen to separate mud from edible creatures they scooped from the bottom of the bay. Occasionally, they would "breach," hurling their great bulk nearly clear of the water, a dramatic movement that still has whale-watching authorities mystified.

And suddenly, three hours had slipped by; it was time to return to the ship for lunch. We bolted our food, anxious to get back to the *pangas*. However, whale watching can be a capricious business. That afternoon, a wind came up, the *pangas* bobbed dizzily in a choppy surf and few whales came to the surface. Those who did kept their distance. We looked about for diversions. A dozen brown pelicans passed overhead, flying close formation in a straight line.

"Beautiful," said one of the passengers.

"They shouldn't fly like that," Pieter said laconially.

"Why not?" the passenger asked.

"The problem is, when the leader crashes, they all crash."

🐦🐦🐦
DAY FIVE

We spent the night anchored in the lagoon, rocked gently to sleep in our berths by the wind. At daybreak, it had subsided somewhat and we were out in the *pangas* by 7 a.m.

We had only one encounter with friendlies this morning, a mother and her calf. It was, however, the closest council I'd ever. The little fellow was particularly friendly and curious, hanging around our *panga* for several minutes. He lounged alongside while we reached out and touched him. It is difficult to describe the feel of a whale's skin; it's rubbery like a wetsuit or maybe an art gum eraser, and yet one can sense the warmth beneath. Junior emitted what seemed to be contented little sighs through his blowhole as we stroked him, misting my glasses with his breath. Then he rolled on his side and stared directly at me with a huge, alert cyclopean eye. I stared back, making good eye contact, and I wondered what he was thinking.

As perhaps did he, about me.

Back aboard the *Spirit,* we were about to settle in for lunch when some of our passengers from another *panga* hurried into the dining room, collectively bubbling with excitement. It was evident that they'd had a good outing. Tomiko, a cute young Japanese woman, wore a particularly wide grin.

"How was it?" I asked her. "Did you pet any whales?"

Her grin got wider. "I kissed one!"

🐦🐦🐦
DAY SIX

Adventure cruises sometimes shift gears from adventure to total relaxation. This often happens when the ship must travel some distance between points of interest.

No shore excursions or skiff runs were scheduled as we headed south toward Cabo San Lucas. However, there are no dull days on or off the Baja coast. Skipper Keating slowed, turned and stopped the boat repeatedly for closer views of dolphins, sea lions, lazily floating sea turtles, pelican flocks

Panga passengers get up close and personal with a young gray whale in San Ignacio Lagoon. The guy on the right uses an old press photographer's trick.

and whales of course. Two killer whales—orcas—appeared some distance away, identified by their near-vertical dorsal fins, although they didn't approach us and they disappeared when Mike swung the ship in their direction.

We paused for some time at the mouth of Magdalena Bay, where from the bow we enjoyed close-ups of humpback whales. Much larger than the grays, they aren't approachable or pettable, making them perhaps a bit more exciting to spot. The *Spirit* didn't enter the bay since the gray whales there had already left for the arctic.

Between wildlife sightings, passengers relaxed in the lounge, nibbled a nonstop parade of snacks from the galley (I have visions of the walking raisins in that TV commercial) and read from the ship's extensive natural history library. Browsing through a book on sea mammals, I learned that *pinnipedia* is the suborder pinniped, which means finned or feathered foot, and that pinnipeds are assigned to three families of the *carnivora* mammalian order: *otariidae, phocidae* and *odobenidae*. Tomorrow, I might learn how to pronounce them.

ß ß ß

DAY SEVEN

We greeted sunrise at *Finisterra*—land's end—the absolute tip of Baja California, after a long night's journey south. The end of land is marked by several nearly vertical sea stacks that appear to have broken free of the peninsula and are marching into the ocean. One is a small natural arch—popular on postcards—and boaters like to thread the needle, although the *Spirit* is a bit large for this game.

First light, which had tinted bands of clouds a hot pink and orange, bathed the monoliths in an eerie glow. It painted them pink, and then a soft orange and finally their proper daytime dress of beige, brown and off-white. A shore stop was not part of this itinerary, so we swung around the tip of the peninsula and rode gentle swells into the Gulf of California—or Sea of Cortez, if you prefer its more colorful name. (Some of these natural history trips terminate in Cabo San Lucas since San Jose del Cabo, about twenty miles north, offers air service to the U.S. and the Mexican mainland.)

Pressing northward, we hugged the east coast of the peninsula. It was comprised mostly of a brushy, hilly shoreline that dissolved frequently into beige sand beaches tucked into small sheltered bays. These were popular for snorkelers, fishermen and yachtsmen who—through wise investment or the luck of birth—could afford to spend much of their lives hanging out on a boat in the Baja. Mainland Mexico, perhaps eighty miles to the east, was out of sight, beyond the earth's curve.

Farther north, the Baja's eastern shore is marked by steep stratified cliffs, evidence of faulting that gradually separated it from the mainland between fifteen and twenty-five million years ago. The Sea of Cortez has many moods. Winds and tidal collisions can bring whitecaps and choppy rides for small boats. On many days, however, it's as smooth as a mountain lake. Even on choppy days, boats can find shelter in countless bays and the leeward side of offshore islands.

About mid-morning, Skipper Keating—who had an infallible eye for the slightest surface ripple—spotted a couple of humpback whales and gave gentle chase. They cruised along lazily, breaking the surface for a quick misty exhalation and then slipping out of sight. After several minutes, they would reappear far to port or starboard or even to stern, where they had become the pursuers and we the quarry.

We encountered several groups of humpbacks this day, marked by their short, stubby dorsal fins, but Mike was unable to approach close enough for decent photos. The passengers lined the bow with cameras, minicams and binoculars in hand, like a well-armed fire team waiting in ambush. Suddenly, a pod of six whales surfaced a few yards in

> *Passengers lined the bow with cameras, minicams and binoculars in hand, like a well-armed fire team, waiting in ambush.*

front of us, blowing, snorting, sighing and diving, offering a splendid display of their great flukes. Later, a hydrophone was dropped and through heavy static we would hear their strange high pitched, moaning, sighing calls. I wondered if they were discussing the fact that it was fun playing tag with this big, harmless boatload of camera-laden landlubbers.

We dropped anchor that afternoon in a pretty little crescent bay called Los Frailes for a few hours of snorkeling, beach walking and exchanging stares with sea lions. A small colony of them occupied a rocky outcropping around the corner from the beach. The *Spirit's* glass bottom skiff came into play at this stop, for those without snorkeling gear could see the garibaldi, angel fish and other finned critters below.

Betty and I joined Pieter on a stroll along the strand, past small Mexican fishing boats and their temporary beach shelters. We were headed for Hotel Bahia Los Frailes, a small resort at the far end of the beach. Pieter wanted to discuss the possibility of arranging shore extensions for future *Spirit of Adventure* groups. The cozy little facility was built by San Francisco stockbroker Wayne Siepman and his wife Ellie. A big, heavy-set man with a sun-darkened face, Siepman wore a full beard, shorts and a loose-fitting shirt, looking—perhaps deliberately—nothing like a stockbroker.

DAS BOAT?

An ominous drone penetrated the calm water.

"What's that strange sound, Dad?"

"I think it's Man, my son. I'll go up and check it out. You stay here."
The adult orca surfaced, blew and looked around.

The younger killer whale soon bobbed up beside him. "Dang, Dad,
that's bigger'n a gray whale! What is it?"

The adult male frowned, not an easy thing for a killer whale to do.
"I thought I told you to stay below! That's Man out there, and he may
be dangerous. He may be on a capture trip."

"Man is shaped like that?"

The big male swished his flukes impatiently. "That's his boat."

"I've never seen a boat! Let's get closer!"

"No, son. It's dangerous."

"But my friend says Man won't hurt us. He and his buddies like to
swim right alongside their boats."

"What friend told you that?"

"Uh...a bottlenosed dolphin."

"Bottle—! I told you not to play with those people!"

"But, they're nice guys, Dad."

"You're a killer whale, Son. You can't think of them as friends! You
must think of them as lunch!"

"But, Dad—"

"Stay away from dolphins, unless you're hungry. And stay away
from Man's boats! They could catch you in a net and take you away.
You'd spend the rest of your life in a tank, performing in some silly
marine mammal show."

The youth's eyes widened in fear. "They'd put me in a tank?
They'd never set me free?"

"Only in the movies, Willie. Only in the movies."

"So, what brought you to this remote place?" I asked, expecting some
kind of detailed commentary on the pressures of urban life and social escap-
ism. I didn't get one.

With a sweep of his big right hand, he took in the bay, the beach, the
rocky sea lion refuge and a small mountain rising behind. "What's not to
like?"

🐾🐾🐾

DAY EIGHT

Another crummy day in paradise?

We awoke early and wandered up to the galley for a cup of tea. At 4:45,
Bubba and Walter already were laying the groundwork for breakfast—waffles, topped with a choice of blueberries or applesauce.

The Sea of Cortez, calm now, was slate gray and gently marbled by
scores of dolphins who arched across its flat surface. Dinner-jacketed frigate
birds passed overhead, distinctive with their white chests, black wings and
long tuning fork tails. We looked to the east just as the sun broke through its
pink halo to emerge over the flat horizon of the sea. To the west, steep ter-

raced and stratified cliffs emerged from night shadows to be tinted pink and orange. We appeared to be cruising through the Grand Canyon that had somehow been filled to the brim.

Later that morning, we parked in a nearly landlocked bay on the northern end of San José Island. It presented a curiously mixed environment. The gentle upslope above the shoreline was thickly forested with *cardon*, (*car-DOAN*), a close kin to Arizona's long-armed saguaro cactus, standing as tall as thirty feet. Just up the beach was a jungle-like mangrove swamp busy with shorebirds—a scene right out of the Florida Everglades. And across the way, above the shimmering jade green and cobalt blue water of the Sea of Cortez, rose the steep seacliffs of the Baja Peninsula.

We poked about the *cardon* forest above the beach and then took to the skiffs to prowl the green-fringed channels of the mangrove swamp in search of birds. Snowy egrets, kingfishers, great blue herons, godwits and reddish egrets added themselves to our growing list. As we skittered our skiff back to the *Spirit*, several pelicans put on a fishing show, streaking downward, wings folded liked World War II Corsairs, slamming into the surf and inevitably coming away with a fish.

The ship later anchored off a rocky spine of an island that looked like a submarine for the Flintstones, for a bit of swimming and snorkeling. We took the glass-bottom skiff on a slow cruise around the island. We'd alternately stare into the water beneath us and then pop up to peer at hundreds of pelicans that were perched on the island. They seemed to be watching our antics as we watched theirs. Silhouetted against the sky, these ungainly looking birds resembled kinetic sculptures.

Back aboard the *Spirit,* our ongoing search for sea mammals took us to a good sized pod of pilot whales—glossy black, blunt nosed critters who circled our boat for two hours. They kept us and possibly themselves amused until just after sunset, when Walter announced "first, last and only call for dinner!" Even though my mind was on pilot whales and pork chops, that silly old ditty kept fluttering through my head:

A strange old bird is the pelican.
He can hold in his beak
Enough fish for a week,
And I don't see how the helican.

฿ ฿ ฿

DAY NINE

The closing days of our voyage of discovery settled into a gentle pace, enlivened by frequent animal sightings. Several times, we posted our "sock alarms" so we could be awakened for some spectacular nocturnal event. We were scrambled from our bunks once to see luminescent dolphins swimming off the bow and another time to witness a feeding frenzy of hundreds of bait fish, thrashing about in one of the boat's spotlights. They appeared to be dining on tiny minnows.

Sock alarm?

It's quite simple. If passengers wish to be awakened at night for some interesting phenomena, they're instructed to tie a sock to the door latch of their cabin.

"You may use a more provocative item of apparel, if you prefer," Pieter had pointed out.

A feeding frenzy erupts in the Sea of Cortez as pelicans, sea gulls and—difficult to spot in the roiling surf—dolphins go after a school of small fish.

Having participated in two sock alarms last night, I passed up an invitation for the 4:30 sunrise hike on Catalina Island, where we would anchor until noon that day. Later, we were shuttled ashore to a beautiful rockbound bay on Catalina to snorkel, take a dip or loaf in the sun. I took a solo hike into the steeply uptilted cactus forest above the gravelly beach. These islands are lonely but certainly not empty places. Many are virtual gardens of desert plant life—forests of *cordon,* remarkably huge barrel cactus, buckhorn cholla, the curious elephant trees with their tiny leaves and thick swollen trunks, pretty little purple blossoms that I couldn't identify and the notorious "jumping cholla" cactus that likes to hitch a ride when you brush past.

From a high ridge, I could see the enticing bay where some of our passengers were snorkeling, about 200 feet below. Lying face down in the Lucite-clear water, they seemed suspended in space over the rocky aquatic gardens.

🦆🦆🦆

DAY TEN

Our cruise was nearing its end, yet there was no end of the continual parade of wildlife in the Sea of Cortez—above and below the surface. Late that afternoon, a legion of bottlenosed dolphins—hundreds of them—sliced through the water toward the boat. They arched through the surf, rode our bow, slapped their tails, and an occasional showoff would clear the water in a spinning pirouette. Up ahead, hundreds of pelicans were engaged in a feeding frenzy so we steered in their direction.

For the next hour, the Sea of Cortez was alive with wildlife. Pelicans, joined by seagulls, plunged into the surf, feeding on a great mass of minnows. The dolphins curved through the culinary chaos, taking their share. Forked-tailed frigate birds, unable to land on water, dive-bombed the smaller seagulls, trying to snatch away their dinners. We found ourselves choosing sides—some rooting for the seagulls, others for the frigates.

Dolphins, pelicans, seagulls and frigates in a wild dinner dance—nature had exploded into splendid chaos all around us. We were witness to something no marine park could duplicate; no movie director could choreograph.

ß ß ß

DAY ELEVEN

On our final day at sea, four killer whales—parents and two offspring—threw the boat into a frenzy, right in the middle of breakfast. We were cruising somewhere between La Paz and Loreto, looking for nothing in particular and anything of interest when they were spotted. Their tall and slender dorsal fins were unmistakable.

For some time they kept their distance, as Mike maneuvered the *Spirit* to get them within camera range. Passengers abandoned their scrambled eggs and bacon and crowded the rail, photographic weapons at the ready. The whales slipped from sight and then suddenly two of them appeared right beside the boat.

"There! Right under us!" From the bridge deck, the usually calm Mike was shouting and pointing.

They passed under the bow, nearly brushing the boat and then disappeared. A stampede of feet forward, but no one got a shot off. Moments later, they appeared to stern, just yards away; another stampede, another missed opportunity.

Didn't it seem odd that we were dashing and stumbling over one another to view creatures we'd seen dozens of times at marine parks, in films and on TV? We had leaned over and scratched killer whales' tummies at Sea World in San Diego. We'd seen the film *Free Willie* and Betty had gotten properly weepy at the end. ("Since killer whales eat dolphins," Pieter had mused earlier, "maybe we should do a movie version of *Flipper* and call it *Free Willie's Lunch*.")

Why did these orcas send the boat and its passengers in circles? Because these Willies really were free, and moving at liberty within their element. This is the challenge of wildlife spotting—to enter their domain, to pursue them on their terms with our cameras and our eyes. They were not our captives and they were not performing for us.

I like to think that we were performing for them.

ß ß ß

But do you know
Of perfumed seas, of tropic trees
Where orchids grow?
Or know the sun can burn as fierce as love?
— Violet Clifton

Chapter eight

THE LITTLE CARIBBEAN

Setting sail with Windstar Cruises

O ur day ended with a touch of elegance. The ship lifted anchor, motored out of the small bay and then unfurled its great triangles of
sails. Pointing its bow toward Grenada, it slipped through a calm sea
at a brisk four knots, leaving the warm oranges and hot pinks of a Caribbean
sunset in its wake.

We took a turn on deck in the fading light and discovered why pure sailing is so grand. There was no drone of engines; only the soft hum of generators betrayed that we were aboard a mechanical device. Lofty sails reached
toward a tropic moon. No wind whipped across the ship's bow, for we moved
with the breeze.

Thus we cruised aboard an elegant yacht, living the lives of the rich and
famous and being neither. Our vessel was the *Wind Star,* one of Windstar
Cruises' three four-masted sailing ships that ply the waters of the Caribbean,
Mediterranean and Tahiti. This small fleet of luxury ships comprise what

CRUISE PLANNER

The cruise ● This is a seven-day "soft adventure" cruise aboard a luxury sailing yacht to some of the lesser visited islands of the Caribbean. Contact Windstar Cruises, 300 Elliott Avenue West, Seattle, WA 98119; (800) 258-7245. The firm also has tall ship cruises in the Mediterranean and the islands of French Polynesia (Tahiti).

For information on Barbados, contact the Barbados Tourism Board, 800 Second Ave., New York, NY 10017; (800) 221-9831 or (212) 986-6516. For a pre or post-cruise vacation at Club Rockley, call (809) 435-7880.

Getting there ● This cruise begins and ends in Barbados, and special air-cruise rates are available on a variety of carriers from several cities. For passengers flying out of Miami, British West Indies Airlines (BWIA) offers frequent service to Barbados.

The ship ● The *M.S.Y. Wind Star* is a luxury sailing yacht with an emphasis on "casual elegance." When breezes are fair, the ship is propelled by sails, augmented when necessary by diesel electric engines. Onboard facilities include a spacious restaurant, pool and hot tub, sports shop and fitness room, casino, library, gift shop, masseuse and hair stylist. The 74 identical cabins—all outside—are quite opulent, done in teak and brass. The ship's officers are British and the hotel staff is international.

When to go ● The dry period from November through May is the most popular season for Caribbean cruising. As in most tropical areas, however, the rainy season has many sunny days, so sailing these islands is a year-around affair for many cruise lines. The Windstar season is November through April.

What to bring ● American citizens should carry a valid passport. Most ports of call are parts of independent Caribbean nations while Martinique is a province of France. Virtually all Caribbean entities have rather informal entry requirements. Dress for the tropics, and bring swimming, snorkeling and scuba gear since water sports are a big part of these cruises. (However, most of these items are available on the ship.) Dress is "yacht casual," meaning informal but a bit dressier than for some other small ship cruises. Cocktail wear and sports clothing are considered appropriate for the evening meal, but no ties and certainly no tuxes.

What's included ● Swim towels, snorkeling masks, tubes and flippers are available, along with plastic sea kayaks, tow-along "banana boats" and other water sports equipment. Shore excursions, not included in the cruise price, are available at many ports, utilizing either mini-van taxis or buses. On many islands, such as English-speaking Grenada, you can choose the option of arranging tours directly with drivers and setting your own itinerary. In Martinique, with its predominately French-speaking populace and air-conditioned tour buses, most passengers prefer tours arranged by the cruise line.

What to buy ● Many Caribbean nations are duty free, with the usual perfumes, liquors and electronics gear available; Martinique offers the best shopping on this particular cruise. Liquor in these islands is relatively inexpensive, but no more so than at most airport duty free shops. The exception is local rum, available at bargain prices.

A giant banyan tree is one of the botanical stars of the Flower Forest on Barbados.

Conde Nast Traveler readers recently voted one of the top three cruise lines in the world.

The "windships" are yacht-like in appearance and attitude—-similar to those sailed by wealthy sea wanderers. Polished woods, brass and beveled glass provide that proper touch of aquatic elegance. Meals are stylishly staged and international in flavor; the wine list is predominately Californian and excellent. Yet, the pace and the dress are casual. Guests pass their days in shorts or swimwear. "Dress casually, as you would aboard your own private yacht," says the brochure. Polo shirts and cocktail casual are the uniform of the evening. (I finally had the chance to wear those Mexican wedding shirts I'd bought a generation ago in Ixtapa.)

Although Windstar ships call on a few larger ports, most shore stops are at smaller, often overlooked islands. The ships follow a leisurely itinerary, with ample time to anchor in a calm bay for an afternoon of kayaking, snorkeling or flitting about in tiny sailboats. Despite their small size, Windstar's sailing ships offer most of the amenities of larger vessels, and some advantages that the love boats lack. Dining is single seating and tables are assigned each night, as they are in a restaurant. Shore excursions are uncrowded because of the ship's small passenger list.

The bridge is always open and passengers are encouraged to stop by and see how a computer-driven sailboat works. Betty and I spent an hour on the *Wind Star* bridge one evening, wrinkling our brows in studied concentration as the first officer patiently tried to explain how a sextant is used to find your location. Something about computing sun and star sightings from the center of the earth. I'd always thought it was too hot down there.

ßßß

A BARBADOS BEGINNING

Since our cruise would begin in Barbados, we decided to build a couple of spare days into our schedule to explore this tropical Caribbean isle. We holed up at Club Rockley near Bridgetown, an older, well-tended resort of two story cottages scattered around extensive grounds. It's an appealing and comfortable all- inclusive resort where meals and even drinks are included.

Unlike most of the Caribbean islands we would visit aboard the *Wind Star,* Barbados is rather thickly populated, with more than a quarter of a million residents occupying 166 square miles. The only city of any size and the only port is the capital of Bridgetown, with about 10,000 residents. The rest of the folks are scattered in scores of small villages.

Most of Barbados is under cultivation---primarily sugar cane and vegetables. However, it was quite different when British settlers arrived in 1627. They fussed that it was "so overgrown with wood as there could be found no fields or savannas for men to dwell in." By 1665, most of it had been cleared for sugar cane and cotton; only a few acres of original rainforest survive.

If you choose to check out Barbados, start with the cute colonial city of Bridgetown. The Barbados Museum, housed in a former military prison, is extensive and quite well done. It traces the history of the island from its development as an uplifted coral reef through its colonial period to its present status as an independent member of the British Commonwealth. Shoppers might like to head for Swan Street, which is closed off as a pedestrian mall, busy with small shops and sidewalk stalls. For an interesting culinary adventure, check out Baxter Road on a Saturday night. More than 20 outdoor vendors cook savory and spicy

"We have a saying here on the island: If a man has done his best, the angels will do the rest."

chicken and fish over small fire pans and serve them piping hot in aluminum foil. Several noisy little cabarets add animation to this street which---on Saturday night at least---never sleeps.

After doing Bridgetown, hire a local guide---easily arranged through your hotel---for a circumnavigation of the island. A good day's outing will get you to a sea-sculpted grotto called the Flower Cave; Barbados Wildlife Preserve and Grenade Hall Signal Station, which is a small swatch of forest with native wildlife and an old British lookout on a knoll; Harrison Cave, a limestone cavern that has been gimmicked up with colored lights and a tram ride; and finally an attractive hillside botanical garden called Flower Forest.

When we ticked off this ambitious sightseeing itinerary to our driver-guide, an old gentleman named Byer, he smiled and said:

"Well of course, I'll do my best. We have a saying here on the island: If a man has done his best, the angels will do the rest."

ßßß

DAY ONE

One cannot miss a Windstar ship in port at night. As our Barbadian taxi skittered briskly through Bridgetown, still nearly a mile from the cruise ship terminal, we saw a splendid garland of white lights on the horizon, draped from the four lofty masts of the *Wind Star.*

We stepped aboard to find a carpeted haven of laminated teak and muted colors—simple and intimate. Our cabin continued the yachting theme, with an art deco aquatic look of rounded corners and a brass-rimmed twin portholes. However, a TV/VCR and CD player confirmed that this was indeed a contemporary retreat. It was a civilized lair as well, with a bottle of wine and dish of chocolate-dipped strawberries awaiting our attention.

Beneath its gleaming white nylon sails, the *Wind Star* is diesel powered. This permits it to navigate easily in port, and to stay on schedule when the winds aren't cooperating. With sails unfurled—mostly for show, I suspect— we glided smoothly from Barbados on a windless evening. Our destination, which we would reach early the next morning after a calm crossing of Tobago Basin, was the tiny island of Bequia (*BEK-way*), one of the Grenadines in the Windward group.

ఠ ఠ ఠ

DAY TWO

As we enjoyed breakfast on an outdoor deck, our yacht slipped smoothly into a sheltered cove that would put Botany Bay to shame. Bequia's Admiralty Bay is rimmed by lush hills into which are tucked tile roofed homes, most surprisingly modest but enjoying million dollar views. Port Elizabeth, Bequia's only town, is properly weathered and tropically funky, offering a few portside shops and an open-air food market.

After breakfast and the requisite lifeboat drill, we boarded shuttle boats to the small pier, where we clambered into the back of Toyotas pretending to be open air buses. We had signed up for a tour of the island which—since Bequia is short on specific attractions despite its tropic beauty—consisted mostly of stopping at viewpoints. Our small caravan of Caribbean-style jitneys zig-zagged up a switchback road chiseled from the steep slopes. En route, our driver stopped to let us absorb the splendid view of our ship in the harbor below, and he told us about his island home.

Although it's only seven miles square, Bequia is the second largest of the Grenadine Islands, with a population of about 5,000. It's part of the principality of St. Vincent and the Grenadines, which gained its independence from Great Britain in 1979. Although off the mainstream tourist route, it does have five small hotels. Just offshore is Mustique Island, perhaps the wealthiest

We enjoyed a proper panorama of Bequia and smaller isles scattered offshore like broken off pieces of jungle thatch.

piece of real estate in the Caribbean. Privately owned, it's a part-time haven for Princess Margaret, Mick Jagger and a few other notables. Cruise passengers who seek closer proximity to these rich and famous digs can book a day sail to the island and its luxury resort.

Content with exploring more plebeian Bequia, we continued to the island's highest promontory, 881-foot Bell Pointe. Here, we enjoyed a proper panorama of Bequia and even smaller isles scattered offshore like broken off pieces of jungle thatch. We then headed back toward Port Elizabeth, pausing en route at a vantage point above Friendship Bay. There, our driver—perhaps not aware that most members of his entourage harbored Greenpeace sympathies—discussed the local whaling industry. Tiny St. Vincent and the Grenadines is one of the few countries still taking whales. Locals have been

All lit up like a sea-going Christmas tree, the Wind Star *basks in the harbor at Bequia.*

hunting humpbacks for generations, using old-fashioned open boats and hand-thrown harpoons. At a recent international whaling conference, islanders were given a bag limit of three humpbacks a year.

"But not to worry," our guide said, perhaps noting some of our frowns. "The only whaler we have left is a 70-year-old man and he's lucky if he even hits one."

Although tiny islands such as Bequia offer few visitor attractions, their villages have a scruffy tropic charm—the kinds of places that invite casual browsing. Because few ships call on them, the occasional visitors aren't part of a crowd of gawking tourists. We walked along the palm lined, coconut husk littered beach, nodding to locals and an occasional chicken. A few Bequians lounged against overturned boats, enjoying the cooling breeze of a gathering evening. Several teenagers played soccer in the sand, with no goal and no boundary except the surf line. Out on the street, an ice cream truck passed by, its chimes playing *My Darling Clementine.*

ß ß ß

DAY THREE

Perhaps you have heard of—or been on—cruises to nowhere, or *erehwon,* as some clever copy writers have written it. We spent this day not cruising at all. The *Wind Star* became a beachside resort hotel—only slightly offshore. Early in the morning, we anchored near a string of emerald islands called the Tobago Cays, each covering only a few acres of ocean. They were too small for habitation although folks from nearby islands, obviously familiar with the Windstar sailing schedule, had set up clothes lines of T-shirts where we would be snorkeling and swimming.

We spent a morning indulging further in this fantasy of a rich and famous lifestyle—loafing in the shade of beach palms, snorkeling among reefs in Lucite-clear water and taking occasional dips to cool the tropic sun. When thirst commanded, we strolled to a bar set up by the ship's crew for a mai tai or Perrier.

And some of us bought Tobago T-shirts.

That afternoon, passengers adjourned to the sports deck on the ship's fantail to check out tiny sailboats, windsurfing rigs and other ocean play equipment. Those who just wanted to go along for the ride climbed aboard a long tube called a banana boat—more resembling a banana slug—that was towed at high speed behind one of the ship's Zodiacs.

Our day ended with a touch of elegance. Our ship lifted anchor, motored out of the small bay and then unfurled its great triangles of sails. Pointing its bow toward Grenada, it slipped through a calm sea at a brisk four knots, leaving the warm oranges and hot pinks of a Caribbean sunset in its wake. On the bridge, dials glowed and radar screens painted orange maps of the surrounding islands. Seafaring had come full circle. Inside that windowed room, computers ran the ship, in response to the deck officer's directions. They could even electronically trim the sails, although our crew preferred to do it manually.

Outside, the *Wind Star* moved as vessels had moved a thousand years before—catching a breeze and running before it.

ß ß ß

DAY FOUR

Beautiful from afar, untidy up close, Grenada's capitol of St. George's was the largest city we had encountered since our departure from Barbados. Weathered stucco buildings with distinctive orange fish scale tile rimmed narrow Carenage Harbour, which was crowded with other cruise ships and paint-peeling fishing boats. Whitewashed homes scaled steep slopes above the town, carving their niches out of thick vegetation.

Teeming with activity, busy with beeping traffic, vibrant in defiance of the torpid climate, the city was something of a jolt after the languid pace of Bequia and the tropic calm of the Tobago Cays. However, the town does display a weathered charm, particularly in its ancient pastel Georgian and Queen Anne buildings with their faded orange tile or rusting corrugated roofs. Occasional wrought iron balconies spoke of grander days when a brisk trade in sugar and spice (and everything nice?) brought quick wealth to these islands.

Our mini-vans danced nimbly through the traffic and climbed into jungled hills.

As we stepped ashore, locals gathered quickly to us, offering with gentle assertiveness taxi tours, walking tours and things to buy.

"You don't have to find taxis on Grenada," our purser had told us before we disembarked. "They will find you."

However, we were with a group that had signed on for one of the shipboard-arranged tours, so we filed into mini-vans. They danced nimbly through the traffic and climbed into the jungled hills.

With annual rainfall ranging from 70 to 140 inches, Grenada is a luxuriant botanic garden and the spice island of the Caribbean. Our driver had taken his botany lessons seriously, and was able to identify as we drove—with no problem—the varied plants that yielded flowers or spice. Beyond St. George's, jungled peaks give Grenada a pleasingly lush appearance, although roads leading from the town are strewn with weathered houses and occasional junk cars. There is almost no level land here, so not all of its rainforest was cleared for sugar cane or cotton—a fate suffered by many other Caribbean islands. Spices, which can be grown and harvested on this tilted land without clearing the forest, thus became the leading agricultural commodity.

This generally untroubled island was the scene of a bloody coupe in 1983, and U.S. Marines and forces from several other Caribbean nations went ashore to oust the usurpers of power. (Listening to CNN's war coverage, we began calling it "Gre-NAW-da" instead of "Gre-NAY-da.") Expect your tour operator, between

Then she turned to me and flashed one of those evil grins that come so easily to skinny old women.

discussions of spices and flowers, to point out landmarks of that invasion, such as the fort where rebels executed the government leaders, the airport and the medical school where several American students had to be evacuated. Peace has prevailed here since, and not surprisingly, most Grenadans are rather pro-American.

Digging deeper into history, you also will recall that Christopher Columbus initially thought he had sailed into the spice islands of the East Indies when he entered the Caribbean Sea. His blunder soon became a boon, for these islands were much closer to the markets of Europe than the East Indies. Early settlers saw that these "West Indies" enjoyed a similar climate, and they began importing spice trees and plants from the East. Lumpy Grenada became an early center for the spice trade.

A requisite stop on any island tour is one of dozens of tiny spice stalls that line the steep road leading into the back country. At our appointed stall, a skinny, animated old woman grated nutmeg, cocoa bean and assorted other spices into our palms. We learned that mace is not its own spice, but the peppery vessel-like filament wrapped around a nutmeg pod.

"So from one thing you are getting two spices," she said, pulling the filament from the pod. Then she turned to me and flashed one of those evil grins that come so easily to skinny old women. "I have the thing for you, man," she said, handing me a bottle of pale orange liquid labeled Double Trouble.

"When a man's business is in trouble, he drinks this and then his woman gets in trouble." She held up a short, thick branch from a *boise bande* tree, whose bark is one of the ingredients. "You drink Double Trouble, and it makes your business look like this."

Our next stop was Annandale Falls, a short, pretty cataract that plunges into a sylvan pool. As we walked the short path to the falls, we were besieged by youths who, for five dollars U.S., would entertain us by jumping fifty feet into the pool.

"I am Flying Eagle. I can jump beautifully for you."

"I am Flying Eagle," said one of the youths, who had the outline of a *cannabis* leaf etched into his crewcut. "I can jump beautifully for you."

Others offering their services included Super Butterfly, Super Splash and Dive Bomber. A policeman back at the parking area had warned us that these dives were illegal and dangerous for the kids, so we refused their dive-for-pay requests. However, other visitors obviously had relented. Flying Eagle spiraled gracefully into the pool, followed shortly by another diver whose poetic name we had not caught.

Our guide shrugged as we drove away. "We try to dis-encourage them, but they do it anyway."

Our tour ended at Fort Frederick, a grassy mass of stone on a hill above the city. Called a "reverse fort," it was built in 1791 by the French, with its guns pointed inland toward the mountains instead of the harbor. They had taken the island from the British by storming the unprotected backside of an earlier fortress. Although the new fort was designed to repel similar approaches, it has never fired an angry shot. The British did get the island back, but through bloodless means at the Treaty of Versailles.

Although we were neither mad dogs nor Englishmen, we braved the noonday sun to stroll about the city after our tour. Spice stalls, similar to those along the highway into the hills, were packed closely together at the pier. They

The chocolate dip on our strawberries hadn't melted.

pleasantly assaulted the senses with aromas of nutmeg, cloves, curry, cinnamon and other savories. A stroll around the curving waterfront delivered us to the Grenada National Museum, housed in an old stone French Army barracks and prison. Small and rather casually assembled, the archive offered an interesting exhibit on sugar, molasses and rum production, a mounted butterfly collection and a rusting cannon or two.

We ended our day ashore with a steep and mercifully short hike up to Fort George, built by the French in 1705. It has been the site of every armed intervention since, including the assassination of Prime Minister Morris Bishop in 1983. From parapets above the fort courtyard, a brace of rusting cannon pointed menacingly toward our ship, anchored offshore. The gleaming white *Wind Star* looked inviting and cool from here, so we hurried back to our stateroom. Air conditioning is wonderful, particularly in the tropics. The chocolate dip on our strawberries hadn't melted.

ß ß ß

DAY FIVE

Carriacou (*CARRY-a-coo*) is one of the three islands comprising the commonwealth of Grenada. This small, low-lying, green-clad coral ridge is rarely visited by larger cruise ships. Its only town, with the lofty name of Hillsborough, offers few of the shops, cafés, shore tours and other amenities that tempt the mainstream cruising community. However, with its sleepy and funky countenance, lack of crowds and great snorkeling and swimming beaches, it provides proper pause for the *Wind Star.*

Several smaller yachts were anchored in the jade green waters offshore when we arrived. Their occupants were members of that fortunate fraternity one encounters throughout the Caribbean. They wander leisurely from island to island, dropping anchor at a whim to slip over the side to snorkel, swim or scuba. They may take a Zodiac to the beach to stock up on grub and rum, and then hoist anchor when the next fair wind blows.

We of the *Wind Star* could emulate that lifestyle, except that we didn't have to shop for groceries. We strolled Hillsborough's single commercial street along the palm-lined waterfront, which was properly weathered but

Relaxing at the rail beneath one of its towering sails, a pair of Wind Star *passengers watch offshore islands glide past.*

neater than the avenues of Grenada. A few grocery stores, shops and small bars were housed in aged stucco buildings, sheltered by rusting corrugated roofs or fish scale tile.

We spent the afternoon perpetuating our saga of the yachting lifestyle. Zodiacs delivered us to tiny, uninhabited Sandy Island just off Carriacou, where the ship's crew had set up a beach barbecue. After consuming hot dogs, hamburgers and remarkably tasty barbecued pork ribs, we were free to swim, snorkel, scuba, sail or kayak in these limpid waters.

⌐⌐⌐

DAY SIX

Our day-long visit to Martinique returned us to the mainstream of cruising, with its attendant crowds. A large Holland America cruise ship was in port, and three other vessels had called earlier. Martinique's main city of Fort de France is one of the Caribbean's most prosperous and tidy communities.

It's a favorite shopping stop, with curio booths just off the waterfront and narrow streets lined with perfumeries, boutiques, dress shops and duty-free liquor stores.

This city of 100,000 offers a pleasing mix of new and well- tended old buildings. Its narrow streets overhung with iron balconies are reminiscent of New Orleans' French quarter or a well-preserved old European town. While the prosperity is real, it's not because this island's inhabitants are more clever than their neighbors. Martinique is a French state, and nearly 70 percent of its gross national product is generated by the mother country. Most of the other islands of the Caribbean are independent and must struggle with limited economic resources typical of the tropics.

This lush volcanic island was settled by the French in 1635, after a brief occupation by the Spanish. Importation of slaves and sugar cane soon followed, while the French literally pushed the local Caribs into the sea. Cursing their conquerors, the natives swore that their "Fire Mountain" would avenge them. A century later, in 1902, the Caribs' prediction came true. Mount Pelée erupted, destroying the capital of Saint-Pierre and killing 29,000 people. The capital was moved to Fort de France, where it remains today.

Only the shattered remnants of the city's now-abandoned fort, and a few other stone wall fragments remain as a reminder of that fateful day in May.

Our tour ashore would take us around the island's fringe and to the site of that awesome volcanic explosion. The mini-bus followed a narrow, twisting highway up the flanks of the Pitons, three conical, jungle-clad peaks that form the island's mountainous heart. Banana groves and other agricultural fields were mixed with thick forest and prim little homes.

As our tour pressed onward, through hilly jungle to the island's northern reaches, the broad-shouldered mass of Mount Pelée filled the horizon. Minutes later, we drove through the narrow streets of Saint-Pierre, paralleling an attractive beach of dark volcanic sand. The once-splendid colonial capital had been the "Paris of the Caribbean" during Martinique's heyday as a profitable sugar cane center. Then, early on the morning of May 8, 1902, a cloud of poisonous vapors swept down from Pelée, followed by a rain of hot ash and lava. Most of the town's residents died within minutes, asphyxiated by the gas. The ensuing blast leveled the town. Only one person was found alive, a prisoner named Cyparis, protected by the thick walls of a dungeon. Badly burned, he survived and later toured the world with the Barnum and Bailey Circus, exhibiting his scars.

After the capital was moved to Fort de France, Saint-Pierre was rebuilt, although in the much more modest version we see today—a small village of narrow streets, tucked up against the sea. Only the shattered remnants of the city's now-abandoned fort, and a few other stone wall fragments remain as a reminder of that fateful day in May.

In the Saint-Pierre Museum, built above the ruined fort, photos, prints and relics recall the days before, during and after the eruption. Photos taken shortly after the blast reveal a stark, Hiroshima-like devastation. A focal point of the museum is the master bell of the Saint-Pierre Cathedral, melted into a flattened oval. Also on display are everyday items such as a charred sewing machine, clumps of nails melted together and even a carbonized bowl of spaghetti.

Our return trip took us along Martinique's pretty west coast, initially at water's edge past palm-lined black volcanic sand beaches, and then up into the lush flower-bedecked hills with views down to the Caribbean. Little pocket villages in sheltered ravines added dashes of orange tile and pastel stucco.

ß ß ß
DAY SEVEN

St. Lucia is perhaps the most beautiful island in the Caribbean. It's lushly green and accented by two splendid jungle-clad monoliths called the Pitons that rise hundreds of feet from the southwestern shore. Petit Piton, although the smaller of the two at 2,469 feet, is impossibly vertical, suggestive of a miniature Matterhorn. Gros Piton, just down the shoreline, is 2,619 feet high but not as sheer. The two monoliths are thought to be plug domes from eroded-away volcanoes.

The tattered, scattered, funky and friendly old fishing village of Soufrière occupies an idyllic little harbor, lolling in the shadows of Petit Piton. With its balconied, corrugated roof buildings lining narrow streets, weathered waterfront and stray chickens, it could be the setting for a Somerset Maugham novel. From the village, forests of banana palms rise steeply toward the island's mountainous interior, to complete this lush tropical scene.

Most cruise ships call on the island's capital city of Castries, farther to the north, since it offers more shopping and other tropically urban lures. However, Windstar ships tie up to the dock at Soufrière. Shopping here consists of good rum prices at several markets, an outdoor fruit and vegetable market on Saturdays and the usual T-shirt stalls. Most of our passengers don't notice the absence of perfumeries and dress shops. They were too busy admiring the idyllic palm-shaded harbor lined with brightly colored fishing boats and that soaring horn of Petit Piton.

The island's first outsiders came by accident, when an off-course ship was blown ashore in 1605. The crew of about sixty- five started a settlement, occupying huts rented to them by the Carib Indians. However, the natives proved to be rather inconsiderate landlords, alternately collecting rent and killing their tenants. Eighteen survivors fled after a few months. St. Lucia spent the next 150 years as a political soccer ball, alternately occupied by the Caribs, Great Britain and France. Through skirmish or treaty, the island changed hands fourteen times until the British gained permanent possession in 1814. It became an independent state within the British Commonwealth in 1979. Soufrière, once a French provincial capital, is the island's oldest city.

Through skirmish or treaty, the island changed hands fourteen times until the British gained permanent possession in 1814.

English is St. Lucia's official language, although many islanders speak a rich *patois*—a blend of English, French and African Creole. With no language barrier, we decided to hire a local guide, accomplished after the usual spirited negotiations. Paired with a couple of new friends from the ship, we placed ourselves in the care of a gentleman named Sylvester and headed inland in his battered Nissan van. After winding up a steep, jungle-shrouded incline, we paused at a turnout for an fine vista of Soufrière Bay. Our gleaming white ship was a grand centerpiece.

The towering cone of Petit Piton fills the horizon as the Wind Star *sails from the harbor at Soufrière on St. Lucia, one of the prettiest islands of the Caribbean.*

We continued first through the thick, mountainous jungle on bumpy roads to the Arts and Crafts Center at nearby Choiseul, touted by a local tourist magazine as featuring an "exciting selection of native handicrafts." Smaller than described and somewhat less than exciting, the center offered a few wood carvings, bamboo and grass weavings and some pottery items. The town was more interesting than its craft center—a tiny fishing village tucked against a pretty if somewhat littered cove. Small wooden fishing boats lined the shore, with names like *No Problem, Lion of Judah, Cool Running* and *Don't Worry II.*

We retraced our bumpy route through the jungle and paused next at Sulfur Springs, a fuming and predictably sulfurous thermal area inside an ancient caldera. A short, steep walk to an overlook was a sinus-clearing experience. Next stop was Diamond Falls and Botanical Gardens, a landscaped woodland that had been the estate of a wealthy French planter. A flower-bedecked trail lead to the falls, a thin and sparkling cataract tumbling over a slickrock face of yellow and cinnamon. The colors came from our just-visited Sulfur Springs, which feed the falls from above. We concluded our day's outing with a pause at a rain forest, so thickly vegetated that its hiking trails were botanical tunnels.

As we returned to the ship, Sylvester offered a running botanical commentary. He paused frequently to pluck samples from roadside trees—aromatic white lilies, nutmeg pods, cinnamon leaves and an oval cocoa bean the size of a small football. (Betty dissected it on the plane home, prompting curious stares from passengers and flight attendants.)

Back aboard the *Wind Star*, we gathered with other passengers at the fantail for a last look at our final port of call. About thirty young villagers swam after the departing ship, urging us to toss coins in the water. One of the passengers floated a dollar bill off the fantail and the youths surged for it in a happy frenzy of roiling water. A few more bills followed and the game continued. Soon, the kids began losing ground as the ship gained speed. Men from the village came out in their fishing boats to ensure that their youngsters made it back to shore.

Our last vision of the Little Caribbean was a palm-lined bay bobbing with smiling, waving children, like friendly seals. Standing by the rail, contemplating the boring flight home, where a week's worth of mail and phone messages awaited, I wished for a fleeting moment that I could slip over the side and join them.

ß ß ß

In the beginning there were no people, no animals, no trees, no stones. There was nothing. In the silence of the mists lived the gods called Tepeu, Gucumatz and Hurakan. They conferred and agreed on what was to be done...and light and life were created in the heart of the void.

— from the *Popo Vuh*, **sacred book of the Quiché Maya**

Chapter nine
BELIZE-GUATEMALA
Exploring Mayan coasts aboard the *Caribbean Prince*

B lame it on the sunshine, lack of wind and quiet surf. It was like swimming in an aquarium. We were snorkeling at a marine preserve just offshore of San Pedro, Belize, where the water was tepid and Lucite clear and the coral gardens were extensive and incredibly varied.

This was the second of eleven day aboard the *Caribbean Prince* of American Canadian Caribbean Line, prowling the Belize Great Barrier Reef, then sailing up the Rio Dulce of Guatemala. Snorkeling off San Pedro was absolutely awesome, some of the best I've enjoyed anywhere. It was a grand beginning to eleven days that would range from stimulating to serene.

ᛒ ᛒ ᛒ

In an isthmus often rocked with chaos, tiny Belize is a sanctuary of serenity. While many other Central American countries seethe with political unrest and often sacrifice their natural resources to feed their poor, Belize is a model of both political stability and environmental awareness. Actually, the two go hand in hand. Leaders of this politically young country—it gained full independence only in 1981—realized early on that tourism offered the great-

CRUISE PLANNER

The cruise • American Canadian Caribbean Line, as the protracted name implies, offers cruises in and about north and central America. These are small ship voyages on rivers and among offshore islands, with a strong focus on exploration, although they are "soft adventures" that appeal to any age group. Our voyage was an 11-day, 12-night exploration of the cayes (pronounced *keys*) of the Great Barrier Reef of Belize, with an emphasis on snorkeling and beach play, plus a cruise up the Rio Dulce into Guatemala to explore its towns and Mayan ruins. For information contact American Canadian Caribbean Line, P.O. Box 368, Warren, RI 02885; (800) 556-7450 or (401) 247-0955; FAX (401) 245-8303.

Getting there • Continental Airlines has direct service to Belize City from its Houston hub. Many other Continental flights converge on Houston from most corners of America and Canada. Early arrivals to Belize City gather at the Radisson Fort George Hotel, near the boat dock; discounted room rates are available for cruise passengers.

The ship • The *Caribbean Prince* is a shallow-draft motor vessel with a special bow ramp devised by company president Luther Blount. The thirty-eight cabins are snug but comfortable, with private baths and large windows. Dining is single seating, unassigned and casual. A BYOB policy eliminates the need to run up a bar tab; mixes are provided free. On-board facilities include a lounge/TV/video area, three open deck areas and a glass bottom boat for those who prefer not to snorkel. Officers and crew are American, plus several Belizeans.

When to go • The dry season in Belize-Guatemala is November through May, although occasional rain can fall during this period. This also is the coolest time of the year—but in an equatorial sense. Average high and low temperatures are around 80 and 65 degrees in December and 85 and 72 in July, with high humidity the year around.

What to bring • U.S. citizens need only a valid passport for Belize; visas for Guatemala are arranged aboard ship at the time of entry. Dress for the tropics—layered cottons are best. Bring broad brimmed hats or visors, beach towels or mats and lotions for sun protection. These cruises are casual, although some folks don jackets or dresses for the captain's dinner. You can bring your own snorkeling gear, although there's an ample supply on the ship. You'll want comfortable shoes for shore explorations, and binoculars and telephoto lenses for wildlife spotting and filming.

What's included • Airport-to-ship transfers, snorkeling and snorkel gear are included, except for a modest fee to snorkel at a marine preserve. A shore excursion to the Mayan ruin of Quiriguá in Guatemala is offered for an extra fee. Also, ACCL can arrange area tours with local operators before and after the cruise.

What to buy • Belize is not exactly a world craft center, although some excellent wood carvings are available at reasonable prices, along with the usual shell jewelry and similar Caribbean style souvenirs. Guatemala offers a better selection of crafts, including carved masks, other woodcarvings and colorful handwoven fabrics that are styled into purses, totes, blouses and skirts. Some Guatemalan crafts are available in Belize shops.

est economic potential. A sliver of land no bigger than Massachusetts, Belize is blessed with the longest barrier reef in the Western Hemisphere and lush swatches of rainforest and mangrove swamps that teem with wildlife. Mayan ruins are sprinkled about the country and more are in next-door Guatemala, including the famous Tikal.

This economy-driven conservation mood has led to the preservation of large tracts of forest and swamp. Cutting and clearing of the rainforest is discouraged. The 150-mile long Belize Barrier Reef and its many cayes (reef islands, pronounced "keys") are protected by strict federal regulations. Scuba divers aren't permitted to spearfish and coral cannot be "mined" by collectors.

Belize suffers no crush of population to threaten its natural resources. Fewer than 200,000 people occupy the country and a third of these live in pleasantly scruffy Belize City. This is a poor but certainly not impoverished country, and its people are optimistic about their future. As tourism grows, new hotels are cropping up among shabby stilt houses and picturesque colonial buildings. With "progress," of course, will come a certain loss of funky charm. Within a decade, visitors to Belize City may no longer feel they've stepped onto the set of a Sydney Greenstreet movie.

If you haven't consulted a geography book lately, you'll remember this country as British Honduras. It's a 180-mile long strip of the Caribbean coast, tucked between Mexico's Yucatan Peninsula to the north and Guatemala to the south and west. The first occupants date from around 10,000 B.C., and from these people evolved the highly sophisticated agrarian-based Olmec and Mayan cultures.

The arrival of Spain's Hernán Cortéz in 1519 marked the beginning of the end of the Mayan empire. He came looking for slaves and in his footsteps followed Catholic priests looking for souls.

British pirates often holed up here between raids against offshore Spanish ships.

Great Britain made several intrusions into central America, looking for timber and other resources, and British pirates often holed up here between raids against offshore Spanish ships. The two countries fought over this small slice of land for decades—while virtually enslaving its people, who were required to decimate their own forests, harvesting logs for export. The bit of land became the crown colony of British Honduras in 1862. In the decades that followed, the mixed population of mostly Creole-Blacks and a few Mayans and Baymen (Belizeans of English descent) agitated—generally peacefully—for freedom. It was granted independence in 1981 and it remains a member of the Commonwealth. The region's original name was restored in 1973 although no one is quite sure of the word's origin. It probably reaches back into Mayan times; *belix* is a Mayan word for brown river, of which rain-soaked Belize has an abundance.

Guatemala, which the *Caribbean Prince* visits during this cruise, is five times larger than Belize, reaching coast to coast across the Central American isthmus. Like Belize, it's a tropical mix of beaches, low swamplands and rainforest. Unlike Belize, it's dotted with volcanoes and other peaks, some reaching more than 12,000 feet. It's much more heavily populated, with eleven million residents. Another major difference between the two nations: English with a Creole lilt is spoken in Belize; Spanish is the national language of Guatemala. To the Maya, of course, Belize and Guatemala were the same

Shore stops on the many islands of the Belize Barrier Reef are a major activity on ACCL cruises to Belize-Guatemala; this one is Man-of-War Island.

place. Both regions fell under the swords of the Spanish, although Guatemala has been an independent nation much longer than Belize, winning freedom from Spain in 1821. It ruled Belize for a few years, then it was pressured in ceding the tiny nation back to Britain in 1859. Assorted liberals, conservatives and an occasional dictator have ruled Guatemala for well over a century. As of the mid-1990s, the country has enjoyed relative peace under a new democratic government.

ßßß
DAY ONE PLUS

Belize City is not a major tourist center. Most of that action is out on the cayes of the Belize Barrier Reef, where several resorts and small hotels thrive. "Out there," an airline passenger said, after sneering at our admission that we planned to spend time in Belize City, "is where the action is!"

Belize City has a waterfront but no beach; some charming old colonial houses but no museums; many shops in its small business district but no trendy boutiques.

However, we like funky old tropical towns so we arrived a day and a half early. We spent the first evening prowling the small downtown area, skipping from broken sidewalk to narrow street, poking about shops, mini-department stores and a good-sized supermarket, and wondering at the curious abundance of Chinese restaurants. (One was in a Texaco service station, sandwiched between the gas pumps and the grease racks.) The people here were exceptionally friendly and helpful and their melodic Creole dialect gave them a special charisma. Strangers with nothing to peddle but friendship greeted us as we walked about and photographed the old city: "What's up, bro. You walkin' your feet?" and "Takin' up some snaps, man?" Although part of the mainland, Belize and its people have a temperament more akin to the Caribbean islands.

The second installment of our early arrival was a day-long tour of interior Belize, which can be booked as part of the cruise package at additional cost.

A bus took us through green pasturelands, swamplands and an occasional swatch of low-lying rainforest to the national capital of Belmopan. The capital was moved fifty miles inland to this site after Hurricane Hattie destroyed the original Belize City capital complex in 1961. It's a rather curious place, more resembling a low-budget country club than a national capital, with a scatter of simple one-story buildings separated by carefully tended swatches of grass. It was laid out with room to grow, although—like a miniature Brasilia—it has failed to attract the expected crowds. Most government officials and workers commute from Belize City or nearby villages. There is little of visitor interest here, although we did encounter a small open air market. A museum to house Belize's rich Mayan treasures is in the works. The gray concrete government buildings are supposed to resemble Mayan pyramids, but the concept doesn't really work and they're rather drab.

A real Mayan ruin, within a mile of the Guatemalan border, was considerably more interesting. Called Xunantunich, this medium sized ceremonial center was discovered in 1882 and assorted archaeologists have been periodically pecking at it ever since, clearing away the jungle and seeking its treasures. A team from the University of California at Los Angeles is currently working here. Its focal point is a 150-foot-high ritual center called El Castillo. The stone ramparts offered a fine view of this profusely green and gently rolling terrain—for those of us willing to climb to the top on a sticky warm

The Belize Zoo is a surprisingly appealing attraction, with animal enclosures tucked neatly into a thick garden of native flora.

day. Surprisingly, after 10,000 years, El Castillo remains the highest man-made structure in this tiny low-rise country.

Our long day in the Belize countryside included two more stops of interest. The Belize Zoo is a surprisingly appealing attraction, with animal enclosures tucked neatly into a thick garden of native flora. It was started in 1983 as the determined afterthought of American Sharon Matola, who came here to manage a native animal menagerie for a wildlife film. When the project was abandoned for lack of funds, she lacked the heart to return the animals to the jungle. After human contact, she knew they probably wouldn't survive. She appealed to locals for help, got a surprisingly enthusiastic response and still remains as the zoo director.

Guanacaste National Reserve protects a small slice of thick woodland near Belmopan. The star attraction in this pocket-sized sanctuary is a giant guanacaste tree, a 150-year-old hardwood whose branches are heavily laden with orchids and other epiphytes (tree-dwelling plants). One could, by tuning out the hum of traffic on the adjacent highway, pretend to be deep within a rainforest, searching the creeper-draped canopy for interesting flora

Life moves at a leisurely pace on the islands of the Belize Great Barrier Reef. This pooch in San Pedro on Ambergris Caye obviously has no worries.

and fauna. I wandered off by myself, following a network of trails and enjoying the solitude of the forest until I accidentally stumbled into the rest of the group.

"Anybody here seen Doctor Livingston?" I asked.

Only a couple of them got the joke.

ßßß

DAY TWO

Don't worry about sharks," said Erwin, our Belizean onboard snorkeling instructor. "I don't think you'll give off vibrations like a lobster."

After overnighting at dockside in Belize City, the *Caribbean Prince* headed for San Pedro on Ambergris Caye. It's the only town of any substance along the Belize Barrier Reef, with a couple of thousand residents and a similar number of visitors. We were scheduled to snorkel here this afternoon, so Erwin conducted a lecture on snorkeling techniques and water safety. Naturally, someone asked about sharks. He explained that they located their prey by sonar vibrations, and that local sharks were rather small and dined only on lobsters and little fish.

We anchored off San Pedro, which from a distance appeared as a string of low-rise buildings fronting a sandy beach, with pink tile or thatched roofs tucked beneath ranks of palms. Closer inspection revealed an appealing study in rustic funk, like a 1930s California beach resort that somehow survived into the 1990s. The town is weathered but well tended and its sandy, unpaved streets are lined with curio shops, rum shops, cafés and small hotels. San Pedro has no sidewalks but no matter; the main mode of transit is by golf cart, so pedestrians are never really at risk.

This cute little beach retreat offers para-sailing, glass bottom boat rides and other water recreation, yet with none of the hustle of jet set resorts. Residents and contented visitors stroll about leisurely, often barefoot and sometimes nipping at bottles of Belikin beer. Although souvenir shops are abundant, commerce here is strictly low key. "You just lookin'? Hey, no problem, mon."

Our first snorkel outing in the Belize Barrier Reef may have been our best. We were taken by small boat to a marine preserve just offshore of San Pedro. Elkhorn, staghorn and fan coral covered the ocean floor like a fantasy forest; brown and purple mountainous star coral suggested Mayan ruins; slender pillar coral reached upward like hundreds of clustered fingers. Scores of fish—some as cheerfully colored as circus clowns—moved about in orderly squadrons or flitted around in random disorder. They ignored our intrusions, having become accustomed, in this popular preserve, to swimming among *homo sapiens*.

I trailed several fish to see where they were going, and soon I realized that—despite their constant motion—they never seem to arrive anyplace.

I began cruising above the coral landscape like a slow, low dirigible, enjoying that sense of free flight that snorkeling provides. Out of curiosity, I trailed several fish to see where they were going, and soon realized that—despite their constant motion—they never seem to arrive anyplace. I followed coral corridors to see where they led. One led to a dramatic cliff—a steep coral wall that plunged more than fifty feet. I explored its convoluted, multihued ramparts, sometimes making free dives to investigate schools of fish or curious coral shapes below.

When I finally returned to the boat I was surprised to see the rest of my group sitting there, unmasked, dried off and waiting with varying degrees of patience.

"How long have you guys been back in the boat?"

"Too long," Betty said, handing me a most impatient frown.

ß ß ß

DAY THREE

Life aboard the *Caribbean Prince* was—take your pick—busy and leisurely. As we motored between islands, purser-cruise director Stephanie Porter scheduled assorted activities—shore talks, videos, stretch and tone exercises and "deck hikes." Of course, those who just wanted to sit and watch the sea slide by could do so. A library in the forward lounge was stocked with books and the dining room—never closed because it also was the social hall and lecture room—was stocked with things to nibble and sip.

Goff's Caye, our next snorkeling stop, is one of those tiny islands that you've seen on TV commercials—a lonely patch of sand where a couple of guys are stranded and desperate for a beer or female fraternity or possibly both. It's even smaller than Gilligan's Island, 113 paces end to end, with thirteen palm trees and a cute little thatched hut.

Despite its lilliputian charms, Goff's Caye was not a welcome spot this day, for it was pelted by rain, driven by a gusty wind. A few brave souls snorkeled briefly and decided it was too chilly and choppy. Others of our group huddled for warmth in the hut. Windblown, cold and dripping wet, we looked very much like genuine castaways on this castaway island. We laughed about our misery, joked about that beer commercial and signaled for the skiff to come rescue us—a luxury not available to bona fide castaways.

Who says adventure cruising consists mostly of lectures and scholarly shore excursions? This not-so-motley crew is all dressed up for a pirates' party aboard the Caribbean Prince.

The storm had spoiled our snorkeling but no problem, as they say in these parts. There would be many more opportunities to view fish and reefs—with calm seas and sunshine. Furthermore, our itinerary would return us to Goff's Caye later in the cruise, giving it a chance to be more hospitable.

ᕝᕝᕝ

DAYS FOURFIVESIX

The weather cleared for most of our other Barrier Reef days, which blended into a pleasant procession of blue skies, bluer water and Technicolor coral.

Our next port of call was Tobacco Caye, a larger island with a few huts occupied by a handful of tourists and Belizean residents. We were skiffed to a rickety pier near a small sandy beach, and found the snorkeling to be fine. As we paddled about, the sun peeked occasionally through broken clouds, bringing sudden brilliance to the fish and coral, as if a considerate King Neptune had turned on a bank of fluorescent lights.

Despite the *Caribbean Prince's* bow landing capability, we anchored offshore and used the skiff for most of our island stops, since a closer approach might damage coral reefs. (The bow ramp is used mostly for landings on the mainland.) Captain Mike Snyder and his crew were zealous about protecting the fragile underwater environment. "Don't touch the coral and don't step on it," Erwin would remind us at each snorkel stop. "It takes a hundred years for coral to grow three inches. One step and you kill all that work."

Later, the skiff took us birdwatching off Man of War Island in the nearby Tobacco Range. We slowly circled the tiny bit of land, which was aswarm with frigate birds and brown boobies. Scores of boobies perched in a thick mangrove thatch, inflating their throat sacs into blood red balloons which, to a lady booby, is a very sexy thing to do. The sky above writhed with the ragged black silhouettes of frigate birds and boobies. It brought to mind some of the nightmarish scenes from Alfred Hitchcock's *The Birds.* However, the only casualties in our boat were a couple of direct hits from passing seagulls. (Captain Snyder *had* advised us to wear hats.)

Time's passage on the Belize Barrier Reef was marked by shore excursions, snorkeling, dolphin sightings and birdwatching, interspersed with ample meals and deep ocean-induced sleep. Yesterday wasn't Tuesday; it was

> *A passenger looked up smugly from her copy of* Marine Life of the Caribbean. *"I'll bet none of you have seen a Spanish grunt."*

Laughing Bird Caye Day, when I saw for the first time a squirrel fish with huge blue-black eyes and an elliptical body with vertical pinkish bands. The day before was Tobacco Caye Day when Betty saw that flight of big angel fish. I think tomorrow is Lime Caye Day. Or is it Punta Icacos Day? Does it matter?

You've heard of barefoot cruises. This is a two-shirt/two swimsuit cruise—one set on the body, the other hung up to dry after rinsing out the saltwater. Between island hops, we strolled about the boat or sat in the sun or shade with something from the library, or we hiked around the Sun Deck; seventeen times is a mile. Evening cocktail hours became games of underwater "Can you top this?"

"I saw a four-eyed butterfly fish this morning."

"Well, I saw *three* blue parrotfish."

"I'll bet you didn't see that fantastic coral garden, out beyond the pier. I went way out this afternoon. It was great!"

"You should've stayed closer in. We ran into a whole school of little striped yellow fish. Dozens of them; maybe a hundred."

A passenger looked up smugly from her copy of *Marine Life of the Caribbean.* "I'll bet none of you have seen a Spanish grunt. I saw one yesterday at Laughing Bird Caye."

"Heck, I saw one three days ago!"

"Where?"

"In Big Daddie's Disco in San Pedro."

DAY SEVEN

After several days of blue sea and palm fringed islands, we were greeted by a new horizon this morning—small, steep and jungle clad hills rising above the red tile roofs of Punta Gorda on the Belize mainland. We had entered the flat calm waters of the Bay of Honduras and would cross this inlet to sail up the Rio Dulce into Guatemala. First, the ship's officers had to clear customs in Punta Gorda (Fat Point), giving passengers an opportunity to prowl about the town.

Although it's in a pretty setting, Punta Gorda, we quickly discovered, was no tourist center. It's a small collection of weather-beaten wooden buildings, mostly on stilts, some listing like tired old men. Equally tired old cars chugged around town or dozed in the grass—some running, some rusting, some doing both. Thick vegetation crawled through the town in a silent invasion from the nearby hills, adding warm green thatch and occasional splashes of bougainvillea to an otherwise drab setting.

Across the Bay of Honduras, the Guatemalan town of Livingston at the mouth of the Rio Dulce was a bit more appealing. A single business street arched steeply up from the waterfront, lined with small stores, sidewalk cafés, curio shops and liquor stores. A fair sized hotel and a couple of restaurants peered out over the bay. The waterfront was busy with a curious mix of pleasure boats, jet skis, shrimp boats, fabric-topped excursion boats and Mayan Indian *cayucas*—dugout canoes. Lake Isabel just inland and the Rio Dulce that flows from it have become popular water play areas. This enticement has pulled Livingston into the touristic present, although it has not yet left its shantytown past.

Several of us from the *Caribbean Prince* hired a couple of the little tourist boats and motored up the river to a lagoon where manatees, those strange off-white sea mammals, were known to hang out. The boat operators spoke no English so one of our group used her high school Spanish to translate.

"He says we'll see many gaviotas," she said. That sounded intriguing until someone pointed out that *gaviota* is Spanish for sea gull. Fortunately, the bird life was considerably more varied. Piers and pilings along the rustic Princeton riverfront were crowded with pelicans, cormorants and—well, yes—sea gulls. Immediately beyond town, white egrets and herons perched in tall mangroves along the river, in shining contrast to the dark foliage.

In less than a mile, we entered "The Gorge," where limestone cliffs soar a hundred feet above the water. Although vertical, they were thickly cloaked with mangroves and other vegetation, like overlapping wall sconces curving out and then immediately upward. When not disturbed by passing watercraft, the river was a flat calm, capturing mirror images of the bankside foliage and the marbled gray sky above—reflections so flawless

We killed the engines and sat in silence for long, reflective moments, listing to the bird calls and the soft whisper of the jungle.

that we seemed to be staring at the sky while peering into the water.

No, we didn't find any manatees. It was mating season and the shy creatures had more important things on their minds than greeting tourist boats. But no matter; it was a fine trip. Cruising into the lagoon where the manatees lived, we killed the engines and sat in silence for long, reflective moments, listening to the bird calls and the soft whisper of the jungle. Heading back toward the ship, we paused at an inlet filled with lily pads, where shorebirds strode across the surface like little saints walking on water. A bit farther along, we paused to dip hands and dangle tentative toes into a hot and sulfuric bankside spring. As we cruised down the river, friendly Mayans waved from shoreline thatched huts and from their *cayucas*.

"I feel like I'm in a National Geographic Special," one of our group said.

≈≈≈

DAY EIGHT

Days aboard the *Caribbean Prince* ranged from leisurely to lively. Today's schedule began with a 6 a.m. wake-up call (not mandatory) to watch shoreline wildlife as the ship cruised up the Rio Dulce gorge to Lake Isabel (Lago de Izabal). Other activities included a visit to an old Spanish fortress on the

Passengers use the Carribean Prince's *bow landing ramp to go ashore at Casa Guatemala, a children's home on the Rio Dulce.*

lake, a stop at an orphanage and finally a cocktail hour marimba concert at the Maramonte Inn, one of several shoreside resorts in this area.

Sailing up the river, we retraced the route we'd taken the day before in the little tourist boat—this time with the advantage of an English narration. Captain Snyder pointed out landforms and birds as we cruised, and he mentioned with obvious pride that the *Prince* was the only cruise ship working these waters capable of crossing the sandbar at Livingston and sailing into to Lago de Izabal.

Castillo de San Felipe is a stone fortress built in the 1600s to discourage pirate forays up the Rio Dulce and into the lake. It's a remarkably complex catacomb. I discovered this the hard way by accepting the invitation of several young Guatemalan boys to probe through the blackness of its interior tunnels. After groping and bumping my way through blackness, I'd emerge blinking into daylight from one burrow, only to see them disappearing into another catacomb, laughing and challenging me to follow.

The day's most interesting activity was something rather unusual for a cruise line—an orphanage visit. Casa Guatemala on the Rio Dulce is a children's home run by a non-sectarian, non-profit group of volunteers from Guatemala, the U.S. and Great Britain. It shelters orphaned, homeless and abused Guatemalan children. ACCL owners help support the home, although the firm does not solicit contributions from passengers. However, a couple on our trip, Frank and Carla Blakely from Colorado, offered to auction off a bottle of bourbon he'd won during one of the ship's games. The crew contributed some ACCL logo items to fatten the pot and nearly $400 was raised.*

---

*Anyone interested in helping the Casa Guatemala orphanage can contact Sandra Seymour, 1716 Anthony Dr., S. Joseph, MI 49085; (616) 429-0255.

Dozens of kids and their care-givers crowded the small dock as the *Prince* nudged up to the shore and dropped its bow ramp. Crew members started a feeding frenzy by passing candy among the kids, and passengers bought generously at the school's gift shop, which featured Guatemalan handicrafts. The orphanage is a self-contained operation and staff members offered to conduct tours of its school, medical clinic, craft shops, greenhouse and other facilities. The intention here is to teach skills that will enable the children to support themselves when they leave the care center.

My tour was interrupted by a tyke about four years old, wearing a Minnie Mouse T-shirt. He attached himself to my left pinkie and offered—in Spanish—to give me his own personalized tour. Although I don't speak Spanish, I let him lead me about. His tour went mostly around in circles as we paused to check out playground equipment, watch other kids play ball and observe the cook preparing lunch. He led me to *Minnie released his grip on my pinkie and disappeared into the crowd of kids. New friendships are fleeting, I thought.* a tabletop Christmas tree with a Nativity scene at its base—we were on a holiday cruise—and he instructed me to rearrange some of the figures. He apparently wasn't pleased with the current grouping and of course he was too short to reach the display. A plastic figure of Darth Vader—I'm not sure of his Nativity connection—had tipped over and it seemed particularly important to Minnie that he be placed upright.

Captain Snyder tooted the *Prince's* whistle and passengers and crew members began returning to the ship. Minnie released his grip on my pinkie and disappeared into the crowd of kids. New friendships are fleeting, I thought, disappointed that he hadn't said goodbye. As our ship moved away from the landing, I saw a little brown face among many brown faces on the pier, pushing toward the front and waving enthusiastically. I waved back and we exchanged smiles; Minnie hadn't forgotten me.

ʚ ʚ ʚ

DAY NINE

The *Prince* had spent the previous evening docked at the Maramonte Inn, and it would remain there most of this day. Passengers could take an inland tour to a Mayan ruin, relax aboard the ship or hang out at the inn, with access to its swimming pool and waterside bar.

A one-hour bus ride through the Guatemalan countryside—lush even where it was deforested and turned to agriculture—took us to Quiriguá ruin. A medium sized Mayan site and now a national park, it's noted mostly for its nine stelae, or carved standing tablets. They're the tallest in the Mayan kingdom; one stands more than 25 feet. The tablets are spaced around a grass-covered meadow so carefully cropped that it would make a decent soccer field. From here, a path leads to the main ruin, a low lying multi-level stone complex called—but bearing no similarity to—the Acropolis.

According to our Guatemalan guide, the site's discoverer, American diplomat John Lloyd Stephens, had wanted to pack up the whole lot—stone by stone—and ship it to New York for reassembly as a tourist attraction. Fortunately, this was the 1840s and he couldn't find the means to haul thousands of tons of stone that distance. Earlier, he'd purchased the magnificent ruin of Copán in next door Honduras for fifty dollars. Fortunately, he left it in place.

Quiriguá ruin, a medium-size Mayan site near Lake Isabel, is one of the regular shore stops on ACCL's Belize-Guatemala cruises.

ße ße ße

DAY TEN

We sailed this day under a bright tropical sun, from the Port of Livingston across the Bay of Honduras and back into Belizean waters. Betty and I almost missed breakfast, having partied the night before with several other passengers and crew members at a Livingston disco. It was one of those pubs indigenous to the contemporary tropics, with a dance floor, thatched roof, no walls and speakers the size of mini-vans. You would not want to live next door to a tropical disco. (I never knew that one could dance to Guatemalan rap music; perhaps one can't but we did, after a sufficiency of local beer.)

Our voyage was to end the way it had begun, with two more days of snorkeling in the Belize Barrier Reef. Today's destination was West Snake Caye in the reef's southern section.

It was a perfect day for play. The sun glittered off the deep blue water and not a whisper of wind disturbed the surf. The *Caribbean Prince* executed a "modified bow landing," stopping offshore beyond the coral zone and dropping the bow ramp into knee-deep water, over a sandy bottom. Our ship thus served as a swimming and snorkeling platform. We had the option of wading across the sugar-white sandy bottom to palm-shaded West Snake Caye and a tiny satellite island nearby. The snorkeling was fine, with the usual array of fish and some striking reef colors, notably purple fan coral, bright orange staghorn coral, and green and lemon yellow brain coral.

When we'd had our fill of snorkeling, we swam, waded and splashed around the bow lander. The crew launched a *cayuca* and we tried our skills at paddling Mayan style. The first challenge was to get into the tippy thing! After we'd accomplish this and could confidently paddle our own canoe—so to speak—crew member Erwin then challenged us to stand up in it. Most of us crashed in the attempt but no matter. A hot shower and mid-afternoon nip of rum were but a bow ramp away.

What a glorious way
To spend a day
On a caye.
No, it doesn't all rhyme.

ßßß

DAY ELEVEN

Goff's Caye was considerably more hospitable on this visit. As our cruise ship approached the tiny island, its palms and white sandy beaches looked especially inviting, shimmering under a bright sun.

We parked our gear in the shade of one of its thirteen palms and headed for the reefs, a short flipper-kick from the beach. They were shallow, easy to reach and offered great stands of tall elkhorn and staghorn coral, resembling giant *bonsai*. We spent most of our final afternoon swimming down coral corridors between these underwater forests.

In a sense, our final day had begun the night before, because that was New Year's Eve and most of us stayed up past midnight. We enjoyed a champagne supper aboard and then several passengers headed ashore to hit the local pubs. We were anchored off the Belizean village off Placencia. Since we'd had our fill of discos earlier in Livingston, we chose to remain aboard and bring in the New Year at a more sedate party on the top deck.

A three-quarter moon, puffy clouds and a scatter of stars decorated the canopy overhead. Ashore, lights of a Christmas tree in Placencia's plaza filtered through the silhouetted palms. As midnight approached, we could hear the distant staccato chatter of strings of firecrackers. Aboard the *Prince*, several passengers danced beneath the stars, to a Sarah Vaughn album piped over the ship's speakers. Others sat and sipped rum punch, talking quietly of the year passed and the one immediately ahead.

As the New Year arrived, several Roman candles erupted from nearby yachts, arching through the night sky like colored comets. They splashed their hues off the side of our ship as they passed, then sizzled into the sea. Our passengers hugged and kissed and did the usual New Year's thing, ending with a ragged version of *Auld Lang Syne*. In the background, Sarah Vaughn's soft voice caressed the gentle tropic air, offering promise for tomorrow: "Somewhere my love, there will be songs to sing."

You can say that again, Sarah.

ßßß

PART IV
Europe

Europe's canals, once essential for cargo traffic, are now popular for cruising.
La Belle Epoque *drifts down Canal du Nivernais in France's Burgundy.*

The ship was cheered, the harbor cleared
Merrily did we drop
Below the kirk, below the hill
Below the lighthouse top.

— Samuel Taylor Coleridge
The Ancient Mariner

Chapter ten

NORWAY'S NORTH COAST
Cruising Viking shores with Bergen Line

Hurtigruten sounds like a word that comic Robin Williams would say with a fake Scandinavian accent. It isn't. Nor is it pickled herring in sour cream sauce, nor a Swedish peasant blouse. This very Norwegian sounding word refers to a very Norwegian kind of boat.

Back in 1893, the Norwegian government hired a steamship company to carry passengers, mail and cargo between coastal settlements that dot the fjords and offshore islands of Norway's far north. This service evolved into the Coastal Express; *Hurtigruten* translates as "fast route" or "fast road." The term eventually was applied to the ships; singular is *Hurtigrute.*

In the days before highways and airports, the *Hurtigruten* offered the only link to the outside world for many coastal communities. Service has continued for more than a century, interrupted only by the German occupation of

CRUISE PLANNER

The cruise ● This is a twelve-day Norwegian Coastal Voyage between Bergen and Kirkenes. Contact Bergen Line, 405 Park Avenue, New York, NY 10022; (800) 323-7436 for booking information or (800) 666-2374 to request a brochure. The local number is (212) 319-1300. In addition to the longer voyages, you can book a seven-day northbound cruise or six-day southbound trips, plus a special one-day cruise from Kirkenes to Russia's Murmansk, which runs in summers only. Book early for summer trips, at six months in advance. Off-season cruises should be booked at least thirty days ahead. Bergen Line is the American booking company for the Coastal Express and several other European ferry operations. The Norwegian liners are operated under government contract by two different firms with unpronounceable names.

Getting there ● Scandinavian Airline Systems (SAS) provides the most comprehensive service between major U.S. cities and Norway. Overseas flights land in Oslo, from where you can catch a short hop to Bergen, or take the scenic Bergen Railway. (See "To Bergen in a Nutshell," page 226.)

The ships ● These are passenger-auto-cargo ferries that ply Norway's north coast. However, some of the larger ships such as the *Nordlys* have many cruise ship amenities—comfortable cabins with private baths, dining rooms, cocktail lounges, workout rooms and saunas. Officers and crew are Norwegian. The 414-foot, 11,200 gross ton *Nordlys* has a passenger capacity of 490 in cabins. Three vessels of similar size, the *Nordkapp, Polarlys* and *Nordnorge* joined the fleet in the mid-1990s.

When to go ● The vessels operate throughout the year. Summer is the most popular time, for two obvious reasons: The weather is more reliable then, and most shore excursions run from May through mid-September. However, the shoulder seasons of spring and fall offer the advantage of less crowded ships.

What to bring ● A valid passport will get you into Norway from America and most other countries. There are no formal dress occasions for cabin passengers; pack casually and warmly, with good rain gear. Much of Norway's north coast lies above the Arctic Circle, so it can get cold, even in midsummer, and it rains a *lot.*

What's included ● Bergen Line can provide all-inclusive packages with air fare, pre-cruise and post-cruise hotel accommodations. Cruise packages include all onboard meals and staterooms. Shore excursions are not included in the cruise price, although they can be purchased individually on board or as a package with your cruise tickets. They range from guided tours at various ports of call to overland coach trips along the fjords. You can choose to wander about on your own since most ports are near city centers, or arrange individual tours through the on-board cruise passenger coordinator.

What to buy ● Because of its affluence and the *kroner's* strength against the dollar, Norway is expensive. Its craftspeople are noted for their crystal, pewter and silver, and the native Sami people produce fine handcrafted silver jewelry.

This is the look of Norway's north coast, as seen from the Hurtigruten. *Even in late summer, the rugged mountains above Soroy Sound are dusted with snow.*

Norway during World War II. The Coastal Express tried to keep operating in the early years of the war but it suffered heavily, losing half its tonnage to German U-boats and mines laid by both sides.

Today, several ships make the eleven-day round trip between Bergen and Kirkenes. Along the way, they make more that thirty port calls in each direction. Many are extended stops, allowing time for shore excursions or exploring on one's own. Although these are modern diesel powered ships, technically ferryboats since they carry both passengers and vehicles, they're still called "coastal steamers." Newest members of the fleet are 11,000-ton vessels capable of carrying 700 travelers, more than half in staterooms. Hundreds travel as deck passengers, primarily Norwegians commuting between communities and backpacking youngsters who unroll sleeping bags in the lounges. The *Hurtigruten* is popular as a segment of a package tour. Bus groups hop on at one port, enjoy a few nights aboard, and then rejoin their land tour down the line.

Newer vessels of the *Hurtigruten* fleet are as modern and well equipped as many cruise ships. Our craft, *M/S Nordlys* (Northern Lights) had comfortable staterooms with writing desks, phones and private baths, plus top deck passenger lounges with picture windows to maximize the views, and a nicely appointed dining room and cocktail lounge.

Meal service is buffet style for breakfast and lunch, with table service at dinner, and the dining room is all nonsmoking. Hefty Scandinavian breakfast spreads include pickled and smoked fish, eggs, assorted breads and crackers, cheeses, patés, fruit, yogurt and juice. Lunch is equally formidable, with the addition of a several other dishes. (Several times during our trip, huge platters of shrimp appeared.) Dinner, generally of a Norwegian persuasion, is accompanied by an interesting if small wine list.

Naturally, the ships are more crowded in summer—often full. Early spring or early autumn are nice times to go if shore excursions and museum hopping aren't critical to your enjoyment; many museums close in the off season and fewer shore excursions are conducted since there are fewer participants. Passenger facilities are uncrowded during shoulder seasons and autumn offers the bonus of fall color that marbles the wooded slopes along Norway's north coast.

If you want to experience the midnight sun, book your cruise from mid-May through July. At the North Cape, the northernmost landfall in Europe, the sun never sets from May 14 to July 30. On the other hand, if you're a night person, the sun doesn't rise on the North Cape from November 18 until January 24. There are no guarantees on weather in these northern reaches, although the odds for sunshine and calmness are better from May through August. Autumn can be sunny, or it can host sizable storms. Winter can turn this already scenic coastline into a white wonderland. However, storms can turn the sea into an angry cauldron in fall and winter, sometimes requiring the ships to bypass ports.

ﾚﾚﾚ

DAY ONE

The *M/S Nordlys* backed gracefully out of its Bergen harbor berth at 10:15 p.m., while a Norwegian-subtitled *Conan, the Barbarian* played on the TV set in the aft lounge. It had been turned on by several happily noisy Norwegian teenagers. The large ship spun slowly on its axis, pointed its bow to the North Atlantic and began its coastal voyage. The rumpled blanket of stars that is nighttime Bergen slipped past the lounge's large port and starboard windows. Meanwhile, Conan was having a terrible time with a bunch of bad guys in leather armor.

Half an hour later, we passed under Nordhordland suspension bridge, Bergan's version of the Golden Gate. I was reminded of San Francisco, almost as beautiful and not nearly as tidy as the city we had just left. Our next port was Floro, where we were due to arrive at 4 a.m. We decided not to wait up.

ﾚﾚﾚ

DAY TWO

We awoke to the first of many miles of stunning north coast scenery—rocky, wooded mountains rising steeply from the sea, veined with glistening waterfalls and dusted in their heights with snow. Tidy farms with white houses and red barns were tucked on coastal shelves; occasional towns cantilevered into the steep slope added more geometry the setting. Rain and sleet veiled the scene and occasional shafts of sunlight danced downward, picking random targets—a red barn, a distant hill, the heart of a whitewashed town. Overlapping layers of peaks and ridges stretched beyond, each shaded differently by the mist and haze, like sections of stage scenery.

Our ship paused briefly at Maloy—too briefly to permit time ashore—and then it entered the open sea. A storm which had been with us since Bergen, gave us our first taste of a turbulent ocean. Betty retired to our cabin and I went to the forward lounge to ride out the swells. A man beside me began slowly pushing antacid tablets into his mouth from their foil wrapper and chewing them solemnly.

A ship cruising a turbulent sea is always a stimulating sight. The *Nordlys* rose and fell through the swells like a slow motion roller coaster, exhibiting a grace than only a sailor can appreciate. Waves slammed into the bow and shattered harmlessly, slipping past like great clouds of steam. Other craft cruised nearby and some bobbed like corks in a flushed potty; I realized that we were aboard a rather stable ship. Waves crashed against the shoreline—just a few hundred yards away—sending white scallops of spray skyward. The ship then heeled as it steered hard a-starboard to tuck between a storm-lashed shoal and the rocky coast. A few minutes later, it entered a sheltered passage where the galloping sea calmed down.

After a brief stop at Torvik, the *Nordlys* entered the open sea again ("For only about half an hour," said our cabin maid, obviously noticing Betty's frown), and then paused at one of the most appealing towns on the entire north coast. Alesund is a jeweled blend of Venice and Bergen, smothering a couple of narrow island and spilling up an adjacent hill. Many of its buildings

Alesund is a jeweled blend of Venice and Bergen, smothering a couple of narrow island and spilling up an adjacent hill.

stand up to their ankles in water, and narrow channels cut through the small downtown area. Cobbled streets tilt up to a low hill, where 418 steps or a brief cab ride will deliver visitors to a stunning overview of this little charmer. Alesund burned to the ground in 1904 and was rebuilt in a pictur-esque *art nouveau* style. Much of this architecture survives today, giving it a curiously prim medieval look. Evergreen-clad peaks rise above the town. Beyond them, the jagged, snowy Alps of Sunnmore add a final touch to this splendid setting.

Next on our horizon, also a brief cargo stop, was Molde, which in summer hosts a popular jazz festival. The rest of the year, its main claim to fame is its sensational view of the peaks of the Romsdalen Alps, across the fjord to the west.

🦜🦜🦜

DAY THREE

We were awakened by a gentle thump and looked out our cabin window to see that we'd just docked at the port of Trondheim. It's the third largest city in Norway, after Oslo and Bergen, with a population pushing past 140,000. Like smaller Molde, it doesn't occupy a spectacular setting. Of course all of these coastal towns, tucked against the shoreline and crawling into wooded hills, are considerably more attractive than most American communities.

A ten-minute walk delivered us to the heart of the town. It's built along the River Nid, where centuries-old peaked roof wooden warehouses contain stores and shops. Beyond the stream, many of its streets are still cobbled, lined with stone and brick medieval style buildings. Our primary targets were two downtown attractions—the imposing high spired Nidaros Cathedral and Trondheim Kunstforening (Museum of Applied Art and Craft). One of the largest Gothic structures in Scandinavia, the cathedral dates from the twelfth century. The museum next door offers an interesting mix of seventeenth and eighteenth century artifacts and examples of postwar commercial Scandina-vian design.

Trondheim is one of Norway's oldest cities, tracing its roots to a Viking settlement in the early tenth century. Originally called Trondelag, then Nidaros, it became the first capitol in late 900 A.D., after Olav Tryggvason defeated other Viking chiefs and unified Norway. It held that post until Hakon Hakonsson gained power and moved the monarchy to Bergen in 1217.

ۿ ۿ ۿ

DAY FOUR

After a quiet night at sea, we awoke in the port of Nesna. This small town is neatly arrayed on a coastal shelf, backgrounded by steep wooded hills and sheltered by offshore islands. On this September morn, the surrounding island forests were marbled with golden yellow.

Just north of Nesna, Hestmann Island—which straddles the Arctic Circle—appeared to port. Legend says the mounded isle with a distinctive tip at the top is the profile of a knight who was turned to stone. However, it more resembles a prominent component of Madonna's anatomy. Just a few miles beyond, on the starboard side, a large wire-cage globe on a small rocky island marks the precise location of the Arctic Circle.

Our next pause—unfortunately brief—was at Ornes, an idyllic gem of a town clustered around a narrow bay at the base of steep, thickly forested hills. Craggy snow-dusted peaks filled the horizon beyond. A tiny rockbound marina sheltering brightly colored fishing boats and pleasure craft completed this pleasing sketch.

Later that morning, as the ship threaded its way between the mainland and scattered small islands, we were invited on a bridge tour. The second officer, who was manning the bridge at the time, proudly demonstrated his electronic, computerized toys. Computer screens displayed—at the touch of a button—fuel and water capacities, indoor and outdoor temperature, even individual cabin conditions. Video cameras flashed images from various parts of the ship (but not from cabins). A control panel resembling a mockup for the starship *Enterprise* could pinpoint a fire in any cabin or anywhere else on the ship, almost before it started.

"We can even tell if you're smoking a cheap cigar," the officer joked. We later discovered just how sensitive this system was. A defective transformer on my notebook computer fried a wall outlet and a crew member knocked on our cabin door in less than a minute, because it had triggered an alarm.

After the bridge tour, we retired to the forward lounge—a favorite spot—and watched the ship dock at Bodo, a town of about 35,000 people. With no craggy peaks rising behind its busy portside business district, we rated it as "ordinary." (Compared with Fresno, California, it would be an absolute jewel.) It's a very young town, says our guidebook, dating back only to 1816.

ۿ ۿ ۿ

DAY FIVE

Merry Christmas!" Betty was kneeling atop her berth, with her undersized Chinese nose pressed to our cabin window. "Come and look!"

I rarely stir at 6 a.m., but she sounded unusually enthusiastic so I dragged myself to the portal. We were gliding into the harbor of Harstaad, a small town which—like most of the others—was surrounded by thick forest, with ice cream scoops of peaks beyond. On this first day of October, the rooftops and streets were dusted white with snow. Autumn color still painted the surrounding forests, presenting a distinctively Scandinavian Yuletide scene.

As soon as the *Nordlys* docked, we took a pre-breakfast stroll through the harborside business district, walking gingerly on sidewalks crusted with snow. After a few minutes, a flurry of fat flakes began pelting us with feather soft touches. Snow crystals clung to our jackets, mittens and eyebrows. Laughing like kids, we took hands and hurried back to the shelter of the ship.

Later that morning, passengers were summoned to the realm of King Neptune, which happened to be the forward lounge. The ruler of the deep, bearing a suspicious resemblance to a Norwegian troll, welcomed us to his cold, wet, windy

Neptune warned us to stop fussing about the weather and choppy seas, or he'd brew up a real storm.

and rainy kingdom and congratulated us for having crossed the Arctic Circle the day before. We landlubbers then received our formal initiation into Neptune's kingdom. Commanded to kneel, we were anointed with a ladle of ice water down our backs, complete with ice cubes. We were then handed a towel, a certificate and a glass of sherry to help ease the shock of entry into this sacred dominion.

"You are now equal to the codfish, halibut, mermaids and crabs," King Neptune proclaimed. However, he warned us to stop fussing about the weather and choppy seas, or he'd brew up a *real* storm.

Tromso, our next shore stop, is one of the north coast's largest towns and it calls itself the Norway's arctic capital. It certainly looked the part when the *Nordlys* glided into port that afternoon. The wooded hills surrounding this island town of 35,000 were blanketed with new snow, continuing the Christmas card scene that had greeted us at Harstad.

Several museums and other attractions mark its arctic role. Tromso Museum offers an outstanding exhibit concerning the Sami people of the far north; the Northern Lights Planetarium features a wide screen film about the *aurora borealis*; the Polar Museum focuses on the exploits of Roald Amundsen and other arctic explorers; and the modern A-frame Tromsdalen Church has polar themes in its striking architecture. Two monuments honor Amundsen, who launched two of his major polar explorations from here.

"Don't be alarmed about the weather," our guide said as we began a Tromso tour. "We had our first snow here at the end of August."

After a drive through the predictably neat and clean downtown area, we were ushered into the Tromso Museum, one of the finest on the north coast. It offers excellent displays of the archeology, flora, fauna and sociology of this far northern region. I was particularly intrigued by an exhibit concerning the native Sami people. I'd learned about them in fourth grade geography as the Laplanders, a name the Sami now disdain. These dark haired people with vaguely Asian features trace their roots back thousands of years. Originally hunter-gatherers, they learned to domesticate reindeer a few centuries ago and became herders. Many still herd reindeer in these parts, although they now use snowmobiles and even helicopters. Others have left ancestral lands to assimilate into urban society.

"Our largest Sami tribes are in Oslo and Bergen," our guide quipped.

The Nordlys *dwarfs the dock at Hammerfest (left), although it appears small from this vantage point on a hill above the town.*

ßßß
DAY SIX

At Hammerfest, one gets an even greater sense of the far north. Only a thin scatter of hardwoods decorate this small community, cantilevered onto a coastal rim around a harbor. Houses and businesses are closely packed, as if huddled together for warmth. Low, rocky hills rise above Hammerfest and special fences protect the town from snow slides.

Rather barren and yet as prim as others on the coast, the town looks better from above. A steep but mercifully short switchback trail delivered us to a high vantage point. From this perch several hundred feet above the harbor, Hammerfest is neatly arrayed around its coastal enclave. The largest thing we could see was our ship, towering over the small waterfront. Visitors can catch similar views and a meal at the nearby Touristura Restaurant, although it's open only in summer. This vista can be reached by road via taxi, but the path offers better vistas.

Hammerfest is the most northern port of call on our route; the ships sail east and slightly south from here. (One guidebook calls it the northernmost city in the world, which would come as a surprise to residents of Resolute in Canada's Northwest Territories and several communities in Siberia and Greenland.)

Our next stop was the gateway to the North Cape or *Nordkapp,* the northernmost landfall in Europe. It's one of the most popular lures in this area, attracting nearly 250,000 people a year. Thousands more see it from the sea, as cruise ships pass beneath its fluted, almost vertical profile. The coastal steamers don't pass the cape, which is located on Mageroy Island. They stay inland, and passengers can take a 21-mile van trip from Honningsvag, across a barren, starkly scenic tundra to this legendary ledge.

"We are very lucky," our shipboard guide told us. "After today, the cape is closed for the season."

How does one close a cape?

He referred to the North Cape Pavilion exhibit center, built on top of—and tunneled into—the 1,007-foot headland. The pavilion is open only from May to early October because snow closes the access road the rest of the year. Hardy souls can get there in winter by snowmobile or cross-country skis, items that cruise passengers generally do not have in their possession.

Honningsvag, supported primarily by tourism and a fair-sized fishing fleet, is attractive despite its bleak setting. The small town is clustered neatly around a harbor with a compact business district rising to brushy, treeless hills. As we started toward the cape on a road covered with new snow, our escort from the ship asked the driver when summer had ended.

"Yesterday."

"How long is your summer here?" I asked.

The driver held up five fingers.

"Five weeks?"

"No, five days." He was kidding, of course.

Sami herders graze their reindeer on the rocky slopes of Mageroy Island during the warmer months. Cape-bound visitors can see their summer camps of skin tents—set up mostly for show—and sometimes the herds themselves. The North Cape Pavilion is an extensive facility, with several view areas, a café and restaurant and a souvenir ship with a good selection of Sami and Norwegian handicrafts. An underground corridor blasted through the stony innards of the headland leads past three excellent dioramas about the cape's history, and to an underground view area in the cliff face.

Back on the surface, a wide path leads to the headland itself, fenced because of the thousand-foot drop to the sea. A focal point here is a large skeletal globe, which most visitors find more interesting than the boundless vista north across the Arctic Ocean. Nothing lies between here and the North Pole except 2,000 miles of water, ice and polar bears.

> *Nothing lies between the North Cape and the North Pole except 2,000 miles of water, ice and polar bears.*

Nordkapp has been around for 400 million years, according to geologists. It's been a landmark for explorers, sailors (including pirates), fishermen and whalers for centuries. The Sami called it *Knyskanes* and Russian sailors referred to it as *Murmanski Noss,* "Cape of the Norwegians." British explorer Richard Chancellor named it North Cape when he rounded the great headland in 1553, searching for a northeast passage. He didn't find one, although others followed his route to exploit the rich fishing and whaling grounds near this juncture of Norway and Russia. And could tourism be far behind? King Oscar II, sovereign of Norway and Sweden, visited the cape in 1873 and shortly after, Thomas Cook, the English inventor of group travel, arranged the first tourist charters.

The cape's first tourist of record was Italian priest Francesco Negri, who was quite taken by the place during a visit in 1664. To quote his journal:

Here I stand at the North Cape, the outer tip of Finnmark, the very edge of the world. Here where the world terminates, my curiosity is satiated. And, God willing, I contentedly return home.

Gee, I didn't think it was *that* awesome!

This globe at the North Cape marks the most northern promontory of land on the European continent.

ᚦ ᚦ ᚦ

DAY SEVEN

The coastal countryside loses much of its contour east of *Nordkapp*. Shorelines and islands bear the characteristic arctic signature—low-lying and brushy, almost treeless and often scattered with stones. At the end of the *Hurtigruten* line, Kirkenes thus does not boast an imposing backdrop, like some of the communities we had seen earlier during this voyage. It is an ordinary arctic town of 5,000 souls who apparently do not mind long, dark winters and the occasional icing up of their harbor. A nearby iron mine and visitors from cruise ships keep them employed. The small airport is busy in summer, since this is the break point for people booking one-way trips on the Coast Express.

The big attraction here—certainly more interesting in concept than in reality—is the Russian border, less than ten miles away. Unless you've arranged a visa in advance, you can't stick your toe into Russia in order to add it to your list of countries visited. (However, summer cruises to Murmansk can be taken without a visa; see below.) Passengers on the regular coastal cruise can join a tour or hire a cab and go to—but not through—the frontier. Most cab drivers speak fairly good English. Ours grinned as we parked just short of the customs-immigration office, which is on the Norwegian side of the border.

"Before the Soviet Union was broken up, the gate to customs was always closed, and people would reach through the fence to pick up a stone, thinking they had a Soviet souvenir. All they had was a Norwegian rock."

"This has always been a peaceful border crossing," our cab driver-guide said. Norwegians, he explained, have a great respect for Russia since it was Soviet troops that liberated Norway in 1944.

Norwegians have a great respect for Russia, since it was Soviet troops that liberated Norway in 1944.

Since the dissolution of the Soviet Union, only a passport and visa are required for entry into Russia. Norwegians routinely cross the border on business. In summer, a passenger steamer makes one-day round trips to Murmansk, which is about 155 miles away. Locals like to take the trip for a glimpse of Russia and to buy liquor, which is much cheaper than their heavily taxed booze.

"But they can't bring it back, so they must drink it all there," our driver said. "And so, of course, they can't remember what they saw."

After a two-hour pause in Kirkenes, the *Nordlys* began its southbound leg. It calls on the same ports, although round-trip passengers don't have to stare at a lot of used scenery. For the most part, the ship makes daylight stops at ports that it reached at night on the way up.

ও ও ও

DAY EIGHT

A nice moment in a Norwegian fjord: As we sailed southward after an early-morning pause at Havoysund, a small motorboat pulled alongside the ship. A Sami man, dressed in a traditional multi-colored knit sweater and four-pointed hat, tossed a bundle up to a waiting deckhand. Then he boosted a woman—probably his wife—onto a rope ladder that had been dropped over the side, and she carefully climbed aboard. The man then pulled away, waving happily at those of us leaning over the rail.

How did the ship's crew know to stop for her? For all we know, this member of Norway's most ancient people had a cellular phone.

Later that day, we called again at Hammerfest, and then the *Nordlys* entered Soroy Sound between Soroy and Seiland Islands, one of the most beautiful passages on the voyage. Ragged peaks dusted with new snow rose abruptly from water's edge, some reaching more than 3,000 feet. They were adorned with rocky ridges and stands of trees, now stripped of their fall color. Our good ship *Lollipop* was sailing between great, rough mounds of rocky road ice cream. Peeking through broken clouds, the sun cast splashes of pale gold on peaks and valleys.

NORWAY'S ABSENTEE WAR

Norway tried desperately to remain neutral during World War II, knowing that the fierce Nazi *Blitzkrieg* could easily overwhelm it. Yet, the proud nation refused Hitler's demands for cooperation; King Hakkon would not be a puppet to *Der Fuher.*

However, he became caught in a political vice between Germany and Great Britain. Winston Churchill wanted to mine Norwegian coastal waters to force German iron ore shipments from Sweden into the open sea, where the Royal Navy could get at them. And Germany wanted naval bases in Norway for operations against Great Britain. Norway sympathized with the U.K. and refused to cooperate with Germany, so Hitler launched a surprise attack on April 9, 1940. Britain landed an ill-equipped, poorly trained force of "territorials" (reservists) in Norway, trying to fend off the Nazi onslaught, but within weeks they and the small Norwegian force were overwhelmed. Since the situation was hopeless, the government decided to surrender on June 7.

Still, Norway did not give up the fight. The royal family and most government ministers escaped to England, where they directed a two-pronged war against the occupying Germans. A home resistance force that eventually numbered more than 40,000 was directed by the Norwegian government-in-absentia based in London. Its members blew up bridges and roadways to harass German troop movements, helped Jews and patriot refugees escape and blew up a German heavy water plant used for atomic bomb experiments. More than a thousand resistance members were captured, beaten and tortured; nearly a hundred were killed. Meanwhile, many members of the Norwegian military had escaped to England, there they united with British forces to battle the enemy. Thousands more young Norwegians slipped out of the country to join this absentee fighting force. Most went to the Shetland Islands, carried by fishing boats that became known as "Shetland buses."

His name was traitor

During the occupation, a minor Norwegian bureaucrat named Vidkun Quisling offered to cooperate with the invaders and he even installed himself as prime minister. Hitler, needing a local puppet, accepted him while privately denouncing him as an incompetent. Throughout the war, Quisling continued working with the invaders and probably was responsible for the betrayal of many resistance troops.

The liberation of Norway began with an invasion by Russians through Finland in late 1944, soon joined by Norwegian troops from England. Hitler ordered a scorched earth policy and attempted the forced evacuation of citizens from coastal communities. Many of the towns we visited had been rebuilt after being burned to the ground by the retreating Nazis, particularly in the northern province of Finmark.

King Hakkon returned home on June 7, 1945, five years to the day after he'd been forced to flee. Quisling surrendered at the Oslo police station and, after a one-month trial, was executed by firing squad, along with several other collaborators. Historians hold him in such contempt that "quisling" has become a noun, meaning a turncoat or traitor who aids a foreign invader.

As I stood on the promenade deck, taking pictures and exclaiming over the scenery, a sudden snow flurry descended, driving me to the fantail. The sun returned a bit later, just in time to cast its rays on our next port stop, the town of Oksfjord. This rustic jewel of a hamlet is tucked into the end of a narrow inlet, cradled by these high peaks. Our northbound stop had been at night, so this was our first good look at this fine scene.

Old Sol, finished playing tag with the clouds, slipped behind high peaks as the Coastal Express slipped out of Oksfjord's inlet. In the half-light, the surrounding peaks with their thin dusting of snow and rocky seams resembled finely-detailed steel engravings. As imposing as this was, that evening brought an even more incredible sight. We saw, for the first time, those fabled Northern Lights. (See box on the next page.)

ß ß ß

DAY NINE

Our ninth day began ridiculously early, or was this the end of our eighth day? We'd signed up for a midnight shore excursion to the Tromso Planetarium to see a 45-minute film on the *aurora borealis*. Having seen the Northern Lights the night before, we decided that this was a required stop, particularly since Tromso is a major research center for the aurora. Watching the film, we learned that the phenomena occurs when the sun's flares generate electrically-charged solar winds that bombard billions of oxygen and nitrogen particles 60 to 100 miles above the earth. The earth's magnetic field creates an "aurora oval" which causes the particles to focus around the poles. Ancient people feared these shimmering bands of light in the night sky and Martin Luther used their presence to keep doubters in line. Early Vikings called the Northern Lights Bifrost, their passage to Valhalla. Superstition says that the lights are angered if anyone waves a white cloth at them; they will swoop down and carry the offender away. Naturally, Norwegian children grab anything white and wave it in the air defiantly when the first aurora visits after the long days of summer.

After a brief sleep following the aurora show, Betty was alert enough to take an optional overland bus excursion from Harstad to Sortland. I wasn't, so this is her narrative:

The tour began with a drive past some of Harstad's upscale homes to an overlook that provided fine views of the city, its harbor and the sea beyond. In nearby Trondenes, we paid our respects to the world's most northern medieval church. Dating from 1250, the simple, thick-walled structure overlooks the sea approach to this ancient Viking city. Although records are vague, it apparently was built by craftsmen from several countries, because it has such architectural curiosities as Roman arch window ports with Gothic windows.

A splendid convergence of three seasons made the drive from Trondenes along the shoreline of Hinnoya Island quite spectacular.

A splendid convergence of three seasons made the drive from Trondenes along the shoreline of Hinnoya Island quite spectacular. Fields of strawberry plants were still green from their summer season, and yet fall colors painted the nearby forests and the early snowfall had dusted the fields and coated

NORDLYS! NORDLYS!

"We saw the Northern Lights last night." The retired English colonel said it rather matter-of-fact, over breakfast, between bites of toast. The English have a way of doing that, of understating the astounding.

"What?" Betty and I exclaimed in unison.

"Why didn't you tell us?" I asked.

"Tell you?"

"We've never seen the Northern Lights. I'm sorry you didn't call us in our cabin." Betty tried not to sound as if she were scolding them.

"Call you?" The colonel seemed puzzled. "Why, it was two o'clock in the morning. Had trouble sleeping, I did. Looked out the window and there it was. This shimmering green light. Woke Maude, so she could have a look."

Maude nodded solemnly. "Quite lovely. Yes."

We'd been hoping to see the fabled *aurora borealis*, but it is visible only on a clear night, and the previous night had been the first clear one in several days.

This evening, the *Nordlys* passed through an unprotected stretch of ocean between Batsfjord and Berlevag, rolling in swells kicked up by a starboard wind. Betty quickly sought refuge in her bunk, fighting her personal demon of seasickness.

"I'm going out to see if the sky is clear," I said as darkness gathered. "I'll let you know if I find anything." I expected nothing, since the sunset had been shrouded in clouds. Too bad, I thought. How nice it would be to see our first *aurora borealis* from the ship whose name means Northern Lights.

Like *Ghostbusters*

I pushed open the door to the promenade deck and stepped into a cold blast of wind. Squinting into the icy squall, I was surprised to see the Big Dipper, standing off the starboard bow. I cupped my hands around my face to shield the ship's lights and stared into the black polar sky. Nothing at first, and then a shimmering vapor appeared, too tall for a cloud. It was ghost-like, long and tapered, like one of those apparitions from *Ghostbusters* without the comic face. The lower portion was tinted a subtle green.

"Wow!" I ran back to our cabin to alert Betty. Still awake, she dressed hurriedly, fighting off her nausea.

The elusive aberration had practically vanished by the time we reached the promenade deck. Then it slowly took shape in our widening pupils. It was blurred by spray kicked up along the ship's side, so we retreated to the relative shelter of the stern. A grand parade of ghosts appeared, like tall, twisting sails. We stared in amazement as they writhed and danced above us. No wonder the ancients thought they were demons!

"This is just absolutely beautiful." Betty's elliptical eyes were wide circles of wonder.

And then she leaned over the side and threw up.

the hills. Jagged peaks tilted skyward, forming a protective wall above these farmlands—a rare vision north of the Arctic Circle.

At the tiny village of Revsnes, our driver somehow managed to squeeze his bus aboard a small ferry to cross Kvae Fjord. A special treat had been arranged for our group: The ferry operator's wife served homemade Norwegian pastries and *Gudbrandsdalsost,* a sweet goat cheese served on buttered waffles. It's tastier than it sounds! As we continued toward Sortland, the driver stopped short of a concrete arch bridge that links Hinnoya to Osknes Island, and just sat there. Several minutes later, we saw the reason for his pause: The vision of our good ship *Nordlys* sailing toward the span, headed for our rendezvous point.

After Betty rejoined the ship in Sortland, we cruised past more marbled ice cream peaks and then docked at the small community of Stokmarkness for a quick shore excursion.

"Anyone who wants to visit the *Hurtigruten* Museum please meet at reception," came the message over the ship's speakers. "We have only forty-five minutes in port."

We hurried into our coats and sprinted through slushy snow to the *Hurtigrutemuseet.* It's a short walk from the dock if you have plenty of time; a long one if you don't. We wondered why the *Hurtigruten* Museum would be in a small town with only a 45-minute shore stop. Once there, we learned the reason. In 1881, a shipping line called

The bluffs blended into a colonnade of sky-piercing pinnacles called the Lofoten Wall; it rivals Wyoming's Grand Tetons in rugged grandeur.

Vesteralens Dampskibsselskab was established here. Then in 1893, its founder Richard With accepted the government challenge to operate year-around passenger, cargo and mail service on the north coast. It thus became the first company to operate a Coastal Express route.

Housed in Vesteralens Shipping Company's original offices, the museum is busy with models of *Hurtigruten* ships through the ages, paintings, historic documents and other memorabilia One could learn a great deal here about the famous Coastal Express—assuming one had more than 45 minutes!

People paid to write books and brochures for the Coastal Express call it "The world's most beautiful sea voyage." A cruise late this afternoon through sixteen-mile Raft Sound, with a side trip into Trolls Fjord, lent considerable credence to this claim. Rocky, scalloped cliffs rose vertically from the narrow sound between the mainland and the Lofoten Islands. The bluffs blended into a colonnade of sky-piercing pinnacles called the Lofoten Wall; it rivals Wyoming's Grand Tetons in rugged grandeur. With a bit of imagination, it resembles a row of upturned trolls' noses. Legend says they were formed when Thor hurled his magic hammer *Mjolnir* during a temper tantrum.

This, we thought, must be the globe's grandest meeting of mountain and sea. Then our *Hurtigrute* made a tight starboard turn and ferried us into an even more impressive spectacle. Troll Fjord is a mile-long slot canyon, barely the width of a football field. The ship managed to fit between these ancient basaltic walls with just a few feet of clearance on either side. Veined with snow, *Trollfjorden's* near vertical walls were particularly stunning in the arctic half- light. At the end of the fjord, a slight widening allowed the ship to do a slow-motion U-turn and slip back out.

🏳🏳🏳
DAY TEN

Most of today's stops were brief—Ornes, Nesna and Sandnessjoen. Wind-driven showers provided an excuse for us to remain aboard and admire their blurry images through rain- streaked windows.

During lunch we saw, through the rain and fog, the Seven Sisters, a chain of rocky promontories south of Sandnessjoen that—according to legend—originally had been trolls. As every Norwegian knows, if these night-dwelling mischief makers are caught in the sunlight, they turn to stone. Thus, like Cinderella, these kids didn't know when to call it a night.

🏳🏳🏳
DAY ELEVEN

Trondheim was the primary shore stop this day, giving passengers who had boarded at Kirkenes their first look at Norway's third largest city. We'd prowled its streets on the way up, so we joined a tour past the city's historic spots, highlighted by Nidaros Cathedral, the most imposing church in the northland. This high-spired structure is one of Norway's oldest buildings, and one of its most elaborate. It traces its roots to 1170, when it was built over the grave of St. Olav, who brought Christianity to Norway. Most of Norway's kings have been crowned here and the royal jewels are displayed in the North Chapel.

This was our last night at sea; tomorrow, Day twelve, we'd go ashore at Bergen. On a normal cruise ship, we'd have to dress up for the captain's gala farewell dinner. However, as crew members would remind us with indulgent grins, this finely equipped vessel was not a cruise ship. Never mind that our staterooms had heated bathroom floors, telephones, writing desks and similar amenities. And don't be misled by the sauna, gymnasium, laundry, cocktail lounge with a small dance floor, or even the guy playing nightly dance music on the electronic organ.

Not a cruise ship? You could have fooled us!

🏳🏳🏳
TO BERGEN IN A NUTSHELL

Although you can book flights directly to Bergen, we recommend flying to Oslo and taking the train, with a side trip down into a beautiful fjord to the tiny hamlet of Flam. Tour operators simplify this Oslo-to-Bergen trek by packaging it as "Norway in a Nutshell," a term coined by the Norwegian National Tourist Office. The route also can be run in reverse, after you've completed your coastal voyage. For Nutshell details, contact the Scandinavian Tourist Boards, P.O. Box 4649, Grand Central Station, New York, NY 10163-4649; (212) 949-2333.

You also may want to include a few extra days in Oslo and Bergen, both fascinating places to explore. Oslo, a charming and comfortable old city caught somewhere between the seventeenth century and the 1960s, provides a good first impression of Norseland. This low-rise Norwegian capital is clean, attractive and easy to navigate. Downtown is compact, relatively level

More than two hundred figures in Oslo's Viegland Sculpture Garden celebrate the lusty fullness of life.

and very walkable. The city has generous wedges of parklands, even in the heart of the business district.

For our base of operations, we chose the medium-priced Rica Travel Hotel, in the heart of downtown, within ten minutes' walk of the waterfront, shops and several parks. A logical starting point for an Oslo exploration is the Norway Information Center in an old mustard colored building on the waterfront. Visitors may find it useful to purchase the Oslo Card, which provides free access to all public transit and admission to most attractions.

The *Aker Brygge*, a restored cargo shed complex adjacent to the information center, offers a plenitude of shops, boutiques and restaurants. From here, you can catch a small passenger ferry to the Bygdoy (bi-DOY) Peninsula, site of Oslo's most interesting archives. Reserve most of a day to visit the Oslo Volksmuseum, a collection of historic structures, many with indoor exhibits; the Viking Ships Museum, where two ninth century Norse vessels and a piece of a third are displayed; and the extensive Maritime Museum. The latter is a complex of several museums honoring Norway's great seafaring traditions; exhibits include the polar exploration ship that took Roald

Amundsun on many of his Arctic and Antarctic exploits, and Thor Heyerdhal's *Kon Tiki* balsa raft.

Before leaving Oslo, find time for the Viegland Sculpture Garden, reached by a long walk or a short bus or cab ride from downtown. Dedicated to the genius of sculptor Gustav Viegland, this landscaped garden is filled with 200 iron, bronze and granite nude and anatomically complete figures. There is nothing carnal about Viegland's works; the bosomy women and properly equipped men exhibit a look of lusty innocence.

The Bergen Railway

One of the world's most scenic train routes, the Bergen Railway provides the first leg of "Norway in a Nutshell." It climbs one of the country's highest mountain passes, ducking through 200 tunnels and seventeen miles of snow sheds and crossing 300 bridges in its twisting run between Oslo and Bergen.

After leaving Oslo, the train passes slender glacial lakes rimmed by neat farms as it climbs toward 4,009-foot Finse Pass in a snow-swept alpine zone above the tree line. At Myrdal, a hamlet just beyond the pass, Nutshell participants transfer to a waiting train for Flam. An engineering masterpiece, this route descends nearly 3,000 feet in twelve miles, dropping into the gorgeous Flam Valley. It's one of the earth's

The Flam River plunges dizzily downward, dropping from one rock-rimmed grotto to the next. splendid places, with steep, rocky canyon walls—some wooded, some cloaked with carpets of moss and lichen. The Flam River, architect of this canyon, plunges dizzily downward, dropping from one rock-rimmed grotto to the next. Far below, patches of green farmlands add a sense of order to this wild scene.

Only 400 people live in this beautiful valley, mostly in the villages of Hareina, Lunden and Flam. Yet half a million visitors inundate the area in summer; 300,000 of them come by rail. Tiny Flam, at the end of the valley and the head of Aurland Fjord, consists only of a train depot, souvenir shop, café, the white clapboard Fretheim Hotel and a few other structures. (Consider booking a night at the hotel for a more thorough exploration of the area. For one of the world's grandest hikes, take the train back to Myrdal and follow a winding trail back down to the valley.)

The next phase of Norway in a Nutshell is an hour and a half ride on a small passenger ferry to Gudvagden, chugging beneath glacial-carved fjord walls several hundred feet high. Dozens of waterfalls cascade down these steep slopes. After cruising from Aurland Fjord into Sogne Fjord, the ferry docks at Gudvagden, where waiting buses whisk passengers along a scenic road to the train station at Voss. A Bergen-bound train arrives shortly to complete the Nutshell journey.

...And so to Bergen

Bergen is one of the most striking urban spaces on earth. Begin your visit by riding the downtown funicular to a low hill for a fine view of this waterbound city. From this high plane, particularly in morning sun, Bergen resembles a table-top model—century-old shops and houses crowding a blue harbor, surrounded by verdant mountains. Two peninsulas reach into the harbor, both thick with stores and warehouses that cast their reflections in the clear water.

Although much of Bergen has succumbed to the realities of modernization and traffic flow, many older buildings survive in the downtown area, which is veined by cobblestone streets. Our hotel of choice here was the Grand Terminus, reached simply by stepping out a side door of the railroad station. From here, you can follow Kong Oscars Gate (Street) to the funicular and just beyond, the Vagen (harbor) and the Bergen Tourist Information Office. As in Oslo, you can purchase a pass good for public transit and museum admissions. Several museums and other lures are just beyond the visitor center along the Bryggen, Bergen's original harborside business district. The street is lined with wooden peak-roofed buildings constructed in the early 1700s, when German merchants of the Hanseatic League dominated local trade. They now house shops, restaurants and an occasional museum. The Hanseatic Museum preserves living quarters, offices and storage rooms of the Hanseatic era. A bit farther down the waterfront, just inland from the SAS Royal Hotel, the Bryggen Museum portrays Bergen in the thirteenth century. The Norway Fishery Museum is housed in the fisheries terminal near the end of the pier beyond the Bryggen; it traces the history of commercial fishing.

Three attractions elsewhere are well worth the taxi fare. (Two of them, Old Bergen and Edvard Grieg's home, can be reached by inexpensive Bergen tours that depart from the visitor center.) Old Bergen is a collection of eighteenth and nineteenth century shops and homes with period fur-

"What a romantic way to fall apart," our young guide said cheerfully.

nishings. Edvard Grieg's Troldhaugen, crowning a low wooded hill above a lake, was the last residence of Norway's Danny DiVito-sized musical genius. Visitors see Grieg memorabilia, furnished rooms and a special low-slung Steinway grand piano used by the five-foot composer.

The third attraction, Ole Bull Castle, can be approached by a $30 cab ride to a ferry dock in Bergen's suburbs. There, a ten-minute cruise across a lake delivers you to an island sheltering the onion-dome mansion built by the famous composer-violinist. Students from the Bergen Music Academy perform works of Grieg, Bull and others in the music room, a stunning study in ornate blonde woodwork and crystal chandeliers. Bull was known for his flamboyant lifestyle, even to the end. When he was near death, he asked to be laid out in the music room, clutching a bouquet of heather; his young wife played Mozart's Requiem as he passed from the scene.

"What a romantic way to fall apart," our young guide said cheerfully.

※ ※ ※

And Noah said to his wife when he sat down to dine
I don't care where the water goes if it doesn't get into the wine.
— **Gilbert Keith Chesterson,** *Wine and water*

Chapter eleven

FRANCE BY CANAL
Floating Burgundy with European Waterways

C aught in the liquid grip of the current, the small boat was drawn
downstream, like a helpless thing on a string. The witch's cauldron of
whitewater rumbled and waited below. The woman gripped the oars
and turned the boat into the tongue of the first rapid, her eyes wide with fear
and fortitude.

Flying Air France from San Francisco to Paris, we watched Meryl Streep
battle the rapids in *The River Wild*. She was being forced at gunpoint to deliver bad guy Kevin Bacon to his getaway car stashed downstream. The airline's *Le Club* business class had offered a choice of inflight films, and how
could we—river-bound as we were—not choose this one?

Of course, our upcoming saga might more properly be entitled *The River
Tame*. We soon would take a lazy barge trip along France's River Yonne and
its adjacent canal aboard *La Belle Epoque*. Hardly a trip to whiten the knuck-
les. It did offer moments of adventure, however, particularly as we tried to
keep pace with four lively couples from Florida while invading the wine cellars of Burgundy. In catching a canal barge, we would be taking one of the
world's oldest forms of water transit. The earliest barges didn't require sails

CRUISE PLANNER

The cruise • European Waterways conducts canal and river barge cruises in England, Scotland, Ireland, the Netherlands, Belgium and France. This particular outing was a six-day voyage along the River Yonne and its accompanying Canal du Nivernais, between the French Burgundian towns of Clamecy and Auxerre. For information on this and other canal trips, contact European Waterways, 140 E. 56th St., Suite 4-C, New York, NY 10022; (800) 217-4447 or (212) 688-9489. The firm also organizes châteaux tours in Europe.

Getting there • Air France offers service to Paris from several American gateways. You can reach your canal barge—wherever it may be parked—via French National Railways or possibly via Air Inter, a French domestic airline. If this is part of a greater European exploration, you may want to obtain a Eurailpass, good for unlimited train travel for specified periods. For information, contact your travel agent.

The ship • *La Belle Epoque* is large as canal barges go. Its 126-foot length allows space for six comfortable cabins with complete baths, a single-seating dining room and lounge area, small bar, spa and fitness room, and a hot tub on deck. The captain and crew members are mostly European.

When to go • There is no set season for canal barging although most travelers prefer to poke about Europe from spring through fall, since winters can be wet and chilly. Late summer through early autumn may be the most reliable weather. Bear in mind that the French often take their vacations in August and many cafés and shops—particularly in Paris—are closed then.

What to bring • Valid passports, casual clothes and hearty appetites are the only prerequisite for a canal cruise. The weather is temperate to toasty from spring through fall so pack accordingly. Some guests like to don jackets and cocktail wear for the evening meal, although these aren't required. Take good walking shoes for hiking along the tow paths and exploring the villages.

What's included • All onboard meals with matching French wines, and all shore excursions are included in the basic cruise price, as well as van pickup from a pre-appointed spot. Excursions consist primarily of van trips into the countryside, wine tastings and strolls through French villages with visits to ancient churches and other time-worn structures.

What to buy • Save most of your credit card limits for the boutiques and designer shops of Paris. In the countryside, you'll have an opportunity to sample and purchase some interesting wines, *foi gras,* cheeses and other local fare.

🐟🐟🐟

or engines, since they were pulled by animals or even people along bankside tow paths. Many canals were—and still are—part of river networks. Small locks and weirs were built to create stair-stepping water levels to permit barge passage. Other canals were dug at sea level to bring water navigation into the heart of coastal cities.

The arrival of trains, trucks and planes put an end to most canal cargo traffic in Europe, although it's still common elsewhere in the world. In recent years, a new form of water travel has become popular—canal cruising in mini-floating hotels. These passenger boats are similar in design to the original wide bodied, low slung canal barges, although with considerably more elegance. Many, including our *La Belle Epoque,* are built into the hulls of old cargo barges.

The French connections

Hundreds of miles of canals interlace the French countryside, linking big cities and rural villages. Most are tended by government lock keepers who live in adjacent and often ancient stone houses. A blast from the boat's horn alerts the lock keeper to its approach. As in the rest of Europe, virtually no cargo barges use these canals today. The meandering waterways are now the dominion of passenger barges, private yachts and "hire boats"— small houseboats that can be rented by the day or week. Canal traffic doesn't get free passage. To maintain the waterways and pay the lock keepers, passenger barges, hire boats and private boats pay an annual fee called a *vignette.*

Our section of the canal between Clamecy and Auxerre was chosen because of its bucolic setting, variety of landforms and access to nearby wine châteaux.

Canal du Nivernais was created alongside the River Yonne to provide navigation between Paris and the Loire river basins to the southwest. Work began in 1783 and continued for more than a century. Our section of the 109-mile route—a 55-mile stretch between Clamecy and Auxerre—was chosen by European Waterways because of its bucolic setting, variety of landforms and access to nearby wine châteaux.

In an English-translation guidebook called *Carte Guide de Navigation,* Canal du Nivernais is described thusly:

In places the canal is made up from the natural channels created by the River Yonne itself and called racles. *There is quite a variety of landscapes: from vineyards and fruit trees covered slopes will succeed steeper and more or less alpine like banks. Then you come to Mailly-le-Château, solidly established on top of its cliffs which yet clear out to let you have a large view.*

ฅ ฅ ฅ

DAY ONE

After landing in Paris, we made our way by train to Auxerre in northern Burgundy. We were picked up in a van by a crewman from *La Belle Epoque,* to be taken in less than two hours to Clamecy, where the barge awaited. It would require six days via the coiling River Yonne and its canal to return. We would sleep and dine aboard the barge that night and then start cruising the next morning.

Motoring southward toward the medieval village of Clamecy, we passed through a countryside with soft, feminine French curves. It was a pleasing landscape—a mix of pasturelands, low tree-thatched hills and brilliant yellow fields of rapeseed. This was open countryside—one of the few places in Europe where one could travel for a kilometer or more without seeing a village or farm house.

One of European Waterways' larger canal boats, the six-cabin *La Belle Epoque* had been outfitted by its captain Leigh Wootten, who shares ownership of the craft with European Waterways. The hull dates back to the 1930s when it began its canal life as a cargo vessel. Its name, which translates literally as "the beautiful time," refers to a particularly happy period of France's history—the years just prior to World War I. On board the craft, which rested in a small boat basin, we found a miracle of condensed convenience and even a bit of luxury. Tucked within a few square feet of mahogany and steel were a lounge with a dining table capable of seating twelve passengers, a CD player, six relatively roomy cabins with private baths and stall showers, and even a small gym and sauna. Two umbrella tables and a hot tub occupied the split-level deck.

Aboard the craft we found a miracle of condensed convenience and even a bit of luxury.

Wootten, an Englishman who has lived in France for the past 20 years, spoke both languages fluently. He was thus an excellent guide-interpreter for his English-speaking guests, who make up much of European Waterways' clientele. Others on the crew were an assistant boatman, a remarkably talented chef and two young women who doubled as dining room aides and room stewards. The crew saw to our every need, providing the same level of service one would receive on a larger craft. The final crew member was Maggie, a spaniel sort of dog who appeared to devote most of her waking hours to finding comfortable places to sleep.

We soon learned that canal barging was cruising at its most intimate and casual level. The small number of passengers—and in our case including four lively and likable jet-set couples from Florida—ensured quick camaraderie. By the first evening—while devouring a cheese souffle salad, excellent tuna steaks and diced melon dessert, accompanied first by a fine regional Chardonnay and then by a light Burgundy—we had become good friends.

Four hours and many glasses of wine later, Betty and I plodded down to our stateroom and slept the sleep of the dead, recovering from a twenty-eight hour plane and train marathon.

🐾🐾🐾

DAY TWO

Since departure wasn't scheduled until mid-morning, we decided on a pre-breakfast exploration of Clamecy. As we walked, we encountered boat captain Leigh, returning with an armload of baguettes, which he carried like kindling wood. He and his chef shopped frequently along the route, ensuring an unending flow of fresh local foods. We walked into town to the cadence of church bells, nodding to women headed to the bakery with their wicker baskets, old men leaning on their elbows in open-shuttered windows to take in the warm spring air, and German tourists in rented canal boats preparing for their morning departures.

Passengers can volunteer to open and close weir gates, one of the rituals of cruising the canals of Europe.

"Good morning."

"Bonjour."

"Guten Morgen."

Like most Bergundian villages, Clamecy is ancient and neatly kept, with cross-timbered homes lining narrow cobblestone streets. A few buildings were abandoned and crumbling, begging new owners, for many children of this generation had left to seek greater opportunities in the cities. Thus, Clamecy was old in both architecture and in the median age of its citizens. There is little new construction in these small French country towns; lack of growth has thus preserved their medieval look. We paid our respects to the local church, prowled several cobblestone streets and returned to the barge.

Back aboard, I sat at the dining table to catch up on my notes. Thus pre-occupied, I was only vaguely aware that Leigh had maneuvered his large craft out of its parking space in the Clamecy boat basin. Then I heard strange voices and looked up with some surprise to see three smiling French ladies at eye level, peering into the barge's window. *La Belle* had been maneuvered into a lock, preparatory to being lowered to river level. The large craft, which cleared the stone walls of the lock only by five inches on each side, had at-tracted this small audience. The ladies and I exchanged nods and grins as the barge slowly sank in the lock. From my prospective, it seemed that the women were rising, until I could see only their dress hems, stocky legs and finally their sturdy walking shoes.

As we got underway, we found that canal barging is cruising that often goes walkabout. Passengers could hop off at will when *La Belle* paused at a lock, and then stroll, jog or bike alongside the tow path and hop back aboard at a later stop. When not pacing the pokey barge, we lounged at a deck table, watching the slow-motion passage of France.

Late in the afternoon we tied up at Lucy Sur Yonne, a tiny farm village where we would spend the night. Accompanying vans drove us to nearby *Ferme de Misery,* a farm dating from the eighteenth century and now used for the production of some of France's finest *foie gras.* We were ushered into the "factory," essentially a strong smelling *corral de canards* in an ancient stone barn, where more than a thousand young ducks milled about. Backlit and silhouetted by an open window at the far end of the long barn, they looked like a crowd of shmoos from the Lil' Abner comic strip. On this earth for only fourteen weeks, the ducks spent the first twelve enjoying a high protein diet of grain pellets, unaware that their livers soon would be spread on bits of bread in better French restaurants.

"They're quite comfortable here, just strutting about and doing ducky things," said Leigh, interpreting for Marie Odile, the farm owner. "Only the males are kept. The females are always quacking about, making entirely too much noise."

We sampled foie gras *and other ducky things, accompanied by a locally produced Chardonnay.*

Their final two weeks of life are spent in another corral in the same barn, where they are force fed corn which increases their liver weight from 50 grams to 500.

"Animal rights groups claim the force feeding is cruel and terrifies the ducks, but actually it's quite gentle," Leigh said. "The handlers are taught to keep them calm. If they panicked, they'd just pack up and die and you'd have a two dollar duck on your hands instead of one worth seventy."

The finished *foie gras* fetches about $40 for a 250-gram packet and the rest of the duck goes to market as well. Just about everything is used except the feathers and feet.

We adjourned to a small sales room, where we sampled *foie gras* and other ducky things on fragments of bread, accompanied by a locally produced Chardonnay. Our Floridian Eight—ever in a party mood—bought generously, packing away several jars of *fois gras,* jams and other specialty foods, plus a couple of additional bottles of Chardonnay that never made it out of the parking area.

ß ß ß

DAY THREE

Despite another pleasantly drawn out dinner the previous evening, the Floridian Eight rose with the sun to take a hot air balloon flight. We'd gone aloft several times before, and chose instead a morning walk. Lucy Sur Yonne is a quiet French country town, and a comprehensive exploration required fewer than fifteen minutes. The sights consisted of an old stone church that was closed, a restaurant-bar with the ubiquitous restaurant-bar dog asleep on the worn concrete steps, and perhaps a dozen houses with typical worn stone walls and window shutters.

Subtle warning? This sign advises motorists to use caution when approaching the end of the dock at the Clamency boat basin.

From the village, we walked a mile up the canal bank to the next lock. En route, we exchanged *bonjours* with a duck-tender who fished as he kept an eye on his small flock; we listened to bird songs; and we admired turrets and towers of a distant castle tucked against foothills. Arriving at the next lock to await our boat, I leaned against a weir gate and absorbed the surrounding countryside—verdant green pasturelands, the blue-brown ribbon of the canal and contoured rapeseed fields, like yellow blankets thrown across the landscape. The French countryside is at once ordinary and beautiful, an impressionist painting that—in its soft impreciseness—never tires the eye.

Time moves slowly here, fitted to the rhythm of our cruise and to French law, which requires that lock keepers take a full hour for lunch. Back aboard *La Belle Epoch,* we continued downstream, sitting on the forward deck, sipping tea and coffee, lulled by morning sun and the rhythmic drum of the engine. We arrived at a lock just at noon and the lock keeper had of course taken temporary leave. But never mind that. His wife had set up a small open-air boutique at lock-side, where she sold pottery and postcards.

When the locktender returned and we were permitted to continue our journey, we were served a fine lunch of seasoned artichokes, lentils and something the French call a California salad—avocados and hearts of palm. We engaged in a heated discussion regarding the merits of California and French wines while drinking copious quantities of the latter. *La Belle* moored for the night beneath sandstone cliffs a hundred or so feet high, adjacent to the wee village of Le Saussios. Several climbers were practicing their art, dangling from thin ropes and working their way about the sheer bluffs.

We were not finished for the day, of course. The vans were brought up and we were driven through the countryside to Vézelay, an ancient village planted atop a low hill. Climbing a winding lane toward the hilltop town, we passed the first vineyards we'd seen in Burgundy; Vézelay was the center of an important wine producing region.

"Vézelay will be one of the high points of your cruise," said Leigh as he hurried one of the vans up the winding road. "You'll particularly want to visit the church for a look at its rather unusual relic—one of the fossilized ovaries of Mary Magdalene." Although Leigh was a font of information about France, one did have to sort out his truths from his fictions.

The village has been clutching this mountain top since the twelfth century and it was an important stopover during the Crusades. The town's roots go back even further; a monastery was established on this hilltop in the ninth century. A Roman style church was built about 1150, followed a century later by a substantial Gothic structure which still stands. It's still an important pilgrimage site, both for Catholics and generic tourists. Reads a brochure which can be purchased at the church:

A splendid vision of weathered city walls and cobbled streets, Vézelay has become a darling of the tour bus set.

Now a tiny town seeming only to preserve the memory of its glorious past, whose steep main street, mixing hardship with tenderness, leads up to the Church of the Magdalene, a massive hulk anchored at the highest point, waiting peacefully for an inevitable here-after.

A splendid vision of weathered city walls and cobbled streets, Vézelay has become a darling of the tour bus set. Its single uptilted cobblestone main street is lined with boutiques, galleries, curio shops and a startling number of wine shops. Many of them offer tastings; the local reds and whites were fine and quite fairly priced.

It was still relatively early in the tourist season, and the town was uncrowded as our small delegation hiked up the main street. The group thinned out quickly as we walked—the shops contributing to a rather high attrition rate. Seeking photographic vistas, Betty and I visited the church and then wandered down a small lane and soon encountered its neatly kept cemetery. A grand slice of Burgundian countryside spread below, with its patchwork fields, clumps of trees, ribboning rivers and tile-roofed towns.

We later returned to the parked vans, saw no signs of familiar life and retired to a nearby sidewalk café. Shortly, members of the Floridian Eight joined us, one and two at a time. Many of them bore packages, having contributed substantially to the economy of Vézelay.

ß ß ß

DAY FOUR

Chablis is perhaps the best white wine of France, and the French insist of course that it's the finest in all the world. Made from the Chardonnay grape, it's produced in a few thousand acres of hilly vineyards around the small village of Chablis. Here, chalky limestone soil, cool climate and even the contours of the hills conspire to produce ideal growing conditions. Several other wine producing nations, including the United States, have played a mean trick on France. They use the word "chablis" to describe any ordinary white wine.

After a lazy morning floating past tree-lined stretches of the River Yonne, we paused for lunch and a quick climb to a castle rampart at Mailly-le-

Ancient vines and an ancient country church are symbols of France's Chablis district, one of the "shore stops" of La Belle Epoch.

Château for a panoramic peek of the Yonne Valley. Then, a bit farther downstream, we boarded the vans for a run to the motherland of Chablis with a capital "C." Driving through softly curved hill country, we saw for the first time on our trip extensive vineyards that reached to distant horizons. Chablis itself is a village of a few thousand souls; signs and numerous wine shops herald its reputation as the center for France's grand *vin blanc*.

We stopped in an older section of the community and inspected the mixed Roman and Gothic lines of the Church of St. Martin, whose ancestry reaches back to 877. We then got to the business at hand. Pushing through a creaking wooden gate into a gravel courtyard, we were led into the dim and properly musty wine cellar of Domaine Laroche. It's one of the largest independent producers of the Chablis region, bottling about 400,000 cases a year. Wine has been produced and aged in this cellar since the tenth century.

From there, we were escorted to a paneled tasting room where four bottles of Chablis and an appropriate number of glasses stood in neat ranks on a stone table. We would taste the four wines in ascending order—a *vin ordinaire* which was hardly ordinary in Chablis country, two versions of *premiere cru* and a *gran cru*. Each was predictably better than the first. We next headed for Laroche's retail shop to pick up a few tasty souvenirs. Members of the Floridian Eight were undaunted by the $60 price tag for a Chablis Gran Cru and started discussing the complexity of getting several cases back to their home state.

ๆๆๆ

DAY FIVE

On this day, nothing happened.

If you are on a barge drifting down Canal du Nivernais, it means that you wake to the song of birds, and that you look out your porthole window into a canopy of trees that drifts slowly overhead. You appear to be stationary in the universe, without motion or concern, and the planet is slowly revolving outside your window on the world.

You wriggle from beneath your down comforter in the cozy cabin, wash and dress and walk the few steps to the lounge where tea, hot coffee, assorted cereals and fresh rolls await. You could have ordered eggs any style from the kitchen. However, you have consumed enough cholesterol-rich food in recent days to send a dietitian into hysterics. You thus decide to limit your intake to a crusty roll injected with applesauce, plus a few bits of French bread blotted with blobs of cherry jam and marmalade.

You then head for the foredeck to sit and sip your tea and watch the trees drift slowly past. Those birds that lulled you awake provide musical accompaniment in stereo, from both sides of the canal. The barge approaches a lock and the warning toot from its horn sends a small herd of horses in quick and brief flight across a nearby pasture.

At the lock, you step ashore for a walk, intending to meet the barge somewhere downstream, although both itineraries—yours and the barge captain's—are rather vague. If you had wanted predictability and a daily printed activity program, you would be aboard a cruise ship, not *La Belle Epoque.*

You walk along the canal bank and shortly encounter several members of the Floridian Eight, approaching from the other direction on bicycles. They're laughing because one of them, confused by the tall grass of the tow-path, had pedaled right into the canal. Her husband had then made an emergency run back to the boat for a bottle of Chablis to set things right. By the time you had encountered the group, even the one who had taken the spill was laughing about the incident.

There is plenty of wine and the more you drink, the more you realize that the birds you heard this morning are still singing.

After a couple of miles, you stop at a lock to allow the boat to catch up. However, because someone forgot to tell you or you forgot to ask or someone did tell you and you forgot what they said, an hour passes and the boat doesn't arrive. You hike back upstream to discover that it had tied up for lunch in one of those tiny Burgundian villages. But it is no problem. The chef has of course saved your food and you dine on the back deck because it's sunny and warm. There is plenty of wine left from lunch and the more you drink the more you realize that the same birds you heard this morning are still singing. They apparently are migrating down the canal—remarkably at the same pace as the boat.

And now the afternoon is gone and you're talking with your shipmates about Le Espérance, the fine three-star restaurant in the nearby village of

Saint Père, where you will go ashore for dinner. This is the one to which French government leaders retreat occasionally from affairs of state. It is not part of the program; the Floridian Eight wants to eat there and you decide to join them. As you discuss dinner plans, Leigh passes through the lounge, headed for the bow where he will pick up a line and try with his usual poor aim to lasso a *bollard* or mooring post. He announces to no one in particular: "Last lock of the day. We'll tie up here."

In this manner, Day Five ends, and nothing has happened.

ß ß ß

DAY SIX

Cruises have a nasty habit of terminating. Fortunately, our voyage aboard *The Happy Time* ended appropriate to its name. We had moored last night in Vermenton, another of those medieval towns dotted across the French countryside. Still recovering from a huge dinner at Le Esperance, we somehow managed to struggle ashore, informed that the town conducted an open air market each Friday.

We browsed past carefully arranged rows of baskets of strawberries, bleached white asparagus, tiny white-tipped radishes, sundry leafy vegetables and fresh fish staring as wide-eyed as they must have been when they were caught. We bought a basket of strawberries for a walk-about breakfast and explored the small town. It dates from the twelfth century, built around an ancient church and a stone watchtower.

This was to be a long day of cruising, for we had to reach Auxerre by nightfall, with a pause for a wine tasting at Saint-Bris-le-vineux. As *La Belle Epoque* hurried flat out along the canal at a reckless two miles per hour, I took to the tow path in one final effort to walk away the week's accumulation of calories.

Since my pace was at least double that of the barge, I found time to detour into small villages along the way. They are similar and yet each is different and I could never tire of walking their cobbled streets. They seem drab at first glance, clothed in ancient gray stone. However, brief explorations reveal bright bits of color—orange tile roofs marbled with green moss, prim lace curtains, window boxes and pots aflame with flowers that seem always to be in bloom, and wisteria spilling over ancient stone walls like scented waterfalls.

This cobweb-laced dungeon de vins, with its moss-draped niches and sinister stone stairways leading only into darkness, would have been a wonderful set for Edgar Allen Poe's Cask of Amantalado.

I found *La Belle* at a lock near Bailly, just in time for lunch—ours and the locktender's. We then boarded the vans and climbed quickly into hill country, passing through a rumpled patchwork quilt of vineyards, orchards, pasturelands and rapeseed fields. We careened carefully through the narrow streets of Saint-Bris-le-vineux and briefly visited the town's requisite Gothic church. The nearby winery, Château Bourgognes Bersan, was tunneled under adjacent stone buildings—a virtual catacomb that crawls beneath much of the town. This cobweb-laced *dungeon de vins*, with its moss-draped niches and sinister stone stairways leading only into darkness, would have been a wonderful set for Edgar Allen Poe's *Cask of Amantalado* or a Stephen King epic. Leigh led us to the crushing tanks—ancient concrete basins fed by chutes from above. In centuries past, he said, the grapes were crushed by naked maidens to produce a fine *La Belle Dénudé*. But after that fossilized ovary business, could this information be trusted?

Madame Bersan's family has been making wine here for seven generations and I suspect that some of the original vintages were still in residence. We saw several *caches* of bottles that were encased in eons of mold and cobwebs. Madame was not here at the moment so Leigh conducted a tasting of white and red Burgundies—pouring from glossy new bottles, not those ancient vessels. Lacking the proper bread to clear our palates between samples, he produced a canister of sour cream and onion Pringles, which he insisted were quite the proper thing for a wine tasting.

The whites were excellent and the reds were young and acidic, not yet ready to drink but showing good promise, so members of the Floridian Eight picked up a few cases for laying away.

"Assuming, of course, they are not devoured on the train back to Cannes," said Bjornar Hermansen, a tall Norwegian who appeared to be the group's ringleader.

Unfortunately, not a single bottle of *La Belle Dénudé* was available for purchase.

ββββ

If, when he reached his journey's end,
He had not gained an honest friend,
And twenty curious scraps of knowledge—
If he departed as he came
Good sooth, the traveler was to blame.
— Praed

Chapter twelve

GERMANY'S ELBE RIVER
Sailing into Saxony aboard the *Dresden*

D eux!" The porter on the night train from Paris to Hamburg held up two stubby fingers and patted one of the six bunks in the tiny compartment.

"Where's the dining car?" Betty asked.

His grin got wider and he patted the bunk more firmly. "Deux!"

"The dining car? Food. *Mangiamo!*" She tried to make eating motions with her hands, but it came out as a chopstick thing and the porter didn't understand. My wife is lousy at Charades.

"Deux!"

"Adieu," I said; it was a signal to Betty to stop trying to communicate with the helpful gentleman. I hefted my suitcase onto one of the bunks and began making night preparations.

The porter was telling us that we had the compartment to ourselves and would need only the two lower bunks. (We had requested the six-bunk com-

CRUISE PLANNER

The cruise • This is a one-week cruise on Germany's Elbe River between Hamburg and Dresden, booked in America by Peter Deilmann EuropAmerica Cruises. The parent company in Germany, Peter Deilman-Reederei, offers a variety of voyages on other European rivers—the Danube, Rhine and Rhône. For information and brochures, contact Peter Deilmann EuropAmerica Cruises, 1800 Diagonal Rd, Alexandria, VA 22314; (800) 348-8287 or (703) 549-1741.

Getting there • Germany's Lufthansa and several other carriers offer service from various American cities to Frankfurt. From there, Lufthansa has connecting flights to departure and arrival cities of Hamburg and Dresden. German Rail also has frequent train service to both cities.

The ship • The *MV Dresden* is a rather opulent riverboat with sixty-five roomy outside cabins with TVs, phones and refrigerators with honor bars. Onboard amenities include a single-seating dining room, cocktail lounge, small gift shop and library, hair salon and sauna, and a rooftop sun deck. Officers and crew members are mostly German; the cruise director and others who deal with the passengers speak English.

When to go • Spring through fall are popular times for river cruising in Europe, and the warmest and driest weather is late August through mid-September.

What to bring • Like most European nations, Germany requires only a valid passport for Americans and most other nationalities. Germany's climate is cooler and wetter than much of America, so bring evening wraps and rain gear, even in summer. Dress is casual aboard ship, although it's customary to don jackets and cocktail wear for dinner. Shore excursions are primarily city explorations that involve a lot of walking but no hiking; bring comfortable shoes. Pack binoculars for spotting items of interest along the riverbank.

What's included • All shipboard activities are included; airfare can be arranged as part of the total cruise price, and airport pickup and delivery are provided. Shore excursions are extra and modestly priced. Most port stops are within walking distance of city centers, for those who want to poke about on their own.

What to buy • These aren't major shopping excursions, although you will have opportunities to shop for the famous Meissen porcelain, other fine china and crystal. Towns in eastern Germany didn't offer a large selection of gift wares when we visited, although this situation is changing rapidly. Because of the general strength of the German mark against the dollar, expect prices to be somewhat high.

partment not out of a need for companionship, but out of consideration for our limited travel budget.) We learned, through further exploration, that the night train to Hamburg had no dining car. Not even a food cart visited the narrow aisles of our sleeperette. We also noted, in the tiny washroom down the corridor, an icon that suggested we shouldn't drink from the faucet. Thus, after an eleven-hour flight from San Francisco to Paris, we would spend our first night in Europe without food or water.

℘ ℘ ℘

The German cruise line Peter Deilmann-Reederei operates sleek "floating hotels" on several European rivers. They're booked in the U.S. by Peter Deilmann EuropAmerica Cruises. We chose the Elbe because this lesser-traveled stream would take us southeast from Hamburg into what had been East Germany. The Elbe, in fact, marked the boundary line of the once-divided Germany for the first several score miles. We were curious to see what changes had occurred since the country was reunited in 1990.

Further, the slow-moving river soaks up a lot of history as it passes through ancient Saxony, where the first Germanic Empire was born with the coronation of Otto I in 962 A.D. Some of its villages trace their roots back to that era and even beyond. Saxons first appeared as fourth century pirates who attacked other European seaports from their homeland at the base of the present-day Danish peninsula. Later Saxons were credited with founding what was to become Anglo-Saxon England. In the eighth century, Saxon tribes were focused primarily between the North Sea and the Elbe River, where they laid the foundations for Germany.

℘ ℘ ℘

DAY ONE

Our morning arrival in Hamburg gave us a day to explore this river port city, since our cruiser, the *Dresden,* would not depart until that evening. Central Hamburg seemed ordinary on initial examination, yet it gained interest with each new corner turned. We left the train, sorted through a confusing wad of dollars, francs and marks to find breakfast money and then took the HVV rapid transit to the river harbor, where the *Dresden* waited at dockside. We dropped our luggage on board and began a walking exploration of the heart of the city. We had been told that the city's outskirts were festooned with parks and fine shopping areas, although those would have to await another, more leisurely visit.

In the process of getting lost in central Hamburg's confusing medieval street tangle, we discovered a fascinating city of monumental churches and interesting museums. In 808, Charlemagne founded a fortress on this site, from where he began the Christianizing and unifying of Germany. Hamburg joined with Lübeck in the early thirteenth century to form the Hanseatic League, leading to Germany's role as a great world trading nation. The city has been for centuries Germany's leading port, even though the ocean is seventy-five miles north. This role proved its undoing in World War II, since it became the frequent target of Allied bombers. Then, in one horrendous raid

The city has been for centuries Germany's leading port, even though the ocean is seventy-five miles north.

The towers of Dresden's Albrechtsburg Castle tower over the riverboat Dresden, *moored at dockside.*

that was later chronicled in the book, *The Night Hamburg Died,* it was blasted to near oblivion.

Thus today's Hamburg is primarily of postwar brick and steel, without the medieval look of some other German cities. However, many churches and several other fine old structures survived the bombing at least partially intact, and most have been rebuilt.

The harbor is the focal point of this ancient Hanseatic city, as it has been for centuries. Since the ocean is far to the north, it is the Elbe, the 625-mile-long river on which we soon would sail, that gave Hamburg its *raison d' entre.* Averaging a quarter of a mile wide with a gentle current, it provides easy freighter passage to the North Sea. Hamburg marks the end of deep water navigation, although barges—including our luxury one—can negotiate its six-foot depth all the way into the Czech Republic, 300 miles upstream.

On weekends, residents and tourists flock to Hamburg's inland waterfront to dine at sidewalk cafés, explore a pair of museum ships and take harbor tours. Late in the afternoon of our first day, we became tourists watching tourists, lounging at a sidewalk café, sipping passable German white wine as the people parade wandered up and down the boardwalk.

ϼϼϼ

DAY TWO

We awoke this morning to find the river dancing on our ceiling.

The *Dresden*, our sleek hotel-on-a-river, was almost soundless and vibration free as it moved along the calm Elbe River. The sun was well over the horizon by the time we awoke, glancing off the river and casting glittering ripples onto our stateroom ceiling. Our large cabin window offered a pleasing picture of the flat, lushly green countryside along the Elbe's tree-lined banks. During the night, we had left the busy, built-up Hamburg section of the river.

We ate breakfast—which we hardly needed—then set about to explore the boat. The *Dresden* is too elegant to be called a barge although it is technically that. Square and basic outside, it is rather opulent inside, done in pastel patterns, light woods and brass. For small ship fans who like the elegance of some larger cruise vessels, it offers an ideal compromise. Roomy staterooms—all outside—have TVs and phones, refrigerators with honor bars, handsome wood cabinetry and marble floored bathrooms. Although the *Dresden* is rather small, its designers managed to find space for a sauna, hair salon, tiny gift shop, a little bookshelf of a library and a comfortable and fair-sized cocktail lounge. The craft's roof is flat, serving as a large sun deck—a fine place to lounge and watch the shoreline slip past.

The dining room is particularly appealing—a glass-walled space that wraps around the front of the vessel for panoramic views. The food, an eclectic continental mix, was generally excellent during our cruise. Dining was single-seating with full silver service and enough food variety to sink a duck.

"They keep bringing different courses until we've run out of tableware," commented our English table mate as he counted up the nine pieces of silver set before him.

Most of the boat's clientele are European, although Americans make up a fair share of the passenger list, particularly in summer. English speaking staff and tour guides are available. Only four of us gringos and an English couple were aboard during an early May sailing. Our cruise director Gudren Weber did a fine job of looking after her small flock of Anglos.

At some point, we crossed into what had been East Germany, although we saw no change in the tile-roofed shoreline towns.

We spent most of our first day on the river watching a lazy panorama of tree-clustered shores, pasturelands dotted white with sheep, German towns with red-orange brick buildings topped by high-pitched orange tile roofs, and churches with copper green spires. Onboard speakers offered brief descriptions of the passing panorama. At some point, we crossed into what had been East Germany, although this was not announced, nor could we note a change in the tile-roofed shoreline towns.

Although this was hardly frontier country, there were few streamside highways to disrupt the parade of green shoreline. Most of the traffic was on the water—barges pushing their cargo upstream and down. Occasionally, our craft's pilothouse would be lowered like a single-floor elevator to allow passage beneath a low bridge. Late in the afternoon, we saw three Germanic Huck Finns playing along the shoreline—one in a tire swing and two in a small boat. The lure of rivers to children is universal.

During dinner, we docked for the night below a fragmented brick castle in Tangermünde, one of the region's medieval towns. Curious for our first look at a former Eastern Bloc community, we skipped dessert and hurried ashore in the fading light. We found in the evening shadows a splendid old Hanseatic town dating back to the twelfth century. Communism's brief tenure, a mere blink of time in Tangermünde's 700-year history, had left no discernible mark. The town looked prim, not grim, with cobblestone streets and tidy old houses adorned with flowering window boxes. Lighted store windows displayed the cameras, camcorders, CDs and other familiar products of Western industry.

ß ß ß

DAY THREE

What has changed since reunification?" Betty asked our guide as we toured Tangermünde the next morning.

She thought for a moment. "Not much in these old towns, except now there is money from the government for restoration from the war damage, and before there was not so much. And for us? The old people—they get a bit more in their pensions and the working people who cannot find jobs, they get less. Jobs are difficult because now there is not so much—what do you call it?"

"Makework?" I offered. "Government jobs?"

"Yes, not so much that. Also, many of our skilled workers have gone to the western part, where they can find jobs."

We looked again into those well-stocked store windows. Capitalism had returned to former East Germany, but not the jobs to support it. About the only obvious leftovers from the communist regime were Trabants. *To get a "Trabie" during the Communist era, a citizen submitted an application and waited up to ten years.* They were dumpy little East German-made cars resembling 1950s Fiats, with skinny fenders and square lines. To get a "Trabie" during the Communist era, a citizen submitted an application and then waited up to ten years. They're becoming rare in larger cities, but still common in smaller communities.

We learned later from an Austrian passenger that West German officials were shocked at the neglected state of industry in the eastern sector after reunification. Many of the steel mills and factories were so outmoded that they were simply scrapped. Some were rebuilt and others still stand idle. The day before, we had seen several barges of industrial scrap iron headed downstream to Hamburg for reprocessing into steel.

A town of about 40,000, Tangermünde is one of the better preserved medieval communities along the Elbe, with cobblestone streets, stone and stucco store fronts and several old brick churches and lookout towers. Its roots have been traced to the eleventh century, and its castle served as a secondary residence for Charles IV, who ruled the German-Czech confederation from 1373 until 1378. It was, like Hamburg, one of the Hanseatic League's trading cities.

Twin spires adorn St. Mary's Church in Wittenberg. It was here that Martin Luther began the Reformation by nailing a list of demands for reform on the church door.

"By and by, 82 breweries arised," read the English language tourist brochure. "They did a roaring trade with the beer called Cowtail."

We followed our guide through the twelfth century Nikolai Church, noted for its elaborate sandstone and polychrome pulpit and altar. We then walked to the 1430 town hall, with a beautifully elaborate Gothic façade. It's now primarily a museum and meeting facility used for ceremonial purposes, including marriages.

"Upstairs, there are bedrooms one can rent," our guide explained. "Marriage ceremony, bedroom and stork on the roof. All very convenient."

She referred to the German custom of building small platforms on rooftops to lure nesting storks, since they were thought to bring good luck. Not to mention babies.

Magdeburg, the capital of Saxony-Anhalt and our afternoon shore stop, offered testimony of Germany's newest and oldest elements. Half a dozen construction cranes marked the skyline of this city of 280,000, evidence of the rapid game of catch-up that eastern Germany is playing with its western sister. Glass and steel office buildings were intermingled with ancient brick and stone. Streets were busy with traffic, including a fair number of coughing and growling Trabants that seemed determined not to be left in the exhaust of progress.

After passing through suburbs where scores of homes were under repair, and then nudging through downtown traffic, our tour bus turned a corner into yesterday. Standing before us, blackened by centuries of chimney soot like a proud old dowager in a soiled dress, was the towering Cathedral of Magdeburg. Built in segments from 1209 to 1520, it's the oldest Gothic cathedral in Germany.

If Germany has a birthplace, it is here—according to the local tourist bureau, at least. Magdeburg was mentioned as a Slavic settlement in the writings of Charlemagne in 805. Otto I arrived in 937 to build a monastery and establish a Saxon frontier to convert or subvert the Slavs. The Pope declared him head of a new German empire in 962 and he confirmed Magdeburg's city charter three years later. In 1296, it became a member of the Hanseatic league and it has thrived as a trading center since. Not without problems, however. It was sacked and burned in 1631 during the Thirty Years War, conquered by Napoleon in 1806, and then virtually destroyed by Allied bombs during World War II.

ßßß

DAY FOUR

Locals like to call it *Lutherstadt*, the town of Luther. Wittenberg dates from 1180 and perhaps before; it was mentioned in early writings as a Saxon castle. It grew into a fortified town and became the capital of the duchy of Saxonia-Wittenberg. Prince Frederic III founded Leucorea University here in 1503 and the community became an important seat of learning.

That might have been the extent of this small town's history had not a young Catholic monk named Martin Luther arrived in 1508 to teach at the university. Troubled by the decadent and capitalistic level to which his church had fallen, Luther began speaking out in protest. He never intended to start a new religion; he merely wanted to reform his old one. His resulting excommunication led to the Reformation, a pivotal period in European history, and to the establishment of the first Protestant church, later named in Luther's honor. He remained at the university for the rest of his life, except for ten months in hiding to escape papal wrath after he publicly burned a church document that branded him as a heretic. Luther died here in 1546 at the age of 62.

Our Wittenberg shore stop consisted of a scholarly hike in Luther's footsteps, from the university where he taught to the church where he is buried.

Our Wittenberg shore stop consisted of a scholarly hike in Luther's footsteps, from the university where he taught to the church where he is buried. We began at the Luther Museum, containing the world's largest collection of Reformation lore, including the great reformer's jowly death mask. Displays fill eleven rooms of his former quarters on the university campus.

Exploring the museum, we learned why Luther was irritated with his church. During this era, 50 percent of all farmland in Europe was owned by the Vatican. Bishops could buy higher posts or combine several bishoprics and create minor fiefdomes by sending proper sums of gold to Rome. Church officials gained wealth by selling "indulgence letters" which forgave sins and exempted the bearers from ecclesiastical punishment. A popular saying of this period, centuries before tele-evangelism, was: "Put the money in the box and your soul goes to heaven."

We walked from the museum past the compact medieval storefronts of downtown Wittenberg to the first of two churches significant to the Luther era. In the twin-towered thirteenth century St. Marys, the "mother church of the Reformation," he regularly preached his new gospel.

A stroll from St. Mary's across a large market plaza delivered us to the fourteenth century All Saints' Palace Church, marked by an imposing crown tower and an ornate spire. Unlike the somewhat cheerless St. Mary's, this is one of the most striking churches along the Elbe, with brightly painted vaulted arch ceilings and

After a multi-course Saxony dinner that hopped from rabbit liver to trout-cucumber tart to pigeon breast, we were offered a tasting of five Saxony wines.

carved wooden pews. Technicolor sunshine filtered through leaded glass windows and splashed about the elaborate altar. It was here that the Reformation formally began, when Luther hammered a list of 95 demands for change to a wooden notice board. And it is here, beneath an elaborate bronze crypt, that the great reformer is buried.

Back on our riverboat, after a multi-course Saxony dinner that hopped from rabbit liver to trout-cucumber tart to pigeon breast, we were offered—for a fee—a tasting of five Saxony wines. The Elbe Valley is one of the world's northernmost grape growing regions and "special care and technical skill in processing" is required to produce wine, according to our information sheet. In other words, it's too cold up here, yet locals still try to grow wine grapes. After sipping four thin, listless whites and a wimpy red, we decided that the Saxons should use their technical skills to reactivate some of those 82 breweries back in Tangermünde. We'd even settle for Cowtail.

❊ ❊ ❊

DAY FIVE

We had always thought—without really giving it much thought—that Dresden was the city famous for porcelain. We learned this morning that Meissen has the oldest and most highly regarded porcelain works outside of China. German kings and princes—and most certainly queens and princesses—had long admired fine Chinese porcelain, whose ingredients were a closely guarded secret. They imported pieces from China and Japan and tried without success to duplicate the porcelain's delicate translucent appearance. Then in 1708, the alchemist Böttger from nearby Dresden discovered by trial and error its elemental ingredients—kaolin clay mixed with quartz and feldspar. Fortuitously, large kaolin deposits were available nearby.

Two years later, Saxony's ruler Augustus the Strong ordered the establishment of a porcelain works, not in Dresden but in Meissen's Albrechtsburg castle. The operation was moved in 1863 to a site in downtown Meissen, where it remains to this day. It's so important to Meissen's economy that it's known as "white gold" and of course it is *never* called Dresden porcelain.

Tours of the state-owned Meissen Porcelain Manufactory are rather cleverly arranged. Instead of being herded through the large main plant, visitors pass through a series of small studios, where individual artisans demonstrate their skills, to the sounds of multi-lingual audio tapes. Most of the work is done by hand, including painting the detailed designs. We then paused in a museum room with more than 5,000 porcelain pieces, ranging from rare examples from China and Japan to works of the Meissen factory through the decades. The tour ended with a visit to an adjacent gift shop. Here, fine porcelain pieces sold for as little as a few dollars, and up to $17,000 for an awesome gold-leaf flowered vase.

Departing the factory, our bus became hopelessly trapped behind a double-parked and deserted truck. Traffic congestion is one of the prices Meissen is paying for progress. Several of us elected to hike to our next stop—the Meissen Monastery and Albrechtsburg Castle, fused together on a nearby hill overlooking the Elbe. The walk took us through narrow cobblestone streets

The market had changed little through the centuries, except for the video cassettes alongside the cucumbers and carrots.

and past a market square beneath the fourteenth century Church of Our Lady, where rare ceramic bells chime out the hours. Surrounded by a virtual outdoor museum of medieval architecture, the market had changed little through the centuries, except for the video cassettes on sale alongside the cucumbers and carrots.

While not as elaborate as Wittenberg's All Saints Palace, the Meissen Monastery has beautiful stained glass windows, the oldest in Germany, dating from the fourteenth century. At the next-door castle, we stepped into one of the most incredibly elaborate rooms we've ever entered. It was a medieval banquet hall, ablaze with a myriad of patterns and colors, with elaborate fluted columns and massive murals of court scenes covering most of the wall surfaces. Lifelike and intricately costumed statues of German noblemen occupied pedestals about the room. We were asked to wear soft slippers over our shoes as we explored this splendid space—a clever ruse to keep the ancient and squeaking parquet floor polished.

That afternoon, we traveled by bus through relatively traffic-free green countryside to what the tour brochure described as a "hunting lodge." Hardly a lodge, it was a huge five-story château with fat domed towers at each corner. To provide a little diversion for his friends, Augustus the Strong constructed this Moritzburg Hunting Lodge in 1723. It was the focal point of an elaborate country estate surrounded by artificial lakes. Here, the

For the "hunt," unfortunate critters were herded into a corral encircled by a linen fence and shot by the so-called noblemen.

royal class wined and dined and wenched in grand rooms decorated with crystal chandeliers and monumental murals painted on leather. Between courses, the guests staged mock naval battles on one of the nearby lakes.

The hunting? It was hardly sport. Royal gamekeepers spent much of the year rounding up deer, stag and elk and fattening them in pens. For the "hunt," the unfortunate critters were herded into a corral encircled by a linen fence and shot by the so-called noblemen. A few managed to escape by crashing the frail barrier. To this day, a term translating as "breaking through the linen" is used to describe a flight to freedom.

From the lodge, we walked to the gamekeeprss' cottage. Again, a royal Germanic understatement. The "cottage" was so large and elaborate that it

A crane towering over Dresden's ruined Church of Our Lady signifies the huge construction project underway to repair the city's damage from World War II bombing raids.

has since been converted into a luxury hotel and restaurant. The place had to be huge, of course. Augustus needed about two hundred gamekeepers to feed all those animals for his sporting events.

ßßß

DAY SIX

Brass numbers set into the altar of a small chapel in the Catholic Cathedral of Dresden mark the two blackest days in the city's history—30/1/33 and 13/2/45. On the first date, the Nazis rose to power. On the second, American and British bombers methodically destroyed the city, bringing more than fifteen square miles to the ground.

Whatever the justification for the Dresden *blitzkrieg,* it devastated one of the grandest cities of Europe. The capitol of Saxony for more than eight hundred years, Dresden had accumulated a treasure trove of palaces, libraries, museums and stately government buildings. Virtually all were destroyed or damaged in the February 13 air raid. They are now being rebuilt in one of the most ambitious and costly reconstruction projects in all of the German east. Completion is projected for the first decade of the next millennia.

A focal point of the project is the rebuilding of *Fraunenkirche,* the Church of Our Lady, once one of the greatest Protestant churches of Europe. Somehow surviving several hits in the bombing raid, it collapsed the next day, leaving only a pair of standing wall fragments. The church is being carefully reassembled, stone by stone, and an international fund drive is underway to help finance the project. Sponsors hope to have Our Lady rebuilt by 2006, Dresden's 800th anniversary.

Although the present city is a mere eight centuries old, the area's history reaches back to 927, when the Duke of Saxony began colonizing Slavic tribes. Variously called "Drezdzany", "Dresdene" and "Neuendresden" in early records, the settlement grew into a fortified castle and then a city, receiving its charter in 1216.

Despite the air raid's destruction, there is much to see in Dresden's government and religious center, called the Newmarket area. Imposing buildings rise above the Brühl Terrace, an elevated walkway atop the ancient city wall that parallels the Elbe. A morning guided walk took us past the ruins of the Church of Our Lady to the still-intact cathedral, an impressive Italianate Rococo structure with a

Saxon rulers made wealthy by the area's silver mines assembled one of the world's greatest collections of paintings, which now hang in the Old Masters Gallery.

soaring barrel-arch ceiling. Another survivor—by something of a miracle—is the 112-foot "Procession of the Princes," an outdoor wall covered with 25,000 porcelain tiles. Individually painted and fired in Meissen, the assembled tiles portray thirty-five members of the royal house of Wettin who ruled Saxony for a thousand years.

Several museums occupy this grand plaza of castles and churches. Saxon rulers made wealthy by the area's silver mines assembled one of the world's greatest collections of paintings, which now hang in the Old Masters Gallery. Despite damage to the building, the paintings were spared because they were spirited away as soon as the war started. The works of Rembrandt, Raphael, Reubens and others hang in this galley which is in itself a showplace, with ornate marble staircases, domed ceilings and fabric walls. Our guide Elisabeth Keiper made it all come alive.

"Look at that face," she said, indicating a portrait of a pouting young boy. "Can't you just imagine? His father must have told him he would have to wear clean clothes and sit quietly, for the portrait painter was coming this day. A little boy sitting quietly to be painted? Look at the picture and you can tell what's going on behind his forehead."

After the tour, I returned to the shattered Church of Our Lady to take some photos. As I approached, I saw a pretty little girl—perhaps four years old—sitting on a nearby patch of grass, gathering yellow dandelion blossoms, with her red bright dress neatly arrayed about her. It would have made a wonderful photo, but—

I walked along the Brühl Terrace toward the boat, thinking about war and innocence.

heeding a call from her parents—she scampered away before I could set up.

I took several photographs of the ruined church, realizing they would be lifeless without her. Then I walked along the Brühl Terrace toward the boat, thinking about war and innocence. When we return home, I decided, I would send a check to help rebuild the Church of Our Lady.

We returned to the boat late that afternoon for the final segment of our journey up the Elbe. Although this cruise is essentially a Hamburg to Dresden voyage or visa versa, the boat continues a few miles beyond Dresden for a

Street musicians in Prague's Government Square try to gain the attention of passing tourists. Prague is an optional side trip on the Elbe River cruise.

symbolic dip into the Czech Republic, the former Bohemia and former Czechoslovakia. We would dock tonight in Germany's resort town of Bad Schandau, ten miles shy of the border, and then continue in the morning to its turn-around point––the small Czech city of Teischen.

As our hotel-on-water pushed further up the Elbe, we approached the mountains which gave it birth, an area locals like to call Saxonian Switzerland. Although hardly the Swiss Alps, it was an appealing area where thickly wooded hills crowd the narrowing river, warping it into pretty twists and bends. Charming little resort towns are tucked between steep slopes and river's edge. In a gesture of elegance typical of this cruise, we were invited to the roof deck as we sailed between towering cliffs. We were handed glasses of sparkling wine and given a running narrative of this scenic passage by our cruise director. In some areas, sheer sandstone cliffs towered 600 feet or so above the river. They draw rock climbers from as far away as America.

This was to be the night of the captain's formal farewell dinner, and most passengers had already donned their dark suits and smart cocktail wear. To an unsuspecting fisherman lounging on the bank or a cyclist on a streamside trail, the sight of formally dressed people standing on the roof of a riverboat sipping sparkling wine must have been rather strange.

ββββ

DAY SEVEN

Passengers had the option this day of staying aboard for the short cruise to Teischen and then touring its two castles, or hopping a bus from Bad Schandau for an all-day trip to the capital city of Prague, a hundred miles east. The drive was a dreary crawl behind smoking trucks on a crowded two-lane road. Our route took us alternately through industrial areas that were busily polluting the Elbe, and pristine farm country festooned with brilliant yellow fields of rapeseed, backdropped by wooded hills.

The towns en route seemed colorless compared with those in Germany, with more concrete block homes and apartments than cross-timbered classics. This was not the Bohemia I had pictured in my mental book of European travel. We soon would learn, however, that Czech Bohemia, as in New York and Berkeley Bohemia, exists not in leiderhosen and cross-timbered chalets but in the spirit and artistic outreach of its people.

We eventually reached an autobahn which ultimately will stretch from Prague to Dresden, and the final twenty-three kilometers were achieved quickly. We were lulled asleep by the singing of our bus tires and then jolted awake by another traffic jam, deep within the Czech Republic's capital city.

In the three brief hours that followed, each of our Czech preconceptions were dispelled. Spared serious bombing during World War II, this is an ancient and handsome city built along the Vltava River; its skyline is marked by church spires and a choppy sea of tile roofs. Our bus crawled with renewed determination through traffic toward a low hill known as "Castle town," topped by the Prague palace and cathedral. Eager to set foot on stable ground, we scrambled stiff-legged from the coach and gathered like anxious students around our Czech guide. She was a vibrant, middle-aged character who spoke at least three languages—each of them at the rate of a mile a minute.

We developed a quick liking for our guide and other citizens of this city. The Czech people have a lively, Latin air about them—-a disposition that manifests itself in a love for art, music and dance. Where large German cities are efficiently run and prim, slightly scruffy Prague seems in a perpetual holiday mood. As we walked about the grounds of the palace and adjacent cathedral, we encountered street artists selling their wares, peddlers peddling souvenirs and sidewalk musicians offering their songs for the toss of a coin.

Although this has been a seat of government since the ninth century, Prague's palace is a rather drab—a low rise stone structure with just a hint of Baroque. The cathedral adjacent is quite impressive, with stained glass windows, an eastern orthodox look to its bulbous spires and a webwork of ornate flying buttresses to hold those spires aloft.

"You cannot see Prague in three hours. Poof, and you're gone! You cannot see it even in a lifetime."

In an elaborate gilded chapel is the crypt of the founder of the original Prague city- state, none other than good King Wenceslaus.

We went next to nearby Gold Street, so named because an alchemist here tried to make gold for a Prague ruler. The "street" is actually a cobblestone strip along the old city barricade, where soldiers once built tiny houses, literally fusing them into the base of the wall. They now contain tiny boutiques—-the darlings of tourists. From the wall, we followed our talkative multilingual guide—-who held aloft a partially opened umbrella as a banner—-to the city's old town area. Hurrying us from this attraction to that, she spent nearly as much time apologizing for the lack of time as she did describing the sites.

"You cannot see Prague in three hours. Poof, and you're gone! You cannot see it even in a lifetime."

Indeed. Prague holds a hundred thousand surprises and we saw only tantalizing samples. She led us at a brisk pace across the ancient stone arched Charles Bridge. It's now a pedestrian way, lined with street hawkers, artists and musicians. The art work was quite good for the most part and fairly priced. Near the end of the bridge, an old puppeteer had drawn a sizable crowd. We peered over heads to watch him turn his creation of wood and cloth and strings into a violin virtuoso. We left the bridge reluctantly, lagging far behind the uplifted umbrella, following it toward the huge town square. The square—rimmed by rococo, Roman, Gothic and Baroque architecture—was an outdoor circus of tented vendors, sidewalk cafés, more street artists, musicians and gently persistent hawkers.

"May I do a caricature of you? Of course there is time. You are from America? I *love* America! From where? California? What a wonderful place! You are so lucky. Please, I would like to do a caricature of you—of your lovely wife, perhaps. There is time. I will go ask your guide to wait. A wonderful place, California. I am from the Ukraine. You have no time for a quick drawing? Well, all right. Thank you."

"A wonderful place, California. I am from the Ukraine. You have no time for a quick drawing? Well, all right. Thank you."

We had lunch of red cabbage, veal and good red wine at a small café near the river. Between courses, we were entertained by a professional puppeteer. He'd been one all his life, said our restaurant host, and his father before him. After lunch, a bit more sightseeing and then, poof! Back to the bus.

To avoid the traffic jams of morning, our driver took a circuitous route through the countryside, passing through—it seemed— every small village in eastern Bohemia. He obviously knew exactly where he was going and we soon skimmed the edge of the two-castle town of Teischen. He took a narrow lane down to the riverfront and came upon our boat.

An old fashion tent circus and carnival was being erected on the bank. It was preparatory to a long weekend holiday to celebrate the country's liberation from the Nazis in 1945. A Czech brass band was playing polka music on our riverboat's rooftop deck and several of the carnies had stopped their work; they were sitting on the riverbank enjoying the free concert.

Betty headed for our stateroom for a quick before-dinner nap and I went up to the deck. One of our waitresses—a pretty one with high cheekbones—handed me a glass of Czech beer the color of dark amber. I settled onto an Exercycle at the rear of the deck, the nearest *Over on the bank, a hippopotamus morosely eyed the proceedings from his cage and the carnies sat near the river, swaying to the music.* available seat, to drink my beer and listen to the music. The band members, dressed in purple vests with lavender lapels—except for the leader, a hefty fellow in an ice cream suit—began playing "La Paloma." Over on the bank, a hippopotamus morosely eyed the proceedings from his cage and the carnies sat near the river, swaying to the music.

I sipped my bitter beer and slowly pedaled the exercycle, going nowhere and contemplating the unreality of this scene. For some odd reason, I thought of that little girl sitting in the grass in Dresden, her bright red skirt neatly arrayed around her, gathering dandelions before the bombed-out church.

I must go down to the sea again, to the lonely sea and sky;
And all I ask is a tall ship, and a star to steer her by.

— John Masefield

STAR FLYER

Chapter thirteen

NORTHERN MEDITERRANEAN

Going full sail with Star Clippers

njoy this, for you may never see it again!" the first officer cried to his volunteers. "This is a ship of sails; this is why you are here!"

The passengers hauled their lines on command and the sails climbed aloft, fluttering and popping in the brisk blow. The topsails and then the jibs snaked skyward. As the ship's canvas filled, she heeled smartly to port and moved majestically across the sea. Then her square-rigged sheets were unfurled and soon she was under full sail. She literally danced across the water.

We'd been aboard the *Star Flyer* for several days and the Ligurian Sea had been remarkably calm, except for a brief blow the first night. This was fine for Betty and others who preferred stable waters, but it was too calm for me. I wanted to see a proper breeze billow those sails and feel this grand sailing ship heel to the wind. Then on the fourth day, a stiff breeze came up

CRUISE PLANNER

The cruise • These are one-week cruises aboard a replica of a square rigged barquentine. Much of the appeal of these cruises is the act of sailing; passengers can help work the sails when a proper breeze blows. Shore excursions on our northern Mediterranean cruise included the islands of Corsica, Sardinia and Elba, where the deposed Napoleon Bonaparte lived in rather elegant exile, and the medieval Italian port city of Portovénere. These vessels also cruise the eastern Mediterranean, Turkey's Aegean Sea, the Caribbean and Far East ports of Malaysia, Thailand and Singapore. For information, contact Star Clippers, 4101 Salzedo Ave., Coral Gables, FL 33146; (800) 442-0551 for booking information and (800) 442-0556 for brochures; the local number is (305) 442-0550.

Getting there • Air France offers service to Paris from New York/Newark, San Francisco, Los Angeles, Washington, Miami, Chicago and Houston. In Paris, the French domestic airline Air Inter flies to Nice, where passengers take a bus to the cruise terminal in Cannes. Those who want to see some French countryside en route can take the French National Railway from Paris; trains stop in Cannes, a short walk or cab ride from the cruise passenger terminal.

The ship • The *Star Flyer* is styled as a classic barquentine, a four-masted, square rigged sailing vessel, yet with modern comforts. With sixty-four cabins—mostly outside—it provides most amenities of larger cruise ships. Onboard facilities include a single seating dining room, library-lounge, indoor-outdoor bar and gift shop. The handsome craft is 360 feet long and fifty feet wide with a mainmast that towers 226 feet. When fully rigged, it's capable of attaining seventeen knots or better in a good wind. Officers and crew members are international.

When to go • As in most of Europe, spring through fall are preferred cruise seasons. The Star Clipper ships sail the Mediterranean in summer, throughout the year in the Caribbean and September through December in Southeast Asia.

What to bring • A passport is all that's needed for entry into France and for the Italian mainland and offshore island stops. Dress "casually smart" with comfortable clothing and good deck shoes for daytime (decks are teak), and jackets and cocktail wear are optional for dinner. There are no formal occasions, although many gents don ties for the captain's dinners. This is a Mediterranean climate, similar to Florida or southern California, so dress accordingly, with something warm for breezy evenings and brisk winds on deck.

What's included • Onboard activities are included, such as sailing lessons, seamanship lectures and the opportunity to help work the sails and even stand watch and steer the ship. Shore excursions are extra, consisting primarily of walking tours of port cities and bus tours inland. At most port stops, you can walk into the heart of the towns.

What to buy • Larger towns on the northern Mediterranean islands have the usual curio shops with the usual tourist souvenirs. Serious shoppers may want to haunt the trendy boutiques of Cannes, Nice and Monte Carlo for the latest in designer clothing, fine French perfumes, watches and jewelry.

as we left the island of Sardinia. Happy and eager passengers hauled on the lines and the great white sails blossomed above. It was one of the grandest visions I could remember. For a silly moment, I wanted to be swinging from the rigging with a sabre in my teeth.

ß ß ß

DAY ONE

We took a train south to the French Riviera to meet our ship in Cannes, after a week in Burgundy aboard the canal barge *La Belle Epoque. As we walked from the train station, we were struck by the contrast between Cannes and the rustic villages we'd just left.*

Our path to the harbor took us down a narrow street past the boutiques, galleries, salons and cafés of this jet-set resort on the French Riviera. It more resembled an affluent southern California coastal city, with red tile roofs, stucco walls and asphalt; there were no Burgundian cobblestones here. The rather compact town was squeezed between brushy hills and the azure Mediterranean. Indeed, the French call this area *Côte d'Azure*, the Coast of Blue. "Riviera" is a term used mostly by outsiders.

After browsing through several trendy shops, we walked past a large, modern theater that hosts the annual Cannes Film Festival; the harbor was just beyond. Somewhere out there, we knew that our ship awaited. Finding it should be no problem. However, the harbor was *huge*. We were looking for a four-masted square-rigger, but the bay was a thick forest of tall masts. Scores of yachts of the idle rich stood at anchor or lazed in over-sized slips. There were no cruise ship docks at the harbor; we knew they had to anchor offshore.

The *Côte d'Azure* airport is in nearby Nice; most passengers fly in and are directed here aboard buses. We'd come directly to Cannes and I'd forgotten the file folder with information about the ship's departure. I remembered only that it left at midnight—an hour and a half from now. What if we couldn't find it? Omygawd, what if we'd gotten mixed up and the ship actually departed from Nice?

I felt my palms start to sweat as we stared in vain through the maze of masts. No *Star Flyer* nameplate appeared. If the ship left from Nice at midnight, we'd never make it! We found an English-speaking French yachtsman and asked him where the cruise ship shuttles came ashore. Well, of course, there was a *The Flyer is a study in varished teak and mahogany, shiny brass, arched windows and paisley prints.* cruise passenger terminal, just down there. We hurried to the terminal and saw the words *Star Flyer* flashing in large letters on a reader board. I felt instantly relieved and quite stupid.

The *Flyer* is a newly built four-masted clipper ship styled in the fashion of mid-nineteenth century barquentines. It's a study in varnished teak and mahogany, shiny brass, arched windows and paisley prints. We learned that this was the first commercial sail vessel of its type built since 1912. On its maiden positioning voyage in 1991, became the first barquentine to cross the Atlantic since 1870. (It makes these crossings annually between the Mediterranean and Caribbean.)

Sails of the fully-rigged Star Flyer reach skyward to catch a Mediterranean breeze.

Should you wonder, a barque is a four or five-masted, square-rigged cargo and passenger ship that was developed a hundred and fifty years ago. The barquentine is a variation on this design, square-rigged on the foremast only; the other masts are rigged fore-and-aft. Because these forward square-sails tend to pull the ship instead of pushing it, the craft is more stable, and there's more deck space for cargo and passengers.

The *Flyer's* comfortable cabins offer modern conveniences with a classic look—decorated in turn-of-the-century appointments in wood and brass. The ship offers the usual dining excess with multiple meals per day, a cleverly fashioned indoor-outdoor cocktail lounge, two small swimming pools and a library. A cruise director organizes shore excursions and a sports staff coordinates scuba and snorkel outings, diving lessons and assorted other water sports.

Such frivolities as fashion shows, dance competitions and talent contests are conducted, and fitness masochists can join in morning workouts on deck. Life aboard is casual and meals are open seating, without excess dressiness. Lunch and breakfast are served buffet style and dinner is a sit-down affair, with a choice of appetizers and entrées offered from the menu.

This all sounds suspiciously like a typical cruise ship, yet it happens aboard a real sailing vessel with its orderly jumble of lines and lanyards, acres of canvas and masts soaring high into the blue Mediterranean sky.

That sky was dark now, as midnight approached, although it was brightened by a full moon behind a disintegrating cloud cover. It had rained much of the day, since one of those unseasonably cold storms had blown in from the British Isles. (Everyone in Europe blames bad weather on the Brits.) On the distant shoreline, a hundred thousand points of light glittered from Cannes and crawled into the night-blackened hills above. We were beyond the reach of the jostling crowds and traffic noise of the resort town. Bustling Cannes was now just a pretty pattern of lights in the Mediterranean night.

The anchor chain clanked and the *Star Flyer* pivoted on its moorage and headed out to sea. No sails yet flew; it relied on its engine for most dockings and departures. Then in the pale darkness the crewmen, aided by the moon and strings of white lights in the rigging, began unfurling the canvas. Curious passengers, bundled against the cold and with nightcaps in hand, gathered to watch. Two great sheets of white, a jib and a staysail, glided skyward to the squeak of pulleys and the tightening of lines. They popped and flapped, caught the breeze, billowed and—like two friendly ghosts—began urging the ship forward.

The *Flyer* heeled a few degrees to port and glided silently across the harbor, her bowsprit rising and falling to the eternal rhythm of the sea. High above, the smiling moon danced in her rigging.

🏴 🏴 🏴

DAY TWO

That little English storm kicked up again during the night, sending our good ship into a rolling amusement park ride. It rode out the choppy seas beautifully and we slept peacefully, knowing we were in good nautical hands. The blow continued into early morning and after breakfast, I settled into a deck chair to watch the handsome ship ride the marbled gray sea.

Sailing ships tilt with the wind, letting the breeze slip off their sails to propel them forward. The stronger the wind, the more the tilt. In a good blow, people move about the deck at odd angles, as if they were in one of those mystery houses where a person loses track of vertical. The tilt remains relatively stable unless the ship changes course; thus its motion is predicable in a strong blow. Motor craft tend to buck and lurch through a storm.

A chubby English lady clutched her deck chair as if she expected it to launch into space.

"Do you think we'll tip?" The timid question came from a chubby English lady nearby; she clutched her deck chair as if she expected it to launch into space.

"Tip?"

"Yes. Do these things ever tip over?"

"Don't worry. Sailing ships are supposed to lean away from the wind; it's perfectly normal. Besides," I grinned, "it's just a little English storm. It's not going to hurt you."

The lady looked puzzled. Then, as if to ease her fears, the *Star Flyer* settled down. We had sailed into the leeward side of Corsica, France's island possession with a strong Italian accent. It was much more rugged than I'd imagined and thickly vegetated, with steep shorelines and snowcaps on craggy inland peaks. Off to starboard stood the small harbor town of Ille Rousse. It was a simple collection of beige stucco and faded orange tile, climbing a slope above a blue slice of harbor. The *Flyer,* now completely calm, headed for her first anchorage of the cruise.

For centuries the island home of subsistence farmers, Corsica has been an historical ping pong ball. It was occupied by Greece, Rome, Byzantium, the Italian city states of Genoa and Pisa, France and England. *La Belle France* has been Corsica's landlord since the late 1700s.

Ille Rousse—whose name means "red" in Corsican, for the ruddy outcroppings in the hills above—is the smallest of the island's three port cities. It was founded in 1758 to handle the overflow from Calvi and D'Agagola, when Corsica was part of the Genoan empire. It was thus and remains today Italianate in architecture and attitude. Its small business district consists of two narrow streets with a mix of old and new buildings of stucco over stone. This is not a major resort since the beach here is rather rocky; nearby Calvi gets most of that traffic. Only the restaurants were open when we arrived at midday, for French Corsica follows the Italian custom of a three-hour siesta. Thus, our exploration was rather brief. Ille Roussse's most appealing area is the packed-earth town square with a few palm trees, a bit of landscaping and weathered architecture.

We inspected the square briefly, and then strolled back to the ship. After lunch, we boarded a bus for a trip inland, where we discovered the island's heart and its fascination. Corsica's first settlers were shepherds and growers of olives and grapevines, so its oldest towns are off the coast, explained our guide. Inland is mostly vertical and its towns are among the more picturesque in the Mediterranean, cantilevered into steep slopes.

As we careened upward, mournful Corsican music played over the bus speakers; I found it to be curiously soothing.

Roads linking these villages are predictably winding and narrow. In some places they are notched into steep cliffs, like slightly oversized hiking trails. Some of the passengers cringed as the driver wheeled his bus around hanging hairpin turns.

"If you're frightened, just close your eyes," the guide said. "That's what the driver does." It's an old gag, but it helped ease passengers' tensions.

Those of us who kept our eyes open were rewarded with impressive views of the distant Mediterranean and the foaming white beaches of Corsica far below. Olive groves, almond orchards, pasturelands and an occasional vineyard formed a pleasing geometry on the sloping terrain. Many of the fields were separated by ancient hedgerows and stone walls. As we careened upward, mournful Corsican music played over the bus speakers; I found it to be curiously soothing. The sad music reflects the hardship of life in this rocky, brushy land, our guide explained.

Our destination was Sant Antonino, a ninth century village clinging like a grasping hand to a Corsican mountaintop; some call it the "Eagles Nest." Only seventy-nine people live here, although they are not lonely and their village is not remote. It's a regular stop on the tourist route; two other buses were parked near the town's simple church when we arrived. This parking

A pastoral scene on the island of Corsica—sheep grazing below a small church in the hilltop village of Sant Antonino.

area, once part of a goat pasture, was one of the few level spots in the village.

There is little to see in "Little San Antonio." It's main appeal lies in its precarious perch and period architecture. After brief strolls through narrow streets past ancient stucco and red tile, most of us retired to the town's wine shop. The owners made a fine sweet muscat and a decent red table wine. We sat in the patio beneath the azure sky, sipping *muscato bianca* and thinking what a pleasant place this would be, were it not so busy with tourists such as ourselves. We bought a bottle of muscat for our stateroom and the shop owner wrapped it in old newspaper, which I thought was a quaint touch. Then it occurred to me that, with the summer tourist traffic, he probably had to special order the papers.

A downhill spiral took us through several tilted towns, with brief stops for visits to churches with Italianate campaniles and dim, hushed naves. We paused at an old olive mill, now mostly a boutique. The owner explained that the millstone was turned by a mule. The mashed olives were then gathered in shallow circular burlap bags resembling artists' berets and squeezed in a hand press to render the oil. We sampled the shopkeeper's olive oil with bits of crusty bread. It was excellent but not mule-rendered, since the dusty equipment had long since been retired.

Our final stop of the day was Calvi. This important shipping port has several miles of sandy beaches, thus attracting a fair tourist trade. The town is well kept except for one wall scrawled with Corsican graffiti which read, as far as we could figure, "The government is run by Nazis." We later learned that a Corsican autonomy group considers the French to be trespassers, although they've been here for more than two centuries. They black out French words on highway signs or shoot holes through them and scrawl their frustrations on old village walls. There have been no serious incidents and no threats to life.

Calvi's focal point is its former citadel, occupying a rocky mass above the city and towering over the sea. It was built during the Genoan era to defend this key shipping point. Only its walls survive today, although it is not abandoned. Shops and homes now occupy this hilltop sanctuary. Many of its cobblestone streets are so steep that they surrender to become broad stair steps.

Back on the ship, passengers were invited to the bridge before dinner for the first of several sailing lessons conducted by the officers. We learned the difference between a jib and a staysail, and that a spanker isn't an irate parent but the aft-most sail on a barquentine. We were told that five miles of line (never call it rope!) is needed for the *Star Flyer's* rigging, and that 36,000 square feet of canvas billows to the breeze when it's at full sail.

೬೬೬

DAY THREE

We awoke this morning to calm seas and a light wind. That pesky English storm had left us and the *Star Flyer* glided through the Mediterranean as if she were on rails.

Much of day three would be spent anchored, giving passengers access to a pair of Corsican communities—one by foot and the other by tour bus. We thought the first, Porto Vecchio, was moderately interesting. The second, Bonifacio, was outstanding. It's one of the most dramatically situated towns in Europe, occupying a limestone ridge high above the Mediterranean. It would be a pity to visit Corsica and not see Bonifacio.

A one-mile walk (cab ride optional) delivered us to the most interesting part of Porto Vecchio—the site of the former citadel. Now the old town section, it occupies a ridge above the harbor, without the impressive views of Calvi, but with an inviting tangle of narrow streets. Betty continued investigating the citadel area's ancient stone while I indulged in my favorite form of sightseeing. I settled at a sidewalk café opposite the church with a glass of local red wine in hand. Never mind that it was called *Café le Tourisme*; I *felt* like a local. The wine arrived with seasoned tortilla chips and a spicy green sauce, an ideal prelude to the hefty buffet lunch that waited aboard the *Flyer*.

I settled at a sidewalk café opposite the church with a glass of local red wine in hand. Never mind that it was called Café le Tourisme; I felt *like a local.*

A post-lunch bus ride took us fifteen miles south to Bonifacio. The heart of the city, enclosed by a high-walled citadel, caps a limestone ridge at the island's southern tip, several hundred feet above the sea. Viewed from the coast, its beige stone walls and tile rooftops seem to have sprouted from the crest of chalky white cliffs.

Bonifacio dates from the late tenth century when it was established as part of the Pisa empire. The natural harbor, cradled between limestone

The harbor at Corsica's Bonifacio, seen here from the citadel, is one of the jewels of the Mediterranean.

ridges, became an important shipping center and the citadel was built to protect it. In 1769, the year after the French took possession of Corsica, a child named Napoleon Bonaparte was born in Ajaccio, a village near Bonifacio. His family had migrated from Italy when Corsica was under Genoan rule and he thus became a French citizen only by chance. Later, as a lieutenant, he served at Bonifacio's citadel and he nearly lost his life when his unit mutinied. A devoted sergeant cut down the lead mutineer with his sword and defused the rebellion—an action that certainly altered the course of European history.

The citadel encloses a wonderful mouse maze of narrow cobbled streets and timeworn stone buildings. Views back down to the busy little harbor are among the premiere vistas of Europe. The best vantage points are from the fortress walls, which require a ten-franc admission. Our local guide, who kept getting lost, was unaware of this fine vantage point, so we found it on our own. She was new to Bonifacio, she said. We suspect that she also was new to Corsica and possibly to the Northern Hemisphere.

🐚🐚🐚
DAY FOUR

A cruise aboard the *Star Flyer* is a lot about sailing. There is, of course, emphasis on water sports and interesting ports of call. When the weather's right, the Zodiacs are lowered for water skiing and banana boat rides or one can simply lounge around one of the pools.

We and many of the other passengers were intrigued mostly with the sailing. Each day, Captain Klaus Muller or one of his officers gathered us novice mariners near the bridge to discuss sailing ships and how they work and where they came from. The captain, a stocky middle-aged man with close-cropped gray hair and an engaging grin, has been at sea all of his adult life. By the age of 29, he was master of his own ship. Born in Germany, he now lives in Scotland, "among sheep herders, far from the sea." He has been master of the *Star Flyer* since 1994 and his identical twin brother Jurgen is captain of the company's sister ship, the *Star Clipper*. Captain Muller loves to discuss the sea and the ships that sail upon it and he frequently breaks into a high-pitched boyish laugh as he talks.

"The history of sailing is the history of man," he said. "At first, there were no roads, no vehicles, only boats. Try to visualize a time when everyone and everything traveled by water. I am convinced that Adam and Eve got about by dugout." Then came that boyish laugh.

"Those who controlled the seas controlled the world. It was the Phoenicians who first sailed, about 1000 B.C., and they ruled much of the known world. But their boats had flat bottoms and square sails, so they could only go with the wind. The Phoenicians may have reached America, and there is evidence of this, but I don't think they got back."

Since trade winds blow from the east in the Northern Hemisphere, it's easy to sail west across the ocean, he said. "Just go south until the butter melts, turn to starboard and catch the trade winds."

He pointed out that the Vikings, inventors of the keel that allows a ship to tack into the wind, made the first round trip to America. As he concluded his talk, the *Flyer* cruised into Porto Rotondo, a luxury resort on the Italian island of Sardinia. It was started in 1962 by Prince Karim Aga Kahn and is now a playground of jet-setters. The place

"This is a halyard, and when you hear the bell go ringy-dingy, it means the anchor is raised. On my signal, you start pulling and the sail goes up."

offered little of interest to us, so we returned to the ship after a brief exploration. Much more fascinating was our departure in late afternoon. The passengers were asked to become part of the action by helping hoist the sails.

First officer Uli Pruesse aligned his troops and placed a thick line in their hands. "This is a halyard, and when you hear the bell go ringy-dingy, it means the anchor is raised. On my signal, you start pulling and the sail goes up; it is as simple as that. Walk quickly backward with the line, but don't walk off the deck." The passengers giggled like a group of collegiates about to begin a tug-o-war.

Conditions couldn't have been better for rigging the ship to sail, for a good stiff wind had come up suddenly. The passengers hauled their lines on command and the sails climbed aloft, fluttering and popping in the brisk blow. The staysails and then the jibs snaked skyward; their snapping in the wind sounded like drum rolls. As the ship's canvas filled, she heeled smartly to port and moved majestically across the sea. Then her squaresails were unfurled and soon she was under full sail. Her engine was silent; we heard only waves washing past her bow, the satisfied laughter of her passengers and—issuing from the ship's speaker—Vivaldi's *Four Seasons*.

"Enjoy this for you may never see it again!" the first officer exclaimed to his volunteers. "This is a ship of sails; this is why you are here!"

Standing on the tilted deck, Betty and I looked up at the towering banks of canvas. We felt the wind in our faces and we listened to Vivaldi and the

"When you hear the bell go ringy-dingy—" Passengers stand ready to haul the Star Flyer's *sheets aloft on First Officer Uli Pruesse's signal.*

sea. We knew then why people love to sail; why tall ships are the icons of poets and painters.

"Today, sailing is so different," Captain Muller said after we were under way. "We have modern compasses and computers and navigation by satellite. Those early sailors, they had to know so much about the position of the stars and the sun. They would watch for shorebirds in flight, for driftwood, for the color of the sea, even, to learn where they were. The first navigation was very crude. They sailed by the North Star and the sun, but they could be as much as forty percent off in their calculations. Can you imagine? So they looked for birds and driftwood, and hoped landfall would come soon."

Since the *Star Flyer* was long and slender, she could not tack effectively without the help of her engine, he explained. The early sailboats were short and chubby, more able to maneuver into the wind. "On this ship, when we turn into the wind and we have a schedule to keep, we give it a little push with the engine, and nobody notices."

He looked up into the rigging and smiled and we knew that he loved this vessel, but that he wished he were sailing into yesterday, sighting on the sun and stars and looking for shorebirds in flight.

🍃🍃🍃

DAY FIVE

One of the attractions of sailing with Star Clippers is that itineraries may be changed—and improved—on a whim of wind and weather. That doesn't mean the ship goes wherever the winds blow, for it has that diesel engine. It does mean that the captain may choose a different port if weather conditions dictate it. We had planned to stop at Giglio, a small island off the Italian coast noted for its beaches; a good place for water sports. However, it was a

THE LITTLE GENERAL AND HIS LITTLE ISLAND

Napoleon Bonaparte was not exactly a prisoner on Elba. His removal from the throne of France was in effect a demotion. He was made sovereign of this tiny island and granted an annual payment of two million francs.

During his nine-month stay, he instituted reforms that radically changed this once backward island's economy and living conditions. He taxed its iron industry, tuna catches, and olive and grape production, using the proceeds to improve roads, replant deforested hills and drain marshes to create new farmlands. He made education compulsory on an island where the literacy rate had been less than ten percent.

And all the while, he found time to plot his comeback. He left the island in March of 1815, rallied a thousand of his faithful soldiers and reclaimed his throne. His glory was brief. Three months later, he engaged British and Prussian troops at Waterloo and lost 25,000 men in a devastating defeat. He was again exiled, this time a virtual prisoner, to the island of St. Helena off the south coast of Africa. Alone and ignored even by his own family, he died there six years later.

However, he is still remembered fondly on Elba, where he left an indelible impression that remains to this day.

bit cool so Captain Muller elected to go instead to Elba, where Napoleon was exiled after surrendering the throne of France. Then a province of France, it is now an Italian possession. (Elba is a regular stop on one of the other *Star Flyer* routes.)

If your vision of Elba is a forlorn rock where Napoleon sat and stared morosely out to sea, you couldn't be more incorrect. It's a beautiful island with lush pasturelands, vineyards and evergreen forests tilting up to a rugged rocky spine, nearly 3,500 feet above the sea. Although not large—just eighty-six square miles—it offers a pleasing mix of modern seaside resorts, a couple of fishing villages and cute vertical towns cantilevered into steep mountain slopes. Napoleon's brief stay here from May 1814 until February 1815 was hardly spartan. He had an elaborate home with a sea view in Portoferraio, the island's main city, and a country estate with terraced gardens a few miles inland, at San Martino. Both are now Napoleonic museums.

Surprisingly, this rather idyllic island once was a major producer of iron ore. Its forests were stripped to create charcoal and its skies were sooty from smelters. Iron production was on the decline when Benito Mussolini dragged Italy into World War II; Allied bombs destroyed the iron smelters and they were never rebuilt. Tourism, olives and wine feed Elba's economy today.

We sailed into the bay of Portoferraio (Port of Iron), a handsome and compact city of pastel stucco row houses tucked between the pretty harbor and the great granite walls of a fortress. It's the kind of city that invites exploration, although we first wanted to poke about the countryside. We teamed with a pair of shipmates, rented a small Fiat for a large daily fee and followed winding roads into the green hills.

Our first stop was Napoleon's "summer residence." As noted above, he hardly suffered in exile. His home was a grand granite villa of multiple rooms and terraced gardens. Little of this elegance remains, for the place begs restoration. Only elaborately coffered ceilings and tile floors speak of the good life he lived here. The main villa is now a museum, with historic Napoleon prints and a nice collection of nineteenth century photographs of the island. The prints are mostly of Napoleon's battles, and in each, he wore the same stoic expression while riding a white horse into the fray. Bonaparte's poker face never changed; his mount usually seemed more concerned about their predicament.

We spent most of the rest of the day careening our little blue Fiat along Elba's winding mountain roads, pausing at assorted *punta panoramicas* for views and photographs of green hills sloping down to azure coves rimmed with tile roofed houses. Our route took us to the village of Marciana Marina, with its charming old pastel waterfront behind a fishhook pier and breakwater, then into the hills to Marciana and Poggio, tilted towns perched dramatically on rocky spurs. Just beyond Marciana, a sky bucket carries visitors to Mount Capanne, one of the island's highest points, for stellar views from Elba to Sardinia to the Italian mainland.

ßßß

DAY SIX

Tomorrow, we would dock in Monaco, sail on to Cannes that evening and leave the ship the following morning—undoubtedly with some reluctance. This would be our last full day exploring the Ligurian Sea, our last real opportunity to watch the sails work, to stand—confidently now—on a properly canted deck or lounge above the waves on the protective netting below the bowsprit—a favorite passenger activity.

We sailed in a good breeze this day, headed for a mid-morning landfall on the Italian coast. During the captain's final "sailing talk" we learned that when you ask for a weather report at sea, you get a wind report. For wind is what settles or troubles the sea; it's what drives the boat. Never mind rain or sunshine; only the wind counts.

Portovénere is a grand medieval jewel; terraced so steeply that its upper streets are traffic-free pedestrian lanes.

"I love sailing the Mediterranean in summer," Captain Muller told us, "because the weather (meaning the wind) is so reliable."

Our final Ligurian Sea port was our favorite—Portovénere. It's the gateway to some of Italy's most famous cities, including museum-rich Florence, tilted Pisa and medieval Siena. However, we didn't expect Portovénere itself to be the jewel that it is. We were so fascinated, in fact, that we canceled our planned bus excursion to Pisa so we could spend the full afternoon here. We'd both seen the leaning tower before and I've heard that it's threatening to topple anyway.

Portovénere is a grand medieval jewel; an easy-to explore town of just a few thousand residents. It's terraced so steeply that its upper streets are traffic-free pedestrian lanes linked by stairway passages. Downtown traffic, and not much of it, is confined to a waterfront street.

That waterfront is part of the town's charm—a stonework embarcadero busy with brightly colored fishing boats, most not much larger than dinghies. Fishing nets were strung about and we assumed that the guys mending them weren't employed by the local tourist office. Narrow row houses four to five

Italy's Portovénere is a splendid example of a medieval city, with rowhouses crowding its picturesque harbor.

stories high and only a few feet wide jostled for position above the waterfront. Their pastel colors—salmon, pink, beige and soft orange—added to the rich texture of the town.

We walked along the shorefront, drawn toward the ruins of a once great fortress and a grand little chapel fused to rocky sea cliffs. The citadel was built of natural stone, not the typical cut stone of most forts, giving it an attractive rough-hewn look. We followed a small herd of chatty, laughing Italian tourists who became suddenly hushed as they entered the Church of San Pietro. It's a simple chapel perched above the sea, with rough stone walls, a few wooden pews, a modest altar and a statue of St. Peter.

Slate stairways took us from the chapel and fortress to the ruins of a castle occupying a higher sea cliff, perhaps 200 feet above the Mediterranean. Little remains of its original luster; it's mostly appealing as a collection of massive walls, stairwells, arches and tunnels. After crawling like kids over acres of age-old stone, we returned to the town and walked through terraced lanes of homes and shops. Finding a promenade that extended for more than a mile along the waterfront, we strolled leisurely, hand-in-hand, allowing our enthusiasm for this charming village to grow. It began drizzling, a very un-Mediterranean thing to do in late May, but it didn't dampen our affection for this charming city. The sprinkle gained intensity and finally sent us in retreat to the ship.

I returned to town later, needing to spend the last of my lira and wanting a final look at Portovénere. At a small market, I bought some boxes of biscotti for friends back home and a bottle of Tuscan wine for dinner, reducing my Italian money to small change.

Although it was now pouring, I walked back toward the fortress and climbed steep slate steps that had become terraced cataracts of runoff.

Soaked to the skin, I stepped inside the chapel and stood quietly, listening to the driving rain patter off old stone. Looking across the medieval harbor at our four-masted ship, I could have convinced myself that I was standing in another century.

On an impulse, I put the last of my lira into the offering box and lit a candle. "See you later, St. Peter," I said patting the statue's knee. Then I stepped into the downpour and headed back to the ship.

For years, Betty and I have talked about spending a year exploring Europe. Of course, we'd want a particularly fascinating town as a base of operations. I knew now that it would be Portovénere.

🏳🏳🏳
SINCE YOU'RE ON THE RIVIERA...

Because the *Star Flyer's* Mediterranean cruises begin and end on the *Côte d'Azure*, we suggest here things to see and do before or after. This strip of coastline—some of it impressive, much of it cluttered and ordinary—stretches from Cannes northeast through Monaco to the Italian border. The best way to commute among the Riviera towns is aboard the French National Railway's *Métrazur* trains, which run twice hourly between Ventimigila on the French-Italian border to Cannes. Other trains, running less frequently, go all the way to Marseille.

CANNES: This is the haunt of the beautiful people of *Côte d'Azure*, with a harbor full of luxury yachts and narrow streets lined with upscale boutiques. Highrise apartments and condos sprout from the hills beyond. However, unless you're here to sun or shop, or you've been invited aboard an oil sheik's yacht, there's not a lot to do. East of the waterfront, you can stroll for two miles along Boulevard de la Croisette, lined with luxury homes, palm-shaded beaches and occasional topless bathing beauties. It ends at Croisette Point, a landscaped park with fine aquatic views. The Cannes tourist office is in the train station, about four blocks inland from the waterfront.

ANTIBES: One of the few cities on the Riviera that retains much of its medieval look, small Antibes is fun to explore on foot. Don't miss the old world Cours Masséna market, where you can buy everything from produce to tourist trinkets. *Place Nationale* is the town's central plaza, lined with sidewalk cafés and shops. Another worthy stop is the *In Monte Carlo, walk along the waterfront and admire billions of dollars worth of yachts.* Picasso Museum in the Grimaldi Castle. Incidentally, Antibes also is a major yachting center, with a harbor full of handsome vessels. You'll find the tourist office at 11 Place de Général-de-Gaulle.

MONACO: This is the fairyland of *Côte d'Azure*, a tiny *Mouse That Roared* principality, where our own Princess Grace lived and tragically died. This city-state of less than two square miles is too modern and too thick with high-rises to have much charm. It is, in fact, one of the most densely populated areas of the world. It does have its attractions, however. In Monte Carlo, Monaco's only city, walk along the waterfront and admire billions of dollars worth of yachts; the one large enough to be a cruise ship belongs to the royal family. Then head for the rocky promontory upon which perches the royal palace, other rococo government buildings and a fine old town area. Catch the changing of the guard at 11:55 each day; it appears to be a scene from a Gilbert and Sullivan operetta. Then walk a few blocks through old town to the Cathedral of Monaco; step into its lofty hushed interior and pay your respects to the tomb of Princess Grace and other Monacan royalty. Just downhill from there, suspended high above the sea, is the excellent Oceanographic Museum and Aquarium.

For a fine walking seascape of the *Côte d'Azure*, take the 2.5-mile coastal trail between Monte Carlo's suburbs and Cap d'Ali to the southwest. To start from the Monte Carlo end, catch a cab to Tahiti Beach, walk across the beach parking lot and you'll find the trail. An easier way is to catch a train from Monaco to Cap d'Ali and pick up the trail just below the train station. First walk to your right a few thousand feet, where the upper end of the trail terminates at a couple of small Cap d'Ali resorts. Then head back along the seacliff past elegant villas toward Monte Carlo until you hit that beach parking lot.

Gaming is conducted in a quiet, dignified manner; no Las Vegas style action here.

A Monaco visit should include a trip to the casino and its adjacent Hotel de Paris. Both are splendid rococo and chandelier-draped structures dating back to the last century. Evening wear (suits and cocktail dresses) should be worn to the elegantly flossy main casino and there's an admission fee of 50 francs ($10 to $12). Dress codes are relaxed in the off-season, but you won't be admitted in shorts and T-shirts. Also, you'll need your passport or a photocopy with the ship's stamp (which is provided by the purser). Gaming is conducted in a quiet, dignified manner; no Las Vegas style action here. You can enter the so-called "American casino" without dressing up, although it's little more than a small room full of slot machines.

NICE: One might say that Nice was here long before *Côte d'Azure*. It's a work-a-day city of 350,000 with a fine old town section, a rustic waterfront and some interesting museums. It's also the base of operations for two dramatic rail excursions into nearby mountains.

The first is the run from Nice to Cuneo, departing the main train station several times daily. It travels into an awesome wilderness of deep canyons and granite peaks, often tunneling through rugged mountains. Stone medieval villages cling to steep slopes or array themselves along pretty river valleys. One of the more attractive is Breil-sur-Roya along the Roya River. If you're in a hiking mood,

The other great rail trip follows the imposing canyons of the Var River toward the community of Digne.

a trail dating back to the Roman era leads into the wilderness along the city side of the river. We don't recommend taking the train all the way to Cuneo; it's a foothill blue collar city on the Italian side of the border. A good place to turn around—before you leave the best of the scenery—is Tende, another of the high mountain villages. With an early morning start, you can explore Tende or Breil-sur-Roya for a couple of hours and catch a later train back to Nice.

The other great rail trip, on the privately owned *Chemins de Fer de Provence* railway, follows the imposing canyons of the Var River toward the community of Digne. The route, nicknamed the *Ligne Digne,* begins at the Chemins de Fer de Provence rail station a short distance from the main terminal. Ask directions at the main station or at the tourist information office, just to the left of the station as you exit. The Ligne Digne trains—narrow-gauge rail-diesel cars—are a bit scruffy and the roadbed is rather bumpy, but the scenery is outstanding. You'll meander through deep crevasses beneath the shadows of high peaks, with stops at stone medieval villages that crawl up steep slopes or cap high ridges. As with the first run, don't go to the end of the line; turn around either at Entrevaux or Annot, both neat little Roman style villages. Entrevaux is particularly imposing, built into a razorback ridge with an old city wall zigzagging up to a hilltop castle. If you get an early morning start, you can hop off for a couple hours' exploration and then catch a later run back to Nice.

Incidentally, both of these trips also can be accomplished in a rental car, since highways parallel the rails for much of the way.

VILLEFRANCHE: Like Antibes, Villefranche has preserved much of its medieval look. Walk through its old town area of steeply terraced traffic-free (but not dog-poo free) lanes. Weathered St. Pierre Chapel is worth a stop; also walk through nearby Rue de Obscura, a street that has become a tunnel through centuries of overbuilding. The attractive crescent harbor below is busy with pleasure craft and lined with sidewalk cafés, boutiques and curio shops. One of the Riviera's longest sandy beaches extends southeast along the crescent bay.

 β β β

Dear are the names of home...
But we have tasted wild fruit, listened to strange music;
And all shores of the earth are but as doors of an inn.
We knocked at the doors and slept; to arise at dawn and go.
— Laurence Binyon

PART V:
Asia

A Chinese street merchant offers his wares at dockside in Wuhan, launch point for cruises through the Yangtze River's famed Three Gorges.

At Yellow Crane Tower I say farewell to Meng
And watch his boat's sail go further, even further,
Until vanishing in the clear blue sky.
But my heart runs with the Yangtze waters,
Flowing, ever flowing.

— Li Bai

Chapter fourteen

CHINA'S YANGTZE RIVER
Sailing the Three Gorges with Victoria Cruises

If America's Mississippi is the Big Muddy, China's Yangtze is the Big Latté. A silty light brown for most of its course, the slow, turbid river reaches nearly 4,000 miles across the earth's most populated landscape. It is the world's third largest in water volume and the third longest, after the Nile and Amazon. The Mississippi-Missouri is slightly shorter, ranking fourth.

It compares in many ways with the Mississippi—busy with river traffic, nurturing villages and major cities along its banks, providing rich riverbottom soil, and finally reaching the sea in a broad, flat delta. In a nation struggling to feed its millions, the Yangtze is more vital to China than the Mississippi is to America. Hundreds of thousands live on the river in sampans; others eke out subsistence by fishing its polluted waters or operating small cargo barges between its hundreds of shoreside communities. The Yangtze River Basin, fed by 700 tributaries, is home to a third of China's 1.2 billion people. It produces two-thirds of the country's rice and nearly half of its freshwater fish.

Yangtze is not the river's Chinese name; it's *Changjiang*, or Long River. Yangtze, which means "son of the ocean," referred originally to the lower reaches of the stream, where it empties into the East China Sea near Shanghai. The Long River begins as a series of crystalline creeks at 20,000 feet in the frigid, treeless and windswept Qinghai Mountains of Tibet. Initially a

275

CRUISE PLANNER

The cruise ● A trip through the Three Gorges of the Yangtze River is one of the world's most popular river trips, taken by more than 300,000 people a year. Most voyages are on smaller, older boats. However, Victoria Cruises, the only American-managed line on the river, operates a fleet of comfortable new ships, offering 850-mile voyages through the gorges between Wuhan and Chongqing. They're six days upstream and four down. For specifics, contact Victoria Cruises, 57-08 39th Ave., Woodside, NY 11377; (800) 348- 8084 or (212) 818-1680; FAX (212) 818-9889.

Getting there ● United Airlines offers service from Seattle, San Francisco and Los Angeles to Shanghai or Beijing, with an extensive network of connections from the rest of the country. Its comfortable Connoisseur Class (business class) provides a preview of the Orient, with Asian entrees offered in its meal service.

The ships ● The firm's three ships, Victoria I, II and III, are designed specifically for river travel, with shallow draft hulls to maximize navigability. Each has seventy-seven outside cabins with private baths and amenities such as in-room TV, phones and oversized windows. Although small, the ships are surprisingly well-fitted, with dining rooms large enough for single seating, a nightclub with nightly activities, a library, beauty salon and fitness center and even a business center. The cruise director is American; officers and crew are Chinese and those who deal with passengers speak English.

When to go ● The "when" takes on special significance, for a giant dam currently under construction will change the river through the gorges into a long, slender reservoir. It won't inhibit cruising, however. Locks will lift ships past the dam, so any interruption in ship traffic will be brief. Estimates for completion of the dam range from 2009 to 2015. The Yangtze flows through south central China, noted for warm, muggy and sometimes rainy summers and chilly winters. Spring and fall are the best cruising months, and fall is the most popular. Wettest period is April through early summer although rain can come at any time, so pack accordingly. Trips run from March through early December.

What to bring ● Americans and most other nationalities traveling to China must secure a visa. Pack as you would for a trip up the Mississippi; the climate along the Yangtze is similar to that in America's South. Light cottons are suggested in summer, since it can be hot and muggy. In spring and fall, days and nights can range from warm to chilly. Dress is casual on board, although some men slip on sport jackets for dinner. Bring binoculars for spotting things on the high cliffs of the gorges.

What's included ● All onboard meals are included and the food is primarily Chinese, with different types of cuisine featured each evening. Some Western selections are available and American style breakfasts are served. Shore excursions can be purchased as an inexpensive package, which generally is included in cruise-tour prices. Many passengers take the cruise as part of a greater China tour, arranged by American companies specializing in this area. You also can book an unescorted tour before or after the cruise, with hotels, transportation and guides waiting at various cities en route. Meals are extra on the land extensions, although breakfast is included at many hotels in China.

What to buy ● See next page.

swift whitewater stream, it gathers volume and mud and slows to a crawl as it crosses a great delta flood plain in China's heartland. In its final ponderous march to the sea, it loses only seventy-five feet elevation in nearly 700 miles. Hundreds of miles of levees are required to keep it within its banks, and it often breaks through with disastrous results.

The Long River divides the country in half, north and south, as it passes through and nourishes major cities such as the former nationalist capital of Chongqing, the great urban sprawl of Wuhan and the major port of Shanghai. It enters the sea just beyond Shanghai, dumping its mud onto a sprawling delta that grows a mile every seventy years. Between Chongqing and Wuhan, the river has carved its way through the Wu Mountains, creating the legendary Three Gorges. And that brings us to our primary reason for coming here.

The Three Gorges cruise is one of China's most popular tourist lures. The gorges, however, are only a highlight of a river voyage that reveals to the traveler the country's vast heartland, from the marshy flood plain of Wuhan to the hilly sprawl of Chongqing. To cruise the Yangtze is to experience much that is China. Today, that is quite an experience.

ಠಠಠ

ON VISITING CHINA

Gone are the days when China tours focused on collective farms and school rooms where students recited Marxist mantras. Today's visitors have complete freedom of movement and first class hotels are plentiful, at least in larger cities. With the world's fastest growing economy, China is a country in fascinating transition. You'll see pedicabs and taxicabs, and street markets in the shadows of high rise office buildings.

Many guided tours are now available in China although it isn't difficult to travel on your own. Arrivals and departures are announced in English at train stations and airports in larger cities. Hotels, tourist-oriented restaurants, handicraft shops and some larger stores usually have English speaking people on staff. Don't expect to become too conversant with most cab drivers, however, since few speak English. Have a hotel desk clerk write down your destination in Chinese, and *always* carry your room key or a hotel matchbook so you can find your way back.

Betty speaks just enough Cantonese to get us into trouble.

Betty speaks just enough Cantonese to get us into trouble. Having a Chinese-American wife in China proved to be no great advantage—particularly a Cantonese-speaking one. Mandarin is the official language, used by the vast majority of Chinese. However, her limited vocabulary did lead to some merry adventures as we were pointed in the wrong direction several times.

What to buy

China is noted for its splendid arts and crafts, from painted scrolls and excellent carvings to delicate cloisonne, jade, and gold jewelry. It is noted as well for ivory carving, but be advised that ivory products cannot be brought into the United States. To counter this, some Chinese artisans are now using animal bone to produce their figurines. The most reliable source for fine giftwares are the government run Friendship Stores. A few years ago, these were the only places where outsiders could buy such items. In the new China, however, department stores also are good sources for art and handicrafts. Many Friendship Stores in fact have been converted to department stores, open both to local Chinese and visitors.

Although prices are increasing with the economy, China is still one of the best places on the globe to buy handicrafts. Prices are more or less fixed in Friendship and department stores, although you sometimes can get a five to ten percent discount. Haggling is expected with street vendors and at shops near tourist attractions. Start at about a fifth of the asking price and work slowly upward. Also, be wary of guides who steer you to gift shops. They may be getting a "finder's fee"; you probably can find better prices on your own.

China's currency is the *yuan* and the exchange rate is around eight to the dollar. You'll find few currency exchanges on the streets; hotels generally give you a fair rate and it's usually a bit better for travelers checks than for cash.

Streets are safe in China, with almost no violent crime and only the occasional pickpocket to fret about. Almost to a man and woman, we found the Chinese to be friendly, and willing to pause and lend a hand when we needed directions or assistance in shopping. The children were like children everywhere. They would pause and stare at this odd looking camera toting gringo with his Chinese companion, and shout the one English word they all knew: "Hello!"

ßßß

DAY ONE PLUS: A CHINA SAMPLER

Victoria river cruises begin in China's interior—far upstream in either Wuhan or Chongqing. Since United Airlines and other overseas carriers fly to Hong Kong, Shanghai or Beijing, one must travel to across China to the board the boat. However, it would be a shame to simply jump onto another plane and hurry through the skies of one of the world's oldest and most fascinating nations.

Aware of this, Victoria Cruise officials work with other American companies who package China samplers in the form of pre- cruise or post-cruise land tours. In fact, most passengers take advantage of these packages. They can be fully escorted or on- your-own with pre-arranged hotels, transportation and private tours. Taking advantage of this program, we stretched our China arrival day into five.

Shanghai: allow yourself to be waylaid

A river port city once so wicked that its name became a verb for involuntary servitude, Shanghai today is a vibrant, inviting and certainly a safe place to explore. It's more colorful than massive and drab Beijing, yet not quite so crowded and chaotic as Hong Kong. Many voyagers on Victoria Cruises' Yangtze river trips will enter China via Shanghai; it is a city that deserves a pause.

Our stay was too brief to thoroughly explore one of China's largest cities, so we focused on the historic downtown area along the Bund. Originally a sea wall to protect the city from floods, it was fashioned into a landscaped, elevated promenade in 1992, part of the city's ambitious redevelopment program. To stroll the Bund is to sample the city—on one side, the Huangpu tributary of the Yangtze River, busy with freighters, strings of little putt-putt barges and an occasional cruise ship; on the other, fine old baroque buildings of the turn-of-the-century international settlement, when Shanghai was China's window on the world. Now protected as historic landmarks, these ornate brick and masonry structures house banks, smart shops and—good grief!—American fast food outlets.

If this city is a window on the world, our room at Shanghai Mansions Hotel was a window on Shanghai, with a splendid view of the Bund and the old city. We awoke to a sound that would not leave our ears until we boarded our cruise ship—a honking symphony of horns as the city beneath us--draped in an ethereal haze—came to life. We

We watched Shanghai stretch and awaken, and then we hurried down to join the fray.

watched Shanghai stretch and awaken, and then we hurried down to join the fray. We walked past silent ranks of men and women practicing their *tai chi,* noisy ranks of school children on outings, street peddlers cooking and selling hot noodles and businessmen jabbering into their cellular phones.

A new park occupies the upper end of the Bund, with a towering Monument to the People's Heroes of Shanghai and a larger-than- life statue honoring heroes of the Revolution. Reads a large sign introducing visitors to the Bund Sightseeing Area:

Any person or organization visiting the Bund should conscientiously observe the law, maintain good manners, follow social order and abide by social morals.

Despite the sign's Marxist tone, we were amazed by the changes since we had visited China several years earlier, shortly after the Tienanmen incident in Beijing. The drab blue and gray quilted smocks had been replaced by bright Western garb; cars jammed streets once crowded only with bicycles; shops spilled over with goods. Pretty young girls, of which China has a delightful abundance, pranced along the Bund in mini-skirts.

Farther along the riverfront, a monumental statue of Chairman Mao glowered down upon the scene; we could understand his concern. Yet a short hike up a side street revealed the China of old—public markets spilling into already overcrowded streets with fruit and vegetable stalls, single-wok sidewalk cafés, silvery piles of dead fish, cages of nervous chickens waiting to die, and some hanging animal carcasses which upon close examination turned out to themselves to be alley cats.

Mao and Communism and perhaps even mini-skirts will come and go; China will forever be China.

Slow train to Hangzhou

Even with the current economic reformation, China is reluctant to admit that it embraces the Western world's decadent class system. At the Shanghai railway station, the place where we awaited our train to Hangzhou was called the "Soft Seat Waiting Room"—a politically correct euphemism for first class lounge.

Our double-deck train, not spotless but comfortable, trundled through Shanghai suburbs that reluctantly surrendered to countryside, although these were hardly wide open spaces. China is a congested land struggling to feed its millions; every square foot is occupied by farmlands, villages or drab new apartment towers. Within the villages and along the railroad tracks, people tended tiny and tidy plots, some no larger than shuffleboard courts.

These raffia-wrapped earthenwear jars being loaded aboard a Yangtze River barge in Wuhan contain dried fish; we could tell by the smell!

Three hours from Shanghai, we entered another urban sprawl. Hangzhou isn't as compact as the bustling port city and its busy streets are wide and tree-lined. Here, as in most other inland cities, bicycles and pedicabs still outnumber taxis and private cars. The clamor of horns and bells, as they fight for space on crowded streets, is cheerfully chaotic.

Hangzhou is a major center for China's silk industry and visitors can tour nearby silkworm farms and silk factories. However, by the time we had arrived in late October, the last of the pupae had been parboiled and unraveled to be woven into fine fabric; no tours were available. We visited the new Hangzhou Silk Museum which traces the industry from its roots in ancient China to modern weaving and dyeing technique. I learned that tie-dyeing wasn't created by 1960s hippies; it was developed in China around 600 A.D.

Later, a rather melancholy guide took us on tour of Hangzhou's other major attraction—Xihu Lake, which borders the city to the west and provides much of its charm. A royal retreat for centuries, it has been dredged and shaped and fitted with parklands. In the dredging, a tree-lined causeway and several islands have been formed. A popular spot, reached by fanciful little pagoda-roofed tourist boats, is Isle of the Fairies. It's a doughnut-shaped island with center spoke dikes, resembling a crooked steering wheel. In typical Chinese verbosity, it's called Three Pools Mirroring the Moon.

Reluctant plane to Wuhan

A small China Southern Airlines turbo jet delivered us from Hangzhou to Wuhan although our delivery was a bit late. We boarded the plane, sat while the engines warmed up, then were asked to return to the terminal briefly because a battery was overheating. "It will take half an hour to change it," we were told. An hour and a half later, midway through a free lunch provided by the airline, we were hustled back onto the tarmac, where our poor little plane was tethered to a tractor.

"You're towing us to Wuhan?" I asked our flight attendant.

No, we lugged our luggage onto a second plane, which got us up into the air and on to Wuhan without further delay. As we approached the city, we could see the great latté colored Yangtze meandering through the mist below. The river and the sprawling city of Wuhan were surrounded by a diked wetland of lakes and paddies. Down on the ground, we discovered that Wuhan was a huge triple city of seven million people, divided into three districts by the merger of the Han and Yangtze rivers.

> "So you see, Chairman Mao has made our fish very much famous," Leslie said brightly.

Our guide here was a remarkable improvement over the melancholy gentleman of Hangzhou. Leslie was a tall and strikingly pretty young woman who led us with firm stride to a few of Wuhan's tourist lures. East Lake, surrounded by parklands, had been visited frequently by Chairman Mao, who was so impressed by a local specialty of steamed fish dish that he wrote a poem about it.

"So you see, Chairman Mao has made our fish very much famous," Leslie said brightly.

We went next to the Hubei Provincial Museum, which displays an imposing collection of relics unearthed in 1978 from a 2,400 year old tomb. Missed by grave robbers, it yielded among other treasures a remarkable set of sixty-five cast bronze bells so intact and perfectly tuned that they can be used to play contemporary music. Museum officials have created a duplicate set of these instruments and on occasion present brief concerts to visitors. Although these are percussion instruments, the sounds from China's misty past are strangely sonorous and resonant, at times sounding like Andean flutes.

We ended our Wuhan day at Yellow Crane Tower, a beautifully rebuilt pagoda on a hill overlooking the city and its surrounding wetlands. We climbed stairs to the fifth floor, with gift shops and exhibits on each succeeding level to encourage our efforts. (A lift is available for about twelve cents for the lame and the lethargic.) As we looked out over the endless sprawl of the city, Leslie told us the story of the tower in her melodic Chinese accent, her eyes arching with excitement as if she were addressing attentive school children:

A beggar asked the owner of a hilltop wine shop for a cup of wine, although he had no money to pay him. The kindhearted man agreed and the vagabond returned several times, receiving free wine with each visit. "You are so kind to a poor beggar," he said after several visits, "so I will now repay you." He picked up an orange peel from the floor, transformed it into a yellow crane and gave it to the wine merchant. A talented bird, it sang and danced, drawing many customers to the shop and making the merchant very rich. Sometime later, the beggar—obviously an immortal—returned. "Your kindness has been rewarded and now it is time for me to depart." He climbed aboard the crane's back and flew off to heaven.

The moral is obvious: Virtue can be its own reward, but it couldn't hurt to have a precocious bird.

A sea of fish, netted from a lake near Yueyang, is spread over burlap to dry.

🏳🏳🏳

DAY TWO

We'd boarded our riverboat *Victoria I* in Wuhan the night before. It shouldered carefully past flotillas of sampans and chugging little barges. Soon, the city's neon and dotted white streetlights faded into the mist and we—weary from an afternoon keeping pace with long-legged Leslie—faded off to sleep.

This was a day devoted mostly to cruising, for we had a lot of river to cover on our 850-mile upstream voyage. However, we paused after breakfast for a two-hour shore excursion to a temple in Yueyang. The contrast between the old and the emerging China becomes more evident as one travels further inland. A "small" city of only half a million, Yueyang offered a mix of mud huts and modern masonry buildings, standing alongside potholed roads.

As our bus bounced along a levee road on Dongting Lake, a pendant portrait of Chairman Mao swung merrily above the driver, who seemed quite adept at seeking out the potholes. We paused at an outdoor fish market, where glittering heaps of still squirming slivers of silver were hauled from boats and spread over burlap to dry in the hazy sun. We continued to Yueyang Tower, a handsome structure gleaming with golden tile. Legend says it was saved from collapse a few centuries ago by Daoist (Taoist) immortal Lu Dongbin. He liked to hang out here, get sloshed on rice wine and write fine poetry. He visited the tower three times and—liking the place—used its powers to ensure that it would endure. A pavilion was built in his honor. The Chinese, with their penchant for the colorfully obvious, have named it the Thrice Drunken Pavilion.

Back aboard *Victoria I,* we fell easily into the lazy routine of river cruising. Despite fancy touches such as a crystal chandelier hanging from the reception hall's atrium ceiling, and a couple of nubile Greek goddesses (Victorian?), this is a casual ship with a pace to match. Breakfast and lunch are served buffet style. Dinner is sit-down, and informal dress is

We did note one difference. You don't find too many sampans on the Mississippi.

acceptable, even for the captain's opening and closing galas. In the style of Chinese hotels, an attendant is posted on each floor, ready to fetch tea water, bring an extra pillow or tend to other needs. Officers and crew are Chinese, except for an American cruise director, who keeps things moving by scheduling lectures, *tai chi* demonstrations, fashion shows and such. Or passengers could simply lean at railside and watch the Big Latté roll past.

Again, we were put to mind of the Mississippi. Well short of the mountainous gorge here, the river flowed through a flat basin that faded to distant, misty horizons. Dike-protected fields and small towns lined the shore and towboats shared the brown current with a few larger cargo ships and other cruise boats. We did note one difference, however. You don't find too many sampans on the Mississippi.

🐾🐾🐾

DAY THREE

The face of China, rarely in vivid tones, is more of a pastel watercolor, like a faded old scroll. We awoke to a hazy sun casting soft rays along the shoreline. Buildings of masonry and faded brown brick—the outskirts of Yichang—stood among thin groves of trees on the shoreline. Narrow bands of vegetable gardens were draped over the low, sloping banks like ranks of fuzzy green caterpillars crawling toward the water.

After breakfast, as we approached Yichang, the low banks rumpled into small, steep hills, forerunners of loftier things to come. Yichang is the gateway to the Three Gorges and the hills became more dramatic with each river mile. We soon realized, as sculpted spires and ridges rose behind this bank-hugging city, that Chinese painters of watercolor scrolls do not exaggerate.

To compare the Three Gorges with the Grand Canyon is to mislead the traveler. The gorges are no less nor greater than *El Cañon Grande;* they are different, and quite dramatic in their own way. They present themselves as a series of sheer walled ravines, stratified limestone terraces, steep and brushy hills and those fantastic spires, buttes and ridges that the artists capture on their rice paper scrolls. Some of the peaks forming the gorge are 3,000 feet high. It is hazy much of the time here, and overlapping ridges—each one less

WHAT'S ALL THE DAM FUSS?

After decades of study and delay, one of the most expensive, controversial and misunderstood construction projects of this century and next is finally underway. Amidst fanfare and debate, the first ceremonial bucket of concrete was poured in 1994 for the Three Gorges Great Dam.

When finished—supposedly around 2015—this giant gravity arch concrete wedge will reach a mile and a half across a shallow valley above Yichang, midway up the lowest of the Three Gorges. It will be the world's largest and most powerful hydroelectric dam, capable of producing 84.7 billion kilowatt-hours of electricity a year. That's 40 percent more than Washington's Grand Coulee, currently America's most powerful hydroelectric dam. Behind the 600-foot-high structure, the world's longest reservoir will extend in a series of skinny fingers more than 350 miles to the edge of Chongqing. Think of a reservoir reaching from San Francisco to Los Angeles or from New York to Norfolk. Cost estimates range from $12 billion to $30 billion and 40 percent of the total budget will go for "inundation compensation."

Thirteen cities, 140 towns and 1,352 villages will be flooded, requiring the relocation of 1.3 million people. Most of the project's funding will come from an energy tax in China; the rest from foreign loans and bonds, although the world community has shown a reluctance to participate financially.

A bankrupt project?

Some say the dam will never be completed; that the staggering cost will bankrupt the Chinese government. Environmentalists and several foreign governments say it never should be completed, for it will inundate one of the world's most dramatic series of gorges. "Inundate" is something of an exaggeration, since it won't actually bury the gorges, whose walls are as much as 3,000 feet high. However, it will raise water levels several hundred feet, turning the free-flowing river into a reservoir. It will not, as some claim, end cruising through the Three Gorges. In fact, a five-step lock and a deepened channel will permit passage by much larger ships. (However, ocean-going vessels can't sail into the gorges unless their superstructures are low enough to get under several downstream bridges.)

Traffic may be halted for construction of a coffer dam to divert the river, although this will be only for a few months, and probably in winter during the off-season. Once that's done, some say that cruise traffic on the river-turned-reservoir will be busier than ever.Cruising's not a major government concern

The cruise industry, of course, is of minor concern to the Chinese government. They list three major benefits for the dam. It will increase electrical generation by 15 percent in a country that is choking on coal smoke pollution. It will improve shipping, a major boon to upriver cities served now only by small barges. Further, officials say it will prevent or at least curtail flooding of the lower Yangtze Delta, which in this century alone, has claimed half a million lives.

So, what's all the dam fuss? Opponents say the project is too expensive, that a series of smaller dams can generate more electricity and help control floods. Further, many of the floods are caused by rainfall below the dam site, so it would have no effect. Silting may become a major problem when the muddy river's flow is blocked, and the reservoir could become a giant sewer since the river won't be able to flush effluent out to sea. Chongqing, a city of thirteen million and growing, has no adequate sewage treatment facilities; its waste is dumped into the river. Also, the dam will impede the seasonal rise and fall of the Yangtze, which deposits fertile soil on streamside farms. Further, rising waters of the reservoir will bury historical and cultural sites and threaten several species of fish and river dolphins. Finally, observers don't trust the Chinese government, with its checkered record on civil rights, to be fair in handling the displacement of 1.3 million of its citizens.

It got the go-ahead

Both the U.S. and Canada, which helped with the original planning of the dam, later withdrew their support and much of the rest of the world community is opposed. But never mind that. After some hesitation and delays, the National Peoples' Congress gave the project final approval in 1992 and construction began two years later. Of course, this massive undertaking might fizzle, and become history's most expensive boondoggle.

The odds are, however, that the late Chairman Mao will get his wish, although it may become a series of smaller dams instead of one big one. Initially proposed by Doctor Sun Yat-sen in 1919, the dam project lay idle as China became embroiled in wars and revolutions. It was resurrected in Chairman Mao's Great Leap Forward program in 1958. He was so enthusiastic about the project that he wrote this poem:

Walls of stone will stand upstream
To hold back clouds and rains.

distinct and more blue-gray as it retreats—present an ethereal scene.

Also unlike the Grand Canyon, the gorges are populated. Yichang, at the lower end of Xiling Gorge, is a good sized city, crawling up the steep slopes. Farther along, tiny villages, terraced fields and lonely huts cling to these inclines. Concrete arch bridges leap across narrow side canyons. The river, narrower and swift flowing here, is busy with barges, sampans, crowded ferries and sightseeing boats. The gorges present a mixed picture and thus mixed emotions from the viewer. Here, a pagoda-roofed temple on a rocky ridge; there a coal loading chute dumping its dusty load onto a waiting barge.

The site of the much discussed Three Gorges Great Dam is about 25 miles upstream from Yichang, although it won't be the first to span the Yangtze here. The small Gezhouba Dam crosses the river just above the city. Passengers were invited to join a lottery, guessing precisely when the dam's big lock gates would open to admit the *Victoria*. Chinese passengers, lovers of gambling, flocked to sign up, although an American—who unscientifically wrote down the time of his first son's birth—won the pot.

Farther upriver, we passed under a Golden Gate style suspension bridge. Just beyond that—the site of The Dam, busy with dusty construction. Above the dust, billboard-sized signs on either bank bore a message in bold Chinese characters:

Build Up the Three Gorges; Develop the Yangtze River!

Just upstream, we passed a contemporary town of poured concrete buildings, looking quite lively but waiting to die. The rising reservoir will inundate this site.

The canyons lived up to their advance billing late this afternoon. After cruising for several hours through the lower gorge with its mix of cliffs, steep peaks, industry and villages, we sailed into Wu Gorge, the second of the three river canyons. Much less populated than Xiling Gorge, it began as a series of overlapping V-shaped ravines, with walls rising 2,000 feet above the water. As the afternoon light faded, it evolved into a spectacular mix of sheer ramparts, overlapping ridges and contorted strata. Etched into the walls were fragments of tow paths where hundreds of men with ropes once pulled cargo barges through the swift currents. If one slipped from the narrow path, we were told, he was cut free of his rope harness and allowed to drop into the river, so as not to impede the barge's progress.

Goddess Yao Ji carved the Three Gorges to divert the river around the petrified remains of a dozen dragons she had slain for harassing peasants.

Shortly after sundown, as fading light added golden tones to the rippled brown water, we passed Goddess Peak, named for the gorge's mythical creator, Yao Ji. She carved the Three Gorges to divert the river around the petrified remains of a dozen dragons she had slain for harassing peasants. Then she positioned herself on a high ridge, where she still stands, a slender finger of rock keeping watch over the gorge. Below her, shaped into dramatic narrow ridges, are the bodies of her victims.

尼尼尼

DAY FOUR

American naturalist Joseph Wood Krutch once wrote that if the planet becomes so crowded that it is impossible for man to find peace and privacy, it will no longer be important. We will then lose the gift of serenity.

We docked this morning off the steeply tiered city of Wushan for a motorized sampan trip up the Lesser Three Gorges. These are narrow canyons of the Daning River, one of the Yangtze's larger tributaries. Several Chinese men, eager to make a fast *yuan*, were selling sedan-chair rides to the street, which was high above the waterfront. Many passengers took this Chinese version of Mr. Toad's wild ride up the tilted muddy bank; they emerged nervously giggling and unscathed at the top. There, as we settled into our bus, the driver shrieked incessantly into a walkie-talkie, apparently communicating with his other drivers. The device seemed redundant; I'm sure his voice would carry unaided into the next county.

The bus howled and shuddered up the steep and narrow street into the heart of this crowded and cantilevered town, its horn blatting constantly to part the sea of pedestrians and motorized rickishas before it. Sidewalks were narrow in old Wushan, and they're mostly filled with commerce, forcing pe-

The majestic, hazy ramparts of the Three Gorges dwarf a river barge. This is Qutang Gorge, smallest and perhaps the most spectacular of the three.

destrians into the streets. (Fortunately, the sampans can navigate right up to the ship most of the time. We were there late in the year when the water was too low at the Daning River's mouth. However, the noisy ride provided an opportunity to view this fascinating old city.)

We crossed over a ridge and lurched down into a narrow bay, where we left the bus and played hop-scotch over a row of parked sampans to reach our designated craft. These were not cozy little family sampans but long and slender motorized launches. They'd been built by the government to haul tourists, locals and light cargo up and down the swift Daning River. Many villages up there are reached by water only. Our craft was similar in length and seating configuration—-though not in cleanliness—to a Greyhound bus.

Our outing became a grand adventure. The slender boat growled and churned through some fair-sized rapids, beneath walls that pitched a thousand feet skyward. Three men were positioned on the bow—two to work, one to supervise—to pole the sampan through the swifter rapids. At one particularly challenging spot, we had to clamber ashore and hike a short distance upstream to rejoin the boats. Souvenir hawkers, anticipating this, had stationed themselves along the trail, offering curios as we trudged past.

Some say these narrow mini-chasms, with their walls rising dramatically from a clear, fast-flowing stream, are more appealing than the main gorges. The perpendicular bastions reminded us of the great inner gorge of the Grand Canyon, although without the terraced buttes and ridges beyond. A brochure provided by our guide instructed us to look for imaginary shapes in the twisted and tilted strata of the walls. We found Monkey Fishing in the Air and Horse Returning to the Mountain, but Pig Worshiping the Goddess of Mercy somehow eluded our gaze.

After pressing several miles upstream, through gorges ever narrowing, past cliffs ever rising, we turned about and practically flew back down.

Within minutes, it seemed, we were back on the groaning bus, honking our way through chaotic traffic. The quiet little gorges seemed part of another time and place. Perhaps they were just a wishful vision in the mind of a poetic naturalist.

Back aboard *Victoria I,* we ended our day with a final and brief encounter with the great gorges of the Yangtze. Qutang Gorge, smallest and perhaps the most spectacular of the three, is a near-vertical chasm rising 2,000 feet above the river. We saw evidence of past history here—tracker paths still etched into the steep walls—but little of the present. This section of the gorges is practically uninhabited, perhaps the closest that crowded China ever gets to wilderness.

Then within half an hour, we emerged from Qutang Gorge. (On the downstream run, the passage takes eight minutes.) Off to starboard was a symbol of China's past, present and future. Fengjie, one of the country's few surviving walled cities, climbed steeply from its busy riverfront. Fragments of the original wall remained, with cluttered tenements and a few modern office buildings towering above. At the town's western end, men with shoulder buckets loaded a coal barge. Behind them, the twin stacks of a factory belched smoke into the air. Within a decade or so, all of this will be history. Fengjie, a city of 350,000, will be drowned by the Three Gorges Great Dam.

ß ß ß

DAY FIVE

We were scheduled for a morning tour of Fengdu, called the Ghost City because pilgrims can visit a temple here and buy their way into heaven. However, heavy fog forced the *Victoria I* to lay at anchor the night before, so the morning shore excursion was rescheduled for 1 p.m. and then 2:30.

But never mind that. There were plenty of activities on board, and the small library was stocked with items of interest concerning China. Cruise director Amy O'Connor maintained two loose-leaf binders—one on current China affairs and another on the Three Gorges Dam—with clippings as fresh as two months ago. We spent much of the morning thumbing through them, and then we attended Amy's thought-provoking lecture on the dam project.

The debate carried well into the noon hour; half-price bloody Marys from the bar helped spur our opinionated fervor.

"I'll give you background on both sides of the issue, and then open it up for discussion."

The debate carried well into the noon hour, even after Amy had left to tend to other duties. The offer of half-price bloody Marys from the bar helped spur our opinionated fervor. Then we were called to lunch, where the food was abundant and good Tsingtao beer flowed freely. Thus, life aboard the *Victoria I* wasn't all that bad, even when she was running five and a half hours behind schedule.

Later that afternoon, we finally reached Fengdu, a compact hillside city of 50,000, and headed for the Daoist temple, God of Hades, where one could purchase a ticket to heaven. The local Chinese guide pointed out that heavenly passage isn't guaranteed, however. If you were a bad person and approached the temple, you were sent straight down to Hades. The temple, crowning a wooded hill over the city, was ransacked during Mao's cultural

*Co-author
Betty shops for
Chinese fans at
a display outside
Yueyang Tower.*

revolution and restored a few years ago. The new version, owned by the city and reached by a sky tram, is no longer an active temple, although the heaven-bent faithful keep coming. It has become more tourist gimmick than religious landmark.

During our tour, our guide put us through three tests to prove our heavenly worthiness. First, we crossed a bridge whose name translates as "Helplessness," which had to be accomplished in three or five paces—no more, no less and nothing in between. The next challenge was to mount a flight of thirty-three steps without taking a breath—no problem. En route to our third test, we passed a walkway lined with the eighteen monsters of the netherworld, representing the Daoist version of Hades. They were so heinous that they looked comical. One was stirring up some skull soup; another was lunching on a recently severed arm. Our final test, after those grim reminders of life in a Daoist hell, was to balance with one foot on a small sphere for three seconds. Our generous guide gave most of us the benefit of a very fast count, but I made an honest four seconds.

"Congratulations!" she beamed. "You are ready to go to heaven."

Thanks, but not right now. I have a book to finish.

GOOD INTENTIONS; BAD ENGLISH

China exhibits a lot of concern for visiting tourists, posting many advisory signs intended to keep us from getting into trouble. Perhaps we shouldn't make fun of them, considering our inability to communicate in *their* language. However, these two in the room of our hotel near the Shanghai Airport were particularly cute.

* * *

Ladies and gentlemen, if you suffer from a serious illness and find urgent accident, please dial urgent telephone 555 immediately. Thanks for your cooperation.

* * *

Dear Guests:
Recently, on the mainland of China, some foreigners were fooled and deceived by evil people in the hotels, street and other places. Please pay attention to the following points:
1. Buying selling some articles forcedly: Such as harmful and false commodity, obscene videotape and magazine, etc.
2. Phenomenon of changing and stealing baggage: Please take care of your handbag and suitcase in the lobby of hotel, airport and railroad station.
3. Phenomenon of calling taxi: Some taxi drivers go around in circle deliberately. They often ask for more taxi fee. Therefore, if you want to take a car please call taxi at the counter of hotel and airport. Be careful of some drivers who induce you to take their taxi.
4. Phenomenon of prostitute: Some prostitutes often seduce you in some hotels or on streets. And some Private Bars and Karoke will ask for much money. You must understand that even if you are victim, you are also responsible for the behaviour of prostitution in mainland China. You will be detained or arrested by the police, according to the seriousness of your case.

We sailed over perfumed waters plumbago coloured, that pale cool blue
of the sea when no breath stirs, and here and there, upon its scented level,
bloomed sudden islands, strange gardens of the ocean, green with palms.
— Violet Clifton, *Islands of Indonesia*

Chapter fifteen

OUTER INDONESIA

Seeking adventure aboard the *Spice Islander*

W hen we go ashore today, look carefully and remember. You'll see things that you have never seen before. Things that no one may ever see again."

Toni Tack, the lecturer on our one-week cruise to several outer Indonesian islands, opened her first-day slide show with this provocative statement. This was not a reference to mystical rites or other exotic tribal customs, but to a primitive way of life that is fast disappearing.

Indonesia is one of the largest and most complex nations on earth. With more than 200 million people from 300 different ethnic groups, it ranks fourth in population after China, Russia and the United States. It's comprised of 13,667 islands, give or take a thatched rock or two, stretching for nearly 3,500 miles across Southeast Asia. This is a land of great cultural and economic extremes, from the oil rich and traffic choked city of Jakarta to rarely visited islands where dwell some of the globe's most primitive tribes. The In-

CRUISE PLANNER

The cruise ● This seven-day "Dance of Welcome" expedition calls on several islands in southeast Indonesia, with the emphasis on tribal villages in transition, plus water sports and a visit to the lair of the famous Komodo dragon. For information, contact P&O Spice Island Cruises, P.O. Box 3581, Denpasar, Bali 80228, Indonesia (0361) 286-283; FAX (0361) 286-284. P&O offers a variety of other Indonesian voyages ranging from three to fourteen days.

Getting there ● Garuda Indonesia, noted for its fine inflight service, is the primary carrier for these cruises, with flights from Los Angeles and Honolulu to Denpasar and Jakarta. Garuda also offers extensive inter-island service and flights from Indonesia to Europe, the Middle East, Asia, Australia and New Zealand.

The ship ● The *MV Island Explorer* is a 134-foot aluminum hulled catamaran with twelve cabins and six suites. Facilities include twin or double beds, private baths and air conditioning. The ship offers single-seating dining, buffet style for breakfast and lunch and table service at dinner. Other facilities include a combination cocktail lounge lecture room with TV and video, and upper and lower sun decks. Officers are English and Indonesian, with an Indonesian crew.

When to go ● "Dance of Welcome" cruises run from mid-March through mid-November. Indonesia straddles the equator, so temperatures vary little from month to month—meaning it's generally warm and muggy. Summer to early fall is the dry season and therefore the most popular for travelers. The calmest seas are September through November, when the monsoon winds aren't blowing.

What to bring ● American citizens need only a passport. This is the tropics, so bring layered light clothing in cottons, linens and other breathable fabrics. Also bring a good head cover and ample sun protection, and binoculars for wildlife spotting and closeup studies of Komodo dragons' eyeballs. The cruise is casual with no formal occasions, although long pants are requested for dinner. There are frequent stops for water sports, so bring swim suits and snorkel gear. Some snorkels, masks and flippers are available.

What's included ● All shore excursions are included, since this is an expedition cruise. Also included is a short flight from Bali to Timor to pick up the ship. Pre-cruise and post-cruise hotels at Sanur Beach near Denpasar can be arranged as part of the package, with airport pickup and return. Scuba diving is available through prior arrangement.

What to buy ● The most popular items are *ikats,* hand woven and dyed cotton wrap-arounds for men and women; each island has its distinctive pattern. Handicrafts include wood carvings, small wooden boxes, bone-handled knives (good letter openers) and hand-crafted jewelry, including hammered and engraved silver items. Craft prices are very modest if one is willing to participate in spirited bargaining. (See box on page 299.)

donesian government is attempting to reach these distant societies with at least rudimentary education and health care. With each contact, the human condition may improve, although a primeval way of life is altered forever.

Most Indonesia-bound visitors hit the highs of Bali, jog around Jakarta and do the dragons of Komodo Island. Most of the other 13,664 islands are more difficult to reach, since transportation is rather limited.

We had done Bali and Jakarta on previous trips. In the spirit of adventure cruising, we wanted to visit some of the country's less developed islands. We signed on with P&O Spice Island Cruises, which has packaged a series of "vacations beyond Bali" that focus on the Indonesia of yesterday. They don't entirely ignore the obvious since many cruises—including ours—feature stops at Komodo Island and Lombok, next door

When first "discovered"
by outsiders, the islands
of Indonesia were called
the East Indies.

to Bali. For the most part, however, they reach out to outer islands and bring to light the Indonesia of thatched huts, dugout canoes and palm tree subsistence.

P&O's voyages are true expedition cruises, with the emphasis not on elegance but on exploration and learning. They feature daily "enrichment lectures" and frequent field trips; nightly talks and videos helped us prepare for the next day's outing. An Indonesian cruise director and an on-board lecturer provided insight to the host country. We selected the "Dance of Welcome" cruise, which calls on the Lesser Sundas along the southern edge of the Indonesian archipelago. Locals call the area *Nusa Tenggara* or the Southeast Islands. More than 500 of them stretch between Bali and New Guinea; only forty-two are inhabited.

This trip focused on rural villages just now entering the current century. The itinerary also included snorkeling and other water sports, a bit of wildlife spotting and a visit to Komodo where we would look those non-fire breathing dragons right in the eye. Our ship, the *MV Island Explorer,* is a squarish 134-foot aluminum catamaran with eighteen cabins. It's of Indonesian registry with local officers and crew members. The food was ample and quite tasty, often with interesting Indonesian accents. Our stateroom, not fancy, was comfortable and roomy.

⌘ ⌘ ⌘

THE SHAPE OF THE LAND

Indonesia is shaped from the summits and high plateaus of a sunken volcanic mountain range. The archipelago extends southeast from the Malay Peninsula, forming a scattered island corridor between the Pacific and Indian oceans. Except for the northwestern tip of Sumatra, the country lies below the equator, with a resultant tropical climate. Its not all hot and humid, however. Although much of it is rainforest, areas of southern Indonesia are arid, with sections almost desert-like.

When first "discovered" by outsiders, the islands were called the East Indies. Early explorers were particularly interested in a narrow string of small isles lying south of Borneo and Sulawesi—a submerged ridge of mountains called the Moluccas. These were the fabled Spice Islands, now collectively called Malaku. Traders were drawn from far corners of the globe to barter for three tasty products found nowhere else—nutmeg, mace and cloves.

Street markets, such as this one on Lombok, an island adjacent to Bali, are typical of the Indonesian scene.

These "Indies" were the destination of Christopher Columbus, who missed his mark by a hemisphere. As a result, he mis-named the collective native populations of north, central and south America.

Although they comprise many linguistic groups and cultures, the people of Indonesia are primarily Malays, a rather handsome blend of East Indian and Oriental. The earliest inhabitants filtered southward from mainland Asia—probably India or Burma—more than 10,000 years ago. Around 1000 B.C., a group called the Dongson culture worked southward from Vietnam through the Malay Peninsula, bringing with them rice cultivation that still dominates Indonesian agriculture and diet. Ancestors of these early rice growers likely had migrated from mainland China.

Isolated from one another by islands and jungle-thick mountain ridges, they developed several distinctive cultures and languages. Like many primitive groups, they were animists, giving spiritual identity and power to the life forces around them. Creatures of the forest, inanimate objects and the forces of weather had their own souls or *semangat*. From this evolved rather structured tribal societies, with special powers attributed to shamans and village leaders. Hinduism and Buddhism filtered down from mainland Asia and gradually took root, along with Islam, brought by Arabic settlers in the seventh century. These remain the dominant religions, along with a thin veil of Christianity, a residual from European missionaries who began coming to the islands in the sixteenth century.

A variety of kingdoms, principalities and assorted other dominions rose and fell during the archipelago's early history. The islands were never unified under a single rule. Trade flourished with various nations for centuries, from Persia to China. European domination began with the Portuguese, after Vasco de Gama rounded the Cape of Good Hope in 1498. Within a few years, the Spice Islands were controlled by Portugal. The Dutch came in 1596 and began a trade war with the Portuguese that led to a shooting war. Their powerful United East India Company controlled trade and Dutch warships began raiding Portuguese ports. By the 1640s, the Dutch had captured Melaka, the heart of the spice trade; the Netherlands East Indies became Holland's largest and most profitable overseas colony. The Dutch would rule for the next three centuries.

Strong Indonesian nationalist movements began in the 1930s, then the islands came under Japanese rule in 1942. At the end of the war, the British came ashore to disarm the Japanese and return the islands to Dutch sovereignty. However, nationalist forces led by Sukarno (single names are common in Indonesia) resisted the return of the Dutch. He declared Indonesia's independence on August 17, 1945. After four years of military and political struggles, the Dutch—spurred by an American threat of sanctions—agreed to pull out in late 1949.

ß ß ß

SAVE A DAY FOR BALI

A tiny, mountainous island of terraced rice paddies, fine resort beaches and mystical Hindu temples redolent of incense, Bali is the most visited of Indonesia's islands. It also is one of the most densely populated, evidenced by the almost constant beehive swarm of motorcycles and cars around Denpasar, its capital and largest city.

However, by retreating to the countryside or simply stepping into a Denpasar temple, one can escape this chaos and discover one of the most ethereal, spiritual lands on earth. The Balinese religion—a gentle blend of Hinduism and animism—is laid over every facet of their lives. More than 11,000 temples and thousands more shrines fill the landscape and incense pervades the air.

> *By retreating to the countryside or simply stepping into a Denpasar temple, one can escape the chaos and discover one of the most ethereal, spiritual lands on earth.*

This land constantly in search of its soul also appeals to the artist, and even simple objects often are given artistic touches. In no other place on the planet are religion, art, work and play so interwoven. The Balinese are noted for their fine woodcarving, painted masks, metal work and incredibly intricate life scenes in paintings and drawings. Tourism certainly has been a spur to art and at times it seems that every earnest young man with a piece of wood and a good carving knife has art to sell the visitor.

Tourism's rampant growth in recent decades may destroy the cultural innocence of Bali, if it hasn't already. The cheek-to-cheek beach resorts of Sanur immediately east of Denpasar resemble Maui's Ka'anapali Coast. Visitors can learn which hotels are presenting *legong* dances and *ramayana* ballets by consulting a free tourist publication called *Bali Now!* Culture is being canned like peaches, put up in Mason jars for display and easy access.

Bali is the assembly point for many P&O Spice Islands cruises—including ours—and we recommend adding a few extra days for exploration. (Thus, even as we decry unabashed tourism, we promote it.) Early arrival also provides opportunity to recover from jet lag, since the time difference is fifteen to eighteen hours for most Americans.

Our Bali habitat was the Surya Beach Hotel, an appealing and lushly landscaped resort in the Sanur area. We strolled its attractive grounds, tempted by its swimming pools, patio dining and private beach. However, we were in Bali to explore so we caught a *bemo* and joined the hornet's nest of traffic headed into Denpasar. Our destination was the Werdhi Budaya Arts Center.

Should you wonder, *bemos* are micro-mini vans that run jitney routes from Denpasar and its outskirts. Tourists can hire them individually at outrageous markups. For instance, normal fare is 250 *rupiah* per person and we were asked to pay 2,500 rupiah for a run to the art center. Before you become too alarmed, the difference is 25 cents and $2.50. Indonesian rupiah, like Italian lira, consists mostly of zeros.

We sat on low benches in our personally chartered bemo, with our knees up around our ears, enjoying the cooling breeze blowing through the window.

We climbed into our personally chartered *bemo* and sat on low benches, with our knees up around our ears, enjoying the cooling breeze blowing through the window. As the tiny van dodged and danced through thick traffic, we watched bits of Bali flash past—tropical plants alive with bloom, temples and altars offering brief whiffs of incense, decorative gateways to opulent resorts, and uncountable shops and tiny stall restaurants.

The art center is a slightly scruffy expanse of galleries, curio shops, food booths, outdoor stages, patios and walkways. One large gallery, which appears to be a former temple, offers splendid examples of incredibly detailed wood and ivory carvings, intricate paintings, masks and such. Some were for sale, with price tags up to $75,000. Yes, that's dollars, not rupiah, although we assume prices were negotiable. Other crafts are considerably less, of course; overall, Bali art prices are very reasonable.

We returned that evening for the *Kecak* (ke-CHAK), or monkey dance, presented every Monday at an outdoor stage. Described by one writer as an *a capella* opera, it tells the story of Sita, a Balinese princess who is captured by Rawana, the king of demons. Her husband Rama, assisted by an army of monkeys, goes to her rescue and naturally the good guy wins. Unlike most Balinese dances that involve only a few costumed performers, the *Kecak* employs a chorus of 30 or more men. They chant, sway and undulate throughout the opera, melding from one formation into another in perfect unison. Their staccato *kecak-kecak-cak* chant, changing in pitch and rhythm, was mesmerizing. Through her ordeal of capture and rescue, the heroine remained remarkably stoic, her face a beautiful painted mask.

Bali high

One of Bali's most interesting features, overlooked by most visitors and therefore uncrowded, is a volcano within a volcano. Mount Batur is a huge caldera with a secondary volcano rising from its floor, and a large lake on one side.

The inner volcano, also called Batur, is a popular climb, with several trails to the top, although it's a tough workout. The more sedentary can enjoy gtand sunrises from one of several hotels or along a terrace in the village

Sunrise over Batur Volcano turns Lake Batur into a shard of silver in this view from the Bali town of Peneloken on the caldera rim.

of Peneloken, perched on the crater rim. All of this is within one or two hours of Denpasar, depending on traffic. Indonesians drive on the right, so you may prefer to hire a driver instead of renting a car. A cab goes for $30 to $60 a day, depending on one's bartering persistence. (See box on page 299.)

One muggy afternoon, we hired a driver and bobbed and weaved his way through Bali's lush countryside and up to the crater rim. The view is superb. Batur, the volcano, is an imposing presence—a rough lava-streaked cone rising more than a thousand feet from the floor of the caldera, hissing steam like a sleeping, restless dragon. Lake Batur is a blue gray crescent, tucked against the caldera's steep eastern wall. The volcano-within-a-volcano has erupted several times in this century, killing villagers and burying homes and temples—most recently in 1993. Still, the optimistic Balinese till the soil and go to bed beneath the dragon's breath.

We checked into the Lakeview Hotel, a tattered old inn terraced into the caldera rim. For about $30, we obtained a room with a relatively clean if rather aromatic private bath. But never mind that. It had a caldera view and we spent a pleasant evening lounging in rattan chairs out front, sipping tea and staring down into the caldera. We watched the scene fade to black, had dinner on the hotel's terrace restaurant and retired for the night.

It must have been 5 a.m. when Betty shook me awake; she was fully dressed and her eyes were wide with excitement. She dragged me tripping outside as I hopped on one leg, struggling into my trousers.

"Look!"

The rough caldera rim was silhouetted against a lavender sky; the volcano brooded darkly on the valley floor; the lake was a gossamer gray. The morning sun, not yet seen, painted cottony tufts of clouds hot pink and orange. Thin wisps of fog spilled silently down the caldera rim and drifted across the face of the volcano like capricious ghosts. Later, a piercing shaft of light suddenly emerged from the far horizon as the sun appeared. We blinked and looked at one another; we'd been staring in silence for more than half an hour.

After an early breakfast, our driver took us down a winding road to the caldera floor for our hike. Balinese guides, all unofficial and mostly amateur, will besiege visitors with offers of their services, although it's not difficult to climb to the crater alone. However, we decided to hire one to help us find an interesting route. Near the village of Pura Jati, mostly abandoned after an eruption, several hopeful guides were clustered at a small parking area.

A sign at the Pura Jati trailhead read:

Come on, help us. Preserve the natural environment of Batur Mountain. Don't throw away your rubbish and graffiti.

We brushed politely past the guides and headed for the mountain, giving them the impression that we were going it alone. They tailed after us, lowering their prices with each step. We finally hired an 18-year-old for about $10; it was a substantial improvement over his starting price of $50. The volcano could be climbed easily in two hours, quoth our guidebook, but it probably was written by a 25-year-old who starts each day of his life with a seven-mile uphill run. We made it in the allotted time, although it was a tough, steep scramble over a succession of broken lava flows.

> *"Come on," he would say in his soft voice. Then he'd start up the trail again before we could catch a good breath.*

We slogged through loose cinders and scrambled over steep slopes, groping for toe-holds while our young guide strolled effortlessly upward—wearing thongs! He carried a cooler of drinks, which he periodically offered to sell us. The price probably would increase with the elevation; fortunately, we had our own water bottles. As we struggled up the steep slope, he would pull ahead easily, sit on a hunk of lava and wait for us, wearing an expression of either pity or disdain.

"Come on," he would say in his soft voice. Then he'd start up the trail again before we could catch a good breath.

At the top, we were surprised to find a small bamboo hut where another entrepreneur, dozing in the shade, had more drinks to sell. We also found a splendid view of the caldera, the lake and Bali beyond—across palm-fringed ridges to some of Indonesia's highest peaks. Bali's 10,188-foot Mount Agung stood boldly on the near horizon. On the adjacent island of Lombok, 12,224-foot Mount Rinjani rested on a soft pillow of clouds. We stood for long moments, pulling cool air into our lungs at this mile-high altitude. It struck me that this was the only place on Bali—with its usual cacophony of beeping traffic, barking dogs and sunrise roosters—where we finally had found absolute silence.

As we began our return trip, our guide hopped down the lava flows with an agility that would have put a mountain goat to shame. We stumbled and slid doggedly behind, trying resolutely to keep pace with this agile young man shod in floppy tongs.

"Come on," he urged in that soft Balinese voice.

He probably wanted to hurry down and pick up another fare before the sun got too high.

BARTERING: THE RULES OF THE GAME

Our Indonesian cruise director Dian Gafar advised us early in our voyage that bartering was a basic way of doing business, not only for tourists but for locals in most public markets. After each welcome dance, we'd have an opportunity to shop for local goods. He urged us to barter vigorously. Sellers won't part with their products at a loss, he said. There is no shame in paying too little, although the buyer who pays too much will appear foolish.

"Don't buy too quickly. Wait until it's time to leave, and you'll get a better price."

Naturally, we didn't follow his advice on our first attempt, and we came away with two bone-handled knives, a fertility pendant and a hand-carved treasure box for which we had paid too much. As we climbed aboard our bus, the spirited sellers crowded around the windows, offering the goods at a fraction of their starting price. These were the lessons learned:

1. First and foremost, do your bargaining in the shade, if possible.

2. When an item is offered, don't appear too interested. Take it politely from the seller, turn it over once in your hand, shake your head and return it. He will step away to avoid taking it back. Place it gently in his hand, turn and start to leave.

3. Take three to nine paces, pause and turn slowly toward him. Take the object again and study it, pointing out its flaws, real or imagined. You must create this impression: "It is a pitiful example of carving, but you seem like a good fellow so I may be willing to take it off your hands as a favor."

4. Start at one-tenth the asking price and work *slowly* upward. Don't increase your bid too fast; you'll meet in the middle with a price that's much too high. If the seller goes down ten, you go up five.

5. Reach your final price and stop. With each new counter-offer, simply shrug, smile and say: "I'm very sorry, but that is all I can pay." Keep repeating this as you work your way slowly toward the bus. As you mount the steps, turn with one final apologetic shrug. You should get your price. If not, that's one less trinket to clutter up the house when you get back home.

DAY ONE

After we flew south to meet our ship on the island of Timor, we were struck by its contrast to lush, crowded Bali. Timor is an arid, lava-strewn brushland with a thin scattering of villages, comprised mostly of thatched roof huts. An hour and a half jet flight from Denpasar had delivered us to Indonesia's yesterday.

For the next week, we would see no fancy resorts, thick traffic or tourist restaurants. We would see thatched villages occupied by friendly souls who greeted us with red betel nut stained smiles, who subsisted on a drought-tolerant palm regarded as their tree of life, who kept goats behind lava stone fences and sometimes piglets tied under their woven mat beds. They would dance for us, costumed in hand-woven cotton *ikats,* with complex patterns

An Indonesian surprise: the people of Savu and some other islands are accomplished horsemen. Look between the pony's front legs and you'll see how the rider stays aboard—at least when he's parked.

distinctive to each of their islands. They would take us into their simple homes and to groves out back to demonstrate the versatility of the lontar palms, so essential to their lives. Residents tap its juice, which can be drunk straight or boiled into syrup or sugar. The tree provides fronds and wood for their thatched roofed homes and utensils, basketry, mats and furniture. The lontar is a member of the coconut family; villagers eat a pulpy fruit in the center of the nut, although the outer white coconut meat is fed mostly to their animals.

After we landed at Timor's one-lane airstrip, we were taken by bus to a craft center at Kupang, the island's largest community, for the first of many dances of welcome. A sword-wielding young man and four remarkably pretty women writhed to percussive music played on wooden and brass drums. The dancers were clad in striking costumes of yellow, red and black. I noted that the lead dancer's scabbard hung from a World War II cartridge belt.

We then adjourned to the craft center to browse among a small selection of artifacts. Several women carded and spun cotton with simple wooden tools; it would be dyed and woven on small looms into the intricate *ikats*. Different versions are worn by men and women, and they're sold to the few tourists who have begun visiting these outer islands. As we shopped, a villager played *Amazing Grace* on a *sasando*, a stringed instrument made of a bamboo rod with a woven lontar palm basket as a sounding chamber. Closer inspection revealed that he was using a cassette tape backup, since the *sasando* can produce only five notes.

Before boarding our ship, we visited the rather spartan Kupang Museum; its most interesting exhibit was a display of typical *ikat* patterns of the various southeast Indonesian islands. We then had lunch at a hillside hotel, one of the few we would encounter on this trip. As we dined on fried chicken, a stir- fried dish that seemed more Chinese than Indonesian and lukewarm but tasty Bintang beer, we were entertained by three more *sasando* players. Their favorite number appeared to be *Amazing Grace*.

ᏝᏝᏝ
DAY TWO

After the captain's welcoming dinner and crew introduction the night before, our little catamaran had set sail for Roti. This small island, the southernmost in Indonesia and rather arid, greeted us at sunrise.

We cruised up a long natural channel in Zodiacs to call on our first village. It proved to be the most basic of our tour, with dugout canoes at the beach, paths instead of roads and simple huts hunkered in the protective shade of lontar palms.

We didn't receive a welcoming dance here, although we certainly were greeted warmly. We were ushered into the chief's house where our cruise director Dian Gafar interpreted his welcome. Little had changed for these folks, with their front yard pigs, chickens and goats and protective lontars. However, a villager wearing a Los Angeles

We were escorted to the chief's back yard where a villager scurried up a lontar with the aid of palm frond toe-holds lashed around the trunk.

Lakers T-shirt suggested occasional contact with the outside world. The Indonesian government was attempting to bring them into the current century. The chief's house served as the village health clinic and various government posters advised against smoking and excessive drink, demonstrated the proper way to brush one's teeth and encouraged birth control.

We were escorted to the chief's back yard where a villager scurried up a lontar with the aid of palm frond toe-holds lashed around the trunk. He tapped the tree for a bit of juice, snipped down a few coconuts and we had an early lunch. The juice was sweet and quite tasty and the nut pulp was soft and squishy, tasting rather bland, with only a slight hint of coconut flavor.

Our afternoon outing was more colorful, if rather contrived. At a second village, obviously more affluent than the first, we were greeted by what appeared to be the entire population and escorted to a dusty arena. A band of costumed horsemen riding small, sleek ponies, galloped about in wild aban-

Pretty village women from the island of Roti, dressed in traditional ikats, offer visitors a dance of welcome.

don, hooting and hollering and kicking up joyful dust. These Indonesian cowboys wore wide-brimmed hats with high Eiffel Tower shaped peaks made of lontar palm leaves. They rode with no saddles, with only small reed mats between them and their ponies. This opening act was followed by traditional island dances performed by a troupe wearing matching *ikat* costumes.

We sat on shaded benches, sipping bottled water from the ship, thoroughly enjoying this premeditated performance. Then, just when we'd gotten comfortable, several of us were hauled into a large circle dance. Linking arms with the villagers, we giggled and tripped and danced happily among the goat pellets and splats of betel nut juice.

ßßß

DAY THREE

We sailed through the night to Savu, smaller than Roti and similar in custom and costume. We spent the morning at a sandy beach for a bit of snorkeling, sunning and swimming. Those with the proper skills went water-skiing behind a specially-rigged Zodiac.

After lunch aboard, we were met on the beach by another band of costumed dancers and horsemen. These riders rode bareback; not even a woven mat sat between them and their mounts. Their ponies moved with a distinctive high-stepping prancing gait similar to that of harness horses. A small procession of dancers advanced on the surf and ceremoniously launched a small palm leaf boat. It was supposed to sail away to a symbolic eternity but an incoming wave brought it back to shore. One of the men on the beach gave it an unceremonious shove back out to sea.

We then boarded an open-bed truck, the island's only public transit, and rode breezily through the village of Seba, ducking branches and utility wires. The horses pranced and danced alongside. Villagers stared in unabashed curiosity at this truckload of camera-draped tourists clutching their sun visors and grinning like kids in the back of a pickup.

Savu seemed more affluent and populated than Roti, busy with rice paddocks, corn patches, groves of lontars, water buffalo and chickens with little marching ranks of chicks. Most of the thatched huts had neat fenced yards; a few were tucked into shaded terraces and splashed with brilliant bougainvillea, like Paul Gauguin paintings. The truck took us to the smaller village of Riloro where we again sat on shaded benches before groups of dancers. Some of the performances were quite elaborate. One mimicked native crafts of weaving, winnowing and pounding rice into flour. Another was sensuously undulating, suggesting a Hawaiian hula in both the graceful movements of the women dancers and their melodic chant.

"Like the chief said, they flew up here and dropped from the sky. Man, don't you believe in the gods?"

When the dancing was completed, *ikats* and assorted handicraft were displayed for sale, and the spirited bartering began. This ritual would follow all village dance visits. (See box on page 299.)

Later, we hiked to an ancient hilltop shrine, where several huge basaltic breadloaf shaped boulders were elevated onto fieldstone altars. These strange stones, which must have weighed several tons each, had been here for ages, said a village elder. Artifacts of the ancients were buried beneath the altars, and perhaps their bones. This was sacred land, where villagers came to study the stars and moon to determine when best to plant their crops and tap lontars for their life-giving juices. Stones identical to these lay at the bottom of the bay. Those at the shrine had been carried up by the gods, the elder said. Our Indonesian guide Dian confirmed that he had seen stones like these while scuba diving offshore.

We explored the shrine and enjoyed a fine panorama of thatched roofed houses, palm groves and the far-away sea. I noted the absence of faulting that might have uplifted this low hill and asked Dian how the huge breadloaf stones got up here.

"How?" He stared at me in mock amazement. "Like the chief said, they flew up here and dropped from the sky. Man, don't you believe in the gods?"

📭📭📭

DAY FOUR

Each day returned us closer to civilization—of sorts. We docked at the port of Waingapu, a busy city of 25,000, the largest on the island of Sumba. Shaped like a bent cucumber, the island is about 120 miles long, with a population approaching half a million—much larger than Roti or Savu.

Its people, a blend of Malay and Melanesian, once were head-hunters who warred frequently with their neighbors. Modern Sumbanese still wage mock horseback battles during their annual Pasola Festival, riding wildly about and chucking wooden spears at one another. A festival isn't considered a success unless blood has been spilled and there are sometimes fatalities.

Marriage and death are ritualistic experiences here, involving expensive dowries for the former and extensive livestock sacrifices for the latter. Burials

A ceremonial palm fron "ship of good luck" is launched by Savu Island villagers.

may be delayed for several years until sufficient animals have been sacrificed to ensure that the departed are wealthy enough to enter the world beyond. Failing this, they hang around and haunt the living. The government tries to deter this practice by levying a "sacrifice tax" on livestock that is killed. It also discourages violence in the Pasola Festival, although old traditions die hard.

Villages are built around central squares occupied by stone-covered burial plots of ancestors. The more important the departed, the bigger the stone monument. We would visit such a village this day, after a trek through the public market in Waingapu. Like most old world market places, it was crowded, hot, fly-ridden and fascinating. Vegetables were arrayed in neat geometric displays on ground mats. Scores of stalls offered meats (unrefrigerated and fly-busy), clothing, pots and pans. Particularly popular were the basic ingredients for betel nut chewers—thin betel nut slices, long seed pods called *sirih* and powdered lime. The user first chews several betel slices, then follows with nips of *sirih* that has been dipped into the lime.

"This makes you not easily sleepy," our local guide said, in describing its effect. Chewing it produces a mild high, deadens the mouth and tongue, eventually softens the gums and then the teeth fall out. Most veteran betel nut chewers are toothless. "But not me," the guide said, displaying his crooked, reddened molars. "I brush twice a day."

From the chaotic market, we went to the small village of Marumata for yet another dance of welcome. It was not the same old showbiz, since it reflected distinctive Sumbanese customs. As we approached the compound, we were "challenged" by the village chief, who emitted a kind of coyote howl, and then demanded to know if we came with good or evil intentions. Another villager, serving as our spokesman, howled back and explained that we had traveled from afar; we came in peace to learn their customs.

This seemed acceptable, so we were led to bamboo benches and offered betel nut, which a few of us accepted. It has a bitter veggie taste and the sliced nut, initially brown, becomes a mealy wad of red fiber in the mouth. Feeling my tongue go dead, I discreetly but quickly disposed of my chaw.

Crew members, who had accompanied us from the ship, passed out glasses of fruit punch which—although refreshing on a hot day—failed to eradicate the betel's cloying aftertaste.

Today's entertainment included a mock wedding ceremony in which agent for a prospective groom offered a bolt of *ikat* and silver ornaments to the potential bride. In proper Sumbanese tradition, these were flung into the dust by the bride's agent as insultingly inadequate. The rebuffed party left and then returned with a pony, additional bolts of *ikat* and an indignant, squalling pig hung by its fours from a pole. This was quite acceptable. Were this an actual wedding, everyone would live happily ever after, except the pig, which would be sacrificed. Fortunately, it was a sham ceremony presented for our benefit, and the piggie was last seen heading south through a nearby corn patch.

In the afternoon, we motored across the bay of Waingapu for another round of snorkeling. It was outstanding. The gardens below were fantasy cities—aquatic Tune Towns of every shape and color of coral, occupied by a population of Technicolor fish. Indonesia had proven its reputation as one of the great snorkeling and diving areas of the world.

> *Lest we starve between meals, bowls of crunchy, habit-forming little peanuts occupied the bar counter.*

Days were kept full aboard the *Island Explorer,* as was everyone's stomach. Breakfast and lunch featured several hot dishes and lots of fresh fruits, and dinners focused on spicy regional fare. And lest we starve between meals, bowls of crunchy, habit-forming little peanuts occupied the bar counter along with an inexhaustible supply of—good grief!—Pringles.

On this eve, dinner moved to the afterdeck. Beneath the Southern Cross, we enjoyed an Indonesian banquet that included barbecued pig, rice cake and satay dipped in peanut sauce. One of our guests was celebrating his fiftieth birthday. Champagne was poured, a candle-lit cake appeared and he was sung birthday greetings—in five different languages.

Later, over tea, I talked with Dian about those dances of welcome that greeted us in most villages. Although they represented authentic folk dances and rituals, they were staged for our benefit.

"As tourist groups keep coming, won't they start embellishing their dances to make them more interesting?"

Dian nodded. "Most likely."

"But doesn't that dilute their traditions? They're corrupting their folklore for the sake of tourism."

He smiled and shook his head. "It would change anyway, without us coming. Maybe not as fast, but it would change. Art and music always change. You aren't still singing *Yankee Doodle* in America, are you?"

ខ ខ ខ

DAY FIVE

Today, we would visit the land of the dragon. Famous in both fact and fancy, the Komodo dragon is one of the most popular attractions for visitors to Indonesia. His lair on Komodo Island is a national park.

Until a few years ago, visitors could experience the joy of watching their ghastly eating habits. (See box on page 308.) They could purchase an unfor-

This face could scare King Kong! A Komodo dragon glowers at intruders in his domain. People observe from a "visitor's corral" while the lizards roam free.

tunate goat at a neighboring village, which rangers would string up in a killing arena, and then step back. This seemed rather contrived for a national park so officials decided to wean the dragons away from these free lunches. They now must fend for themselves. Timor deer, goats and an occasional careless chicken from the island's only village are their diet now. Visitors may be fortunate enough to witness a natural killing, although it's unlikely.

Although Komodo Island is on the regular tourist route, only small ships and special charters call on it with regularity. Travelers must visit the dragon area in the company of a ranger, who carries a long forked stick to keep the critters at bay. The beasts, generally lazy and lumbering, can move in quick bursts and have been known to take down humans. They either topple their prey with a swift swat of their long tail or go for the *viscera*. In past years, before the escort service was established, tourists occasionally disappeared, and villagers still come up with missing children now and again.

The best viewing time is early morning, after the dragons have crawled from their dens to lie in the sun and warm their cold blood for their day's activities. (Yes, they live in dens, just like pretend dragons.) The *Island Explorer* obliged us by sailing into the harbor near the rangers' huts before dawn. Several of us stood on deck, coffee and tea cups in hand, to watch the lighting of a stark, ragged and arid landscape. This certainly *looked* like the land of the dragon. After breakfast, we headed ashore to meet our guides. As we gathered before a ranger hut, Dian turned to passengers Jack and Tila Malay, a Caucasian-Indonesian couple with four delightful children.

"Keep an eye on your kids," he said, trying to hide a grin. "If you go in with four, you must come out with four."

We walked single file along a path canopied with palms and tropic hard-woods. Dian cautioned us to be silent to avoid spooking wildlife—not the liz-ards, who seemed indifferent to human intrusion—but the timid deer who shared the forest with them. Our silence created an air of unease; I kept thinking of that stalled tram car in *Jurassic Park*. A sign on the trail added to the drama:

Danger! Komodo Crossing. Be Silent.

After less than a mile, we entered a clearing, where we were herded into a fenced enclosure; a gate was closed behind us. How appropriate, I thought. We were caged and the dragons were free to roam outside. And dragons there were! We saw a dozen of these impossibly large lizards, lazing in the sun, taking the air with their evil-look-ing forked tongues or simply staring off into space with beady, scowling eyes.

The dragons wouldn't have taken notice if we had marched into that compound behind the Marine Corps Band.

We spent nearly an hour there, tak-ing photos and watching them shuffle si-lently about. One lounged so close to the fence that we were able to get mug shots with ordinary lenses. For the most part, they showed very little activity. They'd occasionally get up and stroll with their curious swinging gait from sun to shade or visa versa. One pair committed the indiscretion of mating right in front of us, to the cadence of clicking cameras.

We continued talking in whispers, which hardly seemed necessary. The monitors ignored us completely. They wouldn't have taken notice if we had marched into that compound behind the Marine Corps Band playing *The Bat-tle Hymn of the Republic*.

We completed our day on Komodo with a beach party—not among the dragons but at a pretty sheltered cove of pink sand elsewhere on the island. The crew hauled a barbecue grill ashore and set up a buffet lunch. We spent a splendid afternoon eating spicy beef-kabobs and barbecued shrimp, rinsing it down with Bintang beer and snorkeling in lazy suspension above a virtual aquarium of multicolored fish and coral.

☞☞☞
DAY SIX

*M*orning *at leisure. You could relax on the sun deck, or start your packing.*

Those awful words appeared on our daily activity sheet. This was the last full day of our cruise. We had sailed through the night and well past noon, drawing ever closer to our debarkation point at Lombok, just below Bali. However, we had one last shore excursion this afternoon; one more chance to sample the fascinating fabric of southeast Indonesia.

Our final day would be our most varied, although it didn't start until 2 p.m. We went ashore at Sumbawa, one of the region's largest and most de-veloped islands, with a population pushing one million. It's also one of the most mountainous; fourth-fifths is too steep to plow. However, with more rainfall than the rest of Nusa Tenggara and extensive irrigation, the tillable land is rich in agriculture, from rice paddies to cornfields.

We landed at the harbor of Sumbawa Basar, the island's chief city. In-deed, we were drawing ever closer to urban Indonesia, for we hit the beach at a seaside resort with mock primitive cottages for lodging. A small, scruffy

HE'S JUST AN OVERGROWN LIZARD

Try not to think about this just before lunch:

Evisceration is the brute's favorite killing technique. Massive bleeding occurs when the dragon rips out the stomach wall. The ora then often buries its head in the animal's abdominal cavity, ripping out and swallowing the internal organs.

This quote describes the table manners of *Varanus komodoensis*, the famous dragon of Komodo Island, called the *ora* by Indonesians. It was taken from the guidebook *East of Bali* by Kal Muller *

Although touted as a living fossil, the critter is just a carnivorous monitor lizard that forgot to stop growing. It attains lengths up to ten feet and can weigh more than 200 pounds. Studying the dragon, one will see a garden lizard magnified a thousand-fold, with one major variation. Unlike most lizards, it has a snake's forked tongue. Naturally, this beast has become the darling of low-budget science fiction films. Already frighteningly large for a lizard, it is easily blown up on film to truly monstrous proportions. Surprisingly, the beast *was* considered science fiction until this century, and it is said to be the model for the Chinese dragon. Its existence wasn't confirmed to the outside world until 1911, when a Netherlands East Indies army officer visited Komodo Island. Later, a specimen was shot and shipped off to the Bogor Zoological Museum in Java for positive ID.

Prehistoric cousins of the komodo have been found in Australia. Archeologists theorize that some were isolated on islands as the ocean level rose several hundred thousand years ago. They found themselves in a happy circumstance—at the top of the local food chain. Succeeding generations just kept eating and growing, like teenagers with insatiable appetites. The dragons live on Komodo, Padar, Rinca and Flores islands. This region is a transition zone between Australian and Asian flora and fauna, mostly grassland savanna and dry monsoon forest.

*Periplus Editions, Berkeley, Calif. © 1992

zoo occupied the grounds, with a sleepy alligator and a few tired birds in residence. We boarded buses and headed inland to Pamulung village for an interesting assortment of amusements. More developed than other Nusa Tenggara towns we had visited, it had paved streets of sorts and elevated tile roof houses with woven bamboo mat walls.

Our greeting party consisted of a singing and dancing group of men wearing what appeared to be Nehru jackets and women in sarongs similar to the type made famous by Dorothy Lamour. A "bride" was being readied for a mock wedding, receiving a facial of rice flour and betel nut paste. Several women of the village wore this curious makeup, which our local guide explained protected them from the sun and was considered cosmetically attractive. Two women, with looms stretched between their waistlines and posts driven into the ground, were weaving fabric for some of the brilliantly colored sarongs we'd seen.

We walked to a large shade ramada to witness two more events—a pretend wedding procession and a muddy spectacle called a bull race. The procession and ritual dance—performed by the lavishly costumed bride, groom and attendants—reminded us that Sumbawa was mostly Hindu. The vivid colors and slow-motion dance styles were similar to those we'd seen on Bali.

The final event was wonderfully silly. Contestants stood on a stick sled drawn by two water buffalo; think of it as a chariot without wheels. They tried to steer their galloping animals through a yucky mud bog toward a doll mounted atop a pole. It had been ceremoniously placed there by the village shaman. If the buffalo team straddled the doll pole and the rider was able to seize it or knock it down, he won. If not, the shaman was the winner. Water buffalo don't take directions very well and most of the riders missed their mark; many fell into the mud.

After we witnessed several races, our local host asked for volunteers. Surprisingly, a young Norwegian passenger offered to give it a try. To our shouts of "Go, Viking, go!" he attempted two passes and was quickly dumped into the mire.

Shaman 2; Viking 0.

Back in Sumbawa Basar, as the Indonesian sun headed for home, we were given rides around town in cute little two-wheel pony carts called *dokars*. They're a popular mode of transit on many Indonesian islands. As we paraded through the city, throngs of children ran from houses and yards to wave in enthusiastic, almost frantic greeting.

ᗷᗷᗷ

DAY SEVEN

Three words—busy, lush and beautiful—describe Lombok, the island immediately south of Bali. It's thickly vegetated in every shade of green, from the kelly green of watercress cultivated in river beds to the yellow green of ripening rice plants.

We bade goodbye to ship and crew, and a bus drove us past a patchwork of rice paddies, cornfields, houses and roadside shops. The island was literally carpeted with crops and the people who tended them. Only the steep flanks of Rinjani, the island's resident volcano, were unoccupied. One of our passengers intended to stay overnight and climb it the next morning. The rest of us would catch a ferry back to Bali to complete our loop. First, however, we were taken to a temple for one last dance of welcome.

Our transportation to Bali was the Mabua Express, a high-speed jetfoil that would complete the hundred-mile trip in less than three hours. Our tickets admitted us to the topside first class lounge—rather plush with tables and comfortable couch seating. Attendants passed out glasses of fruit juice and small box lunches. As we got underway, *The New Karate Kid* movie flickered to life on a pair of TV sets flanking the lounge bar. After a fascinating week in Indonesia's outback, our return trip to Bali would be rather luxurious.

We looked to starboard as the jetfoil slipped out of the harbor and saw the *Island Explorer*, moored several hundred feet away and awaiting the arrival of the next passengers. Crew members waved enthusiastically, their wide Indonesian grins quite visible, even from this distance.

As we hurried out to the jetfoil's small afterdeck to return their waves, it occurred to me that we were on the wrong boat.

ᗷᗷᗷ

*I will wander all the world over and
return to the home of my fathers
to muse on the strange and
beautiful things I have seen.*
— Pierre Loti

PART VI
Africa

*Four feluccas, ageless sailboats so common to Africa and the Mediterranean,
create a pleasant geometry on a hazy Nile morning in Luxor.*

Chapter sixteen

LEGENDS OF THE NILE

Pacing among pyramids with Abercrombie & Kent

E ye contact," said our Egyptian host Khaled in his careful English. "I know the traffic seems confusing, but we have very few accidents. That is because we maintain eye contact with other drivers, and with the people on the streets."

The Abercrombie & Kent information sheet had warned that "traffic lights do not have a great deal of meaning" in Cairo and that traffic is rather chaotic. We'd arrived late in the afternoon and the A&K host who met us at the airport recommended that we catch the evening sound and light show at the pyramids of nearby Giza. Seeing the pyramids has been a childhood dream, so we readily agreed. Now, as the driver attacked the Cairo traffic with casual abandon, Khaled turned to us in the back seat, trying to reassure us that we would live to see our dreams come true.

As our car lurched toward a large parking lot filled with buses and taxis, the pyramids' familiar shapes flashed past and disappeared, like a subliminal TV advertising message. Had we seen them or just imagined them?

Moments later, the pyramids of Giza stood before us, bathed in artificial light that succeeded in giving them a ghostly glow. Even though we were more than a hundred yards away, sitting in bleacher seats and awaiting the start of the sound and light show, they seemed overwhelming. Cheops, the largest and oldest, built around 2690 B.C., towered more than 460 feet. To the left stood the pyramid of Cheophren, a bit smaller and half a century

CRUISE PLANNER

The cruise ● Abercrombie & Kent, which specializes in worldwide, upscale expedition travel, offers a variety of Egypt packages built around Nile cruises; some have air and land extensions to Israel, Kenya, Syria or Jordan. Our outing, the Nile Explorer, combines coach and air excursions with a five-day Nile cruise on A&K's Sun Boat II. Land portions include explorations of Cairo with its Egyptian Museum of Antiquities, the great pyramids and the legendary Sphinx of nearby Giza, Memphis and the necropolis of Sakkara. The firm's Egypt trips are limited to 24 participants and each group is accompanied by an English-speaking Egyptologist. For information on this and other outings, contact Abercrombie & Kent, 1520 Kensington Rd., Oak Brook, IL 60521; (800) 323-7308 or (708) 954- 2944; FAX (708) 954-3324.

Getting there ● TWA has nonstop flights from New York to Cairo and several other carriers also serve Egypt's capital city. Intra-Egypt segments of A&K's programs are provided by EgyptAir, which has an extensive network of flights in the Mideast.

The ship ● The 32-cabin Sun Boat II, built in 1991, is designed specifically for Abercrombie & Kent's Nile cruises. All cabins are outside, with color TV and mini-refrigerators. Other onboard facilities include a barbecue and games area, cocktail lounge, single-seating non-smoking dining room, and a sun deck with a small pool and poolside bar. Officers and crew are Egyptian; those dealing with passengers speak English.

When to go ● October through April is considered the high season in Egypt, although A&K cruises are scheduled the year-around. Spring is temperate, although it can be windy. Predictably, summer days are hot yet quite bearable since it's a dry heat and summertime outings are scheduled in the cool of the morning and late afternoon.

What to bring ● American and Canadian citizens must have passports valid for six months beyond their arrival date and Egypt tourist visas. Dress for the seasons and bring a flexible wardrobe of lightweight, loose clothing that can be layered, since temperatures can vary greatly from day to night. Daytime wear is casual on A&K trips, with jackets and cocktail wear suggested for evening meals. Bring binoculars for spotting interesting things along the Nile, plus high speed film for photographing inside tombs, since flash isn't permitted.

What's included ● These are all-inclusive trips, covering shore excursions, sightseeing, transportation within the tour, airport transfers, entrance fees and all gratuities except those for the Egyptologist. Hotel rooms and some meals are included on the land portion; all shipboard meals are included. (Some A&K Egypt programs include all meals in the land portion as well.) Although tips are covered, carry small denomination bills in your pocket for baksheesh, little gratuities sought by Egyptians for small favors—showing you a good photo angle at a temple, posing for a photo or giving you directions.

What to buy ● Traditional paintings on papyrus are populars. Make sure they're genuine papyrus which rolls up smoothly, and not "banana papyrus," a coarse fiber that crinkles at it rolls. Other popular items include gold and silver jewelry, alabaster figurines, leather goods, carpets, and wood crafts with mother-of-pearl inlay. Bartering is part of shopping; start at a fraction of the asking price. That look of troubled sincerity in the seller's face—as you undercut his price or question his product's authenticity—may be a measure not of his honesty, but of his acting ability.

younger; beyond it, the still smaller pyramid of Menkaru. Dominating the foreground, paws stretched toward our bleacher seats, crouched the most familiar figure of all, the Sphinx. Somewhere in the hazy Egyptian night, we heard the wailing voice of a *muezzin,* calling his people to prayer:

"Allah is great! Oh, come Worship him!"

It was a memorable moment in this ancient land. Before us stood some of the earth's oldest structures, reaching back nearly 3,000 years. And from the darkness came the voice of Islam, the "new" religion adopted by Egypt a mere thirteen centuries ago.

And then the spell was broken because the Sphinx started talking. With a proper baritone voice, it became the storyteller of the sound and light show, relating the tale of the pyramids and the great river Nile, while squiggly laser figures flashed on a nearby stone wall. Other lasers outlined the dimensions of the pyramids and sketched their inner chambers. All of this happened to the tumultuous din of background music and a booming narration filled with clichés about eternal journeys and sailing with the sun.

The booming narration was filled with clichés about eternal journeys and sailing with the sun.

"The Nile be praised, for it is the father of all our harvests," cried a voice as the show swelled toward its climax. "The Nile be praised for it bears all of our prosperity and happiness," wailed another.

It was all rather corny, we agreed as we were driven back to our hotel. Then Betty pointed out the car window.

"Look! A camel!"

Although we were in Egypt, the critter looked out of place in this busy Cairo suburb.

Khaled smiled. "In the city, they're used mostly for tourist rides."

"In this traffic?" Betty wondered.

"They maintain eye contact," I said.

ßßß
THE ENDLESS DECADES

The oldest country on earth, Egypt traces its recorded history back an astounding thirty-three centuries. Beyond that, its roots disappear into the mists of time. People first drifted into the Nile Valley, then tropical and richly vegetated, around 10,000 B.C., probably migrating from present-day Libya and Arabia.

Through the centuries, weather patterns changed and the forests vanished, yet those early settlers survived. They did as Egyptians do today. They turned the Nile, relying on it to nourish their crops and quench their thirst. As the land became burning desert, the river became their salvation.

The Nile figures into every facet of Egypt's history; it divides, unifies, nourishes and defines the land. Today as yesterday, more than ninety-nine percent of Egypt's people live along its banks. In no other country in the world is a single geographical feature so dominant and essential.

By 4000 B.C., while Europeans still wore animal skins and lived in crude shelters, the paleo-Egyptians had laid the foundations for a civilized agrarian society. It was nurtured by the Nile's annual floods that brought new silt to their fields. They devised a 360-day calendar of twelve thirty-day months,

This face of Egypt has changed very little for thousands of years. The Nile basin is a lush, narrow garden while the hills immediately beyond—just visible through a haze—are barren.

with the spare five days set aside to celebrate the harvest. This early civilization is simply called the "Red kingdom" by archaeologists, a reference to the ruddy soil along the river. About the same time, a "White kingdom" developed upriver from the present site of the Aswan High Dam; again, archaeologists named it for the chalky soil of that area. Since the Nile flows south to north, these regions are now called Upper Egypt—the southern headwaters area; and Lower Egypt—from Aswan north to the great delta at the Mediterranean.

A shadowy ruler known to Egyptologists as Menes—probably not his real name—united the Red and White kingdoms through conquest. It is from this point—about 3100 B.C.—that scholars trace the country's history. Thirty consecutive dynasties ruled a nation that remained little changed politically until Egypt fell to Alexander the Great in 332 B.C. For most of those centuries, the country had been ruled by a pharaoh, regarded as both mortal and divine—a being who walked the earth and walked with the gods.

At times, it disintegrated into fractured, warring feudal states, only to be reunited by a powerful new pharaoh. Like most ancient people, the Egyptians venerated the animal kingdom and regarded the sun as the giver of all life. Animals became symbols of their gods—some depicted with human bodies and animal heads. The most powerful god was *Re* or *Ra,* who carried the sun across the sky and returned it to the east during the night. It traveled along the dark corridor of an underground river that was the netherworld twin to the Nile. Other gods dealt with assorted earthly and heavenly matters.

During these endless decades the Egyptians, protected by desert wastes that surrounded their river basin, developed a remarkably sophisticated civilization. They became master sculptors and metalsmiths, they built history's first ocean going vessels and, of course, they erected grand shrines to the pharaohs, employing hundreds of thousands of workers. Historians still aren't sure how the pyramids were built, although sand ramps and pivot cranes probably were used. And how did the pharaohs find the means to feed all of those non-producing citizens?

For generations, the magnificent monuments of Egypt have whetted the imaginations of every school child, museum curator and camera-clutching tourist. Visiting the pyramids was the one grand objective of my many travel goals. Never mind that I saw them first as pawns in a corny laser-fed sound and light show. Those things were absolutely awesome.

ᐯ ᐯ ᐯ

DAY ONE

Like most large old world cities, Cairo is at once modern and ancient. Highrise office buildings, hotels and apartment towers mark the skyline and cast shadows over mosques and old stone houses and shops. Bursting with seventeen million people, the city sprawls over the river-ribboned upper delta of the Nile, reaching to and absorbing neighboring Giza. The great pyramids which once stood in open desert are now hedged by suburbs.

We watched the city awaken from the window of our room at the Semiramis Inter-Continental Hotel, which overlooks the Nile. Unlike the Yangtze, the Nile is not thick with barge traffic; most of the country's cargo is hauled over busy streets and highways. There was little movement on the river as the sun rose through the Cairo haze. A few traditional *feluccas*—small wooden sailboats—lay at anchor, along with several live-aboard barges and excursion boats. Most of the morning traffic—and it was chaotic—was on the Tahrir Bridge just below our window.

The Cairo Museum offers a huge collection of antiquities that initially overwhelms the senses.

After breakfast, we met Hesham, the Egyptologist who would spend the next several days with us, and the rest of the Abercrombie & Kent guests. We traveled by mini-bus to the nearby Egyptian Museum. Built at the turn of the century, it is not a modern interpretive; it offers a huge collection of antiquities that initially overwhelms the senses. Sarcophagi, mummy cases and statues jam the main floor; thousands of other exhibits crowd the mezzanines above. Fortunately, Hesham sorted out the museum's most interesting highlights during our three-hour visit. We followed him through its crowded corridors like obedient, attentive students.

We went first to the Mummy Room, an exhibit of more than a dozen embalmed pharaohs or their queens, which wasn't opened to the public until 1994. Centuries earlier, priests had spirited their bodies from tombs to hide them from grave robbers and this stash of stiffs wasn't discovered until a few years ago. Some of the leading players in the Egyptian drama are here, including Ramses II and V, two of the country's greatest monument builders. Two queens lie side by side, their braided hair still intact; artificial eyes stare vacantly at the ceiling.

Most visitors find these beings with their blackened, shriveled faces and gnarled hands fascinating; I found these silent messengers from the past to be decidedly spooky. They resembled relatives of the narrator on TV's *Tales from the Crypt.*

From this crypt, we followed our guide to the Tutankhamen display, the largest single exhibit in the museum.

"Tutankhamen's tomb was very small, not yet finished because he died very young—before he was twenty," Hesham explained. "The tomb had only a about a thousand and seven hundred funerary objects."

As any beginning Egypt scholar can tell you, the significance of King Tut's tomb is that it was missed by grave robbers. When it finally was discovered in 1922, its treasures went to the Egyptian Museum. What treasures they were! Folks who saw the King Tut exhibit on tour of America several years ago saw only fifty- five pieces, a fraction of the tomb loot. The Cairo display contains hundreds of items, including a solid gold coffin, several huge wooden funerary shrines, the king's chariot and gilded throne, life-sized statues of the boy ruler, leering gilded jackal heads and—perhaps the most famous museum artifact in the world—the solid gold, lapis inlaid mask of Tutankhamen. Its flawless craftsmanship would challenge the skilled hands and modern tools of a contemporary sculptor. That it was molded in 1324 B.C. is difficult to believe.

ᚹᚹᚹ

DAY TWO

To students of Egyptian history, Memphis is not the mecca of Elvis fans, but the earliest capital of pharaoh Egypt, founded by King Menes in 3100 B.C. Nothing remains of the original city; nothing here marks the passing of that shadowy figure who first united Egypt. Visitors are drawn to this area southwest of Cairo by vestiges of a much later ruler, Ramses II. His fifty-foot alabaster statue is the focal point of a large collection of broken sculptures. Once standing, it was toppled and wounded by Ramses' enemies and now lies face up in a sheltering museum structure. It's surrounded by an outdoor garden of other fractured statues, tired-looking dogs and souvenir hawkers.

From Memphis, our A&K van took us to nearby Sakkara, a rather desolate area where several tombs and temples currently are being excavated. The setting reminded us of that expansively dusty archaeological dig scene from *Crusaders of the Lost Ark.* In the region around the dig, Egypt began to look like Egypt—a rolling expanse of sandy wastes, within sight of a green agricultural belt irrigated by the Nile.

At Sakkara, we explored the tomb of Mereruka, a high priest of the Sixth Dynasty. Its walls are covered with incredibly detailed *bas relief* carvings and here, the importance of traveling with an Egyptologist came into play. Tracing the carvings with his trusty pencil light, Hesham painted a vivid picture of life in the Egypt of 2000 B.C. Scenes of hunting, fishing the Nile with nets, tending crops, stomping grapes and dancing came to life. He translated a scenario to which we can all relate—citizens refusing to pay their taxes. In ancient Egypt, however, they weren't assessed penalties; they were whipped.

Monumental statues of King Amenophis III and his wife Queen Tye dwarf three Cairo Museum visitors sitting at their feet.

Just across the dry wasteland from the tomb stands a worn-at-the-edges pyramid that is hardly monumental, but is perhaps the most significant structure in Egypt. The Step Pyramid, a simple tier of building blocks, was erected around 2500 B.C., predating the great pyramids of Giza. The tomb of an emperor named Zoser, it was the first pyramid ever built, the world's oldest surviving manmade structure and possibly the world's first large edifice made of stone.

 β β β

No matter how much you prepare yourself to be impressed by the pyramids of Giza, you likely will be awe struck—as silent as a Sphinx—when you stand before them. Superlatives flow like the desert winds and your mind is quickly emptied of adjectives. The Great Pyramid—the tomb of Emperor Cheops—is an incredible stack of cut stone rising more than forty stories and covering four city blocks. It contains 2.5 million tons of material and remains after twenty-eight centuries the largest stone structure in the world. Standing at its massive base, we found it difficult to see the top, more than 460 feet above.

The Great Pyramid is equally imposing from within. A narrow inclined shaft—low enough to require stooping and guaranteed to give visitors a backache—leads about 250 feet up to the burial chamber. The pyramid's interior has been stripped of adornment, although this vaulted corridor that tapers toward a granite infinity again conveys the immensity of this structure and the incredible skill of the workmanship. It is vaulted to bear the billions of pounds of weight above and the stones are so carefully fitted that my Swiss army knife blade wouldn't slip between the seams.

Although the two smaller pyramids and the famous Sphinx also occupy the dusty Giza plateau, they seemed puny compared with *Le Pyramide Grande*. In daylight, the Sphinx was something of a disappointment—disfigured and standing a mere sixty-six feet tall. Perhaps I was still put off by his hackneyed narration of the sound and light show the night before.

Hordes of souvenir hawkers blunted much of the passion of visiting the pyramids of Giza. They swarmed like bees, quickly encircling us when we paused to take a picture or to try and reflect on the grandeur of the scene. Camel riders galloped into our camera lens, wanting to be part of the picture—for a fee. Dusty kids pushed postcards into our faces.

"Where you from?"

"America."

"Good place. I like America. You want postcards? Ten for a dollar."

"No, thank you."

"Where you from?"

"California."

"Good place. I like California. You want postcards? Ten for a dollar."

"No!"

"Where you from?"

"Lower Slobbovia"

"Good place. I like Low Slobber---uh. You want postcards? Ten for a dollar."

"Oh, all right."

There were only nine cards in the packet.

฿฿฿
DAY THREE

And suddenly we were 760 miles south of Cairo at Abu Simbel, the massive monument that was moved to higher ground to avoid flooding by the Aswan High Dam. Well, not suddenly, although an EgyptAir flight and a bus delivered us to the base of this monument within two hours.

Considered by some as the grandest temple of Egypt, it was built by Ramses II around 1300 B.C. It was intended to serve as a self aggrandizing monument and as a reminder to pesky enemies from the south not to mess with him. Ramses spent much of his reign battling with the Hittites and Nubians of Upper Egypt so he built this colossus on their doorstep. Nubians are black Egyptians who still predominate in the Aswan area. Four massive seated statues of Ramses—each sixty-five feet high—flank the entrance to the temple chambers. Several inner rooms are exquisitely decorated with hieroglyphics. A smaller temple honors Ramses' favorite wife Nefertari, again with larger than life figures guarding the entrance.

We then went backstage to learn how effectively we had been fooled. Hesham took us through a tunnel that led into a gigantic chamber with a high domed ceiling; think of it as an Egyptian Superdome. The "mountain" housing Ramses' temple is in fact made of concrete and steel and covered with dirt and stone. The dome keeps the weight of this *faux* mountain from

Two of Egypt's most famous monuments are only hours apart if you happen to be on a tour with air connections. *At right*, huge statues of Ramses II guard his temple at Abul Simbel above Aswan. *Below*, the Great Pyramid of Giza is difficult to capture even with a wide angle lens.

crushing down on the temple itself. Two years and millions of dollars were invested in the 1960s to disassemble the original temple and drag it, in multi-ton chunks, to this higher ground. Here it was reassembled above the water line of Lake Nasser.

Men indeed can move mountains and even the temples inside them.

That afternoon, we caught a short flight north to Aswan to transfer to our floating hotel, the *Sun Boat II*. After checking in, we took a late afternoon ride in a *felucca* to visit the mausoleum of the Aga Khan. Although not an Egyptian, he was a frequent visitor to Aswan and asked to be buried on a hill high above the city.

The boat ride, silent and blissful after a busy morning, transported us into Egypt's past. Unchanged from drawings we'd seen on temple walls, the *felucca* is a small boat with a crossed mast and boom, and a triangular sail truncated at the downward end. Two cigarette-smoking Nubian crewmen—

We were among a small squadron of feluccas—a flight of white winged moths drawn to the fading light of sunset.

barely teenagers—piloted their weathered boat expertly into an upstream breeze, leisurely tacking from one side of the Nile to the other. We nudged ashore below the mausoleum and hiked to its hilltop perch to admire its simple cut stone elegance. Beyond, the soft brown contours of the desert again reminded us that dry wasteland is never far away in Egypt.

As we sailed back upriver, *Ra,* the sun god, slipped below the horizon, painting wisps of clouds blood red and tinting the Nile pink. We were among a small squadron of *feluccas*—a flight of white winged moths drawn to the fading light of sunset.

After the *felucca* cruise, we finally found time to explore our floating Nile resort. The *Sun Boat II*, roomy and comfortable, is at once modern and traditional. It's a sleek craft dressed in teak and other woods, trimmed in brass and cheered by bits of color. Floral prints in the public areas, potted flora and planters along the deck railings provide a homey touch.

This attractive movable shelter would remain at anchor here in Aswan until noon the following day, and then begin its downriver journey.

ßßß
DAY FOUR

Several tourist-laden *feluccas* were already at play along the Aswan riverfront as we left in a van for an introduction to the Greco-Roman phase of Egypt's long history. We would learn that, even as the Greeks conquered the Egyptians, they emulated their art and architecture and adopted their gods. We also learned—and most of us didn't know—that there are two Aswan dams, and we visited them briefly this day. The original was completed at the town of Aswan in 1902 by the British and the second—called the High Dam—was built with Russian aid in the late 1960s. It was this structure that created Lake Nasser—the world's second largest reservoir—and required the relocation of several temples.

Our first stop was at one such displaced structure. The Temple of Philae, occupying an island in a reservoir between the two dams, is of typical columnar Greek design, with elements of Egyptian and Roman architecture. It was built in the fourth century B.C., and remained a place of pagan worship un-

The Temple of Philae on an island near Aswan offers an interesting blend of Egyptian, Roman and Greek architecture.

til the fifth century A.D., when it was occupied by Eastern orthodox Christians called Coptics. They defaced many of the Egyptian-Greek gods and carved their Coptic crosses into the stone. As Hesham led us around the elaborately detailed—although scarred—temple, he related a story of the temple gods:

Seth so hated his brother Horus that he chopped him into fourteen pieces and buried thirteen of them at different places around Egypt. The fourteenth piece, his—uh—private part, was thrown into the Nile. Horus' faithful wife Isis managed to find and reassemble all of the parts except for that one item which, unfortunately, had been devoured by a catfish.

"So Isis, being a great goddess, was able to put heem back together and bring heem back to life. But..." Hesham added with an Egyptian shrug, "...the marriage, it was never quite the same."

After lunch, the *Sun Boat II* sailed from Aswan, cruising past assorted *feluccas* and a virtual armada of other Nile riverboats. None was quite so sleek, we decided, as ours. We paused at a second Greco-Roman temple, Kom Ombo, standing within a few hundred feet of the shore. Carvings on its walls and columns were incredibly detailed. Interestingly, many had been spared mutilation by the Coptics because—Hesham pointed out—they resembled Christian religious scenes. These were the most ornate carvings we had seen thus far. In this land of superlatives, what would tomorrow bring?

Ramses the First clutches a crook and a flail, symbols of royal power, in this tomb painting in the Valley of the Kings.

ᚠᚠᚠ

DAY FIVE

Today brought the most fully intact temple in Egypt, although it isn't the most elaborate. Relatively small as monumental shrines go, the Temple of Horus in Edfu was started by the Greeks around 200 B.C. although it wasn't completed until shortly after the birth of Christ. It's essentially one huge square with a forty-foot sandstone slab ceiling still in place. Unfortunately, its fine condition attracted squatters who lived inside for decades after it was abandoned. No fans of Egyptology, they bored holes for their coat hooks, gouged loopholes out of the walls to tether their animals and blackened the lofty ceiling with their fires. Fortunately, much of the finely detailed *bas relief* wall carvings, relating the exploits of Horus, are relatively intact.

Today's second temple, a shrine to the God Khnum in Esna, just downstream from Edfu, also is still intact. It's noted particularly for the complex capitals at the top of its supporting columns. Hieroglyphic records suggest that Khnum's temple originally was much larger. However, houses have been built atop a portion of the temple that was buried under—well—the sands of time. The interloping houses are several hundred years old and crumbling but still intact and occupied.

"The government keeps waiting for them to fall down, so they can dig beneath," Hesham said, "but as you can see, they are still standing." He indicated one with a large vertical crack down the middle. "Very stubborn houses."

Between and beyond the two temples, as the *Sun Boat* cruised toward our overnight stop at Luxor, we witnessed a slow motion panorama of life along the Nile. Mud hut villages huddled beneath sheltering palms. Women wearing scarves and full-length *galabeyas* washed their clothes in the river or walked with water jars balanced on their heads. Their men worked the cane fields, fished the river or jogged along the banks astride cargo-laden donkeys. Children played in the water as children do everywhere in the world. It was as if some magical Disneyesque brush stroke had brought the ancient temple carvings to life.

ß ß ß

DAY SIX

Egypt's first pharaohs built the great pyramids as their tombs and since they were rather conspicuous, they were promptly looted by grave robbers. The next generation of monarchs went underground, hiding their magnificent tombs in two desolate, mountain-rimmed valleys six miles west of the Nile near Luxor. Sixty-four pharaohs are buried in the Valley of the Kings; more than fifty queens and a young prince are entombed in the nearby Valley of the Queens. There are so many tunnels leading to the tombs that the two valleys resemble abandoned mining districts.

Going underground didn't work. Every tomb has been looted, with the notable exception of the crypt of Tutankhamen, whose discovery by Howard Carter in 1922 rocked the archaeological world. Tomb robbers are still at work in the area. Through the generations, residents of a mud-hut village near the two valleys have turned looting into a cottage industry, despite heavy security. Egyptian President Honsi Mubarrak, after visiting the site in 1994, was so disturbed that he initiated steps to have the village relocated.

Our first stop—in the Valley of the Queens—was at the tomb of Nefertari, favored wife of Ramses II. By a grand stroke of good timing, the tomb had been reopened only three weeks before our arrival, after being closed for decades for restoration. Visitation is limited to a hundred people a day to lessen the impact on the stunningly beautiful wall decorations, and our A&K hosts had managed to get us tickets at scalper's prices.

This is the most flamboyant tomb in the Valley of the Queens and its colors are the most brilliant of any tomb or temple in Egypt. Hieroglyphics literally leaped from the wall with their vivid reds, greens, blues, yellows and browns. *Bas relief* portraits of Queen Nefertari were so expertly painted that we could see the soft tones of her arms showing through her gossamer white gown, and a touch of rouge on her cheek. The unknown artist even suggested that the beautiful, willowy queen had a slight double chin.

In the Valley of the Kings, visitors get potluck. A single ticket gives them a choice of three tombs, again to lessen crowding and impact. We checked out the digs of three of the Ramses, whose wall decorations are as extensive as those in Nefertari's tomb, although more faded. An extra fee—included as part of our tour—got us into the most famous tomb of all. Ironically, the final resting place of Tutankhamen is one of the smallest and most modest crypts in the valley. He was a minor luminary and he died young—at age 19 or 20—so there was little time to prepare his final resting place. Only the main burial chamber is decorated, with a scene showing Tut accompanied by gods and friends as he prepares to enter the next world. The quartzite sarcophagus containing Tut's mummy is still in place.

This modest tomb's treasure trove included a solid gold inner sarcophagus weighing 1,170 kilograms, the stunningly beautiful golden death mask and hundreds of other objects. Imagine, said Hesham, what must have been in the major tombs, some containing more than fifty rooms!

Sadly, these objects are lost forever, since they were taken many centuries ago. In the valleys of kings and queens, the only things left to steal are pieces of the decorated walls, which thieves still try to gouge loose and sell to unscrupulous collectors.

ß ß ß

DAY SEVEN

Perhaps even more than Cairo, Luxor is the tourist center of Egypt. In this city of 250,000, more than seventy-five percent of the work force is involved with the tourism industry. Nearly 250 tour boats work the Nile and it appeared that half of them were moored along the Luxor riverbank during our stay. Our A&K boat was isolated from the crowd, parked alongside the Isis Hotel, one of several luxury resorts in the city.

Luxor's popularity is no surprise. The burial grounds of the pharaohs occupy the west bank of the Nile and Egypt's two largest temples—Karnak and Luxor—dominate the city on the eastern shore. This was the site of ancient Thebes, the capital of Egypt for fifteen centuries. It finally fell to ruin just before the birth of Christ. Those ruins, partially restored, are splendid. We were mightily impressed when we visited Luxor Temple, for this was the largest we had yet seen, with a massive forty-foot portal and a long processional colonnade. A double row of sphinxes once led two miles to Karnak. Several hundred yards of this promenade are still intact.

However, Luxor Temple paled when compared with the Temple of Karnak, nearly twice its size. During Thebes' long reign as the capital of Egypt, Karnak was embellished and enlarged by a succession of pharaohs. Covering sixty-four acres, it's Egypt's largest temple and some say it's the largest in the world. Its focal point is an incredible forest of 134 huge decorated columns standing about forty feet high.

ß ß ß

DAY EIGHT

An EgyptAir flight had returned us 400 miles north to Cairo the afternoon before, and we now prepared to spend our final day in the world's oldest country. That 400 miles also bridged many centuries, for today's tour began with Islamic Egypt, which dates only from the sixth century A.D. Cairo itself is a mere 1,000 years old.

Pyramids and pharaohs' temples are hard acts to follow, and the first of

THE HAUGHTY QUEEN HATSHEPSUT

As we toured the monumental temple of Karnak in Luxor, we met—through our guide Hesham's lively descriptions—Queen Hatshepsut, one of the more fascinating characters in Egyptian history.

When her husband Thutmose II died in 1300 B.C., she tried to assume his throne, but she was a mere woman and it rightfully belonged to her stepson, young Thutmose III. She convinced powerful priests that she was the mortal daughter of the god Amon, and to prove her claim, she went to the Temple of Karnak and had this information carved in stone. (Could this have been the origin of that expression?) She also insisted that Amon had come to her in a dream and directed her to erect two obelisks. This she did, and dedicated the first one to her father-god.

Successfully wrestling the throne from her stepson, she became the first pharaoh to be regarded as both a ruler and a godhead and the first to wear the double crown of upper and lower Egypt. She wore men's garments and some images even portray her with the traditional false beard of a pharaoh. Hatshepsut ruled for about twenty years, greatly enlarging the temple of Karnak and expanding the borders of Egypt through trade and military might. And, of course, she kept her stepson in her shadows.

When she finally died, a petulant Thutmose III had her name obliterated from Karnak and he destroyed or defaced all of her monuments there except one. He couldn't touch the obelisk of course, because his stepmother had cleverly dedicated it to the powerful god Amon. So he did the next best thing; he built a wall around it.

Ironically, the wall served as a protective barrier and that splendid 97-foot obelisk still stands—Karnak's only surviving monument to a remarkable woman.

several mosques we visited this day was something of a letdown. The fourteenth century edifice of Sultan Hassen is one of the world's largest mosques, although it seemed rather grim with its dark monastic stone and dim corridors with high barrel arch ceilings. We were reminded by Hesham, who is a Moslem, that mosques contain no statues, paintings or other illustrations that might suggest idolatry. Their decor consists of floral and geometric patterns and writings from the Koran. It is of course a one-god religion and Moslems recognize Abraham, Jesus and other Biblical figures as prophets of Allah.

The second mosque, Ali-Rafaii, was newer and its colors more vivid since it dates only from 1912. The marble crypts of King Faruk, his father and grandfather are located here, along with the simple yet elegant onyx crypt of Muhammad Reza Pahlavi, the deposed Shah of Iran. Why is he here? Because it was the late Egyptian president Anwar Sadat who offered him sanctuary when he was forced to flee.

We went next to the huge Mosque of Muhammad Ali, located within the city's walled Citadel. This multi-domed edifice is perhaps the most attractive mosque in Cairo, rich in marble, crystal chandeliers and ornamental columns more sugestive of a French palace than a temple of Allah. Muhammad Ali was a Turkish military leader of Albanian ancestry, sent by the Ottoman

Turks to rule Egypt in 1801. His first act was to massacre all the priests of the Mamelukes. These were descendants of former Turkish and eastern European soldiers and mercenaries, who had been ruling Egypt for several centuries. One of Ali's aides protested this rash act, saying that there were good men of God among the priests.

"Do not let it concern you," Ali said. "God will know his own."

We took a noontime break at Cairo's huge Khan el Khalili bazaar, a maze of narrow streets, stalls and shops that some say is the world's largest marketplace. Several miles of covered shopping streets overflow with brass and copper wares, silver and gold jewelry, clothing, souvenirs, spices, nuts, fabric and anything else that a human being could possibly ponder purchasing.

We're convinced that the term: "Babble of many tongues" refers to the dozens of multi-lingual tour guides herding their charges through Egypt.

In the afternoon, we headed for Old Cairo, an ancient neighborhood of skinny cobblestone alleys where the city began a thousand years ago. In a sense, the tour brought us to the present, for this is Cairo's Christian and Jewish quarter. Although the city was founded by conquering Muslim Arabs, its roots go deep into Christianity. Long before Cairo was established, Mary, Joseph and the Christ child fled to this area from Israel and hid in a cave. Coptic Christians honored their hiding place by building St. Sergius Church at the site in the fifth century. It survives today as Egypt's oldest Christian church—a simple and sturdy chapel of stone.

Two other lures in Old Cairo—which may or may not be on your regular tour—are definitely worth a visit. Both are uncrowded, offering a refreshing break from the often chaotic tour bus scene that simmers around most attractions. (We're convinced that the term: "Babble of many tongues" didn't originate in the Bible. It refers to the dozens of multi-lingual tour guides herding their charges through Egyptian antiquities.)

The Mosque of El Ibn el-As, built around a huge courtyard, is the oldest Islamic religious site in Egypt, dating from the seventh century. It's now abandoned but fully intact and fascinating for its long colonnades with lavishly embossed arches. For those not concerned with heights, a visit to this mosque offers a rare privilege. Since it isn't in use, visitors can

We spotted a shabby "penthouse" where a man relaxed while chickens and a turkey wandered about his rooftop yard.

climb 194 steps to the top of the minaret, where in earlier days the *muezzin* issued his call to prayer. (They now use loudspeakers.) The view of Cairo from this lofty perch was imposing—and fun. We spotted a shabby "penthouse" atop a nearby building, where a man relaxed with his water pipe while chickens and a turkey wandered about his rooftop yard.

The other Old Cairo attraction, a short walk from the abandoned mosque, is a lavish sixty-room home built by Hajj Muhammad al-Jazzar in the seventeenth century. It was occupied early in this century by wealthy British Major Gayer Anderson and is now the Anderson House Museum. The palatial residence displays a mix of Byzantine, Egyptian and English furnishings. The original house contained a harem. While the proper Major Anderson did not partake of such earthly pleasures, Muhammad al-Jazzar retained at least six ladies in waiting.

"From theese room he would send for them," said a museum guide in his thick accent as he ushered us into a large room with cushioned benches and settees. Using appropriate gestures, he concluded: "Een summer, he would send for a skinny one, and een winter, a fat one."

Being a class operation, Abercrombie & Kent had hired a police car to escort us through traffic-ridden Cairo on our last day of touring, complete with blinking lights and sirens. However, other motorists and even donkey cart drivers ignored it for the most part, certainly proving that Egypt is no police state. The vehicle also made several wrong turns and at one point, Hesham suggested that the policemen follow the bus, so the escort wasn't really that useful.

But never mind that; it provided a festive finale to a memorable tour of Egypt. And besides, it's the thought that counts.

ß ß ß

I have bathed in the Poem of the Sea...
Devouring the green azures.
—Arthur Rimbaud, *Le Bateau Ivre*

Chapter seventeen

SEATALK

Talking (but not swearing) like a sailor

When I was a Marine, we called sailors "swabbies" because, with the Navy's penchant for cleanliness, it seemed that they were always swabbing the decks. If you're from Kansas, that translates as mopping the floors. Ships have no floors, nor do they have walls, ceilings or stairs. They do of course have bulkheads, overheads and ladders.

If you're going down to the sea in ships, or up a river in boats, you might want to learn some nautical language. We've also included some contemporary "cruise lingo" in this glossary. Thus, when your travel agent asks you about ad-ons, you'll know she's not talking about the weight you might gain from overeating aboard ship.

Incidentally, swabbies also had a name for Marines, but never mind that.

Abeam — At right angles to another ship, usually off to one side.

Ad-ons — Additional charges added to a cruise price for airfare or shore excursions.

Aft — The rear of the ship.

Allyway — Passageway in a ship, also called a companionway.

Amidships — Just what you think it means; toward a ship's middle.

Astern — Same as aft; it often implies an action: "Going astern."

Awash — The point at which a ship's deck reaches water level; not a pleasant condition unless you're in a submarine.

Ballast — Weight placed in the hold of a ship to stabilize it. After a long cruise, most passengers could be very useful as ballast.

Bar — My favorite place on a ship. Also short for a sandbar, which isn't a captain's favorite place in shallow water.

Barge — A boat with a flat bottom.

Basis two — Cruise talk for double occupancy or a cabin that holds two people. Most cruise and tour prices are quoted as "per person, double occupancy." If you go it alone, you'll have to pay a single supplement, because you're taking up a room with two pillows. "Pillows" is hotelier talk for two beds or a bed for two people.

Barquentine or *barkentine* — A barque or sailing ship in which the foremast is square-rigged or set square across the ship, while the masts behind it are fore-and-aft side-rigged.

No, they're not on an ocean-going trampoline. These passengers on Star Clippers' sailing ship, Star Flyer, *have learned where the bowsprit is, since they're sitting in a netting attached to it—giving them a great ride over the waves.*

Batten down — To secure something on a ship. Sailors "batten down the hatches" during a storm to keep waves from flooding into the hold.

Beam — The widest part of a ship, usually measured amidships. Also an unkind reference to the *derrière* of a person who's been to the midnight buffet too many times. ("He's getting a little broad in the beam.")

Bearing — The direction of a ship's travel, measured in compass degrees. Also used as a verb: "We are bearing 45 degrees."

Bells — A traditional seafaring measurement of time. Watches were divided into six four-hour shifts and one to eight bells were rung by the watchkeeper every half hour—probably to prove that he was still awake. Thus, "Eight bells and all's well!" can be translated as: "Hot diggity! My watch is over and I'm heading for the rum keg!"

Berth — The dock space or slip were a ship parks; also refers to a cabin or crew's quarters.

Bilge — The lowest part of a ship's hull. Old wooden ships often leaked and the water became quite foul, giving rise to the expression: "That's a lot of bilge!"

Boat station — The place where passengers and crew are directed to gather in an emergency, usually near a specific lifeboat; "station" for short.

Bow — The pointy end of a ship or boat.

Bowsprit — A tapered shaft extending forward from the bow of a ship, used to connect lines for forward sails such as the foresail or jib.

Bridge — The ship's control center and command center.

Brigantine or ***brig*** — Midsize sailing ship with two or more masts.

Bulkhead — Ships don't have walls or partitions; they have bulkheads.

Bunker — A ship's fuel tank, usually filled with a coarsely refined diesel called bunker fuel.

LITTLE BOATS FROM YESTERDAY

These are some of the small, specialized vessels you may encounter during your voyage, particularly on an adventure cruise.

Cayuca — Dugout canoe made from a palm trunk, little changed for centuries, still used by the Mayans of Belize-Guatemala and the Caboclo Indians along the Amazon. Cayuca rides often are part of Amazon or Belize-Guatemala cruises.

Dhow — Small Arabian craft with a triangular lateen sail, similar to the Egyptian *felucca.*

Felucca — Small open sail Egyptian boat with a crossed mast and boom, and a triangular sail truncated at the downward end. They have sailed the Nile for centuries and still are used, for cargo, short-haul passenger ferries and to haul tourists about. One company, Egypt National Tours, packages live-aboard cruises on these tiny boats; see Chapter two, page 24.

Gulet — Small Turkish wooden ketch-rigged motor sailers, usually hand-built, varnished and beautifully finished. They're popular for "Blue Cruises" on the Aegean and Mediterranean seas off Turkey's coast.

Kayak — This now-familiar term actually is an Inuit word. The people of the far north, who no longer like to be called Eskimos, developed kayaks with bone frames covered by animal skins many centuries ago. For modern adventurers who like to get close to the water, two types are available, usually made of Fiberglas or plastic or a new lightweight material called Kevlar. Sea kayaks are long and slender, sometimes equipped with a foot controlled rudder, for voyages over open water. River kayaks or whitewater kayaks are short and maneuverable for dancing through the rapids, but they don't "track" well on flatwater trips.

Panga — Small open boat used in many Latin American countries for fishing, transport and light cargo. They were originally oar powered, although most are now fitted with outboard motors. They're used along the Baja peninsula and Galápagos Islands to get cruise passengers closer to wildlife.

Pirogue — A canoe made from a hollowed out log. The word is French and originated in Caribbean or America's southern bayous.

Capstan — A large motor-driven spool mounted upright on the deck, around which a rope or cable is wrapped to haul up an anchor or other heavy object. Early capstans were turned by men who inserted levers or "capstan bars" into slots and pushed with their chests to rotate the capstan.

Caravel or *caravelle* — A European sailing ship of the fifteenth century, originating in Spain and Portugal, with a high deck, broad bow and stern and two or three masts rigged with triangular lateen sails. Adding square rigged sails resulted in the transition from caravel to carrack (below), and the terms later were used interchangeably.

Carrack — The first fully-rigged sailing ship, developed about the fifteenth century, with both lateen sails for maneuvering into the wind and square-rigged sails for speed. It was the breakthrough in ship design that permitted men to explore the far reaches of the globe. Columbus' ships were technically carracks.

Chart — Ships don't have maps, but they have lots of charts. More specifically, they're navigational charts, showing the depth of waterways, sandbars and reefs, navigational beacons and compass bearings, as well as landfalls.

Chow — Sailor talk for food. To eat is to "chow down," but don't use that expression in front of a stuffy dining room host.

Clipper ship — Fast cargo or passenger ship with sleek lines, a concave bow and lots of sail for its size. Clippers were developed in Baltimore shipyards in the 1880s. They were the fastest sailing ships afloat and ruled the waves for decades. "Clipper" is a generic description; these ships can be rigged as brigantines, barquentines or schooners.

Colors — The flags flown from the mast and astern; generally a ship flies the "colors" of its nation of registry and of the nation it is visiting.

Companionway — Narrow corridor or passage in a ship.

Course — The direction in which a ship is traveling, expressed in degrees of the compass.

Crow's nest — Any kid knows that's an observation platform high in the rigging, where the lookout stands and shouts: "Thar she blows!"

Davit — Curved poles or brackets from which lifeboats are hung, which can be swung out to lower them into the water.

Deck — There are no floors on ships; only decks.

Derelict — A ship that has been abandoned at sea.

Disembark or **debark** — Go ashore, or leave the ship. (To a salty old sailor or Marine, "going ashore" also refers to leaving a military post.

Draft — The depth that a ship's hull extends beneath the water. Also used as a verb: "The ship drafts sixteen feet."

Embark — Obviously, the opposite of disembark; to go aboard or start a cruise. And now you know why that waterfront street in San Francisco is called the Embarcadero.

Even keel — The term "keeping everything on an even keel" comes from the upright position of a ship; it's sitting vertical to its axis.

Fantail — The rear of a ship.

Fathom — A nautical measurement of depth; six feet to a landlubber.

Figurehead — A decorative figure—often a bosomy woman—molded to the bow and bowsprit of a sailing ship. Because it's ornamental, the term is applied to someone who is given a highly visible position, but with no real authority.

First seating — The first of two meal sittings on a ship with a dining room too small to accommodate all of its passengers at once. If you like to dawdle over dessert, *never* take first seating, because the second seating people will be hammering at the door.

Fore — Forward part of a ship; on sailing ships, forward of the main mast.

Fore and aft rigged — Sails rigged to the length of the ship, instead of across it, which is "square rigged."

Foremast — The mast on a sailing ship nearest the bow.

Forward — The forward part of a ship; often used as an action word: "I'm going forward."

Free port or **freeport** — A port city where no duty is charged on your purchases. However, they are still subject to customs duty when you take them home.

Frigate — It originally referred to a mid-sized eighteenth century warship with twenty-eight or more cannons; many frigates were combined warships and merchant ships. The term is now used generically to describe any small to mid-sized sailing vessel.

Funnel — The ship's chimney.

Galleon — An early sailing ship with two or more masts and a high stern that contained several decks. This was the standard merchant ship and warship of the fifteenth and sixteenth centuries.

Galley — Kitchen. ("Galley slave" takes on new meaning when you're in mess duty in the military.) Also an early vessel propelled initially by oars and later by a combination of oars and sails. Some of history's first sailing ships were galleys.

Gangway or **gangplank** — Ramp for embarkation and debarkation.

Halyards — The lines (sailors never call them ropes) used to haul sails up and down.

Hatch — An opening into the cargo bay of a ship, and the cover over that opening. Thus the old salt's term when he slams back the last of his drink: "Down the hatch!"

Hawser — Cable or very thick line used to tie up a ship.

Head — A pottie on a vessel or at a military base.

Helm — The steering and control center of a ship. "Who's at the helm?" means "Who's driving this thing?"

Hold — The space deep inside the ship's hull, generally used for cargo.

House flag — The banner with the symbol or logo of the company that owns the ship.

Hull — The basic body of a ship, without its rigging or superstructure.

Jib — Sail or series of sails forward on a ship, often rigged between the foremast and the bowsprit.

Jacob's ladder — A rope ladder used for climbing up into the rigging, or up to the crow's nest.

Jigger — A small mast nearest the stern on a four- masted sailing ship. Or if you hang out at the ship's bar a lot, it's an ounce and a half of liquor.

Knot — Things sailors tie when they're bored. Also a measure of speed. A nautical mile is 6,080 feet, compared with a land mile of 5,280 feet. The term is used mostly to measure speed, not distance: "We're doing about seventeen knots."

Ladder — Aboard a ship, a stairway is always called a ladder. So, what's a ladder called on a ship? We'll have to think about that one...

Laniard or **lanyard** — A short line used to secure something on a ship or boat.

Lateen — Small Portuguese sailing craft utilizing lateen sails (see explanation below).

Lateen sail — The forerunner of modern fore-and-aft sails, tracing its roots to the ancient Mediterranean. It's a triangular sail, loosely hung and rigged so that it can be swung on a pivot to catch a breeze coming in at different angles. This and the later development of the keel—probably by Vikings—allowed ships to tack and sail into the wind. The word comes from "Latin," because Europeans first noticed the sail being used by Latin-speaking countries.

Lateener — Any sailing ship rigged with lateen sails.

League — An archaic term used to measure distance; 3.45 nautical miles.

Leeward — The side of a ship or island opposite from the direction of the wind, and therefore the most sheltered side.

Line — There are no ropes on a ship, but there are lots of lines.

Log — A detailed record kept by the ship's watch, or the officer on duty.

Mainmast — The second and often the largest mast on a multi-masted ship.

Manifest — It has nothing to do with destiny; it's the list of a ship's passengers, cargo and crew.

Mast — The long pole that holds up the sails, supported by rigging. On sailing ships of old, the crews' quarters were in front of the foremast—the one closest to the bow. Thus the name for Richard Henry Dana's book recalling his days as a crew member on a sailing ship: *Two Years Before the Mast.*

Masthead — The top part of a mast. For some odd reason, the term also applies to the information box in a newspaper that lists its name, chief editors, circulation and other specifics.

Missenmast — The third mast on a three or four- masted sailing ship.

Muster — To assemble all hands (crewmen) and or passengers. This occurs during lifeboat drill, which is required by international law. "Muster station" is another term for boat station.

Nautical mile — A knot.

Open seating — Unassigned seating on a cruise; much preferred to assigned seating if you've gotten stuck with a boring mail carrier from Omaha.

Overhead — There are no ceilings on ships; that flat surface above you is an overhead, which makes sense when you think about it.

Pilot — Snoopy, when he's fighting the Red Baron. Also, a person familiar with a particular waterway who is licensed to steer ships or boats through it. Ship captains entering or leaving a harbor or sailing up a tricky channel often have a pilot brought aboard. It may be required by local maritime law. By tradition, riverboat captains are called pilots, and indeed they are, since many river channels are quite complex.

Pitch — The action of a ship rising and falling in rough seas, bow to stern, as opposed to *roll,* which is to sway from side to side. Either motion will send some people for their Dramamine.

Port — The left side of the ship when you're facing forward. Also a sweet wine whose name comes from Oporto, Portugal. Too much port and you won't know port from starboard.

Prow — The ship's pointy end.

Purser — Either the chief financial officer or hotel manager of a ship. On cruise ships, it's likely to be the latter.

Quay (kee) — A pier or dock.

Registry — The country in which a ship is registered.

Rigging — All those ropes and cables and chains and things that support a ship's masts and sails. However, they're not called ropes and cables and chains; they're lines and halyards and lanyards and stuff like that.

Running lights — A red light to port, green to starboard and white at the top of the highest mast. International law requires that they must be lit when a ship is underway at night.

Schooner — A glass beer mug with a large handle. Also, a vessel with two or more masts, rugged fore and aft. If it has four wheels and it's headed west, it's a prairie schooner.

Screw — A ship's propeller.

Spanker — Not a child abuser, but the fourth mast on a four-masted sailing ship, or the sail on that mast. However, if it's quite small, it's called a jigger. And no, we don't know why.

Spinnaker — Large, billowy sail, rigged forward on a ship to increase speed during a race.

Square rigged — Sails that are rigged port to starboard, across the ship, instead of fore and aft.

Stabilizers — Retractable fins that move in and out below the water-line, to help keep a ship from rolling in rough waters. They're controlled by gyroscopes or computers and are sometimes called Denny Brown stabilizers because he's the guy who invented them.

Stack — The funnel.

Starboard — The right side of the ship when you're facing forward.

Stateroom — A passenger cabin. The term comes from custom of naming cabins after states on early American paddlewheelers.

Steward — A shipboard employee on a cruise line; room steward, wine steward and such.

Stem — The most forward part of a ship's prow; on sailing ships, it's the bowsprit.

Stern — The rear end of a ship.

Stowaway — Actually, it's not a noun describing someone hiding on a ship. It's a verb referring to a cruise passengers' ability to eat six lemon tarts at the midnight buffet.

Superstructure — Any structure built above the deck of a ship other than the masts and sails, which are referred to as rigging.

Tender — A small craft used to move passengers and crew between a ship and port. A lifeboat often is employed as a tender.

"Thar she blows!" — A description of your wife's reaction when she sees your bar bill.

Tipping — On most cruises, you are told that tipping is a very personal matter, strictly up to your individual discretion. Then you are given specific suggestions on how much to tip.

Wake — The ripple of water left in—well—in a ship's wake.

Waterline — The point at which the ship's hull is even with the surface of the water. Anything below that is the draft.

Weigh — A verb, meaning to haul up the anchor. Also, something passengers avoid doing after too many midnight buffets.

Windward — The side of a ship or island exposed to the wind direction.

Yaw — Rotational movement of a ship caused when waves approach from an angle.

ßßß

INDEX: Primary listings indicated by *bold face italics*

REMARKABLY USEFUL GUIDEBOOKS
from *PINE CONE PRESS*

Critics praise the "jaunty prose" and "beautiful editing" of Pine Cone Press guidebooks by Don and Betty Martin. In addition to being comprehensive and "remarkably useful," their books are frank, witty and opinionated. They're available from book stores, or directly from the publisher.

ADVENTURE CRUISING
It's the first book of its kind—a guide devoted exclusively to adventure, specialty and other small ship cruises. Scores of cruise lines are listed, with hundreds of itineraries world wide. Special "Cruise closeups" provide an intimate look at more than a dozen different voyages. *— 352 pages; $15.95*

ARIZONA DISCOVERY GUIDE
This detailed guide covers attractions, scenic drives, hikes and walks, dining, lodgings and campgrounds in the Grand Canyon State. A "Snowbird" section helps retirees plan their winters under the Arizona sun, and special "RV Advisories" help steer RVers around the state. *—408 pages; $15.95*

THE BEST OF THE GOLD COUNTRY
It's a remarkably useful guide to California's gold rush area in the Sierra Nevada foothills and old Sacramento. This comprehensive book covers attractions, historic sites, dining, lodging and camping. *— 240 pages; $11.95*

THE BEST OF THE WINE COUNTRY
Where to taste wine in California? Nearly 300 wineries are featured, along with nearby restaurants, lodging and attractions. Special sections offer tips on selecting, tasting, serving and storing wine. *— 336 pages; $13.95*

COMING TO ARIZONA
This is an all-purpose relocation guide for job-seekers, retirees and winter "Snowbirds" planning a move to Arizona. It provides essential data on dozens of cities, from recreation to medical facilities. *— 232 pages; $12.95*

NEVADA DISCOVERY GUIDE
This guide covers all of Nevada, with a special focus on gaming centers of Las Vegas, Reno-Tahoe and Laughlin. A special section advises readers how to "Beat the odds," with casino gambling tips. *— 352 pages; $15.95*

More books and ordering information on the next page

NORTHERN CALIFORNIA DISCOVERY GUIDE

Our new Discovery Guide series focuses on driving vacations for motorists and RVers. We steer our readers to popular attractions and little-known jewels, along with great places to play, eat and sleep. — *356 pages; $12.95*

OREGON DISCOVERY GUIDE

From the wilderness coast to the Cascades to urban Portland, this book takes motorists and RVers over Oregon's byways and through its cities. It's another in the Martins' new Discovery Guide series. — *352 pages; $12.95*

THE ULTIMATE WINE BOOK

It's the complete wine guide, covering the subject in three major areas: wine and health, wine appreciation and wine with food. It's loaded with useful information for both casual and serious wine lovers. — *176 pages; $8.95*

UTAH DISCOVERY GUIDE

This remarkably useful driving guide covers every area of interest in the Beehive State, from its splendid canyonlands to Salt Lake City to the "Jurassic Parkway" of dinosaur country. — *360 pages; $13.95*

WASHINGTON DISCOVERY GUIDE

This handy book takes motorists and RVers from one corner of the Evergreen State to the other, from the Olympic Peninsula and Seattle to Eastern Washington's wine country and great rivers. — *372 pages; $13.95*

MARTIN GUIDES ARE AVAILABLE AT MOST BOOK STORES, OR YOU CAN ORDER DIRECTLY FROM THE PUBLISHER

VISA & MASTERCARD ACCEPTED

Phone, FAX, e-mail or write, giving us your credit card type, number and expiration date. Or you can mail us your personal check. For each book, add $1.05 for shipping ($3.05 for priority mail). California residents please include appropriate state sales tax.

Send your order to: *Pine Cone Press*
P.O. Box 1494, Columbia, CA 95310
(209) 532-2699; FAX (209) 532-0494
e-mail: pinecone@sonnet.com